THE MAN
WHO
REMADE
INDIA

MODERN SOUTH ASIA

Ashutosh Varshney, *Series Editor*
Pradeep Chhibber, *Associate Series Editor*

Editorial Board

Kaushik Basu (Cornell University)
Steven Cohen (Brookings Institution)
Veena Das (Johns Hopkins University)
Patrick Heller (Brown University)
Niraja Gopal Jayal (Jawaharlal Nehru University)
Ravi Kanbur (Cornell University)
Atul Kohli (Princeton University)
Pratap Bhanu Mehta (Centre for Policy Research)
Farzana Shaikh (Chatham House)

The Other One Percent
Sanjoy Chakravorty, Devesh Kapur, and Nirvikar Singh

Social Justice through Inclusion
Francesca R. Jensenius

THE MAN WHO REMADE INDIA

A BIOGRAPHY OF P. V. NARASIMHA RAO

VINAY SITAPATI

OXFORD
UNIVERSITY PRESS

Published in the United States of America by Oxford University Press
198 Madison Avenue, New York, NY 10016, United States of America

© Oxford University Press 2018

Published first in India by Penguin India

All rights reserved. No part of this publication may be reproduced, stored in a retrieval system, or transmitted, in any form or by any means, without the prior permission in writing of Oxford University Press, or as expressly permitted by law, by license, or under terms agreed with the appropriate reproduction rights organization. Inquiries concerning reproduction outside the scope of the above should be sent to the Rights Department, Oxford University Press, at the address above.

You must not circulate this work in any other form
and you must impose this same condition on any acquirer

Library of Congress Cataloging-in-Publication Data

Names: Sitapati, Vinay, author.
Title: The Man Who Remade India : a biography of
P.V. Narasimha Rao / Vinay Sitapati.
Description: New York : Oxford University Press, 2018. | Series: Modern south asia | Includes bibliographical references and index.
Identifiers: LCCN 2017030117 | ISBN 978-0-19-069285-8 (hardback) |
ISBN 978-0-19-069287-2 (epub) | ISBN 978-0-19-069286-5 (updf)
Subjects: LCSH: Narasimha Rao, P. V., 1921-2004. | Prime ministers—India—Biography. | India—Politics and government—1977- |
BISAC: HISTORY / Asia / India & South Asia. | BIOGRAPHY & AUTOBIOGRAPHY / Political.
Classification: LCC DS481.N312 S58 2018 | DDC 954.05/2092 [B]—dc23
LC record available at https://lccn.loc.gov/2017030117

A prince ... must imitate the fox and the lion. For the lion cannot protect himself from traps, and the fox cannot defend himself from wolves. One must therefore be a fox to recognise traps, and a lion to frighten wolves.

Niccolò Machiavelli, *The Prince*, circa 1513 AD

The demon king Hiranyakashipu performs penance to achieve immortality. He is granted a boon that he will die neither on earth nor in space, neither in the day nor night, neither at home nor outside—neither by a human nor animal. Confident of cheating death by this clever device, the demon starts believing he is God and unleashes terror. His devout son Prahlada continues to worship Lord Vishnu as all-pervasive. Enraged, Hiranyakashipu points to a pillar and mockingly asks if Vishnu is present within. He shatters the pillar with his mace. Out of the shards emerges Narasimha, an incarnation of Vishnu. Narasimha—half-man, half-lion—kills Hiranyakashipu. The time is twilight, the place is the courtyard, and Hiranyakashipu is killed on Narasimha's lap, neither earth nor space. The ambiguities and contradictions of Narasimha, half-lion, are precisely why he is able to slay the demon.

Story from Narasimha Avatar, *Bhagvata Purana*, 900 AD[1]

Contents

Preface to the US Edition	ix
1. Half-burnt Body	1
2. Andhra Socialist, 1921–71	12
3. Puppet Chief Minister, 1971–73	32
4. Exile, 1973–74	42
5. Delhi Durbar, 1975–91	53
6. Monk to Monarch	84
7. Rescuing the Economy, 1991–92	107
8. Growing the Economy, 1992–96	140
9. A Welfare State?	169
10. Surviving Party and Parliament	182
11. Managing Sonia	212
12. The Fall of Babri Masjid	225
13. Look East, Look West	257
14. Going Nuclear	279
15. Lion, Fox, Mouse	296
Acknowledgements	319
Notes	327
Index	379

Preface to the US Edition

Narasimha Rao flew to the United States in 1994, an anxious man. His chief diplomat remembers India's prime minister being "unsure of himself [and] perhaps [he] felt inadequate to handle President Clinton." Rao rewrote his talking points "like a nervous student," his doctor recalls. For America had high expectations of the leader of the world's largest democracy. He had spent the last three years remaking India—opening her economy, creating a welfare state, building a nuclear program, and moving foreign policy towards the United States, Israel, and East Asia. As he landed in Washington D.C., the *New York Times* welcomed P.V. Narasimha Rao as the "Deng Xiaoping of India."

Two decades later, it is time to revisit that assessment. Like the man who transformed China in the 1980s, the diminutive Rao was an apparatchik who disassembled the very system that brought him to power. Deng understood that a country of China's size needed symbolic continuity while undergoing change. He justified his capitalism as an extension of Chairman Mao's communism. So, too, did Narasimha Rao dress up his radical policies as those of Jawaharlal Nehru and Indira Gandhi. His 1991 New Year's greeting card had a sketch of a spinning wheel morphing into mechanical gear. Typed below was the slogan: "Change is the only constant."

PREFACE TO THE US EDITION

Where Rao was most like Deng Xiaoping was in the results of his rule. When he took power in 1991, India was just weeks away from a global loan default. Its ally on the world stage, the Soviet Union, was folding. And with civil war in Kashmir and Punjab, swathes of the country were heedless to Delhi's writ. The assassination of Rajiv Gandhi, the very reason for Rao's elevation, embodied this shriveling of national power. That Rao converted this inbox from hell into good news and transformed a basket case into an emerging power has only one other historical analogy. In fact, it was a book on Deng—the historian Ezra Vogel's magisterial *Deng Xiaoping and the Transformation of China*—that inspired me to weave twined narratives: the story of India opening in the 1990s, and the story of the man who did it.

The scale of this makeover places Narasimha Rao among other twentieth-century reformers who shaped their country's internal politics as well as place in the world. Apart from Deng Xiaoping, others include Charles De Gaulle of France, Margaret Thatcher of Britain, Franklin D. Roosevelt and Ronald Reagan of the United States, Lee Kuan Yew of Singapore, and Jawaharlal Nehru of India. This illustrious company makes it all the more baffling as to why Rao has been forgotten in India. In the United States of America, he is an unknown, a cipher. When I told a political scientist researching South Asia at an Ivy League about my new muse, he professed to having never heard of Narasimha Rao.

There are many reasons for this amnesia. But most inexcusable is that Narasimha Rao has been disowned by his own party. Deng is venerated by the Communist party of China, Democrats are still nostalgic for the New Deal. But the Congress party—led by the Nehru-Gandhi dynasty—has disowned its most consequential leader since Nehru. A second reason why Rao is lesser known is academic bias. Scholars prefer structural explanations to the vagaries of personality. Researchers on contemporary South Asia have long put down the tectonic shifts of the 1990s to external earthquakes—the fall of the Soviet Union; IMF pressure—or to intellectual swings within Indian policy makers. The role of politicians, of leadership, stands diminished.

The concluding culprit for Rao's erasure is the man himself. Aware that survival hinged on distancing himself from unpopular yet necessary policies, Rao avoided taking public credit. Instead, like Deng, he pretended to continuity—citing the very predecessors whose legacy he was dismantling as justification for it.

Luckily for Narasimha Rao, we have more than his public words to rely upon. Rao's family made available to me 45 cartons of his private papers. This paper trail, along with more than 110 interviews and 200 books and articles, is the bedrock on which the arguments of this book rest. This palette of material enabled me to not just vividly portray Indian politics; it allowed me sketch the inner man. The picture that emerges is of a micro-manager consciously shaping history, rather than a disinterested politician who chanced upon the right place at the right time. I was also lucky that Rao's family did not insist upon their opinions, enabling me to criticize my subject (his corruptions, his affairs, his misjudgments) with the same passion reserved for his triumphs.

"All my life," Charles De Gaulle began in his *War Memoirs*, "I have had a certain idea of France." Narasimha Rao was not as certain of his idea of India. As this book chronicles, the early Nehruvian socialist had long since abandoned any pretense that static convictions could grapple with the country's chaos and cacophony. He was, in particular, no free-market ideologue. The political scientist James Manor asked Rao whether he was the next Margaret Thatcher. He replied that his model was Willy Brandt.

The reference to West Germany's first social democratic chancellor was a pointed rebuttal to right-wing admirers as well as left-wing critics. For Rao was neither a devotee of socialism nor a convert to capitalism. That Narasimha Rao did not have the luxury of ideological posturing stemmed from his disposition, that of a wily survivor in the Delhi court. But it also arose from his mandate—the weakest any world reformer has had. To truly understand the genius of Rao, therefore, one must fathom how he converted weakness into strength.

The German sociologist Max Weber emphasized charisma as an ingredient of leadership and authority. Narasimha Rao was arguably the least charismatic, most boring prime minister India has produced—in what is a competitive list that includes H.D. Deve Gowda. He could not work the room like Bill Clinton, nor could he match the soaring rhetoric of Barack Obama or the folksy optimism of Ronald Reagan. He was not a conspicuous man of action, the way Lee Kuan Yew and other East Asian strongmen were. He possessed, as his critics never tired of pointing out, "the charisma of a dead fish."

Nor was he an organization man. Unlike Deng, Stalin, Nehru, or Margaret Thatcher, Rao did not control his own party. As this book shows, Rao was selected as prime minister as a compromise candidate—precisely because he did not threaten any of its power brokers. Some even expected the diabetic and heart patient to not live through his tenure. Scarcely a month passed in which party members—and later Sonia Gandhi—were not rebelling against his leadership. Subduing the Congress's querulousness to lead them for an entire term required patience and acuity.

Rao's ability to turn foible into force extended to parliament. In India's Westminster-style system, the party with a majority of seats runs the government. But Narasimha Rao's Congress was a minority in parliament. A single vote by a united opposition was enough to sink the ship of state—as was done to the two minority governments that preceded Rao, and the four that succeeded him. In such choppy seas, being the first minority government to survive a complete five-year term required a flair for navigation. Rao's ability to manipulate opposition parties—through coercion, bribery, flattery, and deception—should remind American readers

PREFACE TO THE US EDITION

of their own Master of the Senate. As majority leader, Lyndon B. Johnson had the pulse of the Senate. His biographer Robert Caro compares Johnson's facility for passing contentious legislation to that of a conductor managing an orchestra. Rao's knack for surviving adversity in the House, including three no-confidence motions, makes him a performer of LBJ's class. That he did so with no charisma, an unsupportive party, and in a fractious democracy, makes his achievements unparalleled among world reformers.

―

This last hurdle Narasimha Rao crossed—that of democracy itself—holds urgent lessons at a time when strongmen are being trumpeted as more conducive to national transformation than elected leaders. With partisan divisions forcing gridlock in the United States and Western Europe, the authoritarian models of Russia and China seem alluring. It is an allure that political scientists have confirmed in their narrative of how poor countries have grown in the twentieth century. First South Korea, Malaysia, Indonesia—then famously China—all have grown with a tyrant at the top. Democracy, with its dispersed power and temptations to populism, has been considered a handicap to economic growth.

India's anemic economy long seemed to confirm this critique. A vibrant democracy with somewhat robust institutions, India's economy grew at a derisory 3.5 percent between the 1950s and 1980s. Competing interest groups, many veto players, and a lack of consensus were blamed for this "Hindu rate of growth." The problem of India, it seemed, was too much democracy.

In these unsettling times, Narasimha Rao offers reassurance that reform can happen through democratic engagement. Where possible, he strived for consensus; where he was convinced he had to go it alone, he did not balk. All the while, he respected the legislature, judiciary, states, and the Constitution. If a man as weak

PREFACE TO THE US EDITION

as Narasimha Rao, with *his* odds, could succeed within the four corners of representative government, others can too.

His are lessons for politicians and political scientists the world over. But he also speaks to those removed from the bustle of politics. After the success of the Indian edition (the number one non-fiction book in the country) CEOs, generals, entrepreneurs, and artists all told me that the book "spoke" to them. A start-up entrepreneur who professed little interest in politics nonetheless loved the book. "Startups are the most dictatorial organizations. [But] Even I can't just walk in and fire employees. Morale would plummet. Even I operate under constraints." The head of a university department had this to say: "The faculty in my department listen to no one. I'm just the ringmaster of the circus. I sympathize with Rao's powerlessness. When I want to bring some change, I read parts of this book." I hope you do, too.

Vinay Sitapati
Delhi, April 2017

1

Half-Burnt Body

The corpse was clad in white dhoti and golden silk kurta.[1] At 2.30 p.m., it was brought from Delhi's All India Institute of Medical Sciences to 9 Motilal Nehru Marg. P.V. Narasimha Rao, prime minister of India from 1991 to 1996, had died at around 11 a.m., 23 December 2004. The doctors had needed a couple of hours to dress the body before sending it back home.

One of the first people to arrive at Rao's house was Chandraswami, the bearded guru who had known him since 1971.[2] Also present were his eight sons and daughters—whom he had kept at a distance—as well as the nephews and grandchildren he had been closer to. Eldest son, Ranga Rao—who had fought bitterly with his father—was inconsolable.

Then began the politics.

The home minister, Shivraj Patil, suggested to Rao's youngest son, Prabhakara, that 'the body should be cremated in Hyderabad'. But the family preferred Delhi. After all, Rao had last been chief minister of Andhra Pradesh more than thirty years ago, and had since worked as Congress general secretary, Union minister, and finally prime minister—all in Delhi. On hearing this, the usually decorous Shivraj Patil snapped, 'No one will come.'[3]

Kashmiri Congressman Ghulam Nabi Azad, another aide of party president Sonia Gandhi, arrived. He too requested the family to move the body to Hyderabad. An hour later, Prabhakara received a call on his mobile phone. It was Y.S. Rajasekhara Reddy, the Congress chief minister of Andhra Pradesh and no friend of Narasimha Rao's. 'I just heard about it,' Reddy said, 'I am near Anantapur, and I'll be in Delhi by this evening. Take it from me. We will give him a grand funeral [in Hyderabad].'

At 6.30 p.m., Sonia Gandhi entered the house in Motilal Nehru Marg, named after her great-grandfather-in-law. Prime minister Manmohan Singh followed, along with Pranab Mukherjee. They walked through the long corridor to the room at the end where Rao's body, now decked in flowers, was displayed. 'What do you want to do with the body?' the prime minister asked Prabhakara. 'These people say it should be in Hyderabad.' 'This [Delhi] is his *karmabhoomi*,' Prabhakara replied, 'you should convince your Cabinet colleagues.' Manmohan nodded. Sonia Gandhi was standing nearby. She said little.

The journalist Sanjaya Baru arrived. His bureaucrat father knew Rao from the 1960s. As Baru entered the corridor, Sonia's political secretary tapped him on the shoulder. 'You know the family,' Ahmed Patel said. 'The body should be taken to Hyderabad. Can you convince them?' Baru continued walking towards the end of the corridor, when he heard someone cry. He turned left to see Kalyani Shankar sobbing in a side room.[4] Kalyani had been Rao's most trusted friend for the last two decades.

Y.S. Rajasekhara Reddy had by now reached Delhi. 'It is our government, trust me,' he told Rao's family. 'Let him be moved to Hyderabad. We will build a grand memorial for him there.' Rao's daughter S. Vani Devi says, 'YSR was playing a major role in convincing [the] family to get the dead body to Hyderabad.'[5]

The family wanted a commitment that a memorial would be built for Rao in Delhi. The Congress leaders present said yes. But considering how the party had treated Rao in his retirement, the family wanted to make doubly sure. At 9.30 p.m., they paid a visit to the one man who had stood by Narasimha Rao in the last years

HALF-BURNT BODY

of his life. Manmohan Singh was wearing his nightdress, a white kurta-pyjama, when Rao's family met him at his official residence on Race Course Road. When Shivraj Patil explained the demand for a memorial in Delhi, Manmohan replied, 'No problem, we will do it.'[6]

Prabhakara recalls, 'We sensed even then that Sonia-ji did not want Father's funeral in Delhi. She did not want a memorial [in Delhi] . . . She did not want him [to be seen] as an all-India leader . . . [But] there was pressure.'

'We agreed.'

The next day, 24 December 2004, leaders from across the political spectrum—from communists to BJP leaders—all came to pay their respects.[7] At 10 a.m., the body was draped in the national flag, put on a flower-decked carriage pulled by an army vehicle, and escorted by military personnel[8] in a slow procession towards the airport. Along the way, they planned to stop at 24 Akbar Road, the Congress party headquarters. Ever since Narasimha Rao had first moved into 9, Motilal Nehru Marg in 1980, he had made this journey countless times.

As the body approached 24 Akbar Road, located adjacent to Sonia Gandhi's residence, the funeral procession slowed. The entrance gate to the compound looked firmly shut. There were several senior Congressmen present, but hardly any cadres had been rustled up.[9] No slogans filled the air, just deathly silence. The carriage stopped on the pavement outside, as Sonia Gandhi and others came out to pay their respects.

It was customary for the bodies of past Congress presidents to be taken inside the party headquarters so that ordinary workers could pay their respects. The family was somewhat dazed when this did not happen. A friend of Rao's asked a senior Congresswoman to let the body in. 'The gate does not open,' she replied. 'This was untrue,' the friend remembers. 'When Madhavrao Scindia died [some years earlier] the gate was opened for him.' Manmohan Singh now lives in a guarded bungalow a few minutes from Akbar Road. When asked why Rao's body wasn't allowed into the Congress headquarters, he replies that he was present, but has no knowledge of this.[10] Another Congressman is more forthcoming. 'We were expecting the gate to be opened . . . but no order came. Only one person could give that order.'

He adds, 'She did not give it.'

After thirty awkward minutes,[11] the cortège moved on to the airport, where the body was placed on an AN-32 plane of the Indian Air Force. The plane reached Hyderabad airport at 4.55 p.m.[12] The entire state Cabinet and bureaucracy, led by the chief minister and the governor, was present to receive the body. The coffin, draped in the national colours of orange, white and green was carefully lowered from the plane, with a guard of honour provided by soldiers of the Gorkha regiment of the Indian Army. The soldiers wanted to place the coffin on a gun carriage, but it would not fit. They improvised, placing rubber sheets under the coffin, and using a nylon rope the soldiers fastened it to the gun carriage.[13] Narasimha Rao, experimenter of objects and ideas, would have approved.

Body secured, the carriage made its way through the streets of Hyderabad, mourners on either side, till it reached Jubilee Hall in the centre of the city. Here the body lay in state for an entire day, as thousands streamed past to pay their respects.[14]

Meanwhile, the Andhra chief minister stuck to his word, and oversaw preparations for the funeral on a four-acre site by the banks of Hussain Sagar lake.[15] The funeral took place at 1 p.m. the next day. Prime minister Manmohan Singh made it a point to attend. K. Natwar Singh, then a senior Congressman, remembers, 'Manmohan was not happy with the treatment of the body [in Delhi].'[16]

Apart from the prime minister, most of his Cabinet as well as former prime minister H.D. Deve Gowda were present. As was

HALF-BURNT BODY

the BJP's L.K. Advani—the man who chose not to become prime minister in 1996, in part after Rao had ordered hawala corruption charges filed against him.[17] Also paying their respects were 12,000 ordinary citizens of India, many of whom had come all the way from Rao's ancestral village of Vangara.

Congress President Sonia Gandhi chose not to be present.

As Ranga Rao lit the pyre, he broke down and was comforted by his younger brothers.[18] When the dignitaries left a couple of hours later, the body was still burning. That night, television channels showed visuals of the half-burnt body, skull still visible, lying abandoned.[19] Stray dogs were pulling at the funeral pyre.

Rao's long-time aide, P.V.R.K. Prasad, was covering the funeral for a local television channel. He rubbishes the claim that Rao's body was only half-burnt.[20] 'The body had been burnt, but the ashes continued to give [an] outline to where the body was.' Prasad adds, 'This was more in [the] minds of the people. They knew he had been forced to come to Hyderabad . . . the body had not been allowed into the Congress office.'

Prasad then slows his speech to emphasize each word.

'The story [of the half-burnt body] was an expression of public anger at Rao's humiliation.'

In the twelve years since his death, P.V. Narasimha Rao continues to be ignored by his party. The Congress was in power in both the Centre and in the state of Andhra Pradesh from 2004 to 2014. No memorial was built for him during this period. The government did not officially celebrate his birthday every year.[21] This was instead done privately by Rao's family in Delhi. They were helped by Rao's personal staff, friends and M.S. Bitta, the Punjab Congressman sidelined for his proximity to Rao. Since filling up a hall for Narasimha Rao in Delhi was not easy, Bitta used to bus peasants from Punjab. 'They were there for free food and drinks,'[22] Sanjaya Baru, who would attend the event, remembers. 'They didn't know anything about Rao.'

The one Congressman who would punctually attend these birthday celebrations was prime minister Manmohan Singh. When asked why he chose to defy an unwritten code of his party, Manmohan replies that Rao gave him full freedom on economic reform. Going for a memorial service one day in a year was a small price to pay. 'I wanted to respect his memory.'[23]

Captain Lakshmikantha, a relative of Rao, is a politician from the regional party Telangana Rashtra Samithi (TRS). When his party was in a coalition with the Congress in Andhra Pradesh in 2012, he remembers petitioning for a statute of Rao to be erected in Warangal. 'The local Congress people blocked the plan,' Lakshmikantha says. 'If the statue is built, then they have to go garland [it]. If someone takes a photo and Sonia madam sees it . . . they did not want that.'[24]

There was one basic reason for Sonia Gandhi's dislike of Narasimha Rao. As K. Natwar Singh puts it, 'Rao realized that he didn't have to report to Sonia as prime minister. He didn't. She resented that.'[25] An aristocrat from the princely state of Bharatpur, Natwar was married to the daughter of the maharaja of Patiala. He had spent much of his life as a diplomat, before joining the Congress party, rebelling against prime minister Narasimha Rao, and then becoming Sonia Gandhi's closest aide. Natwar would end his career like Rao, abandoned by Sonia, cast out by his own party.

The subtle sidelining of Rao has been accompanied by more blatant attempts to tar his legacy. On economic liberalization, the Congress narrative seeks to credit Rajiv Gandhi for the ideas, and Manmohan Singh for the execution. As Sonia Gandhi said during the 125th anniversary celebrations of the Congress party, 'Rajiv-ji did not stay with us to see his dreams being realized, but we can see reflections of his thoughts in the party manifesto for the 1991 elections. That became the basis for economic policies for the next five years.'[26]

The other criticism of Rao has been on his role in the fall of Babri Masjid in December 1992. Congress leader Jairam Ramesh—otherwise an admirer of Narasimha Rao—says that '99.99 per cent of the Congress party believes that Rao connived in the destruction of the Babri Masjid. And that clouds the judgment of every Congressman.'[27] Rahul Gandhi publicly claimed that had his family been in power in 1992, the Babri Masjid would not have fallen.[28] Since the Congress was anxious to denounce its own for the demolition, other parties felt no need to contest the claim.

This absence of a political constituency meant that Rao was also blamed for other sins—from letting Union Carbide chairman Warren Anderson go free after the Bhopal gas leak,[29] to allowing Sikhs to be killed in Delhi in 1984.[30] As Congress leader Salman Khurshid says, '[Rao] is a tragic figure, remembered for so much that went wrong, but not for so much that went right.'[31]

The Congress assault on Rao's record has been supplemented by left-wing parties and intellectuals. They blame Rao for 'pro-rich policies', which, in the words of veteran communist Somnath Chatterjee, 'had brought untold miseries to the people'.[32] It is essential to this intellectual project that Rao also be blamed for Babri Masjid. For, communalism and capitalism, Marxists believe, are two sides of the same coin.

With no group willing to stand up for him, these criticisms have contributed to Rao's public disgrace.

That has been changing in the past few years, with newly converted devotees—as hagiographic as his detractors are blistering—attempting to resurrect his legacy.

In Telangana, the TRS has adopted Rao as a local icon in a newly formed state looking for regional heroes. Starting in 2014, the Telangana state government has chosen to officially celebrate his birth anniversary in Hyderabad every year. It has announced that Rao's life will be taught to schoolchildren,[33] and a district and university renamed after him.[34] In 2015, the new BJP Central government built a memorial ghat for Rao in Delhi. The BJP's finance minister, Arun Jaitley, calls Rao 'India's best Congress prime minister'.

'He showed it is possible to be a Congressman without being from the Family,' he says.[35]

This nascent political revival is anchored in ideological waters. As a 'right-wing' intellectual discourse takes shape in India—loudly on Twitter and television, more subtly in think tanks and some universities—Rao is being sculpted as the hero who freed India's economy and ended Nehruvian socialism. Subramanian Swamy, a poster boy for this emerging discourse, has demanded a Bharat Ratna for Narasimha Rao.[36]

These disagreements over Rao's legacy—between left and right, the Congress and its opponents—are really contestations over competing ideas of India. They revolve around a few key questions that deserve well-researched answers. What was Rao's role in the liberalization reforms? Have they transformed India for the better, or have they made the poor worse off? Why was he selected prime minister? Did he secretly want the Babri mosque demolished? Why did Sonia Gandhi and Narasimha Rao fall out? How did he survive a hostile Parliament and party to last a full term in office? Did he set India off on a new foreign policy path, or was the shift inevitable? Are the corruption charges against him true? And is Narasimha Rao India's most transformational leader since Jawaharlal Nehru?

That Rao's five years in office transformed India is hard to dispute. When Rao became prime minister in 1991, the economy was folding up. By 1996, India was growing at 7.5 per cent. Narasimha Rao inherited a 'welfare state' that was inefficient and underfunded. Many of the large social schemes that India has now undertaken—from employment guarantees to food security—were first initiated during his reign. Rao came to power when India's main global partner, the Soviet Union, was in slow collapse. By the time he left, India had improved relations with the US, Israel, China as well as East Asia.

The India of 1991 was fraying at the edges. The Liberation Tigers of Tamil Eelam (LTTE) had just killed Rao's Congress predecessor. Elections had to be postponed in Kashmir and Punjab, because the Indian government could not guarantee peace in either state. And insurrection in the North-east showed no signs of easing. By the time Rao left office, Punjab and Assam had been pacified, and the worst of the violence in Kashmir was over. Narasimha Rao also transformed the very idea of the Congress. A party that had grown used to anchoring itself around a single family was—even if briefly—prospering without them.

The reforms Narasimha Rao unleashed have also transformed India in the everyday. In 1991, the middle-class numbered no more than 30 million,[37] compared to 300 million in 2013.[38] There were only 2.3 million kilometres of roads in 1991, compared to double that in 2012.[39] Flying was expensive, with only one option, the state-owned Indian Airlines. A mere ten million passengers travelled by air in 1991[40]—compared to 82 million in 2014.[41] Train travel was cheaper but meant waiting in queue for months, with no certainty of a confirmed berth. The one accomplishment was telephone connectivity, a result of prime minister Rajiv Gandhi's target of a telephone booth in every village. But so low was the bar for 'accomplishment' in the India of 1991 that the number of subscribers was only five million.[42] Compare that to 2015, where India has nearly a billion phone subscriptions.[43]

The India before Rao was also a place without broadcast entertainment. Entire neighbourhoods would huddle around a single television to watch serials of the Hindu epics, the Ramayana and the Mahabharata. These would be carried on the nation's only television channel, Doordarshan, thanks to a state monopoly over broadcasting. Compare that to 2015, where viewers can choose from 832 channels.[44]

In terms of the quantum of transformation brought about, Rao ranks with other twentieth-century revolutionary figures such as Jawaharlal Nehru of India, Deng Xiaoping of China, Franklin D. Roosevelt and Ronald Reagan of the United States, Margaret Thatcher of Great Britain, and Charles de Gaulle of France.

But these leaders had advantages that Rao did not.

Unlike Deng, Narasimha Rao operated in a fractious democracy with several limits on his powers. Unlike FDR and de Gaulle, Rao lacked charisma and popular support. And in contrast to Reagan, Thatcher and Nehru, Rao did not control Parliament or even his own party. Scarcely a week went by when he was not challenged by dissidents within the Congress. And Rao's government survived multiple ordeals in Parliament to become the first minority dispensation in Indian history to last a full term. That he survived is itself noteworthy. That he did much more than survive is nothing short of a miracle.

A few other Indian leaders have ushered change while working under constraints. Despite being the first non-Nehru-Gandhi prime minister, Lal Bahadur Shastri won a war, encouraged some private enterprise, and launched the Green Revolution.[45] But he was respected within the Congress and enjoyed a dominant majority in Parliament, while Rao had none of these luxuries. Prime minister H.D. Deve Gowda, perhaps as weak as Rao, was able to push through some reforms. But nothing of the scale of Narasimha Rao.

Understanding how prime minister Narasimha Rao achieved so much despite having so little power is the central puzzle of this book.

To answer this, it is necessary to know what prime minister Rao did vis-à-vis the economy, welfare schemes, Babri Masjid, foreign policy, nuclear deterrence, and internal security. One must also analyse how Rao managed party, Parliament and Sonia Gandhi.

One must begin, however, by drawing out the early Narasimha—his childhood in Telangana, early years in the Congress, fight against the Nizam, experience in Andhra politics, disastrous stint as a socialist chief minister, introspection in exile, resurrection as loyal number two in the Delhi durbar, and retirement in 1991 to almost head a Hindu monastery.

These formative years shaped Rao's politics and personality, providing him the talents to change India when he became prime minister. Rao's final words before he died had to do with memories of his mother's room in his ancestral village.[46] This is no coincidence. To understand how Narasimha Rao transformed India, one must begin, as he began.

In the village of Vangara.

2

Andhra Socialist, 1921–71

He was named after his grandfather, Narasimha Rao.[1] Pamulaparti was the family name, and following Telugu convention, preceded his own. In between was god, Venkata, after the presiding deity of Tirupati. A Sufi master knocked on the door of his father's house soon after he was born. 'Your son will become a *baadshah*.' A king.[2]

Pamulaparti Venkata Narasimha Rao was born on 28 June 1921 in British India. His family lived in Vangara, a settlement of rice fields in Karimnagar district, in what is now the state of Telangana. As was custom, his pregnant mother travelled to her parents' home in nearby Lakinepally to give birth.[3] Both villages were in a part of India that was, in Rao's telling, 'geographically... a bridge between the North and the South'.[4] Living on the edge of five linguistic cultures, villagers here spoke Telugu, Hindi, Marathi, Kannada, and even some Oriya. And in this the land of the Nizam, the language of power was Urdu, while the language of courtly life was Persian. Narasimha Rao would go on to speak ten languages.[5] These were the tongues he inherited at birth.

His parents were of the Brahmin caste. Father Sitarama Rao owned 200 acres of dry land. The only other Brahmin family in the village was related to Narasimha's family in three ways: by blood, a common wall, and a daily routine. This other family owned 1200 acres of rice fields and mango orchards, making them the largest landlords of the village—a fact that would matter to Narasimha, who would soon make this family his own.

The village where Rao was born was in the princely state of Hyderabad. Its peculiar politics, at odds with mainstream Indian nationalism, is critical to appreciating the influences on young Narasimha.

For, the princely states of colonial India were a world unto themselves. By the early 20th century, they comprised more than 500 principalities[6] and covered a third of the subcontinent.[7] Some kingdoms were no more than a handful of villages; the state of Hyderabad was close to the size of England, Scotland and Wales put together. Ruled at the time by the ornately wealthy Nizam, Asaf Jah VII, Hyderabad state's mostly Muslim officials administered a population that was 85 per cent Hindu.[8]

Along with this religious bias came a second inequity. Land ownership in Hyderabad state was skewed even by the standards of colonial India. British treaties with the Nizam had guaranteed that 'a political and social structure from medieval Muslim rule had been preserved more or less intact'.[9] This ensured many middlemen between the tiller of the land and the Nizam. Formal ownership of land was in the name of *jagirdar*s. But actual power over tenant and tiller was with the village agents, known as *deshmukh*s, or *dora*s. The Nizam often had a direct relationship with these doras, who paid him a share of the land revenue, a portion of which was then passed on to the British. Many doras were Hindus—from the Reddy, Velama and Brahmin castes.[10] The Reddys and Velamas would typically deal with village administration, while the Brahmins would handle revenue collection.[11] Narasimha Rao's ancestors, Brahmins from Telangana, were also doras,[12] and as such, embedded in this structure of exploitation.

By 1921, pan-Indian nationalism was challenging these injustices. Mohandas Gandhi had just given a call for 'non-cooperation' against the British, transforming the Congress from a debating club of the Indian elite into a mass movement. A panicking Nizam responded by banning political meetings and entry of outsiders into his state without prior permission.[13] This was the political situation at the time of Narasimha Rao's birth—a surge in both nationalism as well as political oppression.

While they would shape his adolescence, his baby years in Vangara were unwet by these waves. The other castes in the village were Yadavs, Gouds, Reddys and Dalits who lived alongside a few Muslim families blessed with royal benefaction. Narasimha would run around the village, mixing, touching and playing with all their children. Some of his closest friends were, in fact, Muslims. The entrance to Vangara today is a tarmac grey road that snakes past green fields of paddy shoots standing to attention.[14] When Rao was a child, this road was a narrow embankment that cut through a pond. Narasimha would swim, leap out and dry himself by running in the sun.

His earliest memories were of stories from the Mahabharata and Ramayana. The monkey god Hanuman was a favourite, and Narasimha would hop from chair to table, setting fire to the evil Ravana's city of Lanka.[15] Ritual chanting in Sanskrit, recitation of epics, and religious holidays were all permitted, perhaps even encouraged, by the Nizam[16]. It was a secularism as much about principle as it was about self-preservation. As Rao observed years later, 'Where no political expression was permitted, cultural preoccupation became dominant, of necessity.'[17]

At the age of four, Narasimha—the first of four surviving siblings—was given in adoption to his Brahmin neighbours. They had no children of their own, and were afraid their heirless lands would be seized by the Nizam.[18] The adoption made Narasimha heir to the richest couple in the village. It was a legal fiction. His birth parents still nurtured him; he still ran around between both houses.[19] When Rao's biological father lay dying fourteen years later, he would remind his wealthier firstborn: 'Just because you are adopted does not mean you can forget this side . . . take care of your mother and siblings.'[20] Rao never forgot, always treating both families as one.

The only thing Rao did not adopt from his new family was the air of a *dora*. He would always identify himself as 'middle class', and years later, would pioneer land reform laws that reduced his own holdings.

While adoption arrangements meant to preserve land were not unusual in the region, what was unusual was the child Narasimha's abilities to read, write and memorize. Southern Brahmins had habitually been clerks or colonial officials, adapting religious learning to a modern education. This was not possible in the state of Hyderabad, where government service was the preserve of Muslims. So there was little motivation for Narasimha to study, especially since his family was tied to land rather than temple.

But personalities are not always explained by structural conditions, and despite having no incentive to learn, Narasimha proved a precocious student. His father would place Narasimha on his chest and 'recite verses from the *Bhagvata* in a long chain'. Within a few weeks, Narasimha was chanting those stanzas from memory.[21] The unschooled Sitarama Rao had a reverence for knowledge, and when he noticed his eldest son surpassing the lone village teacher, he sent Narasimha away to the nearest village which had a full-fledged school.

The separation of seven-year-old Rao from his family would haunt him for the rest of his life. Shaken from the settled rhythms that centuries of cultivation had given his family, he was now on his own, visiting his parents only once every five months. Education would propel Rao from village to town to city. Into politics and into power. It would make him prime minister of India. But it would also cut him off from clan and community. It would make him remote, squirrelled away amongst ideas and words from which he could never be sent away. He would develop a distant relationship with his children, a beleaguered one with his eldest son, Ranga.

The early separation from his parents would torment him seventy-six years later, when he lay dying in a hospital bed in Delhi. 'I am walking on the bund in [the] village,' the semi-conscious former prime minister told his children, 'Father is wearing white and [is] on the other side. He is beckoning to me. Let me go. Let me go to him.'[22]

In 1931, Rao was married off. He was ten. His wife, Satyamma, was related to his adoptive mother, a calculation meant to keep his lands within that family line.[23] She would bear and raise eight children, remain in Vangara to take care of the family lands, and show little interest in Rao's political career. Rao would later describe his arranged marriage as an act beyond his control, as so much of his later life would be. He was 'disappointed but not shocked'; his 'inner self remained unaffected'.[24]

By the age of ten, Rao had experienced adoption, separation and marriage—all thrust on him without his choice. It gave him, early on, the serenity to accept the things he could not change. As Rao later wrote, 'As he went through life, he found that less and less of his self determined his action.'[25]

In 1937, Narasimha Rao completed high school, 'higher secondary education' as it was called back then. He had stood first in the entire state of Hyderabad.[26] It was an achievement so singular that it vindicated—to Rao and to others—his decision to study further rather than cultivate land.

The year 1937 was also a time of political unrest in Hyderabad state. In elections held that year in (directly-ruled) British India, the Congress came to power in Madras and Bombay presidencies, both of which shared boundaries with Hyderabad. This gave a fillip to movements working against the Nizam. Marathi, Telugu and Kannada associations began organizing to protect their linguistic groups within the state. The conservative Hindu Mahasabha as well as the reformist Arya Samaj began working together to end the Nizam's rule. The Hyderabad State Congress was formed that year with the aim of 'attaining responsible government under the aegis of H.E.H. the Nizam by peaceful and legitimate means'.[27] In 1938, the state Congress organized a satyagraha on the very same day that the Arya Samaj and Hindu Mahasabha launched theirs. They were countered with uncommon ferocity. The Nizam was determined to protect his temporal power. He also wanted to shield Muslim rule from a national movement that was largely Hindu.

Nothing symbolized this latter concern more than the song 'Vande Mataram'. Written in 1882 by the Bengali poet Bankim Chandra Chatterjee, the song used Hindu imagery of a mother goddess as an allegory for India. Religious Muslims refused to worship another god, while the Congress adopted it as a secular creed. Singing the song was banned in the state of Hyderabad.

Narasimha Rao's tryst with India's destiny began during the 1938 satyagraha, when the seventeen-year-old Rao sang 'Vande Mataram' with other Hindu students in his college in Warangal. The Nizam's officials ordered them to stop, since the song was associated with the banned Congress party. When they persisted, 300 students—including Rao—were expelled by the principal.[28] Rao's resumé until then had been a carefully crafted ticket to a secure government post. That had ended on a song.

The expelled students scrambled to complete their degrees elsewhere. The chancellor of Nagpur University, a nationalist, agreed to take in the brightest of the bunch. Rao was, of course, among those selected.

His Nagpur years were the start of a long association with the region. Rao brushed up on his Marathi, and by the time classes began, was speaking like a native.[29] Forty-six years later, his Marathi skills would be put to use when Rao left his constituency in Andhra Pradesh to stand and win from Ramtek in Maharashtra.

When he finished his degree, he moved to another Marathi-speaking city, Pune, to study astronomy. Marathi-speakers were at the forefront of the intellectual currents of the time. Rao swam in them with ease. He read the works of the Hindu nationalist V.D. Savarkar, and also subscribed to the communist weekly *New Age*, where P.C. Joshi was acclimatizing Karl Marx to the specific misfortunes of the Indian peasantry.[30] But it was to the mainstream of the national movement that he was most drawn. He read the moderate Gopal Krishna Gokhale as well as the radical Bal Gangadhar Tilak.

In 1938, Rao also attended a session of the Indian National Congress in Haripura, Gujarat. The session was pertinent to Rao, for it marked an emboldened Congress attitude towards princely states such as Hyderabad. The party resolved that 'Purna Swaraj or complete independence, which is the objective of the Congress, is for the whole of India inclusive of the States'.[31] The Congress 'Left'—headed by the young Jawaharlal Nehru—wanted to act on that declaration, and organize protests in the princely states. But the 'moderate' Mahatma Gandhi was worried that an escalation might stretch the party. He ensured that the resolution also stated that 'under existing circumstances, the Congress is not in a position to work effectively . . . within the States'.[32]

The only memory of Narasimha Rao's that survived from Haripura was of hearing Jawaharlal Nehru speak 'with his earnest voice, now halting with emotion, now surging like a river in flood'.[33] Nehru's advocacy of militant action in the princely states must have resonated with the impressionable seventeen-year-old—and goes some way in explaining his early association with the left-wing of the Congress party.

In 1940, Narasimha Rao's wife, Satyamma, gave birth to their first child, Ranga. They would have seven other children: two sons and five daughters. Satyamma could barely read and write.[34]

But she possessed an earthy practicality that the intellectual Rao lacked. Satyamma chose to remain in the village, looking after Rao's lands as well as their children. Until her death in 1970, she was to provide for the family, leaving Rao free to pursue his dreams.

Meanwhile, Rao graduated from Pune with a first class, and was tempted by a career in law. He also considered pursuing astronomy in England, the terminus of the Empire. Years later, when disenchanted with politics, he would tell his youngest son, 'I never wanted to be a politician. I wanted to go to the UK to settle as an academic, in Oxford or Cambridge.'[35] There was also pressure to return to the family business, to join his wife and look after his acreage in the village.

These career options reflected the contradictions already visible in the young Narasimha Rao's personality. The inward gaze of a five-foot-short scholar was coupled with curiosity about the ways of the world. In the scuffle between the introvert and the extrovert inside Rao, the latter won. He chose to pursue a law degree in Nagpur.

The decision imposed financial costs on Rao, and Vangara's largest landlord began working part-time as a food-rationing inspector, living on the fifty rupees he earned.[36] But the legal profession unlocked to Rao a universe that stargazing never could. A black coat and white neckband was the costume of anti-colonialists across the British Empire. The Indian freedom movement was brimful with lawyers, among them Gandhi, Nehru, Patel, Ambedkar and Jinnah. After Rao stood first in his law exam, he returned to Hyderabad to begin legal practice as a junior to Burgula Ramakrishna Rao, a Brahmin lawyer and future chief minister of Hyderabad state.

With World War II over, the British were keen to leave India. They faced two knotty questions. What to make of the princely states that had enjoyed autonomy within the British Empire? And how to address the demands of Muslim politicians for a separate country? The state of Hyderabad posed both questions at once. It was one of the largest princely states, complete with its own insignia, air force, army and police. The Muslim Nizam also wanted the right to choose where he belonged. Soon after the announcement of Partition on 3 June 1947, he declared that he preferred independence,[37] ignoring the detail that his subjects were mostly Hindu, and his kingdom surrounded by India. When the rest of India became independent in August 1947, negotiations between the state of Hyderabad and the Union of India remained unresolved.

The ensuing struggle against the Nizam brought together the unlikeliest of allies. The Indian National Congress wanted to dethrone him and integrate Hyderabad state into secular, democratic India. The Hindu Mahasabha and Arya Samaj disliked the Islamic ruler. And in Telangana region, an armed insurrection against landlords had morphed into a communist rebellion. These three elements gave rise to an anti-Nizam movement that was secular, religious and radical. All at once.

These features were embodied in the man who led the movement. Bald and clean-shaven, with penetrating eyes and saffron garb, Swami Ramananda Tirtha was a Hindu sadhu who was half-saint, half-politician—a persona which Mohandas Gandhi had perfected nationally. He spoke many languages, and was active in Telangana. He was president of the Hyderabad State Congress,[38] and had attempted to convert it into a mass movement. Tirtha argued that land ownership should vest not just in the hands of the village agents (who were from the dominant castes)—land should pass on to the actual tiller (many of whom were low-caste Hindus). These radical views were resisted by party 'moderates' such as Mohandas Gandhi in Delhi and Burgula Ramakrishna Rao in Hyderabad. But Tirtha's vision, infused with spirituality and socialism, proved irresistible to the twenty-six-year-old Narasimha Rao.

Rao would later describe the left-wing Ramananda Tirtha as someone whose 'saffron robes scared [some people] as Red rags'.[39] Tirtha was to be the first of many religious figures with whom Rao would share a political relationship. But unlike the Chandraswamis and N.K. Sharmas who would come later, this power broker was guru first. Tirtha would mentor the future chief ministers of three states: Virendra Patil of Karnataka, S.B. Chavan of Maharashtra, and Narasimha Rao of Andhra Pradesh.[40] No one would be more grateful than Rao. Before meeting him, Rao would wash his mouth carefully to make sure there was no trace of paan.[41] In his later years, Rao would create a memorial for his dead guru, and when he himself died in 2004, Rao's beloved books would live on there.

Ramananda Tirtha's influence over his young protégé is central to understanding chief minister Rao's zeal for land reforms in the 1970s. It is also crucial to appreciating prime minister Rao's attitude to the BJP and Hindu nationalists in the 1990s.

That was to come later. In the struggle against the Nizam between August 1947 and September 1948, Narasimha Rao worked under Ramananda Tirtha, who was deploying the methods of both Gandhian resistance as well as violent struggle. Rao moved to a Congress camp in Chanda, Maharashtra, where he worked as a gunrunner, ferrying arms to groups plotting the Nizam's downfall.

These groups were opposed by the Nizam as well as a Muslim militia called the Razakars. Through this period, the Indian press reported atrocities by the Razakars against the state's Hindu population, incidents which were used to make the case for military action.[42] That came in September 1948, when India's home minister, Vallabhbhai Patel, sent in troops to annex Hyderabad into the Indian Union. This 'police action' ended the 224-year rule of the Nizams. It also brought retaliatory violence against the state's Muslims. According to a government report commissioned by prime minister Jawaharlal Nehru, between 27,000 and 40,000 Muslims were murdered after the liberation of Hyderabad.[43] The

Indian Army stood by and in some cases even participated in the killings.

After September 1948, those who had fought the Nizam searched for a new career. Narasimha Rao, once again torn between his inner and outer ambitions, once again sided with the latter. His choice of a career in politics was not an affirmation, merely the preclusion of other alternatives. In his own words, he was a 'hopeless misfit'; but a 'mundane existence' would have driven him mad.[44] Politics was where Rao would finally belong.

By 1948, the Indian National Congress had already transformed itself from a freedom movement to a political party. Since there was little opposition from other parties, political differences began to be reflected *within* the Congress. The contradictions of India—regions, castes, religions, personalities—were represented by groups arguing and manoeuvring inside the same party. As the political scientist Rajni Kothari first pointed out, this 'Congress system' made for energetic inner-party democracy.[45] In Hyderabad state, for example, landed castes such as the Reddys and the Velamas began to compete with Brahmins for power within the party. There was also rivalry amongst the Brahmins. Rao's former employer, the 'moderate' Burgula Ramakrishna Rao, was pitted against the 'radical' Ramananda Tirtha and his supporters.

Narasimha Rao had to choose between master and mentor. He selected neither, cleverly cultivating a relationship with each bloc without alienating the other. As his career advanced, Rao was to perfect this quality, one that his daughter, S. Vani Devi, described as that of *'ajathashatru'*—someone whose enemies are yet to be born.[46]

As a reward, Rao was made president of the Karimnagar district Congress, and given a ticket to contest in the first elections of free India.

The elections were scheduled between the final months of 1951 and early 1952. They were, in historian Ramachandra Guha's words, 'an act of faith'.[47] Of the 176 million Indians of voting age, about 85 per cent could not read or write. These voters cast their preferences in 2,24,000 polling booths to choose representatives for 500 Parliament seats and 4000 seats in provincial legislatures. To supervise the process, there were 56,000 officers, 2,80,000 helpers and 2,24,000 policemen.[48] History provided no parallel.

P.V. Narasimha Rao contested the first Lok Sabha election as the Congress candidate from Huzurabad constituency in Hyderabad state. His party prevailed nationwide, winning 364—74 per cent—out of the 489 seats. But the party did below average in Hyderabad state, only winning 56 per cent of the seats.[49] Rao lost his election to a communist party candidate. The thirty-year-old could not fathom the results. His family was 'sullen and disapproving'; his party demoted him.

Rao also lost his guide within the party. Ramananda Tirtha had attempted to become the first chief minister of Hyderabad state in 1952. He was defeated by Burgula Ramakrishna Rao. A full lion, if ever there was one, Tirtha had been able to scare away the wolves, but was not fox enough to avoid traps. He chose to retire from active politics in 1953.[50]

In the elections of 1957, Rao was given a state legislature ticket, not a national one, from Manthani, a constituency far away from his village. It was a ticket to oblivion.

To avoid that fate, Rao campaigned hard. He would drive from village to village in an olive-green military jeep, humming Hindustani raga tunes from film songs.[51] This time he won easily, and never lost Manthani for the next twenty years. His eldest son-in-law, Venkat Kishen Rao, who managed the campaign, remembers Rao's appeal: 'He used to speak in a colloquial language. He would always give one or two simple solutions to some of the people's problems. If they took long to travel, he would talk about building a bridge. And after [the] elections, the bridge was built.[52]

Compared to the suitcases of money that would tarnish Narasimha Rao in later life, the early Rao was a stickler for rules. Those days, candidates would commandeer Mahindra jeeps from Madras. But few would be returned, and the company dared not ask. Before one of his election campaigns, Rao took 200 jeeps from Madras for the entire state. He returned them after the election. 'The owner was shocked,' Rao's son-in-law remembers. 'No politician ever did that.'[53]

Ever since Rao moved to Hyderabad to pursue politics, he would see his family infrequently. As he grew successful, he saw even less of them, not more than once in six months.[54] It was almost as if a busy public persona was meant to compensate for a lonesome personal life.

Soon after he won his first election, Rao returned home to Vangara village for a rare meeting with his family. While walking in his mango orchards one evening, Rao was shown a new Kirloskar motor, bought to pump water from the well. The expensive motor was refusing to start. The next morning, Rao dismantled it. Examining the inner parts in the glint of the sun, he noticed that the steel was too dry to rotate. He bathed that part in kerosene, lubricated it, then put the motor back. It worked. Rao composed a technical letter to the company, asking them to make changes in their pump motor in 'public interest'.[55] It was duly acknowledged.

In 1956, after a fierce agitation, Hyderabad state was cut on the lines of language. The Marathi- and Kannada-speaking regions were included in the newly formed linguistic states of Maharashtra and Karnataka respectively. The remaining part—Telangana, where Rao was from—became part of Telugu-speaking Andhra Pradesh, along with the coastal Andhra and Rayalseema regions of the erstwhile Madras state.[56] The belief was that a shared language would bind these diverse regions together. But those in hinterland

Telangana suspected landlords from the coast of dominating their region, and demanded a state of their own. The grievances of the Telangana region against Andhra Pradesh would never go away, and would reshape the political career of Narasimha Rao within his new state. To his many political identities—being a Brahmin, a landlord, a socialist, a scholar—another one was added in 1956. He was now from the poor, disgruntled region of Telangana.

The other politician associated with Telangana was Lakshmi Kantamma. Kantamma would be the first of many women to provide political acumen as well as companionship to the professionally and personally lonesome Rao.

The wife of a forest officer, she was a Kamma, a landed and entrepreneurial caste that had only just begun to organize politically. By 1957, she was working the Congress machine, lobbying to become a member of the legislative assembly. Years later, in his fictionalized memoir, Rao would remember the first time he saw her: 'Although she was plain and rather dark, she had a captivating presence.'[57] As he came to know her, he saw reflections of his own loneliness. In his words, 'she was a typical example of many people who had access to university level education for the first time in the history of their families, with no specific idea of what to do with it . . . And having achieved academic success, they felt an acute sense of alienation from the feudal, semi-literate, traditional environment they were trapped in.'[58] He might as well have been describing himself.

Like Rao, Lakshmi was attracted to socialism; like Rao, she was a writer and Sanskrit scholar. While Rao would almost become a Hindu monk in his later years, Lakshmi would make the complete transition from politician to *sadhvi*, a female renunciate in the Hindu tradition. Though they shared many interests, their personalities could not have been more different. While he was cautious, she was voluble, warm and full-blooded. She needed the approval of others; he looked inward for happiness.

In 1962, Lakshmi Kantamma became a member of Parliament. In that same year, the forty-one-year-old Rao became a minister in the state Cabinet. His name was not on the original list, but was pencilled in to accommodate someone from the backward region of Telangana.[59] All eight children and Satyamma moved to Hyderabad to live with him in his spacious government bungalow.[60]

Narasimha Rao's nine years as state minister would be marked by an impulse to fix and 'modernise' the rusting mechanisms of Indian society. But it was a socialist version of modernization that Rao adopted, the version that his idols Ramananda Tirtha and Jawaharlal Nehru espoused. To be a 'moderniser' in this idiom meant suspicion of private enterprise and belief in the modern state as the sole instrument for social change.

Rao began as state minister by holding dual portfolios of law and information. In 1964, he was made minister in charge of Hindu endowments and temples. A colleague of his remembers: 'Temples were not managed well . . . they were encroached, and tenants never gave rent. Even pujaris were not behaving. He regulated them, put them in their place.'[61] Three years later, in 1967, Rao moved to the ministry of health. Here, he monitored government doctors by paying unannounced visits to hospitals, and forbade them from private practice.[62] In 1968, when he was made education minister of Andhra Pradesh, Rao banned private colleges. He also thrust Telugu as the medium of instruction on all government schools,[63] a populist decision that placed poor children at a disadvantage compared to their English-speaking counterparts in wealthy private schools.

Narasimha Rao's time as Andhra minister taught him how government worked at the state level, a skill he would take with him to Delhi as Union minister and prime minister. Where the Andhra Rao was markedly different from the later Rao was in his impeccable socialism. The Nehruvian in him believed that only the visible hand of the state could pull India into the twentieth century.

During these years, Rao took care to keep his wife and children away from politics. This was especially hurtful to Rao's eldest son. Ranga wanted a political career of his own and could not understand why his father would not promote him. He was even angrier that Lakshmi Kantamma, not family, seemed to be benefitting from minister Narasimha Rao's career.[64]

The state Congress was then led by the Reddys, and the Kammas wanted a toehold in the party. Lakshmi became their self-appointed spokesperson. When a minister sacked an irrigation engineer for corruption, Lakshmi stalled the dismissal because 'under this administration, all Kamma issues go through me'.[65] A rare woman of the time trying to make it in a man's world, Lakshmi was the target of sexist jokes and innuendos. While she did not care, the gossip upset Narasimha Rao. By 1968, he was in need of a break.

He visited Madras, south India's only metropolis at the time, for a writing holiday. Since Rao was by then a senior politician and head of the Telugu Academy, the local Telugu association decided to honour him at Mahabalipuram, a beach town on the outskirts of Madras. The programme began in Telugu, but then shifted to the local language. Rao, who did not know Tamil, felt excluded from his own felicitation. He went back to his temporary home in Madras, pored over Tamil grammar books, and improved his reading by walking around the city, translating street signs. By the time he returned to Hyderabad, he was fluent in the language.[66]

Rao returned home to the changing colours of politics. It was 1969, the world was turning red. In the US, students had already occupied colleges protesting the Vietnam War. Activists in Paris had shut France down. In India, prime minister Indira Gandhi was pulling down the shutters in her own way.

She had come to power in 1966 after the sudden death of prime minister Lal Bahadur Shastri. The regional heavyweights—the 'Syndicate'—who ran the party wanted a surname that brought in national votes, and a novice who did their bidding. Indira Nehru Gandhi, at the time quiet and introverted, seemed just that person. But in the national elections held a year later, her middle name did not bring in the votes. Backward castes and other marginalized groups were unwilling to mechanically back the Congress any more.

Indira Gandhi's remedy was socialism. The hesitant prime minister, termed a 'dumb doll'[67] by a political opponent, transformed into a convincing protector of the poor. Painting her rivals in the Congress as right wing, she presented herself as a messiah of the marginalized, and split the party in 1969. In response to Opposition slogans calling for 'Indira *hatao*' (remove Indira), she coined the unopposable slogan, '*garibi hatao*' (remove poverty), and potent symbols—bank nationalization, and the abolition of privy purses. Indira Gandhi was in full control.

She began to use her power to promote economic socialism. In the Indian context, this meant strengthening state control over the economy, cutting businessmen to size and isolating India from the world market. It is vital to understand the origins of this licence raj, since these were the very controls that prime minister Narasimha Rao would abolish in 1991.

Contrary to perception, it was Indira Gandhi and not her father who was responsible for many of the most stringent economic controls.[68] Nehru's preoccupation was rapid industrialization of his poor country, and when he looked around in the 1950s, the obvious inspiration was the planned economy of the Soviet Union. Western economists broadly agreed with his 'soft-left' vision in the late 1940s and '50s.[69] By 1965, however, many parts of the world were searching for new models of growth. Nowhere was this more evident than in East Asia where authoritarian governments in Thailand, Singapore, Malaysia and South Korea began working with business houses to increase exports and achieve rapid growth.[70] It was at this very moment when India should have opened up to domestic entrepreneurs as well as encouraged exports, that Indira Gandhi's political compulsions closed the economy off.

This closure was achieved in three ways. First, large parts of the economy were reserved for public sector enterprises, thereby limiting the industries where private entrepreneurs could operate to a few 'open areas'. The wristwatch industry was one example of this. The government had placed restrictions on local manufacturers and banned imported Swiss watches. To meet domestic demand, therefore, the government tasked the state-owned Hindustan Machine Tools, or HMT—established to build heavy machinery—with making precision wristwatches. The results were ungainly and unsightly, like many Indian industrial products of the time. But a near-monopoly ensured that through the 1960s and '70s, HMT made eight out of every ten watches sold in India.[71] Some of these state monopolies were an extension of the logic of Nehru's 1956 Industrial Policy Resolution. But it was Indira who converted the mild suspicion of the private sector into active animosity.

The second set of changes was designed to limit the size of business houses so that they did not threaten the hegemonic power of the Congress party. This was done through licences, anti-monopoly laws, labour laws and nationalization of banks. Mandatory licences ensured that, in the few areas where the private sector was permitted, allocation decisions on what a businessman could make—how much, where, and at what price—was done by a bureaucrat sitting in Delhi. Licences, in particular, reduced entrepreneurs to a hobble. In the years 1966–68 alone, the Birla group of companies had to apply for 325 different licences.[72] Indira Gandhi also passed anti-monopoly laws that curtailed the growth of companies. In addition, she nationalized private banks. The aim was to improve rural credit, but the move starved industrial houses of capital. Laws meant to protect labour also ended up having the opposite consequence: companies hired fewer workers.

The third and final pillar of Indira's socialist economy was isolation from the global market. Protection from foreign competition became integral to the government's strategy of self-reliance. Entry of foreign money, companies and consumer goods was limited. There were also import restrictions on the raw materials and technology that Indian factories desperately needed. And exports were made unprofitable due to an artificially valued currency. This need for self-reliance was, in economist I.G. Patel's words, 'our cardinal sin'.[73] It consigned India to produce second-rate rather than get the best from the world.

These three pillars of the licence-permit-quota raj led to public sector dominance over the Indian economy. But state-run companies worldwide are not known for their efficiency, and the Indian public sector was particularly incompetent and corrupt. As Manmohan Singh put it, public sector-led investments were chronically unproductive,[74] and the few products they did make—such as HMT watches—would perhaps have never been purchased by customers if they had other options. The result of these controls was a 'Hindu rate of growth'.[75] Between 1960 and 1979, humble Malawi grew by 2.9 per cent per capita, while the world's largest democracy grew at just 1.4 percent.[76]

More striking—for a policy ostensibly for the poor—was that government revenue was so low that welfare schemes were unable to make a dent in poverty.[77] Indian socialism was more bark than bite.

Narasimha Rao, the Andhra minister, ideologically supported Indira Gandhi's leftward turn. While prime minister Rao would decisively dismantle the licence raj, the early Rao was genuinely sympathetic to economic controls. At a conference of the Andhra Pradesh backward classes, he even declared, 'We will not tolerate capitalists, even if he is a Harijan [Dalit].'[78]

Narasimha Rao's loud support for economic socialism spoke of a dual personality. At one level, the mouse-sized Rao was introverted and cautious. His childhood traumas—adoption, having to leave home, and early marriage—had made him solitary. He could connect with neither village nor wife. Rao's education and natural curiosity had also distanced him from rustic family and friends. In his political career, this isolation had translated into never choosing one party faction or personality cult over the other. It was a strategy that won him few friends or followers, but it also made him very few enemies. Such a restrained disposition would have normally made for a circumspect policymaker—with neither durable principles nor abiding concerns.

But such were the paradoxes of Rao that when it came to running the education, health, law, and endowments ministries, he had acted like a lion. His childhood observation of feudalism as well as the Nizam's tyranny had exposed him to the inequities of India. The influences of Ramananda Tirtha and Nehru had uncovered for him the inadequacies of gradual reform. Like the rest of the Congress-left, Rao supported an all-powerful state battling unjust feudals and unscrupulous businessmen.

There was yet another socialist policy on which Narasimha Rao's beliefs coincided with Indira Gandhi's political calculations. This was land reform, which, by the early 1970s, was a burning issue through much of the country. It was a cause for which Narasimha Rao was prepared to stake—and burn—his own career.

3

Puppet Chief Minister, 1971–73

At Indian Independence, 40 per cent of all land was owned by revenue intermediaries, known as zamindars or *jagirdar*s.[1] Breaking the power of this class was a vital plank of the freedom struggle. By 1966, not only were these lands freed from intermediary control, the government estimated that 200 million tenants of former intermediaries had been brought into a direct relationship with the state.[2] Some of these new owners were the former village agents (i.e. the *dora*s or *deshmukh*s) who anyways had exercised control over the land. They became the new title holders, and employed others to till the land. Various states had attempted to pass on ownership to the tillers and the millions who were still landless.

These reforms had failed mainly because the new landlords belonged to the dominant castes who were the spine of the Congress in the villages.[3] Land ownership was especially lopsided in Telangana, a bequest from the Nizam's rule. These inequalities persisted even after the first phase of land reform laws. 'It was largely the Reddy ryots and tenants who benefitted from land redistribution, while Dalits and lower castes had to be content with common pastures and wastelands.'[4] Renewed land reform was Indira Gandhi's bait to lure the poor and lower castes back to her party.

Narasimha Rao approved of his leader's strategy. He had always spoken in favour of land reform, a persistent theme in his guru Ramananda Tirtha's politics. What gave Rao new purpose was the agitation, in 1969, for the separate state of Telangana. Narasimha Rao felt that underlying the demand was the clamour by the landless for land of their own.

Captain V. Lakshmikantha remembers meeting Rao in his village during the height of the agitation. Rao came back after a dusty day's work, washed his feet outside, then walked in and said, 'There must be land ceiling [against large landowners]. Or there will be blood.'[5]

It was an insight that also occurred to Indira Gandhi, as a pro-Telangana party defeated the Congress in many constituencies in the region in the 1971 national elections.[6] Land redistribution was a way for the Congress party to score three wins—reduce the power of the landlords, prevent blood being spilt in Telangana, and wrest seats back for the party.

The chief minister of Andhra Pradesh at the time was K. Brahmananda Reddy. He was liked by local Congressmen, was from a landed caste and came from a coastal district. In the eyes of prime minister Indira Gandhi, these made for three arguments against him. She wanted someone whom she could mould, someone who would attract backward castes and landless peasants, and a Telangana man who could placate the region.

Indira began to look for a 'nominated' chief minister. It was a concept that Narasimha Rao would explain some years later in a speech at the School of Oriental and African Studies, London.[7] A 'nominated' chief minister would have no local power base, thus ensuring loyalty to New Delhi and its socialism. Indira was looking for a powerless devotee. One who would sing only her hymns.

Chief minister Brahmananda Reddy was asked if he was okay with being replaced by D. Sanjivayya, a past chief minister who was also a Dalit. Reddy 'strongly opposed' the suggestion since Sanjivayya might threaten Reddy's hold over the party machinery in the state. Instead, the chief minister lobbied for his unambitious education minister to replace him.[8] Rao had no faction backing him. His advocacy of land reforms and socialism—not to mention the fact that he was from Telangana—made him especially attractive to Indira Gandhi.

Caste was another factor in Narasimha Rao's favour. Narsa Reddy, the state party president at the time,[9] recalls that since southern Brahmins were numerically few, they were seen as on the side of the other politically weak castes. It also helped that the national leadership was run by north Indian Brahmins, Indira Gandhi and Union minister Uma Shankar Dikshit amongst them.

Another person claimed credit for Rao's anointment. Lakshmi Kantamma, then a Lok Sabha MP, convinced Rao that she had lobbied for him in Delhi.[10]

And so it was that P.V. Narasimha Rao became chief minister of Andhra Pradesh in September 1971. Years later, in 2010, when Congress President Sonia Gandhi faced yet another agitation for a distinct Telangana state, she made an Andhra man chief minister.[11] It was a sign that, unlike in 1971, New Delhi had a separate Telangana in mind.

As chief minister, Narasimha Rao seemed to fulfil the first condition under which he was nominated: he appeared pliant and unassuming. Rao made no effort to promote his own family. In order to appease warring factions of the party, he included twenty-nine MLAs in his Cabinet—the largest in the state's history until then.[12]

Every morning at seven, he would descend from his house on the first floor to greet visitors. His secretary, P.V.R.K. Prasad, remembers the durbar. 'Ministers could walk in at any time . . . Although people continuously streamed into his chambers, thousands continued to wait outside.'[13] Rao would never ask someone to leave his office,[14] but was also careful to never overtly agree with anyone. Photographs from that period show Narasimha Rao in a perpetual half-smirk, neither fully committed to a smile nor fully to a frown. Narsa Reddy remembers: 'When you go to meet Narasimha Rao, it is as good as talking to the wall. The wall does not reply, nor does Narasimha Rao.'[15]

To push Rao into taking decisions, his secretary, Prasad, had rehearsed an act. Whenever the chief minister had an open file in front of him, Prasad would chime in and reassure Rao about the contents of the file. 'Even after arriving at a decision, he vacillates wondering whether he has overlooked something in the process. If someone he trusts backs him at that exact moment, he takes the decision promptly.'[16]

As a chief minister without a base of his own, Narasimha Rao needed guides and informants. He was learning that even if he eschewed factions, he needed his own channels of information. This became even more necessary after guru Ramananda Tirtha died in January 1973, a few months after his protégé reached the position he never could. The chief minister was inconsolable, and ordered a state funeral, proclaiming, 'I owe everything to him.'[17] Rao was in need of new eyes and ears.

These were provided by Lakshmi Kantamma. Just before he was made chief minister, Narasimha Rao's wife had passed away, ailing from diabetes and blood pressure; overwork too had taken its toll.[18] They had been married for around forty years, during which Satyamma had uncomplainingly taken care of the family land and children, while her husband pursued his own ambitions. Rao was filled with guilt and swore to end his relationship with Lakshmi. When the bureaucrat B.P.R. Vithal paid him a condolence visit that morning, he was told, 'I will be a changed man.'[19]

Rao did not change, and, as chief minister, had lunch with Lakshmi on most days. Secretary Prasad remembers that Rao would eat only after she joined him, sometimes waiting long until she appeared.[20] Narasimha Rao may have been an unfaithful husband but he was no hypocrite. He made no attempt to hide his relationship with Lakshmi, and the daily political gossip she brought was valuable. But their intimacy tarred his reputation. M. Narayan Reddy, who was secretary of the Congress Legislative Party, remembers going to the chief minister's office one day. 'There were 150 visitors waiting outside his office. Also the film star N.T. Rama Rao, who had come to give his son's marriage invitation to the chief minister. He was made to wait for one hour, and [he] went off to sleep. I went inside the CM's chamber to see what was taking so long, and found Narasimha Rao listening to Lakshmi Kantamma talk. It was a henpecked atmosphere. I told her, with folded hands, "Kindly allow people to see PV *gaaru*." She got up and went away.'[21]

Another source of information and advice for chief minister Narasimha Rao was Chandraswami, a man unusual even among the astrologers and soothsayers who hovered around Indian politicians. Born as Nemi Chand Jain, Chandraswami was from Hyderabad and knew many Andhra politicians. Rotund, with long hair and a beard hanging below eyes that never left you, Chandraswami radiated an unsettling air. Even in 2015, living in a baroque, wood-engraved mansion in the heart of Delhi, he spoke little, but exuded an aura which the secular call 'charisma', and the religious describe as 'presence'.[22]

Now a spent force fighting off allegations of corruption and human sacrifice, in the early 1970s he was a man on the rise. He claimed to have spent five years meditating in the jungles of Bihar, a penance that gave him mystical powers.[23] He would seduce politicians with predictions, then provide them with contacts ranging from Britain's Margaret Thatcher to the Saudi arms dealer Adnan Khashoggi. Aware of the insecurities of the powerful, Chandraswami would size up a politician or bureaucrat within five minutes of conversation, then connect him with someone whom the person respected in his own world—a senior party leader or bureaucrat. The effect was other-worldly as well as of this earth.

Narasimha Rao met him for the first time in 1971 when Chandraswami was performing a yagna in the temple town of Tirupati.[24] With his collection of contacts in Delhi and abroad, Chandraswami expanded the horizon of the provincial Narasimha Rao. Since many Andhra politicians were his devotees, Chandraswami kept the chief minister informed of the goings-on in his state. And the godman's access to Indira Gandhi and her coterie in Delhi gave Narasimha Rao, anxious to please his political patron, an alternative line of communication.

Rao's reliance on Lakshmi Kantamma and Chandraswami would set a pattern that would continue into his time as prime minister. For a leader to judge his own relative strength and weakness at any given point, he requires a network of spies and informants. He always needs extra pairs of ears.

While Rao was mostly conciliatory as chief minister, he was coming to terms with a contradiction in Indira Gandhi's concept of a 'nominated' chief minister. Being politically weak was the reason he was chosen, but as chief minister he was expected to be strong in implementing Indira's orders. It was a paradox that would bedevil Manmohan Singh in 2004. He was selected by Sonia Gandhi as prime minister precisely because he lacked any power of his own. But executing her will required him to be powerful. This inconsistency would similarly trouble Narasimha Rao in 1991. He was chosen as prime minister because he was submissive, while the circumstances that besieged India at the time required him to take initiative. Prime minister Narasimha Rao would resolve the contradiction by transforming India's economic and foreign policies, all the while pretending to be doing little. But this Narasimha Rao, the young chief minister, had much to learn about the politics of reform.

This Rao felt that he had to justify Indira's faith in him by carrying out her policies on land reform, and he would do whatever it took to achieve that end. To implement these policies, Rao threw caution and subtlety—the very qualities that made him chief minister—to the wind. The introvert gave way to the extrovert, the vacillating Hamlet gave way to the charged Don Quixote. Rao became, in his own words, a 'wild boar'.[25]

Gone were his customary silences or indecisions. On land reform, his colleagues recall, 'Rao had a sudden sense of importance at becoming chief minister at a young age.'[26] His party was in control of the state, and the few opposition 'communist members here and there were welcoming his reforms'.[27] The national leadership was backing him, and land reforms were sure to win votes. There was nothing to rein in the wild boar.

So, on becoming chief minister, Narasimha Rao, used his drafting skills to craft legislation that limited land ownership to a 'ceiling' of between thirty and fifty-four acres for dry land, and between twelve and twenty-seven acres for wetland.[28] Land in excess of the ceiling would be taken over by the government and distributed to the landless. The ceiling was uncomfortably low, given that Rao himself owned 1200 acres, and other landlords—including his Cabinet colleagues—had many times more. More dangerous still, in the eyes of the landlords, was that Rao plugged the loopholes in the law.

Congressman M. Narayan Reddy, who was assisting Rao at the time, remembers: 'After the announcement of the land ceiling, people started manipulating records. When we used to visit villages, Rao said, "Patwaris and revenue officers are colluding with the landlords.'"[29] Rao worked to plug these loopholes, and after introducing a new law in the state legislature, he resorted to theatre. He got up from his seat in the assembly, and went to the gate. 'All those in favour of land reform can stay,' he bellowed. 'The rest can leave.'[30]

Narasimha Rao's actions angered landlords and politicians, who bided their time. A colleague remembers that Rao's enemies extended to his own Cabinet. 'Because of Mrs. Indira Gandhi, those opposed were silent in the cabinet, they never opposed violently.'[31] But the tide was turning. Even Brahmananda Reddy, the man who had made Rao chief minister, now wanted him replaced.[32] Prime minister Narasimha Rao, wiser and older, would have paused. That reformer would never have taken on too many enemies at the same time. But chief minister Rao mistook silence for submission. He pushed on.

In the early years of the state, Brahmins had directed Congress politics until they were displaced by politicians from the more numerous Reddy caste. Now the Brahmin Narasimha Rao was ushering in the next revolution. He removed Reddys and other forward castes from his Cabinet, increasing the percentage of scheduled castes, backward castes and minorities from twenty-five to forty.[33] He was also the first chief minister of Andhra Pradesh to induct a tribal into his Cabinet.[34] The elite were not just losing land, their political tentacles were also being slashed.

To add salt to their wounds, Rao gave incendiary speeches. In his home district of Karimnagar, he told the young people who were listening: 'You are to indicate who is saving the lands . . . pass on information about law breakers.'[35] It was understood as a call for vigilante justice. In May 1972, Rao swore that he would implement land reforms 'whatever be the consequences'.[36] The subtext of violence was present in another speech. Narsa Reddy remembers the fiery chief minister declaring: 'All these big landlords have grown like babul trees under which no other tree can grow. I want to pluck out all these big trees to make way for the smaller trees to grow.'[37]

Intemperate speeches, consciously evoking caste, and provoking many enemies at the same time—this was not the quiet prime minister that New Delhi would know two decades later. But Narasimha Rao the chief minister was pouring kerosene all over himself. All that was needed was a matchstick.

Ignition came in the form of a Supreme Court judgment on 3 October 1972.[38] The question concerned the validity of *mulki* rules, a Nizam-era law that allowed for quotas in government jobs for those from the Telangana region. State employment being one of the few ladders for social mobility, these mulki rules were unpopular in the other regions of Andhra Pradesh. Rao was returning from one of his many Delhi visits when the court delivered the judgment declaring mulki rules to be valid. Ambushed by the press, Rao brusquely replied that the court ruling 'will bring finality to this matter',[39] and he would implement the judgment. His words were spun to imply that a Telangana chief minister was favouring his own region. Street protests followed.

This was the chance his enemies were waiting for. Landlords and high castes, still smarting from being targeted by Rao earlier, provoked, then joined, the agitation. They even demanded an independent Andhra, an ironic reversal of the demand for a separate Telangana. Eight Cabinet ministers resigned.[40] Rao's government crumbled.

As the state machinery screeched to a halt, the chief minister's bureaucrats gave him a list of 100 leaders to arrest.[41] Rao dallied. 'What can I do?' he griped to his secretary. 'There is no clearance from the High Command. I have been speaking to Delhi once an hour. However only rarely do I get an opportunity to speak to that great lady . . . I am awaiting her clearance because it is a serious political issue.'[42]

'That great lady' was rethinking socialism, at least as applied to the state of Andhra Pradesh. The agitation against Narasimha Rao had morphed into a protest against Indira Gandhi herself. Slogans were raised against her. Some leaders even threatened to quit the Congress. The Central minister Uma Shankar Dikshit, who had played a role in Rao's elevation, now wanted him sacked. Indira's socialism was a means to power. But in Andhra Pradesh, these policies were eroding her popularity. Ideology and self-preservation clashed. It was the latter that won.

Indira Gandhi decided to remove Narasimha Rao and impose Central rule on the state. Rao had misjudged his own context, failing to satisfy Indira's need for a chief minister both powerless as well as powerful. On 16 January 1973, Narasimha Rao was ordered to come to Delhi for 'urgent consultations'. The Congress president, Shankar Dayal Sharma, told him that the Central leadership was of the view that President's rule for a brief spell might help.[43] Rao disagreed, but did not rebel.

The next day, 17 January, he took his resignation letter to the governor in accordance with constitutional custom. Then, 'he got into the car, sighed, massaged his head with his hands, and commented, "Thank God, I am rid of the curse of being the chief minister."'[44]

Rao had been chief minister for two years, state minister for nine, and legislator for sixteen. He was being put out to pasture.

4

Exile, 1973–74

At the same time that Narasimha Rao was being retired in 1973, China's Deng Xiaoping was making a political comeback. In the late 1960s, angered by the reforms that Deng was championing, communist party chairman Mao Zedong purged Deng from power. He was sent to work at the Xinjiang County Tractor Factory in 1969. Deng was woken up at six-thirty every morning and forced to read the writings of Mao. He and his wife would then walk to the tractor repair station where Deng performed manual labour.[1] It took four years in the wasteland for Deng to find favour with Mao again. These years gave Deng the time and distance to recognize the problems of Maoism, and analyse what reform would eventually entail. As Harvard historian Ezra Vogel writes in his magisterial biography of Deng, 'Like Churchill, de Gaulle, Lincoln, and other national leaders who fell from high positions and then spent time in the wilderness before returning to high office, Deng found that the time away from daily politics allowed him to achieve clarity about major, long-term national goals.'[2]

Narasimha Rao spent the first months of his political exile hoping for a comeback. The circumstances of his removal in January

1973—through the imposition of Central rule—meant that the Congress party still retained its legislative majority. He had led his party to a spectacular victory in the 1972 assembly elections in Andhra Pradesh, and many of the legislators—personally chosen by him—remained loyal. Rao assumed he would be back as chief minister once the violence subsided in Andhra Pradesh. State legislators continued to visit him at his house in Hyderabad's MLA colony.[3] A group of forty legislators met prime minister Indira Gandhi and asked her to reappoint Rao as chief minister, to lead a Cabinet filled with 'weaker sections.[4] Some hotheads even declared that if Rao chose to split the party, they would side with him. He shushed them, saying, 'You do not know [the] power of the PM. We cannot do that.'[5]

J. Vengala Rao, Rao's competitor for chief ministership, also met with Indira Gandhi. In his memoirs, Vengala Rao recalls the prime minister telling him: 'I made [PV] chief minister hoping that he would work hard. But he has greatly disappointed me. He was so obsessed with Lakshmi Kantamma, that he sits when she asks him and stand when she asks him to . . . His eldest son P.V. Ranga Rao came to me and related all the woes of his family caused by Lakshmi Kantamma.'[6] Lakshmi was to dispute this claim when Vengala Rao published his memoirs decades later. 'Indira Gandhi is not alive to testify to the rot written by this coward.'[7]

The months dragged on. When Central rule was lifted in December 1973, Indira Gandhi appointed Vengala Rao chief minister. A Cabinet colleague of Narasimha Rao recalls why Indira chose one Rao over the other. 'Vengala Rao was born in coastal Andhra, settled in Telangana. He would be able to convince the Andhras and there would be no upheaval.'[8] The elevation of Vengala Rao, from the landowning Velama caste, ended any possibility of land reform.

The Congress high command was sending a message, and the rats below took notice. Rao's house, once suffocated by favour seekers, now breathed emptiness. The only audience that remained were Telugu writers who would spend hours occupying Rao in literary criticism.

Narasimha Rao felt the loss of status keenly. 'It gave him perspective,' his son Rajeshwara remembers. 'The moment you step down, people do not take much notice and are not bothered about you. Father saw all that.'[9] The fifty-two-year-old started complaining of blurred vision and toothache.[10] He developed diabetes and had to cut down on after-dinner sweets, and stick to a regimented diet of soup and vegetables.[11]

He retreated to New Delhi, to the state guest house, Andhra Bhavan.[12] While hungry locals would come to gorge on the thalis served in the ground-floor cafeteria, Rao lived and ate frugally in a suite on the floor above. National leaders, only a few kilometres away, ignored him. State politicians would visit Andhra Bhavan without paying their respects to him. Lakshmi Kantamma, then an MP in Delhi, would join them in card games that would go on late into the night. Rao would wait in an adjacent room while Lakshmi played cards with his rivals. When he asked her to hurry, she would put him down. '*PV, atla kuuchoo.*' ('PV, sit here.')[13]

With the public man in forced retirement, the introvert turned to paper and pen. Rao would wear a thin cotton kurta with a blue or green 'Madras checks' lungi, and sit on a small chair in front of a desk crowded with books and files. 'If we tried to move it, he would get angry, saying, "No, no, no. I have marked them,"' recalls his daughter Vani Devi.[14] The files would be piled so high that Rao, at a little over five feet, could barely be seen as he sat reading. The assortment of papers reflected his interests. Government reports competed for space with Telugu, Hindi and Marathi literature, all marked in red ink in flowing hand that survive to this day among his private papers.

Rao began scribbling away at an idea for a novel. It would be the story of an impassioned boy who leaves his village, joins the anti-Nizam movement, enters politics, and becomes the chief minister of the fictitious state of Afrozabad. The idealism of the protagonist would be tested by a party hollowed out by cliques, cash and personal ambitions. Though names and dates were veiled, the reader could easily part it to glimpse the author's own life.

The semi-autobiographical nature of the plot, neither faithful fact nor fully fiction, revealed something of Rao. As writer and former governor of West Bengal Gopalkrishna Gandhi put it: 'He was too shy of his own truths to put them straight, but he was too honest to hide them. He was too proud to be a hypocrite.'[15] The book ended with a question that troubled Narasimha Rao during these years out of office. Why was a devout chief minister, protected by Goddess Durga, sacrificed for implementing her holy writ? Rao moped over this question in Delhi, in Hyderabad, in Vangara village. The answer would give Prime Minister Rao the dexterity to navigate the politics of reforms twenty years later.

Narasimha Rao realized that Indira Gandhi had wanted a chief minister who was both powerless and powerful—and that could never be. 'If you consider the hurdles the nominated chief ministers had to face precisely for the reasons for which they were chosen, and only the limited extent to which they could . . . be underwritten by the High Command eventually,' Rao explained some years later, 'you will not be surprised that their regimes proved to be short lived.'[16] Ruminating in his suite in Andhra Bhavan, he complained to M. Narayan Reddy, a young legislator from Andhra Pradesh: 'Even though I did all, Madam Gandhi treated me so badly.'[17]

Rao brooded over his failed attempt at land reform. He told Narayan Reddy, 'I never expected so much opposition from [the] landlord section.' Forty-two years later, Reddy remembers, 'He was prejudiced against Reddys and Kammas. That was too open.

If he had maintained good relations with them, he would not have been removed.'[18]

Rao had also provoked multiple enemies at the same time. He had coupled land reform with the removal of high castes from his Cabinet. He had simultaneously supported sops for the Telangana region, angering other parts of the state. When his enemies made common cause, chief minister Narasimha Rao had been unable to manage the fallout.

All reforms take place under constraints and involve battling entrenched interests. Rao's mistake was that he had misjudged the opponents of change.

He would introspect on these missteps in an academic paper he wrote in the late 1970s. It was on the role of chief ministers in India, and Rao identified a range of roadblocks to reform. He called them 'unforeseen problems of the time', 'opposition from vested interests', and 'politics of the street'.[19] He deplored in particular the tendency to 'depose chief ministers by resorting to large-scale violence on the street . . . if force is used, it is condemned as repression; if it is not used . . . the chief minister [is] dubbed as inept.'[20] The trick, he was learning in his time out of power, was that to have the impact of a 'wild boar', one must have a light footprint.

The chief minister's other gaffes had been verbal. He had given inflammatory speeches, endorsed vigilante justice against landlords, and threatened violence. He had also spoken out of turn when the Supreme Court judgment on the validity of mulki rules was delivered. His words had been misinterpreted to imply favouritism towards his region of Telangana. From now on, Rao would say little. As prime minister two decades later, his silence would be lampooned as 'analysis until paralysis' and 'when in doubt, pout'. But as Narasimha Rao was learning in the lonely months after his removal as chief minister, silence was sometimes the ideal decoy to distract from radical action.

While Rao was licking his political wounds in early 1974, family beckoned. Daughter K. Saraswathi, now living in the United States, was pregnant. Rao had a barbed relationship with his children. They had grown up in Vangara village, away from their busy father. Rao had wittingly kept his family away from politics, and his ambitious eldest son, Ranga, felt neglected. By 1974, father and son were not on talking terms. Rao had a healthier relationship with his daughters, and now, with time on his hands, he decided to travel to New York for the birth of his grandchild. It was his first journey outside India.

A medical doctor, Saraswathi was part of the early wave of Indian professionals to be allowed into the United States. The Immigration and Nationality Act of 1965 had replaced national (i.e. racial) quotas with professional ones, allowing educated foreigners entry into the United States.[21] With wounded veterans returning from the Vietnam War, the demand for doctors was acute. By the early 1970s, India-born physicians like Saraswathi were much in demand in the United States.

Rao landed in New York, went to Saraswathi's house, and when his grandchild was born, wrote a perfunctory letter back home. 'This was the first time I got a letter from him,' Rajeshwara remembers. 'He wrote that Saraswathi has been blessed with a son, and that mother and child are good.'[22]

In what was becoming a pattern, Rao's laconic façade was covering the modifications within. In New York, he would spend the day reading local newspapers—the *New York Times* was a favourite—and watching US politics on television. He saw an America being transformed. The long noon of American liberalism had since given way to a Republican President, Richard Nixon, who had shaken up the verities of the Cold War. Nixon opened up relations with China, which had defeated India in a border war. He even signed an arms reduction treaty with the Soviet Union. And in early 1973, peace accords were reached between the United States and Vietnam, ending a decade of misadventure.

The Nehruvian alignments that had guided foreign policy in the early years of the Indian Republic were being subtly redrawn, and Narasimha Rao—who would someday be foreign minister—was seeing them first hand.

While his three months in the United States seems to have been spent absorbing American politics, Rao would occasionally wander the streets. One day, he walked into a Manhattan restaurant and asked for vegetarian cuisine. The waiter did not understand, so Rao had to explain that it was food without any animal meat in it. The waiter nodded and came back with a plate of raw corn, *bhutta*. When he returned to India, Narasimha Rao would narrate this story to his children, ending with a laugh.[23]

The one visit Rao made outside of New York was to the University of Wisconsin in Madison.[24] The university, nestled among the cheese factories of the American Midwest, was famous for scholarship on India. Velcheru Narayana Rao is today one of the world's experts on Telugu literature and early modern south Indian history. In 1974, he was a young lecturer at the University of Wisconsin. He remembers meeting Narasimha Rao on that trip.[25]

'We spoke about literature. He [Narasimha Rao] had very original ideas. I remember thinking to myself even then: he should be a professor in a university.' The books that Narasimha Rao was attracted to are revealing. 'He was particularly interested in the sixteenth-century Telugu text *Raghava Pandaveeyam*,' Narayana Rao recollects. 'One can, with the same set of words, read the story about either Ramayana or Mahabharata. The same words are capable of dual meaning. [Narasimha] Rao kept talking about the importance of dual meaning . . . how the same words can mean different things.'

In an interaction with other Indologists at the university, one professor asked Narasimha Rao a detailed question on caste in Andhra Pradesh. Rao replied, in part humour, 'You are talking of the things that we have already forgotten [in India].' Narayana

Rao, who was part of the conversation, remembers, 'He was pointing out that the way India was studied in the US was not right.' For dinner that night, Narayana Rao and his wife hosted the former chief minister in their small apartment in Madison. They ate flavoured rice, spicy powders and other staples of Telugu cuisine. Narasimha Rao wondered how these ingredients, so hard to find even in north India, were available in pastoral America.[26]

When he returned to India, Rao carried with him electronic equipment—a lifelong hobby—and stories of American technological prowess. His youngest son, Prabhakara, was an engineering student at the time. Rao bought him a calculator made by Texas Instruments.[27] When Rao's lackeys gathered in his Hyderabad home to greet their US-returned leader, Rao showed off the calculator to them. So enamoured was he by the United States that he even delivered lectures in Telugu on three occasions, telling his perplexed audience of American industrial success. When he travelled to America once again in 1979, for the birth of Saraswathi's second child, he was an old hand, explaining the working of mixies and dishwashers to his eldest daughter who had accompanied him from India.[28]

Jawaharlal Nehru, schooled in the West, was an Englishman who had moved back to discover India. His idea of India was moulded by this reverse journey. Narasimha Rao's path was more straightforward. In the words of K. Natwar Singh, '[Rao's] roots were deep in the spiritual and religious soil of India. He did not need to Discover India.'[29] It was the West he was noticing, at the age of fifty-three, and he liked what he saw.

Most Indian leaders of the nationalist period had been schooled in the United Kingdom, shaped by the Fabian socialism of the time. Peculiarly enough, this formative experience had led many to a fascination for the Soviet Union and its model of state controls. As state minister and chief minister, Rao had internalized this Nehruvian ideology as the only route a traditional society could take to modernity. His 1974 visit to the United States was to subtly change his mind.

Over the years, Telugu-speaking migrants to the US would reshape the relationship between their lands of origin and work. By 2015, they would account for the single largest group among Indian immigrants to the US.[30] This migration would have, what the scholar on migration Devesh Kapur calls, a 'cognitive impact' on what Telugu speakers back home thought of America.[31] Narasimha Rao's own interactions with his American family members—a second daughter was to migrate a decade later—would deepen his admiration for American capitalism. The economist Montek Singh Ahluwalia, himself a product of Washington, remembers a briefing on the global economy when the prospects for oil prices came up. Prime minister Narasimha Rao asked his assistant to connect him to a 'Mr Rao' in New York, explaining, 'He is someone I know very well and he knows a lot about oil.'[32]

Soon after his return from the United States, and hardly welcome in Hyderabad, Rao returned to Vangara village to look after his ailing mother.[33] For much of the remainder of 1974, he would live in the mud house he spent his childhood in, working on his book. The house, designed to Hindu architectural rules, was hardly suited for a former chief minister, a US-return. Rao made plans to replace mud with brick and mortar, the hay roof with tiles.[34] Rao could have simply broken down the house he had grown up in and built it anew. Instead, he chose to stick to the old measurements, shifting the walls not an inch. While modernizing the house, Rao chose to keep tradition intact.

In Vangara, Rao loved walking in the fields and talking to villagers.[35] Since he was the largest landowner in the village, his own law expropriating excess land from landlords had been used against his own fields. Of his 1200 acres, he had surrendered 1000 to the district magistrate, who had then distributed it to the landless. Almost every villager received two acres. These villagers, who had earlier bowed to their landlord, now learnt to love their saviour.

As their euphoria subsided, Rao saw something disconcerting. Villagers had used their new land to grow rice, a food crop with little market value. Two acres of rice fed a family for a year, but did not earn much money in the bazaar. While land reforms had provided dignity to the landless, it had not increased their disposable income.[36]

Narasimha Rao advised the villagers to move from growing rice to cash crops that would give them higher returns in the market. From Gujarat he sourced cotton, which he then planted all over his land. Cotton came with its own problems. Since the male and female parts are in the same plant, there is a chance of self-pollination, sometimes resulting in weaker new plants. The risks were considerable for poor farmers with no access to insurance or credit. In order to encourage his villagers to use the cotton seeds he had procured, Rao turned to his talent for innovation.

Captain Lakshmikantha, a relative, remembers how Rao solved the problem. 'He put a straw on each cotton plant, so the pollen would only fly to the next plant, not the same plant.'[37]

Rao's success in growing cotton set the other villagers thinking. Mallaiah lives next door to Rao's ancestral house in Vangara. He was one of many landless farmhands who gained two acres from Rao's largesse. Learning from Rao, Mallaiah started to grow cotton in his fields, and began earning three times what a rice grower would.[38]

For a socialist who had staked his career on land reform, the insight unsettled Rao. Handouts to the poor did not solve their problems unless it also connected them to the market.

By the end of 1974, calm had returned to Andhra Pradesh. Things began looking up for Narasimha Rao. Uma Shankar Dikshit, the Central minister who had supported Rao's elevation as chief minister in 1971 only to bring him down in 1973, now lobbied for Rao to be brought into national politics in Delhi.

Rao abandoned work on his confessional novel in anticipation of the discretion that a political future entailed. Meanwhile, Lakshmi Kantamma felt her own career had stalled. A Lok Sabha MP for the past twelve years, she had not yet been made Union minister. She complained publicly of being ignored by prime minister Indira Gandhi. Lakshmi would eventually leave the Congress to join the rival Janata Party. Their political estrangement caused her to spend less time with Rao.

Around this time, Narasimha Rao met a young reporter working in Hyderabad.[39] The soft-spoken Kalyani, whose husband worked for a nationalized bank,[40] would never betray her sources. K. Natwar Singh says of Kalyani, 'She is utterly discreet, utterly loyal. Your secrets are safe with her.'[41] She would remain Narasimha Rao's closest confidante for the rest of his life.

In October 1974, Narasimha Rao's fortunes turned. He was called to Delhi as Congress general secretary, an influential national position within the party. Like with Deng in 1973, Rao was heading back to the centre of power, a changed man. And as with Deng, these changes would reveal themselves only later— once Narasimha Rao became his own man.

5

Delhi Durbar, 1975–91

Delhi has been capital of empire through much of its history. For centuries, its ruling dynasts controlled Delhi-wallahs through a mixture of patronage and fear. This grease and acid seeped into its stones. Threat, flattery, hierarchy—and above all, power—defined the contours of the city.

For a brief while in the 1950s, it seemed as if Delhi would have to change to accommodate the ideals of newly independent India, as reflected in the democratic sensibilities of the new prime minister. The Delhi durbar seemed to be closing down.

But habits of ancient cities die hard, and Indira Gandhi brought to Delhi none of the egalitarian impulses of her father. By 1974, she was more monarch than leader, with total power over party and Parliament.

Almost imperceptibly, the Old Delhi returned. Rather than representing India, the city regressed to its historical self. Courtiers fawned, brokers promised access, and the writ of the queen ran unchallenged across the empire. When Narasimha Rao was appointed Congress general secretary in October 1974, it was to this Old-New Delhi that he moved.

Rao was listening to the radio in New Delhi on the morning of 26 June 1975 when 'there was a sudden interruption in the All India Radio programme with a special, grim sounding announcement. Some unfamiliar terminology, called Emergency was heard.' These words are part of Rao's private diary that remain undisclosed to this day.

On hearing the announcement, Rao 'found himself completely confused'. He couldn't, 'at least at first, identify any compelling reason that could lead to the invocation of the Article [352 of the Constitution, that allows for a national Emergency]'.[1] When he 'reached the meeting hall, it looked like Sanjay Gandhi's durbar, not Indira Gandhi's . . . he was shooting off questions in an aggressive and intolerant tone, and all others meekly answered them.' Rao 'was shocked beyond belief, to find Indira Gandhi giving a halting, diffident explanation to every question the young prince fired at will. So much for Durga and Kali.'

This sudden announcement of the Emergency was, in fact, long in the making. Indians had begun to notice that their prime minister was more unresponsive ruler than accountable representative. For all her talk of 'garibi hatao', poverty in India had actually increased since the 1960s, from 33 to 40 per cent in villages, and from 49 to 50 per cent in cities.[2] Student movements in Bihar and Gujarat began demonstrating against their chief ministers, agitations that devolved into remonstrations against the prime minister and her younger son, Sanjay. Government employees, unhappy with their work conditions, joined in. From early 1974, the movement was led by Jayaprakash Narayan, a seventy-one-year-old veteran of the freedom struggle. One of the many groups aiding the protesters was the Hindu nationalist Rashtriya Swayamsevak Sangh (RSS), a convenient fact that allowed Indira to mischaracterize the entire movement as a vast right-wing conspiracy.

In order to emphasize that the struggle was merely ideological, Indira restructured her party in late 1974 to appoint overtly left-wing Congressmen to senior positions.[3] Narasimha Rao had dual claims to a high-ranking post. As chief minister, he had been an orthodox socialist—exactly the kind of fig leaf Indira needed at the time. Rao had also demonstrated that personal loyalty meant more to him than ideology. When Indira Gandhi had removed him as chief minister, he had not rebelled, despite his own fury and the initial support of state Congressmen.[4]

As reward, Indira appointed him as one of four general secretaries of the All India Congress Committee.[5] Rao claimed this elevation had caught him unawares. 'I had resigned as Chief Minister and was slowly slipping into my favourite literary activity when the High Command perhaps decided that such drift was not on.'[6]

This cosmetic surgery did not change Indira's appearance from empress to democrat. Protests continued through the early months of 1975, and were rejuvenated on 12 June when the Allahabad high court found the prime minister guilty of a minor election offence. Her election was cancelled and she had twenty days to find a successor. When Indira appealed to the Supreme Court, the high court judgment was conditionally stayed on 24 June 1975. But she could not vote in Parliament until her appeal was fully heard. Some of her own partymen thought she should resign.

The next day, 25 June, Jayaprakash Narayan addressed a considerable rally at Delhi's Ram Lila grounds. He declared Indira's prime ministership illegal. And then he crossed a line: he asked the police and army to disobey her 'illegal orders'. That night, Indira Gandhi declared a national Emergency and suspended fundamental rights. The largest democracy in the world was now a constitutional dictatorship.

As Rao noticed in the first days of the Emergency, it was Indira's second son, Sanjay Gandhi, who called the shots more than the prime minister. Meanwhile, Indira's eldest son, Rajiv, was living in a cocoon insulated from politics. In 1968, he had married an Italian girl he had met in Cambridge. Her name was Sonia Maino. They lived together in Delhi, while Rajiv worked as a pilot for Indian Airlines, soaring above the tumult and casual violence that was the defining feature of the Emergency.

In private, Narasimha Rao told his close friends such as the Karnataka politician Satchidananda Swamy that he was not happy with the imposition of Emergency.[7] But the public man was mum.

This duplicity served Rao well, and the Emergency improved his political fortunes. He was now celebrated as a martyr for land reforms. At a meeting prime minister Indira Gandhi called in late 1975 to discuss using her Emergency powers for further land reforms, the Andhra politician Narsa Reddy told her, 'General secretary Rao was the architect of our Land Reforms Act. So there can be no fault in the law. The fact that big landlords put up such a fight means that it was well drafted.'[8] There was even talk of Narasimha Rao replacing the Congress president—and high priest of Indira worship—D.K. Barooah.

Rao's ascension to the top party post would have marked a dramatic return from exile. But he was still a state politician schooled in the Nehruvian sixties. He was unused to the new rules of the Delhi durbar of the seventies, where flaunting ambition was the surest route to downfall. When Rao misjudged his context and deployed associates to lobby on his behalf, the backlash was swift.

Barooah's faction spread rumours about his competitor. Rao had earlier obliquely criticized the Emergency, noting that 'only a dialogue would help but not detentions'.[9] This was spun as treason. The prime minister was also told that Rao was spending time with Lakshmi Kantamma, by then Indira's opponent.[10] Rao had, in fact, seen little of Lakshmi in those years. But the gossip fell on paranoid ears. Instead of becoming party president in 1976, Rao was removed as general secretary.

He spent the next few months lecturing abroad as well as working on his writing. Meanwhile, the Emergency was proving unpopular. Trains may have run on time and bureaucrats may have run to work, but that was only the shawl of terror. As the historian Ramachandra Guha chronicles, 'Thousands were arrested under the Maintenance of Internal Security Act (MISA), known by its victims as the Maintenance of Indira and Sanjay Act.'[11] The absence of press freedoms as well as pressure on bureaucrats to meet impracticable targets led to awful abuses of human rights. This was captured in the public imagination by the forced sterilization of men in the name of 'family planning', the emasculation of India by a cruel dictator.

And so when Indira Gandhi ended the Emergency by calling for national elections in March 1977, she was trounced by a united Janata Opposition. The Congress won only 34.5 per cent of the vote and just 154 of the 543 Lok Sabha constituencies.[12] Indira Gandhi lost her own seat.

While the Congress had been decimated in northern and central India, it had held its own in southern states such as Andhra Pradesh. This was probably because the effects of the Emergency in the south had been less brutal. Southerners were also worried that the predominantly north Indian Janata Party might impose Hindi as the sole national language.[13]

Narasimha Rao had contested the Lok Sabha seat of Hanamkonda in the Telangana region of Andhra Pradesh, the first time he was fighting a parliamentary election after losing in 1952. Bucking his party's national rout—but in line with the Congress's performance in Andhra Pradesh—he won easily, polling 59.3 per cent of the votes cast.[14] He had already won four straight state elections; this was to be the first of six consecutive national elections he would go on to win. Rao's career in the Congress might have been wobbly, but he was always sure-footed when it came to winning elections.

Rao entered the 1977 Lok Sabha as a member of the Opposition. He was soon made chairman of the Public Accounts Committee (PAC), a parliamentary group meant to keep tabs on government accounting. In the 2000s, the PAC would gain prominence in the way it went after the Manmohan Singh government. Back in the late 1970s, it was a sleeping dog. And Rao let it lie. Instead, he spent his energies defending Indira in her time of need. The Janata government was unleashing commission after commission to investigate misdeeds during the Emergency, and within her party, devotees turned into apostates and left to form their own cults. Narasimha Rao, only half a lion, chose to remain loyal to Indira.

In his spare time, he turned inwards, taking courses in Spanish at Delhi's Jawaharlal Nehru University. A visitor to the university library recalls Rao parking his own car, and walking, unescorted, to the languages department.[15] Most politicians do not know how to take a break from politics. They hanker after influence long after they have lost it. Rao's exception to this rule gave him his exceptionally detached view of how power worked. Distance allowed him to see the trees as well as the forest.

A few years later, in 1980, the Janata government collapsed. Its internal splits could not be stitched together by a shared loathing of Indira Gandhi. Elections were called and Rao once again won from Hanamkonda. This time, his party shared his success, winning 362 of 520 seats—a gain of 208 from the 1977 elections.[16] Indira was back as prime minister, and the man who had stood with her in the wilderness was about to be rewarded.

Indira Gandhi offered Narasimha Rao the position of foreign minister of India. The ministry is one of four that sit on Raisina Hill, right beside the prime minister's office. It was a signal to Rao, an outcaste just seven years ago, that he was now part of Indira Gandhi's inner circle. Rao was nonetheless dissatisfied. He was an expert in education and health, ministries he had held in Andhra Pradesh in the 1960s. But he had little experience in world diplomacy.[17]

Rao's youngest son, Prabhakara, was with him at the time. He remembers his father asking Indira Gandhi's personal secretary and man Friday, R.K. Dhawan, to fix a meeting with the prime minister. Dhawan briefed Indira, and when Rao was brought into the prime minister's office, Indira asked him bluntly, 'Are you not happy with Foreign Affairs?' 'Yes,' replied Rao, 'I would prefer some other portfolio.' 'In that case,' Indira said, 'you have the job of finding your own replacement. You have two days to think about it.'[18] Rao mulled over it that night, telling Prabhakara, 'The leadership has given me so much confidence, I do not want to disappoint them.' The next morning, he accepted the offer.[19]

This early foray into foreign policy would serve Narasimha Rao well as prime minister a decade later. For, Rao had become foreign minister at a time when India was recomputing its Cold War calculus. The Indira Gandhi of 1980 was different from the Indira of 1969. During her years in the Opposition, from 1977 to 1980, the Soviets had cosied up to the Janata government and ignored her completely. The diplomat Ronen Sen (later ambassador to Russia) remembers, '[The Soviets] even erased Indira Gandhi from their history books.'[20] Upon her return to power, a peeved Indira first visited the United States before travelling to Moscow.

As foreign minister, Rao was also witnessing a revolution in China, with whom India shared a 3500-km-long border.[21] After Mao's death in 1976, Deng had emerged victorious in the succession struggle. Deng opened the economy to domestic and foreign enterprise in late 1978, and Rao was primed to watch China abandon Maoism for the Market, all the while paying lip service to the glories of the first chairman of the Communist Party of China. Rao's admiration for Deng's ability to wrap change in the garb of continuity was evident in a later interview: '[Deng's] thinking was the single largest factor in giving a new orientation to the Chinese political philosophy, still not doing away with prevailing beliefs in their external manifestations. I am reminded of the genius of the Hindu Law, which brought out different practical results from a particular Sutra to suit different areas and customs prevalent in them—by the method of multiple interpretation of the same Sutra by different commentators. Deng's miracle is an object lesson to those wedded to different interpretations.'[22]

Years later, in 1991, prime minister Narasimha Rao would prove an apt pupil of Deng, praising the socialism of the Nehru-Gandhis, all the while adroitly abandoning their policies.

Despite Rao's initial hesitation on foreign affairs, he proved an able apprentice. Having learnt from his debacle as chief minister, he was now calibrated rather than impulsive. This Narasimha Rao was a natural diplomat. He was also, by 1982, one of Indira's most trusted advisors, along with Pranab Mukherjee and R. Venkataraman. Party papers and government files from other ministries would be redrafted by him.[23] Rao's emollient style also made him Indira's point man with secessionist groups, many of whom prime minister Rao would outwit in the 1990s. When Rao was prime minister and Pranab Mukherjee was making a meandering return from his own exile, Pranab would gushingly remember Rao's relationship with Indira Gandhi during the early 1980s. 'Mrs Gandhi depended on him so deeply that [on] any major issue . . . be it the problem of Punjab or that of Assam or that of Sri Lanka, P.V. Narasimha Rao was the first person to be consulted . . . and to be entrusted with the job.'[24]

Rao selected a young diplomat to assist him. The unassuming Ramu Damodaran, son of a freedom fighter and storied diplomat, later worked for the United Nations in New York. In 1983, he helped Rao navigate the twin roles of foreign minister and domestic troubleshooter. Damodaran recalls that this dual responsibility once had unintended consequences.[25] 'I suggested that Rao as foreign minister meet new Indian Foreign Service [IFS] officers one-on-one for fifteen minutes each. Rao agreed, and it was pencilled into his diary. Meanwhile, a minor flunky working in the prime minister's office called up Rao and told him that he had to meet with leaders from Punjab, a state where separatism was a growing concern. This assistant scheduled these meetings at the same time that Rao was supposed to meet with the IFS probationers. The probationers were not told of this, and at the appointed time, went to meet with Rao. The first ranking man walked into the foreign minister's office, and Rao spoke for fifteen uninterrupted minutes about the importance of staying within the Indian Union. When the perplexed diplomat left, the next one walked in to be lectured about the importance of non-violence. It was only when the third one came in that Rao realized something was amiss.'

So thoroughly had Rao gained Indira's confidence, that in 1982, she considered him for the role of President of India. P.C. Alexander, then Indira Gandhi's principal secretary, recalls that Zail Singh's and Narasimha Rao's names were both floated.[26] But southern politicians, especially Tamil Nadu's Dravidian parties, preferred a Sikh over a Brahmin, and Zail Singh was made President. Rao had seen so many U-turns in his career that he did not show his disappointment, remaining Indira's trusted problem-solver.

The one problem that Rao's diplomatic skills could not solve was Punjab. By 1984, the state was ungovernable. Sikh separatists, led by Jarnail Singh Bhindranwale, had taken over the Golden Temple in Amritsar, from where they directed attacks on Hindus in the rest of Punjab. Told that ending the violence meant taking control of Sikhism's most revered site, Indira ordered the Indian Army to storm the Golden Temple on 3 June 1984. By the time the operation ended five days later, Bhindranwale, 700 soldiers and more than 2000 others had been killed.[27] The shrine itself was bulleted and burnt.

Throughout the military operation, Narasimha Rao was in Jakarta on an official visit along with K. Natwar Singh, then a senior diplomat. When news of damage to the Golden Temple reached them, Rao was exasperated. He had presided over the largest number of meetings with Sikh leaders,[28] and had invested much in a negotiated solution. He had always believed that faced with so emotional a regional and religious issue, the centre should play fox instead of lion. But he had by now learnt the first rule of the Delhi durbar: the monarch is never wrong. When an angry Natwar told Narasimha Rao, 'This is a great tragedy. It could have been avoided. The Sikhs will neither forget nor forgive,' he remembers how Rao said much while saying nothing. 'Deep in thought, Narasimha Rao's silence was eloquent enough.'[29]

Internal security was now prime minister Indira Gandhi's priority. In July 1984, a month after the damage to the Golden Temple, she decided to move her trusted foreign minister to the critical ministry of home affairs. Narasimha Rao was now in charge of protecting the nation from enemies within.

On 31 October 1984, three months into his new job, Narasimha Rao was visiting the city of Warangal in Andhra Pradesh. Around 10.15 a.m., he received a message that Indira Gandhi had been shot.[30] She had been walking to a television interview within her guarded house in New Delhi an hour earlier, when her two Sikh bodyguards sprayed her with bullets. Her daughter-in-law Sonia had rushed her to hospital, but to no avail. On hearing the news, Narasimha Rao recollected that he 'left Warangal at about 1.00 pm by special plane of BSF, reached Delhi airport around 5.00 pm and state way [sic] went to AIIMS [hospital]'.[31]

Rajiv Gandhi was sworn in as prime minister that evening, despite the protestations of his wife. Rajiv had become the heir apparent of the party after the sudden death of his brother, Sanjay. As darkness fell, armed Congress thugs fanned out from AIIMS hospital, where Indira's body was kept, to meet local supporters and arm them with kerosene, knives and voter lists that located where Sikhs lived. A pogrom was being planned.

Delhi was a union territory at the time, and the police chief reported directly to the Union home minister, Narasimha Rao. That evening, as police dispatches began to report attacks against Sikhs, Rao was in his office in the home ministry in North Block on Raisina Hill talking to a bureaucrat from the ministry. This bureaucrat recalls vividly what happened next, though he has never spoken about it publicly for fear of forfeiting his career. His evidence is crucial in assessing Rao's complicity in the killings that followed.

According to this bureaucrat, the telephone rang at around 6 p.m. On the line was a young Congressman known for his proximity to Rajiv Gandhi. He told Narasimha Rao about the attacks against Sikhs living in Delhi, and spoke of the need to 'coordinate a single response to the violence'. Henceforth, 'all information [on the violence] should be sent to the PMO [prime minister's office]'. The reason was one of efficiency, but the result was that home minister Rao was bypassed. Reports from local police stations were now sent directly to the prime minister's office.

An hour or two after Rao had been sidelined, the lawyer Ram Jethmalani met him and urged that the army be called in to protect the city's Sikh population. Jethmalani was struck by the fact that Rao appeared unconcerned. He also noticed that throughout the thirty-minute meeting, Rao was not in contact with police officers, by phone or in person.[32] With the prime minister's office in direct control of the police, the home minister knew he had been made redundant.

The next morning, the first Sikh was reported killed. He was to be one of an official total of 2733 knifed, burnt, shot or beaten to death in four days of mob fury. Later that day, the former law minister Shanti Bhushan met Narasimha Rao in his house to ask him to stop the violence. He remembers the home minister picking up the phone and talking to someone to convince them to take action.[33] Bhushan infers from this that there was a higher-up who had given instructions to the police to stand by.

Rao spent that first day, 1 November, as well as the next, evaluating the change of guard within the party, as well as preparing to receive foreign leaders arriving for the funeral. Rao's behaviour on these crucial days recalls the lines of Tacitus, the first-century CE Roman historian: 'The higher a man's rank, the more eager his hypocrisy, and his looks the more carefully studied, so as neither to betray joy at the decease of one emperor nor sorrow at the rise of another, while he mingled delight and lamentations with his flattery.'[34]

Meanwhile, policemen did little while Congress mobs roamed the streets of Delhi, killing turbaned Sikhs, setting fire to their houses, and looting their shops. At Indira's funeral on 3 November, Narasimha Rao, eager to display devotion, headed the procession.[35] The violence eventually subsided. For the Congress party, the taint had just begun.

Rajiv Gandhi became prime minister on the evening of 31 October, before the slaughter had commenced. One public word from Rajiv would have ended the violence. There is no evidence that he directly ordered the killings; rather, his silence allowed party thugs to loot and murder in his name. The investigation into the murder of Sikhs, by successive Congress governments, would be abysmal. Convictions were few, and the implicated leaders continued in the party.[36] A fortnight after the killings, Rajiv would dismiss the violence with 'whenever a mighty tree falls, it is only natural that the earth around it does shake a little'.[37]

It is true that commission after commission investigating the massacre have cleared Narasimha Rao of any role in the violence and, as the evidence suggests, he was under a direct order from the prime minister's office to stand down. But he was home minister of the nation, formally in control of the Delhi Police. He could have defied his prime minister's henchmen, ordered the police to act, and called in the army on 31 October itself, before the killings began. A public statement by him may have shamed Rajiv into acting sooner. Such an open revolt against his party would have meant political oblivion for Narasimha Rao, who had by now perfected the art of being a loyal number two.

DELHI DURBAR, 1975-91

Rao's career in the Congress would have surely ended had he ignored instructions—both categorical and couched—from his party. But it would have set him apart from the others who allowed evil to take place in those four days of 1984. It was his vilest hour.

~

A month after the murder of 2733 Sikhs, a pesticide plant in Bhopal, operated by the multinational Union Carbide, negligently released 30 tonnes of methyl isocyanate. At least 5000 people were killed, and 6,00,000 thousand more affected.[38] It was the world's largest industrial disaster,[39] and was to spark a global movement against western MNCs exploiting the Third World.

Four days after the catastrophe, when prime minister Rajiv Gandhi visited Bhopal, he spoke with the chief minister of Madhya Pradesh, Arjun Singh. In his autobiography, Arjun Singh says, 'Even today I cannot reveal what he told me. It's a state secret that I shall carry to my grave.'[40] When the chairman and CEO of Union Carbide, Warren Anderson, landed in Bhopal the next day, he was arrested. What remain controversial to this day are the circumstances under which Anderson was then allowed to leave for the United States, never to return. Arjun Singh claims that the orders for Anderson's release came from the home minister.[41] Even if Singh is to be believed—and given his later attack on prime minister Rao, this is a big if—the cautious Rao would have only acted on the orders of his boss, the then prime minister of India.

National elections were held later that month. The Congress party campaign resorted to innuendos against the entire Sikh community. One political advertisement warned, 'India could be your vote away from unity or separation'.[42] Narasimha Rao contested from both his old seat of Hanamkonda, as well as the constituency of Ramtek in eastern Maharashtra. This was done on the advice of Indira Gandhi, who had told Rao before her death: 'I am getting indications that you will not win in Hanamkonda. I would like you to contest from Ramtek also.'[43] Narasimha Rao convinced crowds in both Telugu and Marathi, and photos from the campaign show an energetic Rao speaking in front of a garlanded photograph of Indira Gandhi.[44]

The results stunned even the Congress. It had gained 49 per cent of the electorate and 404 of the 543 seats. Rajiv had won more seats, and won over more Indians, than his mother or grandfather ever had. The Bharatiya Janata Party (BJP), established in 1980, was reduced to just two seats. There was a surge of affection for the young prime minister. Many Indians felt that an honest man with a modern outlook had received the mandate necessary to transform their country. Narasimha Rao's own election results were mixed. He had won from Ramtek, but lost from Hanamkonda. Death approaching, had Indira Gandhi turned prescient?

In prime minister Rajiv Gandhi's new Cabinet, Rao was shifted from the home ministry to defence. It was an ever so subtle demotion, and Lutyens insiders noticed. There were rumours that Rajiv was planning to move away from the ageing coterie which had advised his mother and cultivate a younger generation of advisors. Rajiv surrounded himself with anglicized friends like Arun Singh and Mani Shankar Aiyar, who like him, had studied at the Doon School and Oxbridge. Satish Sharma, Rajiv's pilot friend from Indian Airlines, was the other entrant into his inner circle. Sharma too had a European wife, and they would all socialize in the rarefied drawing rooms of Delhi. This world was aeons away from that of the more vernacular Narasimha Rao. At sixty-three, he was also twenty-three years older than his prime minister. He had mastered Indira's mind, but was yet to fathom his new master.

Some months after the elections, Narasimha Rao was present in the room when Rajiv Gandhi told a friend that he intended to open up electronic and computer imports to India. 'But the old guard in my party will not understand,' Rajiv complained within earshot of his defence minister. Narasimha Rao said little.

That evening, he called up his son, the engineer Prabhakara. The home computer revolution had only begun in the late 1970s, and computers were a novelty even in the United States. 'You keep talking about this computer thing. What is it? Send me one,' Rao said.[45] The next day, Prabhakara sent a prototype to Delhi. Prabhakara also hired a computer specialist to teach his father. Ever the technophile, Rao bought manuals to read on his own, and within fifteen days, told the specialist he was redundant. Over the years, Rao would master two computer languages, COBOL and BASIC, and would also go on to write code in the mainframe operating system UNIX. Narasimha Rao's love for learning had merged with his instinct for political survival.

And survive he did. Indira's handyman rebooted himself to be in sync with Rajiv's programme of technology and modernization. In the words of Pranab Mukherjee, '[Rao's indispensability] was clearly demonstrated when Mr Rajiv Gandhi formed his government and he wanted to have a new team. But it was recognized that without P.V. Narasimha Rao there cannot be a team. Therefore, he not only continued as minister in various ministries with which he dealt, but also he proved to be indispensable in the Congress ministry.'[46] During Cabinet meetings, Rao would be seated to the left of Rajiv.[47] Other Indira loyalists such as P.C. Alexander were soon eased out. Pranab left to form his own party. But Rao remained, as prominent in the new republic as he had been in the ancien régime.

Dr V.S. Arunachalam was then leading a number of India's nuclear and covert technological programmes. He remembers telling Rajiv Gandhi about the need to talk to the Israelis to exchange information on the F-16 planes and other US technologies that were being sold to Pakistan. India did not then have full diplomatic relations with Israel. 'Have you told the defence minister [Rao]?' Rajiv asked. When Arunachalam said that he had, Rajiv was reassured.[48] When Rajiv gave Arunachalam and Naresh Chandra the secret approval for nuclear weaponization in 1988-89, Narasimha Rao was the only other politician (apart from President R. Venkataraman) Rajiv thought fit to inform.

The new prime minister was passionate about raising the education level among Indians. In September 1985, Narasimha Rao was told that Rajiv Gandhi wanted him to take charge of the education ministry, which would be renamed the 'Human Resource Development Ministry'. His secretary, Ramu Damodaran, remembers Rao asking for a list of all ministries and any pending files at the defence ministry. When the files returned the next morning in a steel box, Ramu noticed a handwritten note that Rao must have inadvertently placed among them.[49]

With 'Human Resource Development' as the heading, it contained an excerpt from an author Rao enjoyed, Antoine de Saint-Exupéry: 'A rock pile ceases to be a rock pile the moment a single man contemplates it, bearing within him the image of a cathedral.' Below this, Rao had written: 'Women and Child Development. Health. Youth Affairs/Sports. Culture. Labour?'

The note was returned to Rao and he slipped it into the pocket of his kurta. Later that morning, he went to see the prime minister. He told Rajiv, 'We see a rock pile of disorganized, underutilized human resources. You see a cathedral. We can fashion it, but we need to go beyond just the Ministry of Education.'

Rao persuaded Rajiv to integrate the departments of culture, youth affairs, sports, women and child development (and later, health) with education into the new 'HRD' ministry.[50] Critically, Rao did not insist on adding 'labour' to the mix. An aide says, '[This was because] the focus of that ministry [was] on protecting the interests of existing workers rather than creating opportunities for new ones.'

After the razzmatazz of defence, home and foreign affairs, the new portfolios would have traditionally been considered punishment postings. But Narasimha Rao was not a traditional man. The former health and education minister of Andhra Pradesh took to his new roles with old relish. They were to provide him the training needed to expand India's welfare state as prime minister in the 1990s.

In May 1986, he drafted the national education policy.[51] What was remarkable about the policy was that it took implementation seriously.[52] Education researcher Akshay Mangla lists the problems in primary education at the time. 'National surveys on education revealed that 40 per cent of primary schools had no blackboards, two-thirds of all classes (grades 1–5) were taking place in one or two classrooms and almost one-third of primary schools had only one teacher.'[53] Rao's policy response ensured that every school would have at least two classrooms, two teachers and instructional materials. Narasimha Rao's time as education minister also saw the creation of the Navodaya school system. A brainchild of Rajiv Gandhi, the aim was to provide centrally run residential schools in every district so that rural children could access quality education.[54] It was not just these ideas that were a departure from the past, it was their implementation. As Rao would demonstrate once again as prime minister, he cared less about lofty words in a policy document, and more about the actual impact on the lives of poor children.

For much of this period, Rao was also in charge of the culture ministry. Like education, it was considered a lightweight. Like with education, Rao's interests made him suited to the task. The minister's expertise, however, did not always make up for bureaucratic clumsiness, as this story reveals.

In preparation for the Festival of India in Moscow in 1987, a film on Ardhanareeshwara, the androgynous depiction of a composite of Lord Shiva and his wife Parvati, was conceived by the dancer Chandralekha and shot by the Kerala film-maker G. Aravindan. The film was to be shown in the 'Stree: Women in India' exhibition at the festival. The staid bureaucrats in the ministry were hesitant to accept the film, worried that themes of sexuality would show India in a prurient light. The cultural critic Sadanand Menon, who assisted in the making of the film, remembers the culture minister being requested to see the documentary.[55]

Narasimha Rao loved it. One of his favourite Telugu books *Veyi Padagalu*—which Rao had translated into Hindi in 1968—describes a scene in which a village artiste dresses up as both Parvati and Lord Shiva, one half of his face portraying the sensitivity of Parvati while the other half depicted a serious Shiva. Similar to his fascination for words with multiple meanings, Rao identified with the ambiguities of Ardhanareeshwara. His own dual personality as well as political experience had taught him that success in life required one to play contradictory roles. Sadanand Menon remembers Rao overruling his bureaucrats, saying, 'Such a film should be screened in schools to educate children.'[56]

Rao ensured the film was taken to Moscow. But nervous officials there replaced the film with a hagiographic documentary on Indira Gandhi. They forgot, however, to replace the banner outside the theatre. So, viewers who thought they were watching a Hindu god who was half-woman, half-man, were treated instead to a film on Indira Gandhi.

On 16 April 1987, a Swedish radio broadcast changed the course of Indian politics. The broadcast alleged that during the purchase of Bofors artillery guns by the Indian Army, bribes had been paid to Indian politicians and defence officials. The needle of suspicion was to turn all the way towards the prime minister and devastate his reputation.

Bofors was only one of many mistakes that Rajiv will be remembered for. Worried that Muslims were disillusioned with the Congress and voting for regional alternatives, Rajiv Gandhi overturned a Supreme Court decision that had enhanced the protections available to divorced Muslim women. This pleased the Islamic clergy, but led to allegations by the rising BJP that he was pandering to Muslim extremists. So, Rajiv decided to win over the Hindu vote bank by completely opening up the disputed Babri mosque in Ayodhya for Hindu worship in 1986. This upset Muslims, so Rajiv's government decided, in 1988, to ban Salman Rushdie's *Satanic Verses* for hurting Islamic beliefs—the first country in the world to do so. Three years later, in an attempt to consolidate his Hindu vote bank, Rajiv allowed the foundation stone ceremony for a future Hindu temple at Ayodhya, enraging Muslims even more. Such competitive communalism reinforced the image of the Congress as playing religious politics rather than standing by its professed secular creed.

There is no evidence that Narasimha Rao advised Rajiv Gandhi against these missteps. In an anonymous article published later, he would be critical of Rajiv's 'naiveté' on Ayodhya. But when writing under his own name, in a book on Ayodhya published after his death, Rao absolved Rajiv of any responsibility.[57] Whatever the inner half of Rao may have thought, his public half never faltered in praise of the Nehru-Gandhis.

Another policy that Narasimha Rao did not publicly oppose, despite knowing better, was on Sri Lanka. As the civil war between the LTTE and the Sinhala-led government endured, Narasimha Rao, careful by temperament, privately opposed any Indian attempt to get involved in its neighbour's wars. He questioned the India-Sri Lanka accord, signed in July 1987, and was critical of Rajiv Gandhi's decision to send troops to Sri Lanka soon after.[58] 'But as usual,' Natwar Singh remembers, 'he was unwilling to confront the PM.'[59] When India finally brought home its 43,000 troops in the last months of 1989, more than a thousand Indian soldiers were dead, 3000 were injured, and a former prime minister was about to be blown up.[60]

On Ayodhya and Sri Lanka, Narasimha Rao knew right from wrong, but chose to keep his own counsel. In the case of the economy, Rao was even more protectionist than his prime minister. When the gently liberalizing reforms that Rajiv began in 1985 sputtered to a stop two years later, Narasimha Rao did not have the conviction to steady his boss. The story of why Rajiv failed to open up the economy provides a vital context to understanding how prime minister Rao eventually succeeded in the early 1990s.

Rajiv Gandhi began with the right idea, that state controls were throttling the Indian economy and needed to be dismantled. But this was an idea whose time had come several years earlier. In 1970 itself, the economists Jagdish Bhagwati and Padma Desai had criticized the three pillars of the licence raj:[61] state control of entire sectors, rules that prevented Indian businesses from growing, and isolation from global economic trade. By the early 1980s, a variety of government reports was advocating some form of liberalization.[62] The presence at the top of the bureaucracy of liberalizers such as L.K. Jha, Abid Hussain, Manmohan Singh and Montek Singh Ahluwalia ensured a critical mass of officials who could implement changes to economic policy as long as politicians gave the go-ahead. Many of the policies that Narasimha Rao and Manmohan Singh would implement in 1991 were, in fact, worked upon during this period. By the mid-1980s, Indian policymakers had become convinced of the need for economic liberalization. What was needed was a political environment to support them.

That political will to reform, somewhat seen in the chastened Indira Gandhi of 1980,[63] was clearly visible in her eldest son. Prime minister Rajiv Gandhi was young, educated abroad, and had businessmen friends. His closest advisors, Arun Nehru and Arun Singh, had worked as executives in multinational corporations.[64]

In his first year as prime minister, Rajiv Gandhi pried open the economy ever so slightly. In the finance budget presented to Parliament in March 1985, the word 'socialism' was not even mentioned once.[65] Tax concessions were offered to corporates and to the middle class, and imports were somewhat liberalized, encouraging entrepreneurs to purchase machinery and raw materials from abroad. The relaxation of anti-monopoly rules allowed companies such as Reliance to grow. Most important, the private sector was allowed to participate in some areas traditionally reserved for the public sector. The Indian business group Tata had long wanted to make wristwatches through its brand Titan. But, in the words of Xerxes Desai, then spearheading the Tata effort, 'Our entry into watches was attempted to be blocked by various lobbies—the anti-big business lobby, the smugglers lobby, Indian manufacturers like HMT, bureaucrats, etc. It was only after Rajiv Gandhi became prime minister that the situation changed and we were given the go-ahead.'[66]

The economic reforms of Rajiv Gandhi were baby steps, not leaps, and helped existing businesses rather than new ones.[67] But so underperforming was the Indian economy that even this slight shift in attitude led to rapid economic growth. Imports grew substantially and exports steadily, and industrial growth grew from 4.5 per cent in 1985–86 to 10.5 per cent in 1989–90.[68]

The problem was that imports grew at a much faster rate than exports, and India lacked the savings or foreign investment to fund the difference. The result was deficit-led growth, with India relying on borrowings from abroad to pay for both investments as well as imports.[69]

Sustainable growth required deep-seated changes—devaluation of the rupee, an end to the byzantine system of licences and permits, tariff reduction, and the removal of anti-monopoly laws—that were opposed by vested interests so powerful that Rajiv was unable to overcome them. As the political scientist Atul Kohli points out, the businessmen who were benefitting from a controlled economy stymied Rajiv's attempts at levelling the playing field, as did Left intellectuals and parties who saw it as a sell-out to capitalism.[70] The most virulent opposition, however, came from within the

Congress. An example makes clear exactly how the party was able to block its leader on economic reforms.

Soon after becoming prime minister, Rajiv had wanted to announce his economic vision in the December 1985 session of the Congress party, to be held in Bombay. In anticipation of the session, his vision was first presented to the Congress Working Committee (CWC), the select decision-making body of the party. But these market-friendly ideas were so bitterly opposed there that Rajiv decided to abandon any further references to economic reform.[71] And so, when Rajiv finally spoke to party workers in Bombay that December, he had the pluck—as is now famous—to criticise the 'power brokers' in the party, but could not muster the courage to criticize economic socialism.

Rajiv's incapacity to achieve economic reform was made worse by his artlessness in everyday politics. Rajiv had come to power with the largest mandate in Indian history. But faced with the usual cycle of state elections, allegations of corruption, and dissidents within his party—in short, the routine turbulence that any prime minister faces—Rajiv lost his appetite for bold changes.

This was particularly so after 1987, when allegations of corruption in the Bofors scam made their way to the very top. A document drafted by the planning commission, circulated in May 1987, called for a larger role for private corporations in industrialization. It was quietly shelved because the prime minister had, by then, limited political capital to expend.[72] A better set of counsellors—such as those that prime minister Narasimha Rao would cultivate around himself—may have steadied Rajiv. But the advisors at Camelot, more school chums than experienced mandarins, were not equal to the task. By 1987, few new reforms were being pursued and the old ones had lost steam. Meanwhile, India continued living off borrowed money, the very problem that would lead to the foreign exchange crisis of 1991.

Narasimha Rao was neither part of Rajiv's early reforms nor his later rollback. He had never worked in the ministries of finance, commerce or industry. His visit to the United States in 1974 had made him question his own socialism, but it had not converted him into a devotee of capitalism as yet. His experience with cotton planting in his village in 1974 had taught him that the poor needed access to the market, not just handouts. But he had only a vague sense of what the Indian marketplace actually looked like.

All he knew of the ills of the licence raj were complaints from his son Prabhakara. A few years earlier, Prabhakara had carped about how licences for the production of aluminium conductors used in the transmission of power were being cornered by monopolists.[73] Those who already had a licence would obtain the other licences under fictitious names, and then not use them. This artificially filled the 'quota' of licences without improving the supply, thereby increasing prices. While Narasimha Rao was appalled at how government policies were being manipulated thus, he did not learn the larger lesson of this story: that the entire system of controls needed to go. Congress leader Jairam Ramesh, who interacted with Rao in this period, remembers him as the 'symbol of procrastination, delay, and the status-quo' on economic policy.[74]

On a visit to London as Union minister in the late 1980s, Rao had asked to meet Dr Manmohan Singh. Manmohan, a former governor of the Reserve Bank of India (RBI), was then secretary general of the South Commission. He travelled from Geneva to meet Narasimha Rao. Nearly three decades later, Manmohan Singh vividly recalls this meeting: 'I had no inkling that Rao was in favour of liberalization, based on his past record.' Manmohan was making a deeper point. In the late 1980s, Narasimha Rao was not an economic reformer.

In 1990, when in the Opposition, Rao would write to the commerce minister, Subramanian Swamy, complaining that the electrolytic manganese metal from abroad was being allowed easy import into India under the 'open general license'.[75] Rao grumbled that this was hurting domestic producers. His complaint reflected economic protectionism at its worst. On foreign policy, 'he had realized that the old shibboleths, that book, had become obsolete. He needed a new approach and vocabulary.'[76] But on the economy, Rao would come to this realization only in the debt-ridden days of June 1991.

By 1987, just as Rajiv's star was on the wane, Narasimha Rao believed his was on the ascent. Rao felt that he was the clear number two in the government, close to the leader, as well as uncommonly experienced. He had served as state minister for nine years, chief minister for two. In Delhi, he had overseen changes to Indian foreign policy towards the United States; as home minister, he had involved himself in the problems of Ayodhya, Kashmir, Punjab and Sri Lanka. Put in charge of education and health, he had stirred up ministries that were traditionally considered backwaters. Where he was given a free hand, he had made an impact. Where his correct advice had been ignored—as in Punjab and Sri Lanka—he had remained a team player, never publicly chiding Rajiv. And where his instincts were wrong—like on the economy—he had neither volunteered advice nor had it been sought. He had, in other words, become the perfect courtier in the Delhi durbar—knowing when to act, when to connive and when to stay silent.

Since he could not express his true feelings publicly for fear of recrimination, he typed his reflections on this period in his life in a digital diary he maintained on his computer (these diary entries—so crucial to accessing Rao's innermost thoughts—remain to this day private): 'For many years now, I have had this dilemma. I have been seen as a wise person, No. 2 to the leader. Sometimes people have been very kind to me, attributing good decisions to me and bad ones to someone else or to some inexperienced adventurist group. This has not always been the case, yet by and large, the hunch was correct. More decisions taken at my instance proved to be good and more taken against my view proved to be bad or harmful. I can say this honestly, although I never said it openly, for fear of creating controversy.'[77]

When President Zail Singh's term ended in 1987, Narasimha Rao's confidence in his own stature led him to lobby for the post. For a man who had built his career by never displaying ambition, this was a rare slip. Kiran Kumar Reddy, who would eventually become the last chief minister of unified Andhra Pradesh, remembers how Narasimha Rao asked him to canvass Andhra MLAs to vote for him for the presidency.[78] All this effort came to naught when Rajiv Gandhi chose R. Venkataraman, the vice president and a close friend of Narasimha Rao's, for the position of President of India.

A reflective Rao took the hint. He had reached the summit of his career, and there were no further promotions that Rajiv had in store for him. The tantrik Chandraswami, known for predicting the political fortunes of leaders such as Margaret Thatcher,[79] met him during this time. He prophesied that Rao would one day become prime minister.[80] Rao did not take him seriously.

He turned once again to writing. Rao had built a parallel reputation as a short story writer and translator from Marathi and Telugu. He had also been an unnamed contributor to *Mainstream*, whose left-wing editor Nikhil Chakravartty was a friend. In 1984 itself he had published an article titled 'Reshuffle', whose sarcastic tone would have cost him his job had his authorship been made public. He wrote under the pseudonym 'The Other Half' or sometimes simply as 'Anonymous'. The October 1987 issue of *Mainstream*, for instance, has pieces by E.M.S. Namboodiripad and L.K. Advani. It also has an essay titled 'Light and Dark' by 'Anonymous'. The essay would later be published as part of Narasimha Rao's novel, *The Insider*.

Rao also began to spend hours alone in his house on Motilal Nehru Marg, watching Dev Anand movies, and listening to cassettes of Bismillah Khan playing the *shehnai*. When public life limited Narasimha Rao, music and writing provided him the space to be himself.

―

In June 1988, Narasimha Rao was reinstated as foreign minister. Eight years earlier, Indira Gandhi had given Rao this job as reward; her son was now giving it to him as consolation.

It was also a ministry quite different from the one he had left. Indira's slight turn towards the United States had become pronounced under Rajiv, whom the historian Srinath Raghavan terms as one of the most pro-American Indian prime ministers until that point.[81] Mikhail Gorbachev had come to power in the Soviet Union, and his policies of glasnost and perestroika were reshaping how Indian policymakers thought of their own country. And in 1988, Rajiv Gandhi made a landmark visit to China, sweetening relations that had soured after the 1962 war.

Narasimha Rao was looking forward to meeting Deng Xiaoping, whose decade in power had already transformed China. He was thus enormously hurt when Rajiv Gandhi decided to meet Deng without either Rao or the foreign secretary, K.P.S. Menon (Jr). It was another signal that Rao was slipping out of favour. He would nurse this slight even after becoming prime minister and transforming Indo-Chinese relations in 1993, accusing an intelligence bureau (IB) man of conspiring to keep him out in 1988.

Foreign minister Rao visited Singapore in 1989. His grandson Shravan recalls, 'He came back and told me, "There is a theme park called Sentosa. There is a sound and light show. There is excellent technology. The way they aligned the lights and sounds is superb. There is one show, that show is conducted on the beach in the night."'[82]

In that same visit to Singapore, he spent the day with an Indian-origin businessman, buying laptops to take back home.[83] These visits to East Asia would shape his 'Look East' policy as prime minister a few years later. It would also shape his dislike for the barriers that technology imports into India faced. Returning from one such visit, the foreign minister was irritated at the level of duty that customs officials levied on the laptop and electronic gadgets he was bringing back. He came away from the airport seething.

Cast aside by Rajiv Gandhi, Rao would spend the day typing away on his laptop, and evenings chatting with friends. Velcheru Narayana Rao, the Telugu scholar whom Narasimha Rao had met at the University of Wisconsin in 1974, came visiting. 'He gave me an hour after dinner,' Narayana Rao remembers. 'I was talking about Henry Kissinger and what was going on in the international [arena]. He knew all about that. He kept up with what was happening in the world very closely.'[84]

In November 1989, general elections were held for the ninth time. Rajiv had squandered the largest majority ever given to any Indian leader. Reformist and eager when he came to power, he had lacked the political skills to navigate the roadblocks to reform in his own party, in Parliament, and among the media and intellectuals. The Congress manifesto for the 1989 elections shows how far Rajiv had moved from the reformist promise of 1985. The manifesto did state that the Congress would continue with removing bureaucratic controls on the economy and industry so that entrepreneurs could concentrate on generating wealth.[85] But it did not mention specific measures—such as disinvestment, devaluation of the rupee, delicensing or removal of anti-monopoly laws—that Rajiv's own policymakers had been advocating.

The people of India expressed their disappointment with Rajiv's leadership by reducing the Congress to 197 seats. Rajiv was replaced as prime minister by a multiparty National Front coalition led by friend-turned-enemy Vishwanath Pratap Singh.

The BJP, meanwhile, won eighty-five seats, a stunning rise from its previous tally of two.

It is a measure of his profile as a departing foreign minister that several world leaders found time to console Rao on this loss. On 6 December 1989, he received a letter from the Australian foreign minister: 'Please accept my commiserations on your loss of office,' Gareth Evans QC began. 'It is always sad to see colleagues and friends become victims of the turn of the political wheel. But congratulations on your re-election: at least your own constituency showed some judgment.'[86] A few weeks later, on 23 December, the American secretary of state, James Baker, sent Rao his commiserations. 'I greatly admired your understanding of issues and the diplomacy with which you handled them . . . As you take up your seat in parliament as a member of the opposition, I want to wish you good luck in your continuing service to India and the world.' Narasimha Rao kept this letter in his archives. His reply, in flowing red ink which was then typed up, thanked Baker and recalled their association.[87]

Aware that twilight was near, Narasimha Rao began to play elder statesman. On 12 December 1990, he sent public greetings to the young Maharashtra chief minister Sharad Pawar on his birthday. 'Being from the generation older than Sharad's, I cannot claim to know him very closely or fully . . . [but] his dynamism was evident . . . and one could have seen in him the makings of a prominence.'[88]

He also introspected, in private, on the Congress's recent loss. Amidst his papers lies a handwritten note on the 1989 elections. In typical Rao fashion, it reveals little: 'There is nothing sacrosanct in being or not being in power. What is important is that out of the 1989 verdict, a complete breakdown should not emerge at the Centre, causing irreparable and permanent damage to the polity. This is the criterion that everyone should keep in mind at this juncture.'[89]

Even in the security of his personal diary, Rao would not say what he really thought: that Rajiv Gandhi had been a disaster.

The truth was that while Rajiv had respected and needed Rao, he was from another social world. Narasimha Rao was a native intellectual, speaking five Indian languages fluently before he even learnt English. He had never studied abroad, and first travelled outside India when he was fifty-three. Rajiv, on the other hand, spoke English as his first language, had studied in elite Indian schools and then at Cambridge, had married an Italian, and moved around in the swish set of Delhi.

These social differences are reflected in a possibly apocryphal story that took place around then. Narasimha Rao was in a meeting with Rajiv and a school friend of the former prime minister. Rao was wearing a dhoti, kurta and leather slippers. Since his feet were aching, Rao placed one foot on the other thigh, and began gently pressing his toes as he spoke to Rajiv. It is a common enough habit among village men in India, but would be considered uncouth in a western setting. The school friend turned and whispered to Rajiv, and on his cue got up and pushed Rao's foot down to the ground. The sixty-eight-year old was being taught manners.[90]

Narasimha—half-man, half-lion—had his revenge. In an anonymous essay published in *Mainstream* in January 1990,[91] Rao identified himself only as a 'Congressman', and was critical of Rajiv's 'naiveté' in handling Ayodhya. He wrote that while Rajiv may not have made money in the Bofors scam, it was 'more probable . . . that Rajiv was concealing something or someone'. More stinging was his description of an inept leader blinded by his own election victory in 1984: 'Thereafter Rajiv Gandhi was right—right all the way, whatever he said or did. So there were no limits any more to what he said or did . . . What he heard day in and day out from his young coterie was nothing but fulsome praise. He became a praise addict. The elders either joined the chorus or looked on, not knowing what to do.'[92]

Narasimha Rao also examined why a leader with the largest majority in Indian history had ended up being so weak. It was an analysis that would also apply to Rao's future strategy as prime minister: 'The other important factor that contributed to Rajiv Gandhi's downfall was a peculiar sense of political insecurity skilfully induced in his mind by whom? ... In fact, he should have shown humility and consolidated his position in the first five years of his Prime Ministership, keeping those whom he considered rivals at bay but in good humour *within* the party.'

Soon after Rao published his unnamed critique of Rajiv Gandhi, the cardiologist K. Srinath Reddy received a phone call in June 1990. It was Kalyani Shankar.

'Mr Narasimha Rao is having problems,' she told Reddy, 'can you come over at once?' Srinath Reddy, whose socialist father was governor of Tripura, knew Narasimha Rao from his Andhra days. He rushed over to 9, Motilal Nehru Marg, and was shown into Rao's room by Kalyani Shankar. 'I found him in front of a laptop typing away. He was in [a] light cotton half sleeves and greenish lungi.'[93] Rao turned when Srinath Reddy entered and he complained of chest pain. 'I realized it was intermittent chest pain, which can lead to a heart attack if care is not given.' Reddy drove Rao to the coronary care centre at AIIMS hospital. The next morning, the cardiologist paid Rao a visit, and found him sitting up on his bed, with the table meant to serve food placed across him. On the table was a laptop, and Rao, in patient's gown, was keying away.

Soon after, Narasimha Rao travelled to Houston in the United States for a coronary bypass surgery. Rajeshwara remembers seeing his father in the recovery room, tubes skewering him from all angles. The patient was reading the *New York Times*. When the doctor asked him what he was doing, Rao replied, 'You do your job. I am doing mine.'[94]

Problems with his heart, in the Congress, and with Rajiv, told Narasimha Rao that forty years of public life were drawing to a close. After he returned to India in late 1990, he received a message that spoke to his soul.

The Siddheswari *peetham*—or Hindu monastic order—was founded in 1936 in Courtallam (or Kutralam), a spa town in Tamil Nadu. The founder, Mouna Swamy, wanted to establish a centre for religious knowledge in the tradition of the eighth-century Hindu theologian, Adi Shankara.[95] For decades, Narasimha Rao had been a devotee of this monastic order, making regular trips to Courtallam. He would pay obeisance to the head of the peetham, as well as take part in its charitable activities—from medical care for the poor to free food.

By late 1990, the Siddheswari peetham was look for a new head. P.V. Narasimha Rao was its most well-known devotee; he was also known for his Sanskrit and religious writings.[96] The monks who ran the peetham decided to offer the religious post to Rao. In a coincidence, Lakshmi Kantamma had by then left politics to become a sadhvi. The Siddheswari monastery demanded that Rao relocate to Courtallam and give up politics, as well as the trappings of worldly life, its material and emotional bonds.

Rao did not agree to the offer. Nor did he straight away refuse.

6

Monk to Monarch

It was the afternoon of 2 April 1991. P.V. Narasimha Rao made the five-minute car journey from his Delhi home on Motilal Nehru Marg to the expansive bungalow at the intersection of Janpath and Akbar Road. The hereditary ruler of the Congress party was distributing tickets for the coming national elections. Rao was nervous.

Over the last few months, courtiers close to the Family had hinted that Rajiv Gandhi was finally planning the transition to a younger Cabinet.[1] These whispers resonated with Rao's own exhaustion with politics. He had won eight consecutive elections, and at sixty-nine, was getting old for the ingratiating namaste. In the aftermath of his 1989 election victory from Ramtek in Maharashtra, he had written to his childhood friend in Warangal of an 'extremely tough . . . last lap of the campaign'.' 'In the process,' he complained, 'my blood sugar shot up very high and I am in need of complete rest and regulated life for several months now. I don't know what to do.'[2] His health, often perilous when out of power, plummeted. After his open heart surgery in 1990, he had told his youngest son that 'God has given me a second lease of life'.[3]

Rao had by now developed a finely tuned sense of political timing. He perceived that his own time was running out.

In the private confines of his diary, Rao wrote that in politics, everyone has a destined level:

'In my case, both with Indiraji and Rajiv, it was the level of a Central Minister—and no Higher. There was talk about the post of Congress President, Rashtrapathi, Vice-President, etc. . . . but every time they eluded me. And this happened several times. Yet, I did not bother, personally, since I still suffer from that phenomenon called lack of ambition.'[4]

Rao must have been rehearsing these thoughts when he was ushered into the meeting with Rajiv Gandhi. Also present in the room was a senior official from the intelligence bureau. This bureaucrat remembers Rao requesting Rajiv to offer his Lok Sabha seat to someone else, because 'I am too sick to campaign again.' That it was Rao who anticipated Rajiv was confirmed by two of his sons and a Family loyalist present in the antechamber.

Subramanian Swamy, a Cabinet minister at the time, tells a different story.[5] 'I was with my friend Rajiv,' he remembered in 2015 in his office in Delhi. '[Rajiv's secretary] Vincent George walked in and said, "Narasimha Rao has been waiting for a long time." Rao came in and Rajiv said in my presence, "Mr Narasimha Rao, you have become very old. I don't think you should contest Lok Sabha. I will bring you eventually to the Rajya Sabha."' Rao's confidante Kalyani Shankar adds, 'Rao wanted to switch places with Rajya Sabha MP N.K.P. Salve, but Rajiv refused.'[6] The conversation apparently ended with Rajiv cajoling Rao into drafting the party manifesto for the coming election, a face-saver, since manifestos are rarely read by party workers, let alone the average voter.

Rao returned home, changed into a checked lungi and short cotton kurta, and ruminated in his bedroom. News began spreading in Lutyens Delhi that a lengthy career had just ended. It reached Ronen Sen, a young diplomat who was already an insider. Sen had worked with Rao the foreign minister and would go on to become prime minister Rao's ambassador to Moscow.

Ronen Sen drove to Rao's house to see him.⁷ Normally bustling, 9 Motilal Nehru Marg was empty, the front gate unguarded. The mannerly diplomat made his way through the house to find Rao slouched in a chair in his bedroom. Feet extended, chin upwards. Sen had come for a short 'courtesy call', a fleeting non-event that is the babble of bureaucratic life. Instead, he listened for hours as a lonely Rao reflected on his youth, his fight against the Nizam, and his early years in the Congress. He interspersed this with details of where the best vadas in Andhra Pradesh could be found. These ramblings were more reminiscence than self-pity. Rao did not mention the conversation with Rajiv earlier that day. Instead, he regaled Sen with stories of how the Mexican diplomat Jorge Castañeda Álvarez 'loved chillies' and would compete with the Telugu Narasimha Rao on who could swallow more. The sun was setting by the time Sen left. An old man was adjusting to the twilight alone.

Rao began to plan for a life outside politics. A life outside Delhi. Worried that he would soon be short of a place to stay when visiting the capital, he had applied to that genteel hospice for geriatrics in the heart of the city, India International Centre.⁸ When he was swiftly admitted to the select club, the former defence, home, health, education, culture, and foreign minister of India, the former chief minister of Andhra Pradesh, was beside himself with joy.

Rao busied himself with Congress meetings to prepare the manifesto. Otherwise, his appointment diary shows that few sought his counsel during this month.⁹ On 16 April, he met Congress president Rajiv Gandhi at 4 p.m., and half an hour later was part of the manifesto release at 24 Akbar Road. Ten days later, when Congressmen filed their nominations for the coming elections, Rao, who already knew he was out, nonetheless recorded his bitterness in his private diary: '26-4-91. At 3.00 P.M. today, a gap has appeared in my legislative career for the first time in 34 years. I am feeling extremely dejected.'¹⁰

MONK TO MONARCH

In early May, Rao began packing his bags. He hired Roger Removals, moving men for Lutyens' elite. The workmen, used to lifting weighty assets beyond known sources of income, were grateful that this old man wanted no furniture or decorations moved. What he was fussy about were books, thousands upon thousands of them. Rao made the workmen reopen already sealed boxes to ensure that his books were carted away correctly categorized.[11] The only other objects that Rao was particular about was his computer and printer models, companions for seven years now. Hardware and hardbound were transported in forty-five cartons to a large truck,[12] which was then driven 1500 kilometres to Hyderabad, into the attic of his second son Rajeshwara's house. The departure of his books from Delhi depressed Rao. A bureaucrat friend who doubled up as an amateur astrologer tried to lift his spirits. 'Leave them here. I predict you are coming back.'[13]

Books were central to Rao's retirement plans. In Hyderabad, he spent hours holed up in a book-lined room, typing away on his beloved computer. He was adding colour to the outline of a novel he had first drawn up in 1973, when, freshly deposed as the chief minister of Andhra Pradesh, he was living in political wilderness. When Rao was drawn back into national politics in late 1974, he abandoned the novel. Now, out of the political scene once again—cynical once again—Rao began adding flesh to those buried bones.

Rao also used his time to rent an apartment in Bombay, since the possible Rajya Sabha seat from Maharashtra would require proof of residency. To confirm to himself where he belonged, Rao sent fifteen cartons of books—recently moved to Hyderabad from Delhi—to his new home in Bombay.[14]

While a part of Rao was hankering after the temporal sinecures of fading leaders, another part was contemplating deeper engagement with the divine. When the Courtallam monastery had first offered Rao the post of head monk in 1990, he had put it off.[15] But now, with few prospects for real power or influence, the life of a monk seemed apposite. He wrote to the monastery indicating that he was considering accepting.

In the run-up to the elections on 20 May, Rao flitted in and out of Delhi, listlessly campaigning for the Congress. On 11 May, his appointment diary shows that he was in Delhi, doing a 'radio recording for Congress party'.[16] His speech was soporific, even by the anodyne standards that Rao set himself. He made no mention of the economic crisis engulfing India or the troubles of her foul-weather friend, the Soviet Union. Instead, he mouthed the platitudes of Congress socialism, promising that if they won the coming elections: '[The] Eighth Five Year Plan will be finalized . . . The welfare of kisans, khet mazdoors and workers will continue to be the main concern.' On 16 May, he left again for Hyderabad on the state-owned Indian Airlines. Taking off at 6 p.m., Rao was flying into the sunset.

Indian national elections are always historic. Each iteration is the largest in the world. The 1991 election was no different: 262 million men and 237 million women were on the electoral rolls, 58 per cent of whom eventually cast their vote in 5,76,353 polling booths across the country.[17] Because it is hard to simultaneously conduct and protect elections all over the country, they are divided into phases, allowing officials and security men to move from hill to valley to plains. The 1991 elections were divided into three phases. It still turned out to be one of the most violent in Indian history, and voting had to be postponed in the militancy-hit states of Kashmir and Punjab.

On the morning of the first phase, Narasimha Rao left for his old constituency in Maharashtra, for the awkward task of campaigning for his replacement as Congress candidate from Ramtek.

The next day, 21 May 1991, Rao woke up at the residence of a local, one Prabhakar Kamble. Rao's appointment diary shows that he left to campaign in nearby Parbhani and Mansar, had lunch at a local engineering college, answered questions in fluent Marathi for a local newspaper, and spoke at a few more public meetings.[18] He returned to Nagpur to have dinner at the house of a local benefactor at 9 p.m., exhausted. Dinner done, Rao made his way to the house of Congress leader N.K.P. Salve to spend the night. Rao had opted out of a Lok Sabha ticket to avoid the strain of campaigning for himself. But here he was, canvassing hard for someone else.

At the exact time that Rao was leaving from dinner in Nagpur, Rajiv Gandhi was at a campaign stop in Sriperumbudur in Tamil Nadu, 1162 kilometres away. Rajiv, whose mother had been killed by separatists, had only a few guards to protect him. At 10.21 p.m., a young Sri Lankan Tamil woman mingled with the Congress supporters swarming around Rajiv.[19] She was a member of the LTTE, and the terrorist group was worried that Rajiv Gandhi would send back Indian troops to northern Sri Lanka if re-elected prime minister. As she approached the son and grandson of prime ministers, and a prime minister in his own right, she bent down to touch his feet, detonating the explosives strapped to her belt.

Narasimha Rao had just entered his bedroom when he was told that Rajiv Gandhi and fourteen others had been killed by a suicide bomber. Rajiv's body had been blown to such shreds that the police were struggling to identify the pieces. Rao recorded his reaction in a terse diary entry: '. . . Just when I was preparing to retire for the night, this news came . . . I was perhaps not looking too well, so they called the doctor for a check-up. However, I was feeling all right and had taken the shock reasonably well. Anyhow, I tried to sleep for a while, but could hardly sleep for about two hours.'[20]

A few hours later, the sun barely up, Gopalkrishna Gandhi, grandson to Mohandas Gandhi and C. Rajagopalachari, was woken up in Delhi by a trunk call.[21] A bureaucrat, Gandhi was at the time joint secretary to the President, R. Venkataraman, and had already heard of Rajiv's death. 'Gopal, what has happened?'

lamented Narasimha Rao from Nagpur airport, in Hindi. *'Itihaas ne karwat badal di hai,'* replied Gopal. 'History has shifted itself.'

'Yes, this is correct,' said Rao before asking for an appointment with the President, an old friend. Conscious of the immense burden he carries, Gopalkrishna Gandhi is a man who weighs his words before pronouncing them. On Rao's dawn phone call, he only says, 'I am sure his coming to Delhi was not just an act of political etiquette.' The pieces of Rajiv's body barely assembled into a respectable corpse, the game to replace him had begun.

An air force plane carrying Rajiv's remains landed in Delhi airport some hours later. It was brought to 10 Janpath, where Rajiv had lived with his wife, Sonia. As soon as he landed in Delhi at around 10.30 a.m., Rao made his way there. 'It was more a coffin than a body,' he noted in his diary later that evening. 'The body had been blown up out of recognition.'[22] Rao was not the only man thinking ahead. As he records in his diary: '. . . while we were hanging around the dead body in 10 Janpath, Pranab [Mukherjee] took me aside and told me that there was general agreement on my being elected C.P [Congress president] and it would be good to clinch it today itself, so as to forestall rumours of internal struggle etc.'[23]

Rao was delighted. But more than four decades of surviving snakes in the pit of politics had taught him to hide ambition. 'I knew that his report was too good to be true. Either he was himself a dupe or he was party to some kind of design and was trying to lull me. He had done this role many times in those crucial years of Indiraji. I did not want to react . . . I mentioned about my health and said I feel a bit diffident. I suggested NDT [N.D. Tiwari] instead, taking care to add that I was not refusing, yet it would be good if he came up after a better consensus. I also knew that NDT would be as unacceptable as, or more so than, myself, in the scheme of things.'[24]

Rao was wise to be cautious. Seven years earlier, Pranab Mukherjee had broken the queue when prime minister Indira Gandhi was killed, setting himself up as successor. For the sin of a commoner claiming a dynastic right, Pranab was sent to the back of the line. He was only now being rehabilitated. The same Family right was being reasserted, as Rao heard 'the loud slogans and shouts of some fellows on the road, asking for Sonia Gandhi to be made C.P'. Rao realized he was being upstaged. 'The picture was complete in my mind.'

He returned to Motilal Nehru Marg to take stock. As his diary entry says: 'Coming home, I first established contact with K and she agreed to come for lunch. She had almost bought the rumours of my being made C.P. [Congress president] that was making the rounds everywhere. She wouldn't have any of my hesitations. I didn't say anything, as I knew it was only a few hours before the cat would be out of the bag.'

At 4.15 p.m., Arjun Singh—who had been chief minister of Madhya Pradesh during the Bhopal Gas Tragedy—and Congress leader M.L. Fotedar paid Rao a visit. They suggested that Sonia be made Congress president to harness public sympathy for the remainder of the elections.

Rao hated the idea, but in his diary claims he revealed nothing. Rao's version is at odds with his bête noir Arjun Singh's own memory of the meeting. On hearing the suggestion to make Sonia Congress president, Arjun Singh claims that Rao 'burst out in anger and virtually yelled out . . . whether it was essential that the Congress Party should be treated like a train where the compartments have to be attached to an engine belonging to the Nehru-Gandhi family or were there other alternatives.'[25] Even if Singh was putting words into Narasimha Rao's mouth, he was echoing Rao's thoughts.

An hour later, the CWC, the apex decision-making body of the party, began its emergency meeting with a condolence resolution. On cue, Arjun Singh pressed for

Sonia to be made party leader. It was not just Rao who opposed Sonia. The ambitious chief minister of Maharashtra, Sharad Pawar, wanted to make clear that the posts of Congress president and leader of the party in Parliament (i.e. prime minister) should be distinct. 'His reasons were obvious and also valid,' Rao wryly notes in his diary. But the rest of the room was chanting Sonia's name, demanding that she contest from the Family pocket borough, Amethi. Sitaram Kesri, a Rajiv acolyte, went so far as to suggest that Sonia be made prime minister. Rao said little, while 'both Sharad and Kesri revealed their thinking'.

Inwardly, Rao seethed. His crown was being placed on another head. He detected a larger conspiracy by a clique led by Sonia, since—in his own words—'such a proposal could not have come without a reasonable certainty of being able to obtain her consent eventually'. Rao felt that he 'had been thoroughly outsmarted by the interested persons, aided no doubt by Pranab'.

The clique that Rao suspected did exist. After the decimation of the party structure by Indira Gandhi in 1969, what remained was an almighty family at the centre, and regional satraps who supplied votes from the states. Nestled in between were unelectable advisors, M.L. Fotedar and Indira Gandhi's stenographer, R.K. Dhawan, among them. They drew their power not from the masses, but from access to the Nehru-Gandhi family. For them to manoeuvre their way into the middle, they needed the dynasty at the top.

Facing defeat with victory so near, Rao managed to remain analytical. Before sleeping that night, he typed a long diary entry, describing the day's events. Though bitter, Rao was still able to objectively analyse his missteps. He had underestimated the court politics around the Family, since as a senior Congress leader, 'I was only dealing with the boss directly. I did not have to bother about the rat race.' More remarkable was his openness to the core argument of the Sonia clique. Though dynasty was 'on the face of it abhorrent and unacceptable', he wondered whether it was, in practice, a vote winner.[26]

While Rao was correct to pretend disinterest, he was wrong in suspecting Sonia Gandhi. The clique was acting on its own. Sonia had always detested the life of politics, and had implored her husband not to become prime minister in 1984. She rejected the CWC resolution, preferring to privately grieve rather than play the public role of party leader. The actor Amitabh Bachchan, then a confidant of the Gandhis, was said to have dissuaded Sonia, and 'In fact,' another close friend recalls, 'it was considered extremely insensitive on the part of the CWC to have made such a gesture when Rajiv's funeral had not taken place.'[27]

Sonia's refusal began a second round of politicking for party leadership. Rao sent a message to P.C. Alexander on 23 May 1991 that he 'should meet him immediately'.[28]

Alexander was a bureaucrat among politicians, and a politician among bureaucrats. An IAS officer from Kerala, he rose to become a powerful principal secretary to both prime minister Indira Gandhi and her son Rajiv. He was with Indira when she had considered, then rejected, Rao for President in 1982. Alexander knew every turn in the Congress labyrinth, making him an ideal guide for a prime ministerial aspirant who had last navigated the party organization (as general secretary) in 1976.

That night, after paying respects to Rajiv's body at Teen Murti, Alexander met Rao, who played the reluctant statesman. 'However,' remembered Alexander, 'he told me unambiguously that since Sonia was not agreeable to becoming Congress president, many people had already requested him . . .'[29] Rao asked Alexander to remain in Delhi and imperceptibly canvass other Congress leaders on his behalf.

The next day, Rajiv Gandhi's body was cremated in front of more than 1,00,000 people.[30] Also in attendance were leaders from sixty-four countries,[31] including Pakistan's Benazir Bhutto—who would herself be assassinated at a political rally sixteen years later. They watched while a twenty-year-old Rahul Gandhi sprinkled water from the Ganga on his dead father lying on a bed of sandalwood. Rahul then circled the pyre seven times and, with a burning torch, set it to flames.[32]

A day later, Rajiv's widow was asked to choose his successor as party leader. With two phases of elections to go, it was likely that a sympathy wave would carry the Congress to power. Even though Sonia was numb with grief, she realized she was choosing the next leader of India.

She also knew the players. Maharashtra chief minister Sharad Pawar, young and pushy, had access to the pockets of his industrialist friends in Bombay. But he had shown disloyalty to the family before, splitting the state Congress to become chief minister in 1978. N.D. Tiwari was in some ways the natural choice. A former chief minister of Uttar Pradesh, he represented the Brahmin face of the north Indian Congress. But, as Rao astutely noticed in his diary entry, N.D. Tiwari was 'unacceptable'. This was because he had displeased Rajiv by disobeying his order and contesting the ongoing national elections (worse yet, he would end up losing).[33] Arjun Singh and Madhavrao Scindia, royals from Madhya Pradesh, were opposed by rival factions within the party. Each one of these regional bosses was polarizing enough to split the party, powerful enough to sideline Sonia and take charge.

There are varied versions of what happened next. The one narrated by K. Natwar Singh (by then a senior Congressman and close aide of Sonia) is believed to be most plausible by Rao's family, Congress leader Jairam Ramesh (reputed to be one of Sonia's speech-writers) and another Congressman so close to Sonia that it is assumed he speaks for her. The story goes like this.

A day after Rajiv's funeral, K. Natwar Singh was summoned by Sonia and asked who the new party leader should be.[34] Natwar suggested she seek advice from P.N. Haksar, Indira Gandhi's virtuous principal secretary who had since had a tempestuous relationship with the Family. Haksar, aged seventy-seven, walked into 10 Janpath. His first suggestion was Shankar Dayal Sharma, the vice president of India. A Brahmin from Madhya Pradesh, Sharma was the most senior Congress leader alive. He had been chief minister of the erstwhile Bhopal state as early as 1952, and was well liked and inoffensive, virtues Haksar felt were the need of the hour. Natwar and Congress leader Aruna Asaf Ali were dispatched to ask Sharma.

He astonished them by declining, resisting the allure of leading the world's largest democracy. 'The prime ministership of India is a full-time job,' he explained. 'My age and health would not let me to do justice to the most important office in the country. Kindly convey to Sonia-ji the reasons for my inability to take on such an awesome responsibility.'[35] A bureaucrat close to Sharma hinted that he preferred the ceremonial pomp of the presidency of India, a post to which he was eventually elevated in 1992.

Natwar and Aruna returned with empty hands. Haksar was called for again.

This time, he suggested Pamulaparti Venkata Narasimha Rao. Rao had spent decades in party and government, Haksar argued. He was an intellectual who lacked enemies, someone who could keep the party united. The other contenders, Haksar hinted, might split the party. Sonia said little, but saw that there was a logic to Narasimha Rao. While no favourite of her husband, Rao knew his place; he had never dissented nor mutinied. With elections ongoing, the party needed someone who could balance the various power equations in the party. No one else fit that bill.

Two decades earlier, similar logic had propelled an improbable Narasimha Rao to the chief ministership of Andhra Pradesh. As a southern Brahmin, he came from a caste too small to usurp state power. Ajathashatru—one whose enemies are yet unborn—had also been careful to avoid factions within the party. This meant no group would fight for him, but it also meant no group would fight against him. In a land of cliques and coteries, castes and communities, Narasimha Rao's greatest virtue was his loneliness.

The next day, Satish Sharma, Rajiv Gandhi's pilot pal and troubleshooter, received a phone call. 'Satish, I want to come over and have tea with you in your farm today evening,' Narasimha Rao said. Sharma did not know that Sonia was considering Rao's name. 'I was most surprised,' Sharma recalled many years later. 'He is not that kind of guy.'[36] That afternoon, at 2.30, Sharma met the grieving widow of his best friend. 'Sonia,' he said, 'I got a call from Narasimha Rao. It is the first time he has called. He is coming to the farm to have tea.' 'I have a suggestion,' Sharma continued. 'There are two people lobbying [for prime ministership]. One is Pawar. The other is Arjun Singh. My suggestion is that you ask Narasimha Rao. He has been Andhra Pradesh chief minister, cabinet minister with Indiraji, cabinet minister with Rajiv. He is a linguist, a scholar with a clean image. Should I ask him when I meet him today evening?'

Sonia Gandhi nodded. 'She agreed.'[37]

Soon after Satish Sharma left, another person visited Mrs Gandhi. This person, currently a senior functionary of the Congress, agreed to speak on the condition of absolute anonymity. 'When I met Sonia, Narasimha Rao's name came up. Sonia had just one concern: Bofors.' Sonia felt that Bofors had led to her husband's loss in the 1989 elections, making him vulnerable to assassination. This Congressman hastened to add that Sonia was not suggesting impropriety; she believed her husband to be innocent. But she wanted Rao to be told that his prime ministership was contingent on his sensitive handling of the Bofors investigation.

Later that evening, Satish Sharma drove to his farm on the outskirts of Delhi. As he entered, he saw P.V. Narasimha Rao talking in Telugu to his mother, who had lived in Hyderabad before. He also noticed another man in the room. This was Chandraswami, wearing a flowing saffron robe, a dark-orange third eye sunk into his temple. 'It was obvious that Chandraswami was playing a key role in making Rao prime minister,' Satish Sharma remembers. Sharma, who prefers the directness of a Boeing pilot to a politician's babbling, cut through the small talk. 'Okay, Rao-ji, let's not waste time.' On that day, in that farmhouse outside Delhi, Narasimha Rao was offered party presidentship, the prelude to becoming prime minister. He wasted no time in agreeing.[38]

On 29 May, at a CWC meeting, Narasimha Rao was elected president of the 105-year-old Congress party. The decision was unanimous—i.e. once Sonia had decided, the rest fell in line. Rumours swirled that Rao, a heart patient, was only a seat-warmer for Sonia. When the election for the next President of India took place in 1992, they said Rao would be finally elevated to irrelevance. Kalyani Shankar remembers, 'The group that was keen on Sonia's selection thought that Rao, who was almost in his seventies, could be a stopgap prime minister until Sonia decided to take over.'[39] Subramanian Swamy puts it more bluntly. He claims that 'Sonia knew that Rao would die soon, and she could take over.'[40]

Genuflection followed. Two days after becoming party leader, Rao got a letter from former Congressman and current foe Devi Lal. 'Though it is an internal affair of your party,' the letter began, 'as an ex-Congressman, I am genuinely interested in the smooth and amicable resolution of the leadership issue in the aftermath of the untimely demise of Sri Rajiv Gandhi.' A politician of a rather different order wished him a week later. In early June 1991, Rao got a congratulatory letter from Soviet leader Mikhail Gorbachev. Aware of the import of the message from India's close ally, Rao replied immediately, assuring Gorbachev that he would work to strengthen Soviet-Indian relations.[41]

There was still an election to be fought, the final two phases of which had been rescheduled by the election commission for 12 and 15 June. Rao, who had opted out of the 1991 elections partly because of the rigours of touring a single constituency, now faced the task of campaigning in more than a hundred. He also had no money.[42] As an aide confided, 'Rao did not know about finances and funding sources of the Congress . . . he was last in the party organisation years ago . . . much had changed since then.' Party treasurer Sitaram Kesri had to scramble to pay for his travels.

Perhaps Narasimha Rao's main shortcoming as party leader—in Jairam Ramesh's words—was that he had 'the charisma of a dead fish'.[43] Engaging in print or in scholarly gatherings, Rao's intellectual parries were lost on a large crowd. The contrast with the man he had replaced, a man with the sex appeal and lineage of John F. Kennedy, was stark.

Salman Khurshid, son of a Union minister and grandson of a president, was at the time a young politician contesting from Farrukhabad in Uttar Pradesh. As part of his campaign, the Oxford-educated Khurshid had originally planned an outdoor rally for Rajiv Gandhi in his constituency. But when the dour new party president turned up to canvass, Khurshid was forced to corral 500 people into watching Rao pout within the safety of a closed compound.[44]

On 15 June, the final vote was cast and the results were due in three days. The Congress expected to win. As party president, Rao was the default candidate for prime minister. But a month earlier, Sharad Pawar had spoken of a distinction between party leader and prime minister. He now began to act on that distinction.

Pawar plotted from Delhi, his henchmen guaranteeing a steady supply of grilled chicken and paneer tikka from the nearby Pandara Road.[45] Pawar was also buoyed by the fact that when the results were announced on 18 June, his Maharashtra Congress provided the single largest share to the party's national kitty.[46] To be fair to Pawar, his strategy was quintessentially democratic: to push for a vote by all MPs, preventing party elites from anointing behind closed doors.

Amidst Narasimha Rao's private papers lies an unsigned yellowing document. It is titled 'CPP leadership' and though no date is mentioned, it was likely written between 16 and 18 June 1991. The letter begins: 'It is becoming increasingly clear that the aspirant from Maharashtra, Sharad Pawar, is keen and may insist on a secret ballot . . . A lot of backstage work has to be done with immediate effect.' It then goes on to recommend: 'The state Congress leaders from all over the country, including the Congress Chief Ministers and members of . . . Working Committee, should be contacted on the consensual proposal for electing PV Narasimha Rao as the CPP [Congress Parliamentary Party] leader.'

Rao took the letter seriously. He met P.C. Alexander, by now his chief advisor, sometimes two to three times a day.[47] A few days before the results, Subramanian Swamy, a Rao supporter, says he chanced upon Sharad Pawar at a diplomatic dinner at the President's estate on Raisina Hill. 'I told him clearly to withdraw. I had intelligence dossiers on him.'[48] Swamy was also making public allegations against Pawar in the press. Another Rao acolyte sent to dissuade Pawar was the astrologer N.K. Sharma,[49] one among the many Hindu godmen and soothsayers who served as the cerebral Rao's eyes, ears, and occasionally, voice. While Rao was deploying the stick on Pawar, he was all carrots for Arjun Singh. Worried that Arjun Singh and Pawar, the two most powerful leaders in the Congress, would reach a deal that would cut him out, Rao sent Alexander to reassure Singh.

Anxious to avoid a protracted fight with power within grasp, the party began rallying behind Narasimha Rao. That signal was sent on 17 June 1991, a day before the election results, when most of the Congress leadership showed up at 9 Motilal Nehru Marg. Rao's appointment diary records that at noon, he was 'Meeting with Sh. Arjun Singh, Ghulam Nabi, Mukherjee'. Then, from 4.30 p.m. to 7 p.m., he met party leaders in one-on-one meetings.[50]

On 18 June, the election results were announced. The Congress had won 232 of the 521 seats, making it the single largest party in Parliament. But even with around eighteen more seats from coalition partners, it was still short of a majority. The BJP had jumped to 120 seats; more tellingly, its vote share had jumped from 11 per cent in the 1989 elections to 20 per cent in these 1991 elections.[51] The third main political grouping was the incumbent National Front, led by V.P. Singh's Janata Dal, and supported by the communists.

It was clear that a Congressman would be prime minister. It was also clear that the party would not allow that man to be Sharad Pawar. Party elites as well as a majority of MPs supported Rao, as did Sonia Gandhi. The bureaucrat-turned-Congressman R.D. Pradhan—who knew both Rao and Pawar well—arranged a meeting between them.[52] Pawar indicated he would withdraw, provided Rao name him deputy prime minister.[53] Rao refused, offering only a 'senior post' in the Cabinet. The terms of surrender were being negotiated.

The world still thought that the race for prime minister was on. The next morning, 20 June, the headline in the *Times of India* blared that the Congress leadership was to meet, and Sharad Pawar was 'very much in the race'.[54] On seeing the news, Sanjaya Baru, then editor of the *Economic Times*, hurried to Rao's house. The gate was open, unguarded. Baru drove his Fiat car inside, entered the bungalow, drew the living room curtain, and peeked inside. Wearing a white dhoti, white banyan and white slippers, Rao was seated on a sofa talking to a visitor. Rao noticed Baru, whose bureaucrat father he knew from their days in Andhra politics, and beckoned him to enter.

'Have you seen this morning's *Times of India*? What do you think?' Baru asked.

'You ask the Maharashtrian editor and bureau chief,' Rao replied. They all laughed, for the insinuation was clear—that

Dileep Padgaonkar and Subhash Kirpekar were from the same state as Sharad Pawar. Baru left, unsure of what the day would bring.

Later that morning, Sharad Pawar announced he was withdrawing from the contest. The newly elected MPs were paraded into Parliament and asked who they wanted as prime minister. One such MP remembers: 'It was all orchestrated. They had already decided who should win.' P.V. Narasimha Rao was elected, unanimously, head of the party in Parliament, the precursor to prime ministership. In the time-honoured tradition of Congress 'consensus', his name was proposed by rival Arjun Singh.[55] The prime minister and his Cabinet would be sworn in the next morning.

It was twilight by the time Sanjaya Baru returned to Rao's house. Power had electrified the place. The gate was ringed with guards; Congress workers jostled outside, chanting *'Narasimha Rao ki jai.'*

⁓

12 Willingdon Crescent housed the Sanjay Gandhi Memorial Trust. Despite a less than cordial relationship with Sanjay, Narasimha Rao had made himself a trustee, giving him access to a large bungalow in the heart of Lutyens Delhi. Rao spent the evening of 20 June there, working with P.C. Alexander. They were deciding who the new Cabinet ministers would be.

Most names suggested themselves. As mere first among equals, Rao had to accommodate party heavyweights, including rivals Arjun Singh and Sharad Pawar. Rao made only two personal decisions. He was determined that S.B. Chavan, fellow devotee of Swami Ramananda Tirtha, be given a senior Cabinet role, ensuring at least one confidant in his inner circle. As we shall examine in detail in the next chapter, he also asked Alexander to suggest, as finance minister, an apolitical economist capable of dealing with the West.

'I want an internationally credible face,' Rao told Alexander.[56] 'You are in such a deep hole at the moment, you need a banker's banker,' Alexander replied.[57]

He recommended two names—the director of the London School of Economics, I.G. Patel, and the economist Manmohan Singh. At 7.30 p.m., Rao called up his friend President R. Venkataraman—who had been finance minister earlier—with both names. '[Rao] said that he would prefer one with some knowledge of the international financial institutions and experience in dealing with them,' Venkataraman remembered.[58] The President of India liked the names of both I.G. Patel and Manmohan Singh.

Rao's decision to ask for an out-of-the-box finance minister was instant brew rather than well-soaked beans. In his twenty years of running ministries in Hyderabad and Delhi, Rao had never once held the finance post. He had said little on the economy, and the few views he proffered were protectionist. Jairam Ramesh says that between 5 and 18 June, he and Pranab Mukherjee had briefed Rao on the economy on three occasions.[59] Rao was aware of his own blind spot, telling Jairam: 'I don't understand economics . . . Pranab and you have to explain.'[60]

But that ignorance changed when, a day before he was to select his finance minister on 20 June, the Cabinet secretary Naresh Chandra bought him an eight-page document, prepared by senior bureaucrats of the previous government, laying out just how imperilled the economy was. Rao put it off, but when Chandra told him that India was on the brink of catastrophe, Rao took an hour to read it.

Then he reread the document. He read it again.

It talked of fiscal discipline, dismantling trade barriers, and removing the licences, permits and anti-monopoly laws that bound domestic entrepreneurs.[61] In short, it contained the core elements of what would be the 'big bang' reforms of the coming months. This blueprint had been prepared before the elections, before Manmohan Singh had even entered the finance ministry.

By the time he had finished absorbing the document, the protectionist Rao had given way to the pragmatic Rao. The first order of business was to choose a finance minister acceptable to the West.

When I.G. Patel declined the job on 20 June, Alexander called up Manmohan Singh at his house that night. A quarter of a century later, Manmohan Singh remembers that he didn't take the phone call seriously, since politicians make all sorts of commitments.[62]

The next morning, 21 June 1991, Manmohan woke up early and made his way to the University Grants Commission, of which he was chairman. His office phone rang. Congress president and parliamentary party leader, Narasimha Rao, was on the line. He asked Manmohan to be his finance minister. The swearing-in ceremony for the new government was scheduled around noon,[63] and Manmohan was asked to come for a meeting on the economic crisis slated just before the oath. Manmohan returned home, changed into more formal attire, and made his way to North Block. Rao was seated at a long table while the bureaucrats who ran India's economy gathered around him. The meeting, held just before Rao was sworn in, indicated what the priority of the new government would be.

Montek Singh Ahluwalia, a former World Bank employee who had briskly risen to the post of commerce secretary, was among those invited to this meeting. 'I felt honoured,' Ahluwalia remembers, 'I felt I was in the new prime minister's inner circle.'[64] Ahluwalia was the cheerleader for economic reform within government. His presence indicated which way the new prime minister was planning to move. As Ahluwalia puts it, 'In the meeting [Rao] knew that economic policies had to change . . . he understood what was going on.' The presence of Manmohan Singh was also telling. Ahluwalia remembers: 'That was when I knew that Manmohan would be finance minister. Why would he be at the meeting otherwise?'[65]

A few hours later, at exactly 12.53 p.m.,[66] P.V. Narasimha Rao was sworn in as the tenth prime minister of India by President

R. Venkataraman at Rashtrapati Bhavan's Ashoka Hall. The British-designed room has an elaborate red Persian painting mounted on the ceiling that is from the nineteenth century. Rao and his Cabinet seemed from that same era, 100 years away from the youth and vigour that Rajiv Gandhi symbolized. One magazine termed it 'Back to the old guard',[67] with an opposition leader sniping about 'old wine in old bottles'.[68] Confirming the impression, a visibly ailing Narasimha Rao drove up to the grand forecourt of Rashtrapati Bhavan in a private vehicle. The man who a month ago was retiring to a life of writing and prayer, left in a cavalcade of cars, emperor of India.

The crown was made of plastic. Though prime minister in name, Narasimha Rao had little real power. His survival depended on the goodwill of other Congressmen who considered him a usurper of the Nehru-Gandhi throne. Rao had no political base within the party and had to rely on the very men out to unseat him.

There were also limits to Congress power. The inheritor of the national movement had been going through a slow decline. The party that once dominated Parliament was now reduced to a minority. It would take just a single vote on the floor of the House, if the Opposition voted together, for the toppling of Rao. And then there was the incapacity of the Indian state, a rope binding even the most powerful of leaders. Undermanned, bankrupt, and for sale, the Indian state machinery had long corroded. The Nehruvian state was no more a vehicle for social transformation. Not only did the latest driver of that vehicle have no legroom, the car was too battered to move.

The road ahead was also potholed. A suicide bomber had just blown up Rao's Congress predecessor. Violence in the states of Assam, Kashmir and Punjab threatened to blow up the nation. With the slow collapse of its patron the Soviet Union, India was being orphaned on the world stage. Its defence forces were teetering; bereft of Soviet-made spare parts, many of India's combat aircraft could not take off. Mass mobilizations around Mandal and Mandir, the demands for reservations for backward castes and a Ram temple in Ayodhya, threatened more violence. Most urgent of all, there were just weeks left before India would default on repaying its foreign loans.

Indians with options began to migrate, and those who remained, resigned themselves to an India destined to be second-rate. It was an acceptance of mediocrity symbolized by the Ambassador car, a 1950s British Oxford Morris knock-off that had survived into the India of the 1990s, courtesy the regulation limiting competition. Outdated yet ubiquitous, the Ambassador crashed into the myth that an ancient civilization had taken its rightful place in the modern world. India was living in the past.

In his first speech to the nation on 22 June, delivered a day after being sworn in, prime minister Narasimha Rao reflected the national gloom. 'The dangers posed to the country by problems in Punjab, Kashmir and Assam are very real,' he warned. He spoke of the threats of communal violence, the failure of social schemes. But he dwelt most on the immediate challenge: the economy. A combination of factors had plunged the government into external debt, and India lacked the dollars to repay. Foreign lenders, the International Monetary Fund (IMF) amongst them, were withholding new loans. India was about to default and lose face in front of the world.

In his broadcast, Rao warned, 'There is no time to lose. The government and the country cannot keep living beyond their means and there are no soft options left.' He then laid out his vision of what reforms entailed. 'We will work towards making India internationally competitive,' he said, promising to remove 'the cobwebs that come in the way of rapid industrialisation'. He challenged the system of controls that had caged the economy, vowing 'to streamline our industrial policies and programmes'.

He also broached the unthinkable. 'We welcome foreign direct investment, so as to accelerate the tempo of our development, upgrade our technologies and to promote our exports.'[69]

The speech was drafted by the man himself, with help from bureaucrats chosen by the previous regime.[70] Manmohan Singh, sworn into the Cabinet just a day ago, had yet to get a grip on the finance ministry. The rhetoric was Rao's, Rao's alone.

But India is a land resonating in rhetoric, where blueprints seldom leave the drawing board. Images of economic reform had been conjured up by politicians and bureaucrats before, most forcefully by prime minister Rajiv Gandhi in 1985. But after revving starts, they had sputtered to a stop, stuck in the swamp of licence-grabbing businessmen, permit-withholding bureaucrats, Left intellectuals quoting Marx, politicians worried about vote banks, and unions threatening strikes. With little power to wield and other crises to handle, how was Rao going to manage the vested interests that had sunk reforms in the past? What was Narasimha Rao going to do?

7

Rescuing the Economy, 1991–92

Two weeks after Narasimha Rao became prime minister, a convoy of vans left the vaults of Reserve Bank in south Bombay. The security around the armoured vans was worthy of a head of state, for inside was India's honour, around twenty-one tonnes of pure gold. The convoy travelled thirty-five kilometres north to Sahar airport, where a plane from Heavy Lift Cargo Airlines stood waiting.[1] The gold flew by plane to London, into the vaults of the Bank of England. In return, the Narasimha Rao government received dollars that allowed it to delay default on its outstanding loans. Gold is wrought with sentiment in India, and when news of the deal leaked,[2] the public uproar was accompanied by private shame. The economy was now so wrecked that India was pawning its family jewellery.

The economic crisis of 1991 was hurtling India towards ruin. But even before imminent catastrophe, the India that prime minister Rao inherited was in disrepair. An elaborate system of government controls gave state-run firms a free run over vast stretches of the economy, stymied private entrepreneurs, and isolated India from international markets. The results were low growth, endemic poverty, a small middle class, broken infrastructure, and few consumer choices. This regime was innately unstable and every once in a while, the system tottered. There had been crises in 1965–67,

1973–75 and 1979–81.³ None, however, was more alarming than what India faced in 1991.

―

The simplest way to explain the financial mess that prime minister Narasimha Rao faced was that, by June 1991, India had enough foreign exchange reserves to pay for just two weeks of imports,⁴ while a minimum safe level was considered six times that amount—enough for at least three months' worth of imports. Manmohan Singh, a former professor of international trade, knew what awaited India. He would say that in 1982, Mexico defaulted on its external debt obligations. For the next six years it was crippled by capital flight, inflation and unemployment. By the time the crisis ended in 1989, real wages had been halved.⁵

Three proximate causes had dwindled India's dollar reserves. The Gulf War of 1990 had trebled the price of oil which India was buying from the world market, and had also diminished remittances from Indians working in the Middle East. The second reason was that Indians living abroad had withdrawn 900 million dollars' worth of deposits from Indian banks between April and June 1991,⁶ panicking at political uncertainty in Lutyens Delhi. A third form of pressure on India's foreign exchange reserves was due to reckless borrowing during the Rajiv years. Many of these were short-duration loans, and by 1991, they were due.

To avoid a default, Rao's predecessor as prime minister, Chandra Shekhar, had taken a loan from the IMF in early 1991. So low was the trust in India's ability to repay that the IMF had wanted India to pledge her gold. That loan had not been enough to solve India's balance of payments crisis. By mid-1991, India was in need of a second tranche. The IMF refused. As Narasimha Rao put it, ' . . . in April 1991 . . . consultations were held with both the IMF and World Bank. The report of the discussions was that no fresh commitments of aid would be forthcoming until basic reforms were undertaken.'[7] India's executive director to the IMF, Gopi Arora, told Jairam Ramesh, 'Our credibility was rock bottom.'[8]

The Gulf War, withdrawal of foreign deposits, and short-term borrowings were the immediate sources of the crisis. The deeper problem of the Indian economy was a weak foundation that left it vulnerable to periodic tremors. The state-controlled economy was persistently inefficient, with scant returns on investment.[9] Anaemic industrial growth, low export levels, and bloated inflation were all symptoms of this chronic malaise. These symptoms, in turn, ensured measly taxation revenue, leading to stingy public spending. As we shall see in a later chapter, the irony was that in Indian-style socialism, there was precious little money spent on education, health and food for the poor.

The argument for reducing state control over the economy would convince the formerly protectionist Narasimha Rao in a single day in June 1991. But that argument had been evident for a decade at least. Despite this, opposition from powerful interest groups vested in the licence raj had thwarted prime minister Indira Gandhi and her three successors from opening up the economy. As Narasimha Rao envisioned the economic changes essential for his country, he also contemplated the barricades he would have to climb over.

The first obstacle was that Rao's party was a minority in Parliament. Unlike Indira Gandhi in 1980 or Rajiv in 1984, Rao did not have the numbers to impose his legislative writ. His very survival was contingent on the opposition BJP and the National Front not voting together to convey their lack of confidence. Some of his adversaries might have privately agreed with him. The National Front leader, V.P. Singh, was Rajiv's finance minister when some liberalizing reforms had been attempted in 1985. And the other opposition, the right-wing BJP, was largely supported by north Indian traders who wanted the government off their backs. These parties also knew that with perestroika in the Soviet Union, India too needed to change.

The problem was that the V.P. Singh of 1991—by now a messiah of the backward castes—was not the reformer of 1985. And the BJP's base of traders and small manufacturers was opposed to competition from foreign companies. The Marxist Left had also done relatively well in the 1991 elections, winning around forty-nine seats. They were against pro-market policies they felt would injure the poor.

This legislative handicap made Narasimha Rao politically feebler than any global leader who had embarked on reforms. Once Deng Xiaoping was in control of the Communist Party of China, he had few checks on his power. The same was true of the East Asian strongmen, from Singapore's Lee Kuan Yew to South Korea's Park Chung-hee. And while Margaret Thatcher and Ronald Reagan had to operate within a democratic system of checks and balances, they had come to power with clear majorities. Narasimha Rao, leading a minority government in a fractious democracy full of veto players, had none of these luxuries.

A second hurdle to economic reform were established business houses, known as the 'Bombay club', and represented through various lobbying groups. Many of these groups had grown fat on the licence raj. Others wanted national controls to go but were fearful of international competition. As Manmohan Singh put it, 'Competition hurts those who are inefficient. And therefore opening up the economy, bringing in domestic competition and competition from abroad does hurt some people, some industries.'[10] Montek Singh Ahluwalia remembers that the message from industry was clear. 'Domestic liberalization today, and external liberalization later.'[11]

Left-wing intellectuals, influential in the media and universities, were yet another impediment to pro-market policies. They had skewered prime minister Indira Gandhi over the currency devaluation of 1966. They also had influence over Parliament as well as within the Congress. Narasimha Rao took them seriously. Many of his left-leaning friends (such as Nikhil Chakravartty, the editor of *Mainstream*) were opposed to opening up the economy. There were also subtler pressures from within the social circles the reformers moved in. Manmohan Singh's daughter Daman Singh recalls that '1991 was the most miserable year of my professional life'. She was working for an NGO, and her colleagues were outraged at her father's reforms. 'They rudely cut me off at staff meetings, and refused to have anything to do with me outside them.'[12]

But perhaps the tallest fence that had closed off the economy was the party of Jawaharlal Nehru and Indira Gandhi, which could not be seen as abandoning its commitment to socialism.[13] The text of the 1991 Congress manifesto gave no hint that the party would pursue radical reform had Rajiv Gandhi lived on to become prime minister again. The manifesto swore to turn the economy around with 'a dynamic and profit-oriented public sector'.[14] It also promised to reduce tax, promote exports, efficiently utilize borrowed funds,[15] and improve nationalized banks. These were vows to improve the licence raj, not eliminate it altogether. To underline just how wary of pro-market policies the Congress leadership was, the alternatives for the premiership, Arjun Singh and N.D. Tiwari, were old-style socialists against any tryst with the West. The one exception was Sharad Pawar, from the industrialized state of Maharashtra. But he was close to Bombay businessmen, and might have preferred oligarchic capitalism to genuine liberalization.

Any attempt to open the economy had to overcome the stodgy Congress party, a divided Parliament, nervous industrialists and shrill intellectuals. Those who benefited from a centrally planned economy—rich farmers, trade unions, business houses, corrupt politicians and bureaucrats—were also powerful.

The reason why a policy that benefitted the many could be held hostage to the interests of a few was because of a dynamic that the social scientist Mancur Olson had first explained.[16] Since liberalization promised only future advantages, it did not yet have a political constituency. Indeed, many beneficiaries were yet unborn. On the other hand, the vested interests benefiting from the status quo were narrow and focussed—because of which they were well organized and formidable. Would Narasimha Rao, like four prime ministers before him, hit these rocks, reefs and shoals while navigating reforms? His first months in power provide the answer.

---

19 June 1991, two days before he became prime minister, was the first time Narasimha Rao realized the magnitude of the economic crisis. As we saw in the previous chapter, he spent the evening reading the eight-page document that Cabinet secretary Naresh Chandra had given him on India's financial predicament.[17] When he left his hideout in Willingdon Crescent that night to make the short journey back to his home on Motilal Nehru Marg, he carried the note with him. Subramanian Swamy, a Harvard-trained economist and minister in the previous government, says he spoke to Rao on the phone that evening. 'I know about the reforms you were working on [as commerce minister]. Send me the documents,' Rao asked. Swamy replied: 'I have one Cabinet note. The rest are typewritten sheets which I will get through to you.' Swamy told Rao what he should do: 'Focus on the economy.'[18]

The next morning, Narasimha Rao was chosen as the leader of the Congress Parliamentary Party, the prelude to becoming prime minister. Rao had grasped by then that his choice of finance minister would signal his intentions to the West.

That he had understood what needed to be done within a day of learning of the problem cannot be explained by economic acumen—Rao had none. It can only be explained by raw political instinct, cultivated through decades in government. What this rapid decision-making at such a crucial moment reveals is that—contrary to stereotype—Rao would dither not because he was unable to tell good policy from bad; he vacillated because sometimes the correct policy did not make for good politics. Where the right decision was also politically defensible—which liberalization was in the early days of his government—Rao could act with remarkable speed.

His first action was to spurn the Congress leaders who wanted the finance ministry for themselves. Pranab Mukherjee had been finance minister from 1982 to '84, a period referred to as the one that saw the origins of crony capitalism in India. Since he had sided with Rao during the tussle for prime ministership, Pranab was confident he would be made finance minister once again. A few hours after Rao was appointed CPP leader on 20 June 1991, Pranab Mukherjee told Jairam Ramesh, '*Joy*ram, you will either be with me in in North Block, or South Block with *Pee Vee*.'[19]

The prime minister-elect had other plans. Rao called up the intelligence bureau that afternoon, says Sanjaya Baru, based on what a senior IB official told him. A few hours later, the official entered Willingdon Crescent carrying the secret file on Pranab Mukherjee.[20] There is no evidence of anything incriminating in the file, or if Rao even used it against Pranab. But one thing is certain. By that evening, Pranab was no longer in the running.

When I.G. Patel had declined to be finance minister, P.C. Alexander had approached Manmohan Singh the same night. The next day, the morning of the swearing-in ceremony, Narasimha Rao called up Manmohan Singh and offered him the unenviable job of the finance minister of India. Twenty-five years later, Manmohan Singh remembers his conversation with Rao: 'I said I will accept this only if I get his full backing. He replied, only half-jokingly, "You will have a free hand. If the policies succeed, we will all take the credit. If it fails, you will have to go."'[21]

A Cambridge-trained economist who had just served as the secretary general of the South Commission in Geneva, Manmohan Singh was very much the 'internationally credible face' that Rao was searching for. Manmohan had also held every significant economic post within the Indian government. The former teacher at Panjab University had risen to become finance secretary and governor of the Reserve Bank. In 1987, he had been awarded the Padma Vibhushan, India's second-highest civilian honour. Like Narasimha Rao, Manmohan was both reformer as well as dutiful deputy. He had been gently critical of the licence raj, but never in ways that upset his political masters. In 1972, for example, he had reviewed the landmark *India: Planning for Industrialization* by the economists Jagdish Bhagwati and Padma Desai. The book was the first detailed critique of economic controls in India. Manmohan agreed with the book that 'the knowledge available to civil servants is not necessarily superior to that of entrepreneurs'. But he was quick to add, 'It would be much too presumptuous to claim that modern neo-classical economics has answers to all economic problems . . .'[22] Manmohan's balancing act was evident even in the late 1980s. As secretary general of the South Commission in 1987, he had overseen the writing of a startlingly socialist report.[23] Yet, once back in Delhi, free to speak his mind, he was once again an advocate of free-market policies.[24]

Rao had met Manmohan several times before. In late 1984, defence minister Narasimha Rao was also holding the position of deputy chairman of the planning commission. He met prime minister Rajiv Gandhi and asked to be divested of the post. Rajiv suggested the names of a few politicians as Rao's replacement. An official working for Rao at the time remembers Rao telling Rajiv, 'The planning commission head is a technical job, you need a technocrat.' Rao suggested the name of the governor of the Reserve Bank, Manmohan Singh. The prime minister agreed.[25]

Six years later, Rao once again chose that same technocrat to man a technical post. Manmohan must have impressed Rao with the same contradictions he himself possessed. Rao wanted a visibly honest reformer whom the West could trust. He also needed a loyalist who could deflect domestic criticism away from the prime minister.

Manmohan Singh would prove to be the perfect foil.

Manmohan was only one of several reformers that Narasimha Rao chose to surround himself with. He wanted a principal secretary who could guide reforms from within the prime minister's office. Alexander suggested G.V. Ramakrishna, a bureaucrat who had worked in finance before, and was at the time the chief regulator of India's capital markets. But Narasimha Rao, whose failure as Andhra chief minister had taught him to be conscious of caste combinations, rejected the name, saying, 'The principal secretary and prime minister should not both be south Indian Brahmins . . . that would send out the wrong message.'[26]

Rao eventually chose Amar Nath Varma, a UP Kayastha who would go on to play as central a role as Manmohan Singh in Narasimha Rao's liberalization reforms. Varma was then in the planning commission after having served as industry secretary. He had acquired a reputation for being a ruthless operator who could get things done, no matter what the cost in bruised egos. A Delhi-based lobbyist remembers the 'Amarnath Yatra' that he took a businessman on. When they entered the room, Varma was reading a file, his face at a downward angle. The businessman explained that he wanted to set up a factory. Varma replied, *'Kal tak approval mil jaayega.'* ('You will get the approval by tomorrow.') Unused to a bureaucratic decision being made so quickly, the businessman turned ingratiating, referring to his ties with Narasimha Rao. Varma cut him short, face still lowered, but eyeballs raised upwards. 'I told you, it will be done.'

The project was approved the next morning.

Also assisting Rao was Cabinet secretary Naresh Chandra. Selected by the previous government, Chandra was a career bureaucrat who knew how to speak his mind without causing offence. He combined the gravitas of Henry Kissinger along with Kissinger's girth. Chandra had shepherded the fleeting economic reforms of the Chandra Shekhar government. A bachelor, Chandra considered the bureaucracy his true home and brought with him an encyclopaedic knowledge of government procedure. He would play a critical role in closing down the administrative tentacles of the licence raj with minimum fuss.

Prime minister Rao had a soft spot for Chandra, and years later explained to an aide why. It was early 1991 and Narasimha Rao, then an opposition MP contemplating retirement, was strolling inside Parliament. He noticed commerce secretary Montek Singh Ahluwalia walking into the building, along with Cabinet secretary Naresh Chandra. Rao saw the security guard at the entrance beckon to only Ahluwalia to move aside for frisking. Chandra, standing behind Ahluwalia, discreetly signalled to the guard that he too wanted to be frisked so that the commerce secretary would not feel singled out. It was a simple gesture, but one that stayed imprinted in Rao's mind.

Montek Singh Ahluwalia was, in fact, the other official whom Rao drew into his inner circle.[27] A Rhodes scholar, Ahluwalia had spent a decade with the World Bank in Washington D.C., before moving laterally to the ministry of finance as an advisor in 1979. This unusual move into the ranks of career bureaucrats had been supported by family friend and finance secretary, Manmohan Singh. Often wearing a reverse-folded blue turban (also Manmohan's favoured turban colour), Ahluwalia was as animated an advocate of reforms inside the closed doors of government as he was sleep-inducing in public. It was a skill that ensured he outlived Rao and became the torchbearer of reform in later governments. Years later, in 1998, when the BJP finance minister, Yashwant

Sinha, visited the United States and faced investors worried about reverses to Rao's reforms, Sinha would reassure them that 'Montek represented continuity while I represented change . . . that was how our system worked.'[28]

Rao also recruited Jairam Ramesh as officer on special duty. Ramesh was a liberalizing policy wonk who would change garb in 2004 to become the left-leaning architect of the UPA's welfare state. In 1991, he was Rajiv Gandhi's point man on the economy. In the words of the economist Rakesh Mohan, 'Jairam was the flag bearer for Rajiv's policy inside Rao's PMO [prime minister's office].'[29]

For commerce minister, the prime minister selected P. Chidambaram, a young lawyer from Tamil Nadu. Chidambaram, who combined a reputation for efficiency with a reputation for arrogance, was an unashamed liberalizer. He would work with Manmohan Singh to pilot trade reforms. But Chidambaram was livid that Rao had made him only minister of state, not a full Cabinet minister. When Jairam Ramesh conveyed this discontent to Rao, the prime minister replied, 'Tell Mr Chidambaram that he will get a post commensurate with his capability.'[30]

Rao also tried to poach liberalizers from other parties. He offered the previous commerce minister, Subramanian Swamy, a Cabinet position. Swamy says he refused to join the Congress. Instead, Rao gave him a post that was 'Cabinet-rank'. The prime minister also wanted the reformist former finance minister—and Subramanian Swamy baiter—Yashwant Sinha to join the Congress, even meeting with him. But, in Sinha's words, 'these meetings did not yield any result'.[31]

Narasimha Rao had chosen to give the finance and commerce ministries to known liberalizers, and selected a principal secretary with pro-market views. To make his intentions even clearer, Rao appointed himself as industry minister. His Cabinet secretary remembers why: 'He was persuaded that if you are not minister for industry, then you cannot implement [industrial policy] reforms.'[32]

The team, all political appointments directly made by Narasimha Rao, was in place. Now, they had to act.

~

On 24 June 1991, four days after becoming finance minister, Manmohan Singh called twelve senior bureaucrats for a meeting in a small room in the finance ministry. Many were resistant to liberalization, but Singh left them in no doubt as to what their new role was. 'This is what needs to be done,' he ended, 'and the PM has given me full authority to get it done. If any one of you have any difficulty with this, speak up now and we can find you other things to do.'[33]

That same day, Narasimha Rao met opposition leaders one-on-one. When it came to the former prime minister Chandra Shekhar, it was Rao who called on him.[34] The following day, opposition leaders, including V.P. Singh of the National Front and Jaswant Singh of the BJP, were briefed by the new finance minister. Rao was present but chose to say little. At the meeting, Manmohan Singh gave details of the crisis: 'I told them all the things that were necessary to control the fiscal deficit, to change the thinking on industrial policy, to liberalise the economy.'[35] Manmohan remembers that the Opposition was stunned; they had not realized the gravity of the situation.[36]

Confiding in political opponents was both magnanimous as well as sagacious for a prime minister who did not have a majority in Parliament. Rao, however, chose not to tell the opposition leaders two things. That he would devalue the rupee soon. And that India's gold was being mortgaged in return for foreign loans. Had they known, they would not have allowed these actions, regardless of how serious the crisis was. Rao later defended this deception. 'About those two decisions, it was not fair, it would not be fair on their part to ask and it would not be fair at all on my part to divulge at that stage.'[37]

RESCUING THE ECONOMY, 1991–92

Having bought some political capital, the new prime minister contemplated whether he should expend it on a symbolic first move. The Indian rupee was artificially valued against the dollar. This discouraged foreign investors and depressed exports. Before committing more funds, the IMF wanted the rupee devalued as proof that the new Indian government was serious. But Rao knew there would be a domestic backlash since the value of the rupee was linked to national vanity. Devaluation would hit imports as well as foreign debt. He also remembered Indira Gandhi's devaluation of the rupee in 1966. Not only was that decision denounced in Parliament and the media as a sell-out to Washington, the World Bank fell short on its promise of aid.[38]

Rao was also under pressure from left intellectuals to not lower the value of the rupee. Nikhil Chakravartty asked him to avoid the move.[39] But Manmohan Singh was adamant that devaluation was necessary, and the prime minister decided to back him. To take the opponents by surprise, they decided to first lower the worth of the rupee and then announce it as fait accompli. Manmohan did not even want the Cabinet to know, and planned to announce it in two phases. Rao agreed.

On 1 July 1991, India lowered the value of the rupee. The change itself was minor, between 7 to 9 per cent against major currencies. In contrast, Indira had devalued the currency by 57.4 per cent in 1966. The next day, 2 July, Manmohan Singh sent Rao a note typed on green paper. The note suggested that Rao should spin the devaluation of the previous day in a way that sounded routine:

'We are living in a world of floating currencies. Most currencies of the world are floating on a daily basis. Some days exchange rates go up next day they come down. India is no exception to this rule . . . we shall do everything in our power to restore the health of our economy and of the balance of payments.'[40]

This dissembling had little effect. While the media cheered Rao, opposition members were furious. The Communist Party of India (Marxist) termed the downward revision of the rupee as a 'very dangerous precedent', while the BJP spokesperson K.R. Malkani said it would compound the already critical economic situation.[41] Atal Bihari Vajpayee claimed that these were 'drastic steps' and that the government 'should have taken the people into confidence'.[42] Congress ministers, who had also been kept in the dark, were uneasy.

To calm his own party, Rao asked the finance ministry to prepare a simple statement that he could read to the inner Cabinet. The chief economic advisor, Deepak Nayyar, sent him a note, explaining that 'if we did not act decisively, default was almost certain by mid-July'.[43]

Though Rao had not let on, there were rumours of a second round of devaluation. Manmohan Singh remembers this as his day of reckoning. Rao was under intense political pressure. But Manmohan Singh was unyielding that a second round take place, since the quantum of devaluation on 1 July had been minimal. Manmohan scheduled the second round for the next day, 3 July. Taken together, the rupee would lose about 20 per cent of its value.

In the early hours of the next morning, the prime minister's feet turned cold. He called Manmohan Singh and ordered him to 'please don't do it'.[44] It was too late. When Singh called up the Reserve Bank deputy governor C. Rangarajan to ask him not to make the announcement, Rangarajan replied, 'The horse has bolted. I have already announced.' Embarrassed, Manmohan Singh offered to resign, saying, 'Let the responsibility lie with me.' Rao had always intended his finance minister as a scapegoat, but he did not want to sacrifice him just yet. 'He backed me,' says Manmohan Singh.[45]

Manmohan used this new-found backing to empower his own team of reformers. He sent Rao a note recommending that C. Rangarajan was the 'ideal choice for the membership of the Planning Commission'.[46] Manmohan also inducted the endearingly irreverent Ashok V. Desai into the finance ministry.

Desai had studied with Manmohan in the Cambridge of the 1960s. As ideologically pro-reform as he was outspoken, he would provide the finance minister with the intellectual ballast to take on the licence raj.[47]

That would come later. On the afternoon of 3 July, Manmohan Singh met his protégé Montek Singh Ahluwalia to ask him to brief the commerce minister, P. Chidambaram, about export subsidies being abolished.

Since an expensive rupee made it harder for Indian manufacturers to sell in the foreign market, the Indian government had created a Cash Compensatory Scheme, or CCS, for exporters—yet another example of how subsidy begot subsidy, i.e. how the Indian state first intervened in the market to create a distortion, then intervened again with a distortion in the opposite direction. But with the rupee now closer to its true value after the depreciation, an export subsidy was superfluous, and Manmohan decided to get rid of it.[48]

Montek Ahluwalia and his commerce minister, Chidambaram, spent the afternoon of 3 July pondering the implications of what was being asked. A ministry meant to promote exports was being told to eliminate an export subsidy. Ahluwalia explained to Chidambaram that there was logic in what the finance minister was proposing, especially since they needed to save money. Chidambaram agreed to abolish the CCS.

The removal of the CCS was sure to worry exporters. In order to assuage them, the commerce ministry decided to offer them an immediate sop. The ministry had already been considering major trade policy reforms involving new incentives for exports. This was in the form of an 'enlarged replenishment licence entitlement' which could be used to import restricted items. Chidambaram and Ahluwalia wanted this policy to be announced simultaneously with the abolition of export subsidy.

Since this could only be done with the approval of the finance minister, they sought a meeting with Manmohan Singh to explain the proposal. He readily agreed, despite reservations from his officials. All three of them visited Narasimha Rao at his house that very night for his consent. In less than twelve hours, the policy had moved from farm to fork.[49]

Rao was now left to carry the political burden. Opposition leaders complained that they had not been warned of these changes. Officials in Udyog Bhavan, the commerce ministry, were terrified that an entire bureaucratic apparatus grown fat on the economy had been dismantled overnight.

Rao placated his adversaries by playing up the crisis. 'Desperate maladies call for drastic remedies,' he said in a speech on 9 July 1991.[50] 'The Reserve Bank changed the exchange rate of the rupee,' he added, shifting the blame on to others. He also argued that the additional foreign exchange produced would be used to import everyday items for common people: 'kerosene and diesel, fertilizers, edible oil and steel'. Finally, he linked this burst of reforms to Rajiv Gandhi's legacy. 'What we have done is a continuation of policies initiated by him.' This was not true. Yet, Rao was hiding behind an icon of the Congress to justify the claim that 'a bulk of government regulations and controls on economic activity had outlived their utility. They are stifling the creativity and innovativeness of our people.'[51]

The speech, drafted by Jairam Ramesh, showcased the rhetorical weapons that Rao had in his armoury. He had alternated between blaming the reforms on the crisis, placing responsibility on others, citing the interests of the poor, and linking reforms to the vision of a deceased leader. Prime minister Narasimha Rao had learnt well from his failures as Andhra chief minister. He was now adept at the politics of reform, able to gauge his own constraints as well as those of his opponents. To avoid the traps set for a lion, he had learnt to tread like a fox.

Devaluation done, the prime minister and his team turned to the next set of reforms. The need to change industrial policy—the red tape that so tightly bound private manufacturers—had been first acknowledged a decade earlier. Even during Indira Gandhi's second term in office, there had been talk of a floating exchange rate, elimination of licensing and the removal of anti-monopoly laws. Rajiv Gandhi had begun his own stint as prime minister determined to make life easier for domestic firms. But the changes had been piecemeal, and by 1987, besieged by scandal, Rajiv lost his appetite for risk.

In 1988, a year after Rajiv abandoned reforms, Rakesh Mohan, a Princeton-trained economist, joined the ministry of industry as economic advisor and began sketching the skeleton of a new industrial policy.[52] The government changed, and Mohan's attention was diverted elsewhere. In 1990, the new industry minister, Ajit Singh, ordered Mohan to work along with Amar Nath Varma (then industry secretary) to write a policy that would end the licence raj.[53] The draft was ready in a few months, and it was revolutionary.[54] In a significant reversal of policy presumptions, the private sector could operate freely in almost any industry, without prior government permission. But the recommendations gathered dust, mired in political infighting.

Now, in July 1991, Prime Minister Rao—in his avatar as the new industry minister—gave Amar Nath Varma (now principal secretary) the mandate to convert that draft into policy. Varma called his friend, the then industry secretary, Suresh Mathur, for a discussion, along with Rakesh Mohan and Jairam Ramesh. He told them this was the chance they had been waiting for, since 'the prime minister had deliberately kept the industry portfolio to himself'.[55] By 7 July, Rakesh Mohan's original draft had been polished into what would become the new industrial policy.

Among Rao's papers lies a copy of that draft, heavily annotated and underlined by the prime minister. The economics dilettante was taking the trouble to master the details himself. He would later say that freeing domestic entrepreneurs from state control was the single most important economic decision he would make.[56]

Rao asked Jairam Ramesh for a summary of the changes so that he could brief his party. A five-page note reached the prime minister around 8 July. The next day, Rao met the CPP and informed it that he would announce comprehensive changes to the industrial policy soon. Rao was careful not to go into the details; he did not want the Opposition to pre-empt him.[57]

A few days later, on 12 July, Rao confidante Kalyani Shankar—who had by now joined the *Hindustan Times*—published an article titled 'Industrial Licensing to Go'. She wrote that 'all industrial licences except for a short negative list' would be removed soon. She even listed the significant features: automatic permission for foreign investment up to 51 per cent; an increase in the exempt threshold under the anti-monopoly law; the removal of phased manufacturing; and an end to other manufacturing limits.[58] Jairam, terrified that he would be blamed for the leak, rushed to the prime minister's office, only to be informally told that the leak had come from the boss himself.[59] Rao was testing reactions to the policy before formally announcing it.

Three days later, Narasimha Rao stood up in Parliament during the vote of confidence in his government. As before, he made use of the threat to the prestige of the nation, urging the Opposition to give up their maximalist ideologies in the face of calamity. He quoted a Sanskrit verse to make his point: *'Sarvanashe samutpanne ardham tyajati panditah.'*[60] ('Faced with total ruin, the wise settle for half.')

That same day, 15 July 1991, Narasimha Rao asked for the note on industrial policy to be presented before the Cabinet—the final step before a policy is put into effect. Narasimha Rao's appointment diary, maintained by his secretary, R.K. Khandekar, shows the following entry for 16 July: '10–11am: Meeting on industrial policy'.[61] The Cabinet meeting was scheduled for 19 July, and a few days before, Rakesh Mohan (along with the bureaucrat N. Krishnan) was instructed to meet Arjun Singh in private to convince him of the merits of the policy. That meeting did not go well.⁶² When the Cabinet met some days later, ministers opposed both the style and substance of the draft policy. Arjun Singh and M.L. Fotedar, in particular, were outspoken in their hostility.⁶³ Rao remained silent, leaving his finance minister to face the fury.

The policy was sent back to the drawing board, but crucially, Rao ensured that the substance remained untouched. Jairam Ramesh worked, instead, to add a longish preamble which linked the new ideas to the fundamental ideals of the Congress, Nehru and Indira Gandhi. It worked. When the Union Cabinet met again, on the morning of 23 July, those who had opposed the policy earlier were reassured by the addition of the preamble.

That afternoon, Rao convened a meeting of the CWC at his house. He began by saying that all that the new policy did was to reverse Indira Gandhi's sharp leftward tilt in 1969, and take the country back to the more flexible 1956 policy resolution of Nehru. The Congress, Rao added, continued to believe in the 'commanding heights of the public sector'.⁶⁴ Having played one Nehru-Gandhi against another, Rao now let his finance minister speak. Learning from his political master, Manmohan invoked the 1991 manifesto to show that within it lay the seeds of the new industrial policy. This was far from the truth, but as Manmohan Singh came out of the meeting, Arjun Singh told him: 'Dr Singh, you have read the manifesto more carefully than we have.'⁶⁵

The ploy had worked. Narasimha Rao, assisted by Manmohan Singh, had been able to take a policy that was in cold storage, make surface changes, and seamlessly link it to a Nehruvian past—all to drag his party behind the most revolutionary economic reform in the history of independent India. As Rakesh Mohan put it, "We had authored this policy before. *Hum to likhte rahte hain* [We keep writing]. But it would not have gone anywhere without a clear political mandate. I would give credit to Rao for his unwavering political backing.'⁶⁶

In parallel to the manoeuvring over industrial policy, was the manoeuvring over the budget, scheduled to be presented to Parliament on 24 July 1991. The budget consists of a report on expenditure, new schemes, taxation plans, and the budget speech itself.[67] The budget is the financial statement of the government, a simple accounting exercise. Most countries do not consider it important. But over the years in India, it has become one of the few occasions when Parliament actually deliberates on policy. In 1991, it was the ideal platform for the government of the day to announce its vision.

Preparations for the 1991 budget were coordinated by finance minister Manmohan Singh. He consulted at length with the ministries of industry, commerce, as well as the prime minister's office. Holding the fort at the PMO was Amar Nath Varma, who had fast established himself as Narasimha Rao's point man on economic reforms.

Early in July, Varma instituted the Thursday afternoon meeting on economic policy in his office in South Block, near the prime minister's room. Varma would lay out an opulent lunch, often with kebabs and cutlets,[68] and ask the chief bureaucrats of various departments a simple question: What was this week's reform? The fruits of the Thursday meeting would then be sent to the Cabinet for final approval. 'Varma Thursdays' would be the engine of reforms for five unbroken years. For the month of July 1991, these meetings were used to discuss budget minutiae, which would then make their way to a super draft, stored in the finance ministry.

Since the budget was a sensitive document that businessmen would pay money to know in advance, its preparation was shrouded in secrecy. In the weeks before 24 July, everyone working on the budget lived locked-down in a basement in North Block. They had to eat and sleep there, with no telephones to connect them to the world.[69] Only a select few, such as the finance minister, were allowed in and out of the basement. The draft would remain secret until it was read out by Manmohan in Parliament on 24 July.

In his speech to the nation on 9 July, Narasimha Rao had hinted that the budget would pursue a reform agenda.[70] But it is possible that the scale of what the prime minister wanted was not known to the mandarins in the finance ministry—some of whom were opposed to concessions to the West.

A few days after, in mid-July, Manmohan Singh visited the prime minister's office with the top-secret draft budget. A senior bureaucrat and visiting Indian diplomat say they were both present in the room when Manmohan Singh gave the prime minister a one-page summary of the draft. They remember Rao sitting in his chair and reading through the page, while Manmohan stood with them, waiting. Then, Rao looked up at Manmohan and said, 'If this is what I wanted, why would I have selected you?'

This explosive sentence has been vouched for by both officials independently. They had not, however, seen the page themselves, and there is no way to verify whether Manmohan Singh's first draft was indeed less reformist than finally revealed. It was suspected, though, that two finance ministry officials tasked with helping Manmohan prepare the budget did not share his ideas.[71] At the very least, however, the story shows that Narasimha Rao had a sharp sense of the kind of message he wanted to send on 24 July.

In the lead-up to budget day, the prime minister met industrialists—many of whom supported internal liberalization but were worried that opening up to external competition would hurt their firms. Rao's appointment diary shows that on 20 July, he met the long-established industrialist K.K. Birla.[72] He also met the poster boy of the new entrepreneurs of the 1980s, Dhirubhai Ambani.

In Rao's archives lies a printed letter bound in light brown paper. While unsigned, on the top right corner, in Rao's precise handwriting, is the word 'Dhirubhai'.[73] The letter begins by referring to the fiscal deficit and balance of payment crisis that

India was facing. It does not suggest delicensing or external liberalization as the solution. Instead, it proposes that India raise 16,000 crore rupees by selling the government's stake in public sector units.

Such a suggestion would be soon implemented elsewhere. After the disintegration of the Soviet Union in 1991, the newly formed Russian republic would opt for the large-scale privatization of public sector enterprises. Many of these state assets were purchased at throwaway prices by businessmen with connections to the new government. This Russian-style privatization was more crony capitalism than genuine liberalization, and Narasimha Rao was being pressured to adopt a similar approach.

The final draft of the budget, ready by 21 July, was groundbreaking. It overhauled the import-export policy, better connecting India to the world market. It also slashed subsidies, and made foreign investment easier. The budget was going to shatter the third pillar of the licence-permit-quota raj: isolation of India from the global economy.

A day before the budget, bickering broke out between the ministries of industries and finance. Manmohan Singh wanted the budget speech to include the new industrial policy. This would send out a clear signal that the government was committed to both external and internal liberalization. But the bureaucrats at the industry ministry, recent converts to reforms, wanted glory of their own. They demanded a separate announcement by the industry minister. The fact that the normally protectionist officials were falling over each other to take credit for reform shows how quickly the Narasimha Rao government was changing attitudes.

The PM brokered a compromise. He sided with his industry ministry and ensured that delicensing was announced separately from the budget. At the same time, agreeing with Manmohan's suggestion that a single signal be sent to the world, Rao ordered that it be announced on 24 July, the day of the budget.[74]

Some commentators question this narrative, since the world was less interested in the internal reforms the industrial policy heralded, preferring the trade reforms that Manmohan's budget contained. They claim that the decision to announce industrial policy on the morning of the budget was entirely Rao's, and entirely Machiavellian.[75] This was before the days of twenty-four-hour news and the Internet, and the day's reforms would first be reported only in the next morning's newspapers. Rao deliberately kept his industrial policy announcement for the morning of the budget, the theory goes, so that newspapers would focus on the evening budget, rather than the more politically sensitive overhaul of industrial policy.

~

24 July 1991 was a hot day, and as parliamentarians streamed into the sandstone Parliament, they expected an evening of fireworks.

The show began even sooner. At around 12.50 p.m., the minister of state for industry, P.J. Kurien, got up to make a bland announcement in the Lok Sabha.[76] Given the weight of what he was going to table, the industry minister should have presented the document. But Rao wanted no part in it. Instead, his deputy got up and said, 'Sir, I beg to lay on the table a statement (Hindi and English versions) on Industrial Policy.'[77]

This innocuous declaration masked the profoundly radical policy he had just announced. Its most famous sentence was that 'industrial licensing will henceforth be abolished for all industries, except those specified, irrespective of levels of investment'. The exceptions were just eighteen industries mentioned in the annex to the policy (which have since been whittled down even further). It also limited public sector monopolies to eight sectors. The second change was to end the official phobia towards large companies by easing anti-monopoly restrictions. The third change was to raise the permitted level of foreign investment from 40 per cent after government approval to unto 51 per cent in thirty-four industries with 'automatic approval'. This was the single most radical economic document in independent India's history, and it was announced without fanfare.

A few hours later, Manmohan Singh, wearing a light Nehru jacket[78] and with the red budget briefcase beside him, got up from his seat in the treasury benches in Parliament to deliver the speech of his life.

The apolitical Manmohan Singh began by confessing that he was 'overpowered by a strange sense of loneliness'. He missed the 'handsome, smiling face' of Rajiv Gandhi.[79] The speech would be peppered with other references to the very family whose ideology the budget was reversing. His next rhetorical tactic was to play up the financial crisis, claiming that it was raising prices on the poor. 'The crisis in the economy is both acute and deep. We have not experienced anything similar in the history of independent India.'[80] In the beginning of the speech itself, Manmohan had cited Rajiv Gandhi as well as the poor—sugar-coating meant to mask the bitter medicine in the rest of the budget.

Over the next few hours, Singh overhauled the import-export policy, pushed for export promotion, slashed import licensing, and reduced tariffs. After another ritual mention of Rajiv's name, the budget laid the foundation for vibrant capital markets.[81] Singh also went ahead and reduced subsidies on fertilizers by 40 per cent. The prices of subsidized sugar and LPG cylinders were also raised.[82] He then referred to the changes in industrial policy announced a few hours earlier, taking care to thank Nehru, Indira and Rajiv for a 'well diversified industrial structure'. Singh warned of difficulties ahead, but ended on a hopeful note: 'As Victor Hugo once said, "No power on earth can stop an idea whose time has come."'[83]

In a single day, Narasimha Rao and Manmohan Singh had done more than anyone to dismantle the three pillars of the licence raj: monopolies for the public sector, limits on private business, and isolation from the world markets.

RESCUING THE ECONOMY, 1991–92

But Rao had learnt from his fiasco as chief minister to neither show exultation nor claim credit, to know when to play lion and when to play mouse. He refused to present his own industrial policy, and throughout Manmohan's budget speech, pouted next to him without speaking at all. At eight that night, after spending the day orchestrating the biggest change to the economy since Independence, Narasimha Rao hosted a perfunctory dinner for the prime minister of Mauritius.[84]

It was to be business as usual.

The next day, newspapers bought the idea that the main reform was in the budget (not in the industrial policy) and its orchestrator was Manmohan Singh (not Narasimha Rao). The *Times of India* called the budget 'Truly Historic', though it made no mention of Narasimha Rao.[85] *The Economist* termed the reforms 'an economic revolution', but headlined the article, 'Singh's new song'.[86] The fortnightly *India Today*'s next issue sported a cover with the heading 'Shock Treatment. Will it Work?'[87] On the cover was just one man: Manmohan Singh.

Narasimha Rao was prescient in disassociating himself from the reforms of 24 July. For, on that day itself, the budget was attacked by opposition politicians. V.P. Singh said that ending subsidies would wreak havoc on farmers. Others reflexively termed the reforms 'anti-poor'. BJP leader Jaswant Singh claimed it did not contain poverty alleviation programmes.[88] In the remaining session of Parliament, the Opposition planned to give Rao's government a hard time.

Narasimha Rao responded with a verbal offensive designed both to exaggerate the nature of the crisis that forced his hand, as well as exaggerate links to the Nehruvian past. In his first Independence Day speech on 15 August 1991 from the ramparts of the Red Fort in Old Delhi, surrounded by bulletproof glass and snipers at the turrets, Narasimha Rao gave his audience a lesson in economics. He first spoke about the unprecedented nature of the crisis, and how this would impact the common man with an increase in the price of fertilizers, kerosene and edible oil.[89] He made no mention of tariff reduction or delicensing, but only of 'slightly changing the exchange rate of the Rupee'.[90] His speeches to Parliament were also crafty. Sensitive to the Opposition's accusation that he was imitating the West, Rao cited examples of pro-business policies in Korea, Malaysia, Thailand and Indonesia.[91] He defended his new industrial policy in other ways too, arguing that it was a continuation of the logic of Nehru's 1956 industrial policy resolution.[92]

This was less than truthful, given that it was this very industrial policy that Rao had demolished the previous month. But this was a prime minister whose favourite Telugu poem was one which could be interpreted to mean either the Mahabharata or Ramayana. It was not the words that mattered, it was the meaning they were given.

Narasimha Rao's other technique in dealing with Parliament was to tap his extensive networks among opposition leaders, many of whom were former Congressmen who had served with him. Rakesh Mohan remembers: 'The difference between Manmohan, Sonia, Rajiv and Rao was that he had worked with everyone for ages. The Gandhi family are completely removed from the hurly-burly of politics. They are not friends with others. [But] Rao and Vajpayee were old coots. He [Rao] knew people in other parties very well. He could deal with them as equals.'[93] To soothe the National Front leaders, Rao kept stressing that his policies were only continuations of those of prime ministers Chandra Shekhar and V.P. Singh. And when it came to the BJP, he used Sanskrit homilies in Parliament to disarm them.[94]

Rao was also pragmatic enough to know the battles which he could not win. When the Opposition was livid that Manmohan Singh had allocated 100 crore rupees—then a considerable sum—to the newly formed Rajiv Gandhi Foundation, Rao swiftly cancelled the grant, but only after Sonia Gandhi had also rejected it.[95] When protests over the removal of subsidies threatened to upturn his entire agenda, he ordered Manmohan Singh to decrease the hike in fertilizer prices from 40 to 30 per cent.[96] The technique of first increasing the price then rolling it back by a meagre amount, punctured the protests while letting the meat of the policy stay.

The one group that was resistant to Rao's charms were the communists. The CPM and CPI had together won around forty-nine seats in the 1991 elections, enough to slow down liberalization policies. On 4 July 1991, right after the second devaluation of the rupee, the CPM government in West Bengal released a document titled 'Alternate Policy Approach to Resolve BoP [Balance of Payments] Crisis'. It called for increasing taxes and cuts to non-developmental expenditures[97]—without having to do any delicensing, rupee cuts, and trade reforms. On 13 July, a group of left-leaning economists—many of them close to the communist parties—issued a statement critical of devaluation and cuts to subsidies.[98] Left economists also wrote articles arguing that the IMF-suggested response to the crisis was not inevitable.[99] This critique was pithily articulated by the Marxist leader E.M.S. Namboodiripad, who compared a loan from the IMF to 'a thirsty man taking a cup of poison on the plea that there is no alternative with which he can quench his thirst'.[100]

Narasimha Rao adopted a multipronged approach with the Left. He realized that public sector workers were organized, and many of them were linked to the communist parties. Any move to fire them would set off a firestorm akin to the riots that followed chief minister Narasimha Rao's land reforms in 1972. This Narasimha Rao, older and wiser, swore to protect the interests of organized labour. He promised that not a single worker would be fired because of his economic policies.[101] His finance minister Manmohan Singh would refer to the successful experience of communist-run West Bengal in pursuing some industrialization, something that flattered the Bengali Marxists while enraging their Delhi counterparts.[102] Narasimha Rao also went out of his way to cultivate Jyoti Basu and other communist leaders. His childhood friend Sadashiva Rao was a long-time member of the CPI, and prime minister Rao would often call him on the phone to find out what the Left was thinking.[103]

While protests against liberalization from Parliament and the communists were to be expected, more unexpected was opposition from business groups. Part of the problem was that Narasimha Rao had hardly interacted with businessmen before. Tarun Das, the long-time head of the industry lobby, the Confederation of Indian Industry (CII), remembers meeting Rao soon after the budget, in August 1991. 'He was a man of few words,' Das remembers. 'He wasn't comfortable with business . . . he was from an older generation.' But the main problem was that local firms were terrified that foreign competition would dislodge them from a cosy existence. A few days after the announcement of the new industrial policy, the business lobbying outfit, the Federation of Indian Chambers of Commerce and Industry (FICCI), expressed apprehensions about foreign companies being allowed entry.[104] Jairam Ramesh remembers telling industrialists at the time that they sounded like radical students from Jawaharlal Nehru University.[105]

In order to allay the fears of Indian businessmen, Narasimha Rao opened his schedule to prominent industrialists, something that the strait-laced Manmohan Singh was loathe to do. Rao's diary shows that he met Dhirubhai Ambani at 7 a.m. on 26 July—two days after the budget—and again on 16 August 1991. Rao would send emissaries—his press secretary, P.V.R.K. Prasad, and principal secretary, Amar Nath Varma—to meet influential businessmen and soothe their immediate anxieties.[106] He also conferred India's highest civilian honour, the Bharat Ratna, on the businessman J.R.D. Tata. This was the first time an industrialist had been recognized as a jewel of India, and the prime minister was well aware of the message being sent. While ignoring the long-term worries of big business, Rao was going out of the way to accommodate their proximate demands.

When Rao was chief minister of Andhra Pradesh, his own Congress had proved the fiercest opponent to his land reforms. Now as prime minister, Rao noted again that the most trenchant criticisms of liberalization emanated from his own party.

Soon after the budget, the party newspaper, the *Herald*, criticized liberalisation for giving 'the middle-class Indian crispier cornflakes or fizzier aerated drinks . . . That could never have been the vision of the founding fathers of our nation.'[107] At a party meeting on 1 August 1991, there was insurrection in the ranks. Narasimha Rao said little, leaving Manmohan Singh, who 'cut a lonely figure' to defend the new policies.[108] In the next party meeting held days later, only two Congressmen got up to defend Manmohan Singh—one of them being Mani Shankar Aiyar,[109] who would later become a visceral critic of the liberalization policies. Once again, Narasimha Rao said little, leaving Manmohan to face the heat.

The apolitical Manmohan Singh was learning tricks of his own. He used Rajiv Gandhi to defend the policies, and in the discussion in Parliament on 6 August, he referred to Jawaharlal Nehru's legacy.[110] When fifty Congress MPs signed a letter critical of the budget, Rao chose not to respond, letting his finance minister do the explaining. When the government later climbed down on subsidies somewhat, the protests dissipated, leaving Rao unscathed and unchallenged.

Behind these pretexts and ploys lay a shrewd political operator, unafraid to use any tool at his disposal. Perhaps the best evidence of just how devious Narasimha Rao was prepared to be to sell economic reforms lies in the existence of a clandestine document that the intelligence bureau sent to the prime minister around late 1991.

This document—which has never been made public—begins by listing the four major kinds of economic reforms that the Rao government had unveiled:

'i. Liberalization of trade and commerce, decontrol of industry, exit policy and IMF/World Bank conditionalities; ii. liberal entry of multinationals, foreign investment, GATT proposals and intellectual property rights; iii. privatisation/dilution of public sector; iv. reduction of fertilizer subsidy and agricultural policy.'

It then lists the names of all the Congress MPs—in the Rajya and Lok Sabha—who were against each of these four measures. There were fifty-five MPs against the liberalization of trade policies, including seven ministers such as Balram Jakhar and Madhavrao Scindia. Six Congress MPs opposed the entry of multinationals, including K.K. Birla. Privatization of public sector firms faced opposition from eighteen MPs, twenty MPs resisted the reduction of fertilizer subsidy, and there were twenty-two MPs against a Congress–BJP understanding on reforms, including Arjun Singh and Digvijay Singh.

This is a remarkable document. The job of the intelligence bureau is to protect the nation against domestic enemies. But Narasimha Rao was using it to spy on his own Congressmen, ensuring that they would not do to him now what they had done in 1973. More than any other single piece of evidence, this report shows how serious—not to mention ruthless—Rao was in pushing through economic reforms.

Narasimha Rao and Manmohan Singh followed up the big bangs of July 1991 with short bursts that were kept muffled from the media. As the political scientist Robert Jenkins explains, the aim in each sector was 'Gradual reform . . . using less transparent means of initiating change in an effort to avoid direct political confrontation as long as possible.'[111]

RESCUING THE ECONOMY, 1991–92

The foreign investment promotion board was set up soon after the budget.[112] Run directly from the prime minister's office, it facilitated the flow of foreign investment. The months that followed saw further changes to anti-monopoly laws and reduction in tariffs. The government also shut down many of the Kafkaesque instruments of economic control, such as the secretariat of industrial approvals, the directorate-general of technical development, and controllers of various commodities. Cabinet secretary Naresh Chandra remembers being tasked with closing down offices and asking babus to leave: 'The buildings were locked. We used to order them to shut down and disband staff by a specific date.'[113]

The 1992 budget, presented by Manmohan Singh in February, made foreign investment in India even easier. In that same month, Rao met the political scientist James Manor. The conversation gave Manor insights into the political logic for these economic reforms. '[Rao] knew that the issues of growth and development were more mundane and less emotive than caste, religious or regional issues. But he welcomed this because . . . the more heated politics became, the less able a centrist party like Congress would be to compete with parties to its left . . . and its right . . .'[114]

The stock market response was euphoric.[115] Within a single month, the Sensex doubled,[116] and the stockbroker Harshad Mehta became a national icon. He would drive around Bombay in an imported maroon Toyota Lexus. A herd of investors would follow his every move on Dalal Street.

By the middle of 1992, foreign exchange reserves—the depletion of which had been the excuse for reforms—were limping back to normal. By April, India's foreign exchange reserves were now enough to buy three months' worth of imports—the 'safe level' that economists agreed upon.[117] S. Rajgopal, who succeeded Naresh Chandra as Cabinet secretary in August 1992, remembers: 'By the time I took over, the economic crisis had abated. Forex situation was improving.'[118] In a speech to the industry lobby FIICI a month after, Rao said, 'The balance of payments crisis is now under control and we have been reasonably successful in reducing the fiscal deficit . . .'[119]

The crisis was over.

The reforms of 1991 are thought of as purely IMF-induced, an inevitable response to what the economist A.O. Hirschman described as an 'optimal crisis'—'deep enough to provoke change but not so deep that it wiped out the means to make it'.[120] This narrative is incomplete for a number of reasons.

India had leaned on the IMF earlier. It had borrowed SDR 3.9 billion in 1981-82, the largest arrangement in IMF history at the time.[121] That optimal crisis had not induced the then prime minister to open up the economy. The ideas behind the reforms of 1991—devaluation, delicensing, trade liberalization—had been agreed upon for at least a decade within government circles. What the IMF did was to provide Narasimha Rao and Manmohan Singh an external political excuse to implement home-grown ideas. It is certainly true that politicians recognized that with India facing a crisis, and with the Soviet Union in slow collapse, some change was inevitable. But Narasimha Rao's response was one of several possible—as the Left parties and intellectuals so correctly pointed out. The fact that opposition parties, as well as sections of the Congress, opposed liberalization shows that they were far from inevitable.

Without Narasimha Rao's political skill in playing up the crisis, disguising change as continuity, and deploying the incorruptible Manmohan Singh's technocratic image, reforms may well not have happened. As Tarun Das puts it, 'Rao was both strategic and shrewd. He knew the difference between what needed to be done, and how it has to be done.'[122]

Perhaps the best evidence that economic reform was not just a straightforward response to calamity is what happened after the crisis ended. Narasimha Rao did not have the excuse of a looming catastrophe after mid-1992. Big business, opposition parties, the Congress, and Left intellectuals could now force the Rao government to declare mission accomplished, and pedal back to the failed policies of the past—until the next financial crisis.

Without further liberalization, the reforms made so far would also be meaningless. While formal restrictions on Indian and foreign entrepreneurs had been eased, the complexity of doing business in India meant that government hand-holding was still necessary. The revolutions in transport, communications and consumer goods were yet to take place, and the first private airline yet to take off. But with no crisis to justify his reforms after 1992, Narasimha Rao could well have chosen to abandon liberalization midway.

8
Growing the Economy, 1992–96

The rule of Chandragupta Maurya stretched from northern India to Persia in the fourth century BCE.[1] In running this unwieldy empire, the king was advised by Chanakya—also known as Kautilya—whose book on the science of politics is titled *Arthashastra*.

Scattered through the *Arthashastra* are a range of *upaya*s (techniques) to prevail upon the enemy.[2] These are *sama, dana, bheda, maya, upeksa, danda*—concessions, bribery, division, trickery, indifference, and finally, punishment.[3] The ruler had to attempt conciliation when success was unlikely. Gifts were a way to win over inferior kings and discontented people without shedding blood. Creating confusion among enemies would neutralize their threat. Pretending moral probity would lull the enemy, as would feigning disinterest. It was only when these failed that the king should punish or resort to war.

Scholars from Max Weber to Henry Kissinger have drawn a link between the fourth-century BCE Mauryan diplomat and the better-known Florentine diplomat of the sixteenth century[4]— like Niccolò Machiavelli, Chanakya was a moralist, though in a complicated sense of the term. As the philosopher Roger Boesche puts it, 'Machiavelli and Kautilya shared the ethical conviction that a leader may, and sometimes must, use morally dubious means to obtain a good end . . .'[5]

In his first year as prime minister, Narasimha Rao had implemented his economic goals by deft use of looming catastrophe. With the crisis over by 1992, he needed new upayas. The 'big bang' reforms of 1991—devaluation, delicensing, trade liberalization—had formally opened up the economy. But industry still needed government help to navigate the hurdles that remained.

The licence raj had also created distinct vested interests in different sectors of the economy. For example, any attempt to privatize banks would symbolically overturn Indira Gandhi's bank nationalization drive. Ideological critics would see red, while bank unions would organize to protect their sinecure. Deepening the capital markets, on the other hand, would be opposed by unscrupulous brokers prospering from the status quo. The same variation in adversaries existed in infrastructure. Road-building had fewer opponents, while electricity reforms would be contested by powerful interest groups—the coal mafia, state power boards and customers. A whole new set of critics would protest the opening up of television and consumer goods, worried that traditional India was being westernized.

The BJP, communists and the Congress had their own complaints against liberalization. The BJP's trader base welcomed delicensing, but was wary of foreign competition. The communists opposed both, while the Congress party was sensitive to charges of elitism that went against the grain of Nehruvian socialism.

On economic reforms, Narasimha Rao and Manmohan Singh had proved exquisite opening batsmen. By 1992, however, liberalization was entering the middle overs. A range of subtler, incremental techniques were needed to deal with concerns unique to each sector, unique to each party. Would Rao be able to play spin as well as pace?

In April of that year, 1992, Narasimha Rao was preparing for the seventy-ninth session of the Congress party, to be held in the temple town of Tirupati in Andhra Pradesh. He was eager to make an impression. It would be the first session addressed by a Congress prime minister who was neither a Nehru nor a Gandhi. Rao was also expected to explain his liberalization policies to uneasy party workers, and he did not have the excuse of crisis any more. The previous session had taken place in 1985 in Bombay, to celebrate 100 years of the Congress. As we saw in an earlier chapter, prime minister Rajiv Gandhi had wanted to use that occasion to argue in favour of liberalization. But party leaders were so aghast at this abandonment of socialism that Rajiv—the man with the largest electoral mandate in Indian history—had deleted any reference to economic reforms from his speech.[6] Seven years hence, would Narasimha Rao, much less in control of party and Parliament, beat a similar retreat?

In the days before the session, Kalyani Shankar saw him consulting assorted drafts before writing his own speech.[7] These remain in Rao's archives. One such draft was from P.C. Alexander, who had guided Rao through the Congress maze during the race for prime ministership. Alexander's note contained the sentence 'Nehruvian socialism did not mean keeping the economy shackled to controls and regulations even after they had outlived their usefulness.' After a year as prime minister, Rao could play this game as well. He struck out the sentence with a red pen and rewrote to exaggerate the point: 'It is a gross distortion to say that Nehruvian socialism meant keeping the economy shackled to controls and regulations even after they had outlived their usefulness.'[8]

The other notes the prime minister drew on while drafting his speech were from the Andhra bureaucrat B.P.R. Vithal and Congressman V.N. Gadgil. Rao read Gadgil's draft and was irritated by jargon that even he barely understood. On the front of the document, he wrote: 'Explain in simple language, words and expressions like—Capital goods, Fiscal management, Balance of payments, Indicative planning, GDP . . . The expressions are used often, but many Congress workers do not fully understand them, including several who pretend to do so. The explanation could be given in the notes at the end of the paper or in the footnote in the text.'[9]

The master of ten tongues was searching for language to explain economic reforms. He complained to Montek Ahluwalia, 'The trouble with you people is you have not found good Hindi words for liberalization. Somebody says that word is '*chhoott*'. This sounds like licence. But liberalization means freedom. We should link it to something inherently positive such as freedom.'[10]

The Tirupati session began on 14 April 1992. Narasimha Rao spent the first days silent on stage, leaving his finance minister to do the explaining. 'Liberalisation was a new thing,' Manmohan Singh later remembered. 'There is always fear of the unknown. There was a feeling that we were departing from the Congress party's philosophy.'[11] On the final day, 16 April, the prime minister finally spoke. He used Jawaharlal Nehru to justify changes to the economy,[12] and likened India's fiscal position to a person using a small blanket to cover himself. When the head was covered, the feet were naked; when the feet were shielded the head was bare. 'It is only to meet that extra length, so to say and to fill the gap that we are taking the help of private sector.'[13]

The party resolution at the end endorsed the prime minister's liberalization policies. Narasimha Rao had done something even Rajiv Gandhi had not been able to. He had sold economic reforms to his doubting party.

The next day's *Times of India* explained how he had done it. 'The party is quite obviously committed to the package of programmes announced by the government in the last few months, marking a major departure from past postures. This has, however, been shrouded in the ritual invocation of the Nehru-Indira-Rajiv vision. Indeed a substantial part of the resolution is devoted to re-interpreting the political-economic thought of Jawaharlal Nehru in a bid to justify the present thrust of government policies.'[14]

When it came to the Congress party, Rao was able to defend reforms with trickery—using Nehru as a shield and Manmohan as a mask. Where reforms concerned technical issues beyond the comprehension of the seventy-year old prime minister, he feigned indifference, relying on those he trusted.

An example of this mellower approach was the reformation of the capital markets that began in April 1992, the very month that Rao spoke at Tirupati.

One of the myriad ways through which companies were pygmied during the licence raj was by making it hard for them to raise money through the stock markets and debt instruments. Insider trading was rife, and brokers were allowed to self-regulate. Since foreign capital was barred, companies had to compete for scarce Indian money. And the Controller of Capital Issues, or CCI, had final say over a company's ability to issue shares and debentures. A bureaucrat remembers comic scenes at the finance ministry: 'At the CCI, someone would come and say, "Birlas, etc. want three crores for capital issue." The person heading [CCI] would say, "Why three, why not two crores?"'[15]

Recognizing these shortcomings, the market regulator, the Securities Exchange Bureau of India, or SEBI, got statutory backing in April 1992. Neither the prime minister nor Manmohan Singh had selected the man running it at the time. But G.V. Ramakrishna, the man who was P.C. Alexander's first choice for principal secretary to the prime minister, would turn out to be a crucial reformer in the Rao era.

The financial journalist Sucheta Dalal terms Ramakrishna SEBI's 'best chairman yet'.[16] Even the best need luck, what Machiavelli called *'fortuna'*.[17] Like with Rao in June 1991, what helped Ramakrishna cleanse the stock exchanges was a scandal, the like India had never seen before.

Days after the creation of SEBI as a statutory regulator, the stockbroker Harshad Mehta was accused of fraud.[18] Mehta was the face of the liberalization stock market, gracing the covers of finance as well as style magazines. The market followed his mantra, until investigations revealed that his investments were made with money obtained by bribing officials from state-run banks. This 'banking' fraud (wrongly described as a 'stock market' scam) was estimated at a billion dollars.[19] The stock market crashed. Liberalization had produced—or so they said—its first casualty.

Narasimha Rao ordered a special court to try the accused; Harshad Mehta was arrested and made to sleep on the cement floor of a Bombay police station.[20] On the morning of 29 June 1992, Rao asked Ahluwalia for a note on the scam. That very evening, Ahluwalia replied, 'As desired by PM in this morning's meeting, briefing notes on the Banking Scam are placed below for PM's perusal.' The note included a 'list of persons arrested' and police complaints filed.[21] Rao's private papers contain other reports on the scam. Clearly, the prime minister realized that reforming the stock market was essential to the credibility of his liberalization policies.

So did G.V. Ramakrishna. He told the *New York Times*, 'Most players in the capital markets felt they were beyond regulation. We are now trying to bring about some sensible regulations of the market in line with other developing countries' capital markets.'[22] He ordered brokers to register themselves and pay a fee, and 'ruthlessly brought order to a rag-tag community of brokers, 20 stock exchanges and a variety of intermediaries...'[23] Ramakrishna is now old and gaunt. But his eyes brighten as he remembers those months in 1992. 'I got threatening calls. The police were worried for my safety. They said there was a plot against you.'[24] Ramakrishna was undeterred, even withstanding pressure from a bureaucrat close to Narasimha Rao. The new rules stayed and the stock markets began to be run professionally.

The exchanges were improved in other ways too. Share pricing was made 'free' from generalist bureaucrats in CCI, and companies were soon allowed to borrow from international markets using financial instruments such as the 'global depository receipt'. Entrepreneurs could also list their companies in the national stock exchange, set up that very year. To make the transformation of markets complete, Ramakrishna wrote a letter to the finance minister, asking for foreign institutional investors to be allowed in.[25] Manmohan Singh checked with his prime minister.

Narasimha Rao was indifferent to the details. A friend of his remembers: 'He used to ask me about [the] stock market; he never invested in it.' But the prime minister trusted his people. And so it was that in September 1992, foreign institutional investors were permitted to enter.[26] In the next twelve years, foreign investors bought a net amount of 163 billion dollars to the Indian equity markets; in just one year, 2014, they invested more than 16 billion dollars—one lakh crore rupees.[27]

While foreign investors were embraced by Rao, he was only half a lion. The government continued to impose restrictions that prevented dollars from flowing out too quickly. Much criticized by financiers at the time, this cautiousness helped India emerge unscathed from the East Asian financial crisis of the late 1990s.

Incorruptibles like G.V. Ramakrishna and Manmohan Singh were necessary to make liberalization credible. Narasimha Rao backed them even when they disobeyed his commands—like Manmohan on devaluation, and Ramakrishna on the broker's strike. It is even possible, though there is no way to tell, that Rao wanted his instructions ignored. The academic V.R. Mehta's son remembers what prime minister Rao told his father when the latter was appointed vice chancellor of Delhi University. 'Sometimes you will get messages from me. Don't listen ... You do whatever you think is right. But I have to call because there will be someone sitting with me who wants that.'[28]

While Rao would support those doing their jobs, he could be unforgiving when he felt that lines were being crossed. This was true of Rao's later treatment of his Cabinet colleagues Arjun Singh, M.L. Fotedar and Madhavrao Scindia. It was also true of his punishment of some fellow reformers—as this story shows.

The wife of commerce minister P. Chidambaram had bought shares in a company subsequently named in the Harshad Mehta scam. The amount was trivial, paid by cheque, and there was no evidence of favours exchanged. But the commerce minister was one of Rao's prominent liberalizers, and the opposition parties had found the perfect target. In response to the clamour, Chidambaram told the press that he would resign if his guilt was proved. In July 1992, he sent his prime minister a letter of resignation. The letter ended thus: 'It is my sincere hope that these small investments will not cause any embarrassment to the government. If they do, I would have no hesitation in stepping down from the office of minister. I leave the matter to your judgment. I also place below a formal letter of resignation.'[29]

It is clear from the text that the letter was only a formality. But that very evening, the prime minister took it to President R. Venkataraman, a mentor to Chidambaram. 'He sent me this letter, and held a press conference before,' Rao told the President.

'Did he take your permission before the press conference?' Venkataraman asked.

'No,' replied Rao.

'Then accept the resignation.'[30]

Chidambaram was shocked. Even twenty-five years later, both Manmohan Singh and Montek Singh Ahluwalia are puzzled as to why Rao rid himself of a reformer.[31] Rao's youngest son,

Prabhakara, provides the answer. 'My father told me that Chidambaram should have taken his permission before giving a press conference.'[32] When Prabhakara told his father that Chidambaram was 'well known in economic circles . . . dropping him will send the wrong message,' Rao replied, 'Let the dust settle, he will be back again.'

While Rao could let pettiness dictate personnel decisions, he never let Chanakya's methods affect the substance of his reform agenda. He ensured this by keeping the engine of reforms where he could see it, in the prime minister's office. The chief engineer was Amar Nath Varma, Rao's feared principal secretary. Varma would chair consultations on reforms every Thursday, as well as regular meetings of the Foreign Investment Promotion Board (FIPB). The journalist Sanjaya Baru calls these meetings the 'cockpit' of economic reforms.[33] As Manmohan Singh put it, 'Varma was a power centre in reforms. I encouraged him. The fact that the PMO was associated with reform gave it lot of weight.'[34]

Not everyone thought this was a good idea. When the FIPB was brought into the PMO, the Cabinet secretary advised that it might be better to locate it elsewhere (as was the past practice) to keep the prime minister at a safe distance from decisions that might result in controversy.

But Rao chose to listen to Varma, whose disposition matched his own. Like Rao, Varma was less bound by rules and protocols. Like Rao, he could get the job done. Prabhakar Menon, then a junior diplomat in the prime minister's office, remembers: 'Rao could be short with people who spoke nonsense, but he always listened to Varma's considered views. I have known five–six outstanding civil servants. He comes to mind. He had a very keen political antenna. He was also very focused in meetings. [He] had a clear agenda, and knew how to achieve it.'[35]

While Varma coordinated with ministers, officials and his prime minister to keep reforms oiled throughout Rao's five years in office, there were moments when the electricity was switched off, and the engine sat idle. One such moment was in December 1992.

As we shall explore in detail in a later chapter, the Babri mosque was demolished by Hindu militants on the sixth of that month. The riots that followed killed over 2000, most of whom were Muslims.[36] Apart from the inexcusable loss of human life, the violence scared external investors and caused internal financial damage. In a speech to students at the Indian Institute of Management Ahmedabad, the prime minister estimated that 'within one month, we have lost what is equivalent to say some two to three hundred million dollars. This is something we cannot afford.'[37] Judging his position to be weak, Rao ordered that no reforms be announced that December. 'If we had let the cat amongst the pigeons in that atmosphere,' Manmohan explained later, 'it would have been misused by our opponents to strengthen themselves.'[38] For any other politician, the demolition of Babri Masjid would have ended any possibility of risky reforms.

Narasimha Rao was not any other politician. He sensed that collective outrage at the symbolic destruction of secularism was an opportunity to manipulate divisions in the opposition ranks. The National Front and the Left were so worried by the BJP that their main enemy changed from economic reforms to religious fundamentalism. As the political scientist Zoya Hasan puts it, 'The primacy of secular politics and the need to contain BJP's further expansion was one important reason why economic liberalisation did not face significant hurdles, even though the Congress lacked a majority in Parliament.'[39] Narasimha Rao was quick to exploit this. A senior CPM member remembers: 'When I used to talk to prime minister [Rao] about liberalization policy, he would talk about Babri and secularism ... He always did [it].'

THE MAN WHO REMADE INDIA

In January 1993, just a month after the flattening of Babri Masjid, the Narasimha Rao government unveiled a reform that would have normally infuriated the Left. The Reserve Bank of India—with a nod and a wink from the government—announced licences for private banks.[40] Ten new banks—HDFC, ICICI and Axis Bank among them—were eventually formed. This was the first such approval after the nationalization of banks by Indira Gandhi in 1969. It was risky—something Chanakya advised kings to avoid—to allow this symbolic shift from the socialist past. But Rao was by now adept at knowing just how far he could go. Afraid that the left-backed bank unions would turn on him, he decided against restructuring state banks, sacking inefficient employees, closing down poorly performing branches, and removing priority sector lending. It could even be that he turned to the private sector precisely because he deemed state-run banks to be untameable.[41]

A month after licences for private banks were issued, a Bangalore-based software company listed itself in stock exchanges across India. By 2015, Infosys would have 1,93,383 employees[42] and a market capitalization of 43 billion dollars.[43] But in February 1993, it was a midsize company hungry for money to expand. Since banks hesitated to help a company whose only collateral was the brains of its employees, capital markets were all the more critical to its growth.[44]

A co-founder of Infosys, Nandan Nilekani, remembers its initial public offering in 1993. 'Four reforms that the Narasimha Rao government made really benefitted us. [The] abolition of the controller of capital issues allowed free pricing of public issues. We were able to price our own shares . . . It made a big difference. The entry of FIIs [foreign institutional investors] helped. The FIIs understood the new economy. We were able to present ourselves as ethical, transparent. They had an understanding of technology.'[45] The liberalization of foreign exchange also made it easier for Infosys—earning in dollars—to expand. But the biggest boost that Narasimha Rao offered software companies was free advertising.

As Nilekani says, 'Just the fact that the economy opened up, was in the news, made foreign companies think of India. That helped us market ourselves to them.'[46]

Software companies employed only a fraction of Indians. But they came to symbolize a newer, younger India where honesty and hard work could make millionaires of the middle class. Narasimha Rao made sure to link software to his reforms. At an information technology exhibition in 1993, he crowed about the success of the Indian software industry. And in a speech in Telugu in the year that followed, he told his audience in Andhra Pradesh that 'we got good name regarding computer software'.[47]

Rao had a personal interest. He knew two computer languages, COBOL and BASIC, could write code in UNIX, and would spend solitary evenings punching away at his laptop. And so, at another public speech while inaugurating IT-ASIA, he could not resist lodging a customer complaint: 'I use one package of word processing. For years the upgrades are coming and when I look into the literature of what the upgrade means . . . I find very little difference . . . I think we should be careful about these things. You skip four upgrades, maybe the fifth will be really useful to you. It will mean a real upgrade. Pardon me, saying so. This has happened to me.'[48]

While foreign investors were naturally attracted to the software industry, they were less sure about the traditional sectors of the economy. Getting them to invest in consumer goods, infrastructure and manufacturing required more than changes to the law. It meant cajoling investors at summits and shaking hands with CEOs. The laconic, dhoti-wearing prime minister could not have been more unsuited to dangle gifts and negotiate with businessmen. So it is all the more creditable that when it came to drawing foreign investment, Narasimha Rao led from the front.

He visited the World Economic Forum in Davos twice, the first prime minister to do so. Tarun Das of the business lobby CII travelled with him both times. 'No Indian prime minister had gone to Davos,' Das remembers. 'For Rao to go twice was huge for us.' In his speech in 1992 at Davos, the prime minister left no one in any doubt as to who was running India. 'My officials and my experts have learnt my languages instead of my learning their language . . . the dotted lines are what I wanted them to be and I sign on them.'[49] He was back again in 1994, quoting Nehru and speaking of a 'middle way' that was not just laissez-faire.

This was for domestic consumption; Rao did not want his audience back home to think that he was selling out to foreigners. But this was also to tell the global leaders gathered in Switzerland in the depths of winter that economic reform in India had to be done without outside pressure. 'Those who wear the shoe and know where it pinches should have full say in deciding how to mend it.'[50]

In his state visits to foreign countries, Rao would play the role of a travelling salesman. Nowhere was this more evident than when he journeyed to Japan. The usual drill on such occasions was that the prime minister would speak to a roomful of industrialists. But Montek Singh Ahluwalia suggested to Rao's principal secretary that the prime minister meet each businessman one-on-one instead. Twelve minutes were allotted to each corporate leader. When Akio Morita, the head of Sony, entered the room, Rao put his hand over Morita and said, 'Every Indian wants a Sony TV, and you are not making it.' Morita shrugged. Sony was willing to invest only if they could own 100 per cent of the local company, which Indian rules forbade. 'You apply,' Rao told him. 'We will give it.'[51]

Without going back to his Cabinet or Parliament, Rao had changed policy. But he was trusted, and Sony soon began selling in India. By July 1993, the Narasimha Rao government had approved foreign equity investment of 3.2 billion dollars from around 1100 different cases.⁵² Ahluwalia explains why these investors took Rao at his word: 'The problem with us Indians is that we make a deal, then we go back on it. We then argue that it was a different deal . . . this irritates foreigners. But people didn't view Rao that way. The sense people got was [that] if this man makes a deal, he will stand by it. Since he didn't say much, when he did, it was taken seriously.'⁵³

While Narasimha Rao worked hard to charm investors, he also realized, as he told Parliament, that 'about investment from outside the Government, the word "foreign" somehow seems to invoke certain pictures, certain concepts . . .'⁵⁴ One of his many tricks to alter these images was to stress the domestic origins of some investors—something that Deng had done so well in China. While inaugurating a steel plant built by the investor Lakshmi Mittal in Ramtek (his former constituency), Rao asked the audience, 'If our own people want to come back, if they want to set up some factories in India . . . should we put obstacles in their way as soon as they land here? It is not fair.'⁵⁵

These tactics worked, and resistance to foreign investment from the public and Parliament was mostly muted through Rao's years as prime minister. More serious was the hostility from Indian businessmen who were worried that they would be swamped by foreign competition. Part of the reason Rao was able to assuage them was that the character of Indian industry was changing.⁵⁶ But part of the story is how Rao and his team nimbly exploited this change.

Industry in India was divided into three lobbying groups. The oldest was ASSOCHAM, or the Associated Chambers of Commerce and Industry of India. Set up in 1920, the chamber represented British-run firms that had given way, after Independence, to local management. The other business chamber, FICCI, or the Federation of Indian Chambers of Commerce and Industry, was set up in 1927, and had Marwari origins—leading some to term ASSOCHAM as 'topiwallas' and FICCI as 'dhotiwalas'. Both groups, however, were shaped in the licence raj. They were both opposed to external liberalization, and worried that internal liberalization would threaten their monopolies. From these traditional groups emerged a third, the CII.

The Confederation of Engineering Industry had changed its name to the Confederation of Indian Industry (CII) in 1992. This change in name was necessitated by liberalization, which was allowing engineering companies to diversify into other sectors, as well as the other way around.[57] The businessmen who supported CII were modern, many of them south Indian exporters. 'There is no doubt in my mind,' Ahluwalia says, 'that CII was the only organization that had a breath of fresh air, and young people.'[58] Its members supported delicensing and were not as hostile to global competition. As a result, Tarun Das concludes, 'We [CII] became cheerleaders for the government's economic policies.'

Narasimha Rao made sure to talk to all three industry groups. But it was CII who were given pride of place, always invited to Davos, always accommodated in the prime minister's aircraft, always the face that greeted foreign investors. Narasimha Rao's conduits to corporate India—P.V.R.K. Prasad and Amar Nath Varma—would go out of the way to court CII. Even the careful Manmohan Singh had links with them. The usual Indian story is of businessmen profiting from fissures between India's political parties. But here was the Narasimha Rao government practising Chanakya's maxim by sowing dissension between old and new industry groups, all to pursue reform.

The changes that Narasimha Rao and Manmohan Singh had so far made were either to move the state out of the way (delicensing, tariff reduction, devaluation) or allow businessmen to grow (foreign investment, capital markets and banking reforms). But by 1992, entrepreneurs as well as the growing middle class were complaining about rough roads and erratic electricity. The average power shortage in 1992 was 8 per cent, while peak shortage was as much as 19 per cent.[59]

Power and roads were not priorities for Narasimha Rao, who had never held these ministries in Delhi or Hyderabad. This is perhaps why his government responded cautiously in late 1992, declaring that 'the public sector will continue to play a dominant role in [infrastructure]'. It did, however, add that 'private initiative' in 'power plants, roads, bridges . . .' would be 'positively encouraged'.[60]

The promise of public sector dominance would fail on its own terms; by 1997, spending on the five infrastructure sectors was 14.4 per cent lower than the target set in 1992.[61] More encouraging, though, were attempts to involve private financing and expertise, especially in road-building. The first private toll road was built in 1993, in Madhya Pradesh, allowing the private partner to 'Build Operate Transfer'.[62] This private sector involvement has transformed the resources available for infrastructure, as well as visibly improved the quality of roads.

If road-building was a relative success during Narasimha Rao's years, the power sector—where control is largely with state governments—remained a failure. States governments provided 70 per cent of all electricity, the Central government contributed 20 per cent, while just 5 per cent was provided by the private sector.[63] Like elsewhere, this public sector dominance ensured that many Indians had no access to electricity.

The Rao government responded with piecemeal changes in the coal sector, through which almost 70 per cent of electricity was generated.[64] Given the power of the coal mafia, the Narasimha Rao government was forced to deny private companies the right to mine coal.[65] But it did eventually allow 'firms investing in power generation, steel, and cement projects to establish "captive" coal mines'.[66] Even Rao realized this was hardly a solution. 'We are today constrained to tell the investor from outside, "If you want power you have your captive power plant." Now whatever he wants, if he has to get captive, then what are we here for?'[67]

Of the many private companies the government courted to invest in electricity, the most infamous was the American multinational Enron. Soon after Rao became prime minister, Enron signed a memorandum of association to set up a natural gas power plant in Dabhol, Maharashtra. Rao eventually agreed to give them assured profits with a sovereign guarantee. The plant became the focal point for mobilization against Narasimha Rao's policies of liberalization. Local farmers complaining of land-grab and ecological ruin joined hands with anti-globalization critics who accused Enron of extracting exorbitant rates. The fact that the contract had been awarded by the Congress government in Maharashtra without a transparent bidding made it a symbol of crony capitalism.[68]

These criticisms have turned out true. Years after Enron failed in the United States, its handiwork lives on in India, continuing to deplete the state exchequer. If there is a single monument of caution to where liberalization could go wrong, it lies on the coast of Maharashtra.

The opacity of the Enron contract fed into a larger criticism that Narasimha Rao and liberalization began facing in 1993. Left intellectuals had long argued that 'neo-liberalism' was shorthand for 'crony capitalism'. From 1993 onwards, an impression was created that suitcases of bribe money were making their way to the very top.

In May of that year, Rao's own Cabinet minister and rival, Arjun Singh, sent him a public letter citing reports of 'a loss of more than Rs. 3000 crore to the Government in the process of disinvestment',[69] and demanding more 'transparency'.[70] That he chose to write this in a letter shows not just how keen Arjun Singh was to damage Rao, but just how damaging he thought these corruption charges were.

A month later, on 16 June 1993, the disgraced stockbroker Harshad Mehta, now out on bail, appeared at a dramatic press conference. He accused Narasimha Rao of accepting a bribe of one crore rupees from him. The prime minister denied these charges, declaring, 'I will emerge out of this trial by fire in the same manner as Sita did.'[71] Mehta's allegations were eventually dismissed by the courts. But the stain would smear Narasimha Rao through his tenure.

Even the scrupulous Manmohan Singh was subject to insinuations. It was whispered in the corridors of Parliament that his children were bankers who had benefitted from the scam. This was a lie, as Manmohan Singh told Parliament: 'I have three daughters but none of them is working in the banking system. And that applies to the officials who are working with me.'[72]

But the hounding of reformists on charges of corruption— some reasonable, some unfair—would not stop. A parliamentary committee formed to investigate the banking scandal questioned finance ministry officials. While most bureaucrats dithered in their defence of liberalization, Montek Singh Ahluwalia was less restrained. 'When you have any period of rule change,' he argued, 'you are bound to get some people who illegally make use of it. That does not mean that the policy is responsible.'[73] The committee chairman—a Congressman—said, jokingly, *'Sardarji bahut bolta hai.'* ['Sardarji talks a lot'.][74]

In the final report submitted in December 1993, the finance minister was blamed for being in 'slumber' through the scam.[75] Attacked in such words by Congressmen themselves, a shaken Manmohan Singh submitted his resignation to Narasimha Rao.

On hearing of Singh's resignation, Rao told his secretary, P.V.R.K. Prasad, '[Manmohan Singh] does not understand that I am the target of their criticism. He assumes that all our MPs are under our control and we can dictate them . . . he does not realise that they want to embarrass me, and not him.'[76] Narasimha Rao was also exasperated at Manmohan's complaints against fellow Congressmen. 'I don't have the mandate of Indira. I have not yet acquired the strength to take action against Congressmen like Arjun Singh.'[77]

Irritated that Manmohan did not understand that he was expected to absorb attacks meant for his prime minister, Narasimha Rao considered accepting his resignation.[78] That meant giving the finance ministry to either P. Chidambaram or Pranab Mukherjee.[79] While Rao weighed his options, Manmohan was pilloried in the media and Parliament. When Rao finally asked Singh to stay,[80] the reaction to the banking scam report had subsided. The prime minister was unscathed.

―

Around the time Rao was fending off corruption charges, a consumer revolution was in the making. The opening up of sectors such as airlines, soft drinks and television was part of the logic of the initial reforms of 1991. But hand-holding by the Narasimha Rao government was needed to attract new players while combatting entrenched interests. This hand-holding took various forms—looking the other way, getting out of the way or paving the way—as the stories of private television channels, airlines and mobile phones show.

The first Indian-owned private channel, Zee TV, had broadcast its opening show in late 1992. But the story of satellite television began earlier, and it was technology rather than Narasimha Rao that lengthened it. A month before Rao became prime minister, an unknown network called Satellite Television Asian Region—or STAR—began broadcasting from Hong Kong.[81] The subscriber base tripled within ten months, from 4,00,000 to 1.2 million.[82]

These new channels were of dubious legality. The nineteenth-century Telegraph Act, enacted by colonial India, had since continued to give monopoly of the airwaves to the Indian government. Narasimha Rao himself was sceptical. He told P.V.R.K. Prasad, 'You don't understand how dangerous this can be ... anyone can install a device on his roof and see anything in the world. We have no control.'[83] But despite his instincts, Narasimha Rao hesitated to ban satellite TV. He was desperate for foreign investment, and realized that it would have sent the wrong signal if he were to ban private channels.[84] And so the prime minister did nothing while technology and popular demand created a proliferation of channels. This legal grey zone continued until 1995 when the Supreme Court held that the airwaves belonged to the people of India and not its government—thus legitimizing these channels.[85]

This backdoor liberalization—where Rao's contribution was to mute his own roar—has had results even he could not have imagined. By 2015, Indian television viewers were watching an astonishing 832 channels.[86] The changing content of TV channels has been as remarkable as their changing numbers. Broadcasters realized that soap operas set in Santa Barbara, California, were not resonating with the Indian viewer. These were replaced by dramas of Indian joint families adjusting to a changing world while struggling to retain their traditional values.

It was also in 1993 that the first private airline since the nationalization of the sector, Jet Airways, took off. Damania, East-West, Sahara and ModiLuft followed—enticing India's middle class to travel by plane. Today, air travel is one of India's fastest growing segments, with 82 million passengers flying in just the year 2014.[87] But this opening of the airline sector was rife with favouritism reminiscent of the licence raj. The businessman Ratan Tata, who wanted to start an airline in the early 1990s, claimed, 'The same government that asked us to start an airline ... made sure that this airline would never happen.'[88]

If Narasimha Rao's reaction to satellite television was to look the other way, and to airlines was to (mostly) get out of the way, mobile telephony was one sector where Rao actively paved the way. The consequence has been the most visible—and arguably most empowering—transformation in India since the 1990s.

With the arrival of mobile technology in the early '90s, the Indian government was grappling with the question: should private and foreign players be allowed to provide mobile phone services? This debate reached policy stage by late 1993, and by early 1994, Narasimha Rao was briefed.

Bureaucrats and politicians were jittery about private involvement in telecom. In April 1994, N. Vithal, the chairman of the telecom commission—and another reformer whom Rao patronized—wrote to the prime minister a private note on the soon-to-be-announced policy. Rao read it carefully, underlining in red ink, and writing comments in his flowing hand. While recommending private sector entry, for example, the document stated: "We are going to put a condition that they should go to rural areas also. On the left margin, Rao made a wry comment: 'Who goes to rural areas? The phones or foreign operation personnel?'[89]

In that same month, news reports claimed the policy was being held up because the telecom minister Sukh Ram 'believed in the old school of government control on the economy'.[90] Sukh Ram—who would later be convicted for accepting a bribe for a telecom cable contract—wrote a clarifying letter to Rao's new Cabinet secretary Zafar Saifullah. 'As you are aware, I am all for the liberalisation of the economy and have used every platform to espouse the government policy and [the] telecom revolution taking place ... under the directive of Hon'ble Prime Minister, Shri P.V. Narasimha Rao.'[91]

The final telecom policy, announced in May 1994, made telephone lines freely available and opened up mobile telephony to private and foreign investment. Narasimha Rao, however, made the mistake of listening to his minister and imposed onerous licensing rules on mobile operators. This was the very practice he had ended in other sectors.[92] It would take later governments to grow the mobile phone market. But Rao's policy, by allowing private operators in telecom, had let the genie out of the bottle. By 2015, 969 million mobile phone subscriptions existed. Of these, a telling 92 per cent—891 million—were serviced by private firms.[93] Provided a choice between public sector and private options on telecom, Indians have voted with their voice.

If there was one 'father' to India's telecom industry, it was not Rajiv Gandhi; it was his Congress successor. Characteristically, though, the prime minister refused the spotlight. He used even these reforms to co-opt his political opponents. When the first mobile phone call was made in July 1995, it was between the telecom minister, Sukh Ram, and Jyoti Basu, the communist chief minister of West Bengal.[94]

By 1994, the opponents of liberalization had been calmed, if not converted. The journalist Sanjaya Baru says that Narasimha Rao had stayed true to his blunt message to Michel Camdessus, the managing director of the IMF: "I am willing to do whatever is good for the economy, as long as not one worker tells me he has lost his job because of me.'[95] Attitudinal changes among politicians were also being achieved through lobbying. Tarun Das of CII remembers that 'state by state we briefed MPs [on economic reforms]. It was all new to them. It was amazingly new to us. That time [there was] no PowerPoint, so we had to use slides. We had to do it in Tamil, Telugu, Hindi. It was very challenging, [but also] very rewarding. You built relationships.'[95] In addition, Narasimha Rao and Manmohan Singh had learnt to carry out incremental reductions in tariffs and licences by executive decisions that rarely made it to the front pages of newspapers. As Manmohan put it, 'After 1992, we did that for which we didn't have to go to Parliament for approval. That was how we were able to go through reform.'[97] As we shall see in a later chapter, Narasimha Rao had also cobbled up a stable majority in Parliament by 1994, and survived three no-confidence motions. The accidental prime minister was now sure of completing his five-year term, the first for any minority government in Indian history.

Making use of this political capital, Narasimha Rao took the final plunge into the global economy. His government engaged in secretive negotiations at the Uruguay round of the General Agreement on Tariffs and Trade, or GATT. The Uruguay round sought to limit worldwide import restrictions, and harmonise domestic laws in areas as diverse as agriculture, textiles and patents. Along with around 122 other countries, the Indian government signed on in April 1994. That agreement stipulated the creation of a World Trade Organization (WTO), to which all signatories would become members. The Opposition was furious. It was as if, a magazine editor noted, 'New Delhi had bartered its economic sovereignty to a latter day East India Company.'[98]

Judging this opposition to be weak, Rao refused to budge. He personally drafted the Congress party's resolution in support of the Uruguay round. He wrote, 'The Congress Working Committee wants to reiterate once again that . . . The Final Act of the Uruguay Round of Negotiations does not compromise the interests of its farmers, scientists and common people.'[99] He even took his case to the public. In 1994, he gave a speech in Telugu in his constituency in Nandyal, declaring, 'I spoke for umpteen hours on [the Uruguay round] Dunkel proposals with the people and farmers. I explained the proposals to all.'[100]

Four years ago, it would have been impossible to envision India tolerating such an opening to the West. In the time since, Rao and his team had helped reimagine India. On 1 January 1995, India became a member of the WTO.

This astute management of the economy had financial consequences. By 1994, macro indicators showed a soaring India.

GDP growth was 6.7 per cent for that year, and would be 7.6 and 7.5 per cent for Rao's final two years as prime minister. As Rao readied to visit the United States that summer, the *New York Times* gushed: '. . . the 72-year-old Mr. Rao has become, in effect, the Deng Xiaoping of India—an aging party leader who, in his sunset years, has abandoned many, if not all, of the economic precepts that had guided earlier governments, challenging not only the old orthodoxies but an entrenched network of vested interests that had built up under the old system.'[101]

Investors were bullish. In a survey conducted on businessmen by CII in April 1994, two-thirds said that they were planning to increase capital expenditure in the near future. Net profits, for 1,200 private companies surveyed, increased by 84 per cent.[102] The iconic western brand Coca Cola had just returned to India, after being eased out seventeen years ago. The Bombay Stock Exchange was back to its high before the Harshad Mehta scam broke.[103] India's foreign exchange reserves—the cause for the 1991 crisis—were now beyond comfortable. As Rao noted in his Independence Day address in August 1994, 'We have foreign exchange reserves worth Rs 51,000 crore. Just imagine, in 1991, we had foreign exchange worth only Rs 3000 crore. It is no mean achievement.'[104]

Behind all these numbers was a psychological transformation that mere statistics could not capture. The India that Narasimha Rao had inherited was used to being second-rate. By 1994, this pessimism had given way to confidence that India could compete with the best in the world without losing her soul. An Indian—Sushmita Sen—won the Miss Universe contest that year, while Aishwarya Rai was crowned Miss World. It was also in 1994 that Sachin Tendulkar opened for India for the first time, hammering a career-defining 82 of just 49 balls in a one-day international match against New Zealand.

Perhaps the best metaphor for this confidence that the Narasimha Rao government had sparked off was the film *Dilwale Dulhania Le Jayenge*. Released in October 1995 and loosely translated as 'The Big-Hearted Will Take Away the Bride', the

Indian-origin characters in the film lived entirely in Europe. Yet they retained their language, family values and tradition—navigating the West without losing their Indian essence. The critic Rachel Dwyer wrote that the film showed 'being Indian is cool, and does not involve pretending to be western'.[105] The movie's most famous lines—at once inane, at once profound—became so emblematic that US President Barack Obama repeated it on a visit to India two decades later. *'Senorita, bade bade deshon mein aaisi choti choti baatein hoti rehti hai.'* ('Senorita, in big, big countries such small, small things keep happening.')

In most countries, a growing economy is a sign of the political strength of the leader. India is not most countries. Even as the economy was booming in 1995, Narasimha Rao was facing rebellion within his party. Arjun Singh and N.D. Tiwari—whom Rao had beaten to prime ministership—went public with their criticisms. In his resignation letter from Rao's Cabinet, Singh wrote that 'A perception has emerged that liberalisation of economic policy perhaps has become liberalisation of corruption.'[106] Shortly after heading a breakaway faction of the Congress, N.D. Tiwari was asked, 'Do you agree with Mr. Rao's economic reforms?' 'I do not agree with their implementation,' Tiwari said. He added, '. . . I have not favoured an unlicensed industrial policy either.'[107]

With the national election due in less than a year, Narasimha Rao responded, by the middle of 1995, by compromising economics for politics. He announced subsidies and populist schemes on rural housing and clothing.[108] The IMF managing director complained in mid-1995 that Indian reforms are 'possibly slowing down'.[109] Rao's finance secretary remembers: 'On reforms in the insurance sector [allowing foreign investment], Manmohan Singh was very clear that we have to keep doing this. By then [Rao] was looking at the next elections. He lost heart on insurance, even though it was a no-brainer.'[110] To give a sense of what it means when a government loses momentum on reform, the 'no-brainer' insurance law was finally passed by the Narendra Modi government in 2015—a full twenty years later. Sensing that reforms were slackening after mid-1995, foreign investment into India reduced.

The irony was that just as Narasimha Rao was slowing down reforms at the Centre, they were picking up in the states. A series of state elections was held in which the Congress did badly. The new chief ministers, however, vowed to continue liberalization at the state level. In Maharashtra, the Shiv Sena-BJP government had come to power opposing the Enron power project. Once in power, they simply renegotiated, and allowed the project to continue. In Andhra Pradesh, the Congress lost to the regional Telugu Desam Party (TDP). The TDP was soon taken over by Chandrababu Naidu, who, it turned out, was more Narasimha Rao than the Congress itself—calling himself CEO of his state and wooing investors.

These were not spontaneous instances of states turning to capitalism. They were the natural consequence of ending the licence raj, as Narasimha Rao, a past chief minister, understood well. As he put it in a speech in Houston, 'A happy development these days is that there is a healthy competition among the various states in the matter of attraction of foreign investment . . .'[111] This 'happy development' has brought prosperity to states such as Tamil Nadu and Gujarat. But it has also increased their distance from states such as Uttar Pradesh, whose politics do not permit investor-friendly policies.[112]

While Rao, the former chief minister, was lauding the federal effects of his liberalization policies, Rao, the election campaigner, was only interested in what would win him votes. A survey conducted just before the 1996 national elections found that those with incomes above 2000 rupees a month were part of the 'consumer boom' of the past five years. But 66 per cent of those earning less than 1000 rupees—classified as 'poor'—felt little change to their lives. Rao refused to engage with this nuanced story of the benefits of liberalization. In his election campaign in March and April of

1996, he stressed poverty reduction and welfare schemes, but sidestepped any conversation on economic reforms.

The election results were announced in May. The BJP was the single largest party, while the Congress had been reduced to 140 seats. On 16 May 1996, a new prime minister was sworn in. Rao's career in government was over.

The young, idealistic Narasimha Rao had been unable to appreciate the conflict between honourable means and ends. Where the older, prime ministerial Rao was more clearly in the 'realist' tradition of Chanakya and Machiavelli was by believing that consistent and moral means were unsuited to the complexities of governing India.

Given that each sector of the economy had distinct problems and interests, Rao's incoherent, crafty approach was perhaps his greatest strength. He continually deployed Chanakya's upayas of dana, bheda (division) and maya to prevail upon opponents of reform. His finance minister was made the face of liberalization, while the mechanism for reforms was kept running in the prime minister's office. When it came to business houses, Rao catered to their immediate interests without hindering the arc of liberalization. He used secularism to divert Left parties from economic reforms. Rao and Manmohan also plotted to bypass Parliament, using executive orders to implement liberalization. And when it came to the Congress party, Narasimha Rao used cunning tools (IB reports) and convenient interpretations (Nehru, socialism) to checkmate his rivals.

Rao also knew when to be equanimous (what Chanakya called upeksa) and delegate responsibility. On capital market reforms, he trusted the advice of Manmohan Singh and G.V. Ramakrishna; on satellite television, he mistrusted his own instinct to regulate. The bang in India's stock exchanges as well as boom in the number of airlines and TV channels owes much to Rao's wisdom in letting technocrats and technology do the talking.

GROWING THE ECONOMY, 1992–96

Even his frontal attacks can be explained through Machiavelli and Chanakya. When it came to reforming banking and telecom, or attracting foreign investors, Rao judged that the Opposition was not strong enough to topple him. He was a lion, leading from the front, using all the resources at his command to noisily push reforms through.

Rao's 'realism' also explains his limitations. A strategy that sought concessions (sama) when the enemy was too strong meant that Narasimha Rao sometimes chose not to fight the good fight. After 1995, with one eye on the national elections, Rao ignored Manmohan Singh's pleas and slowed down reforms. His halting approach to infrastructure reform—scared off by entrenched interests—brought little electricity to Indians. The Enron and Harshad Mehta scams tarred liberalization with charges of corruption that still persist today. More damaging was Rao's unwillingness to sack a single public sector official, because he feared a backlash from the unions.

His failure to enact labour reforms—making it easier for companies to hire and fire workers—has, ironically, forced firms to employ less. Manufacturers continue to be hobbled by a slew of smaller regulations that has pushed India to the bottom end of the world 'ease of doing business' rankings. India is the only country moving directly from agriculture to services, bypassing manufacturing.

In many ways, Rao's inability to 'make in India' ranks as his single biggest economic failure. While China, Vietnam and even Bangladesh have had some success in making products to meet world (and domestic) demand, India has botched the opportunity to leverage cheap labour and become a manufacturing hub, creating millions of factory jobs.

This let-down has meant calamity for farmers stuck to unproductive land. The lack of factory jobs for them has been made worse by the failure to reform agricultural markets where the licence raj still persists. Farmers are forced to sell their produce at predetermined prices to predetermined middlemen; laws passed in the name of food security prevent them from exporting to the world.

Even these shortcomings can be explained by the prime minister's fear of instability. As we shall see in the next chapter, the agricultural sector—with its entrenched lobbies of rich farmers and middlemen who supply rural votes in return for subsidies—was a giant that Rao preferred not to awaken. Besides—and like in the case of the power sector—land and agriculture are controlled mainly by the state governments. Rao realized he was too weak to take them on.[113]

The most toxic legacy of this Machiavellian approach to reforms, however, has been the lingering belief that the Indian voter is not to be trusted to vote for liberalization. The Congress's indifferent performances during the state elections held between 1991 and 1996 led Rao to conclude that the public was not ready for reform, a conclusion that his successors have also come to.

While 'realism' does explain these retreats as well as victories, it does not explain *all* of Rao's actions.

His decision to stick with liberalization even after the crisis of 1991 abated, cannot be explained by the need to acquire and consolidate power. He ran a minority government in a divided democracy, and was not even in control of his party. As we shall examine later in this book, in his five years as prime minister, Narasimha Rao was a besieged fort, withstanding three attacks from outside—in the form of no-confidence motions in Parliament—while dealing with never-ending rebellion within. No other reformer in modern history has had these handicaps.

Chanakya and Machiavelli not only advocated wicked means to achieve the common good, they also felt that the ruler should not attempt those 'good' policies that endangered his stability. They would have advised Rao to abandon liberalization—unpopular with party and Parliament—far earlier than he actually did.

That P.V. Narasimha Rao was still able to *cause* (there is no other word for it) the most sweeping economic advance in Indian history is proof of his political genius, of course. It is also a testament to his idealism.

9

A Welfare State?

Narasimha Rao's commitment to liberalization policies even when it threatened his government cheered pro-market ideologues. They began applauding him as the next Margaret Thatcher, someone who would encourage business, shrivel the public sector and cut welfare spending. The Left were coming to the same conclusion. As the communist politician Somnath Chatterjee said in February 1992, 'We contended that the [1992] Budget was nothing but a faithful implementation of the fiats of the IMF and the World Bank that compromised India's sovereignty. The market economy of the Western world became the mantra of the government.'[1]

In that same month, the political scientist James Manor spent a week with Narasimha Rao. He asked the prime minister about his ideological inclinations. 'My model is not Margaret Thatcher but Willy Brandt,' Rao replied. 'I do not believe in trickle-down economics.'[2]

Rao's choice of exemplar was curious. The Nobel-prize-winning Willy Brandt was Germany's first 'social democratic' chancellor. At the heart of this vision was the mundane question of public finances, i.e. government revenue and expenditure. These European welfare states would promote private capitalism, ensuring higher tax revenues. They would then lavish the money on expensive public goods such as education and social protection schemes. It was not just the scale of these social schemes that was vast; smartly designed policies and a competent 'last mile'—i.e. teachers, doctors, welfare officials and other frontline bureaucrats—ensured that benefits actually trickled to the poor.

This social democratic vision, where growth and redistribution went together, was nothing like the 'socialism' of Indira Gandhi.

For all her talk of 'garibi hatao',[3] an economy that grew at around 3 per cent did not have much tax revenue to redistribute to the poor. The result was that government schemes were too underfunded to touch the lives of India's poor.

The sources of tax revenue were also skewed. Since companies and the middle classes were intentionally kept pygmied during this period, the little taxes collected were from indirect (sales and excise) taxes rather than direct (income and corporate) taxes. By 1991, direct taxes contributed to just 23 per cent of total tax revenue while indirect taxes took up a whopping 75 per cent.[4] Since the poor save very little and spend almost all their income on consumption, indirect taxes tend to hurt them more. In contrast, the rich and middle class save more than the poor, and therefore pay less indirect tax as a percentage of their income.[5] What was doubly ironical about Indira-style socialism was that not only was there little money to redistribute to the poor, the poor actually paid relatively more in taxes compared to the rich.

India's 'socialist' schemes were also badly designed. Indira's left-leaning advisors were telling her to constrict business, nationalize banks, and partner with the Soviet Union. But when it came to the education, health and social insurance schemes that really mattered for the poor, they had little to contribute. This lack of expertise led to welfare policies that rarely reached their intended beneficiaries. For example, fertilizer subsidies benefitted rich farmers, not landless peasants. And even a study sympathetic to bank nationalization found that formal credit was still 'concentrated in the hands of the rich and the already developed

A WELFARE STATE?

regions. The poor still depended in a big way on the informal sector."[6] The final, endemic drawback of Indian-style socialism was a bumpy 'last mile', populated by grasping middlemen and venal officials.

The results were unsurprisingly stark. Forty-four years after Independence, around 36 per cent of all Indians were still classified as poor,[7] 47 per cent as illiterate,[8] and 26 per cent as undernourished.[9] These were the statistics that prime minister Narasimha Rao inherited in 1991. He also inherited a number of vested interests who—like with the liberalization—would resist any attempt at reform. To judge whether Rao was more Brandt than Thatcher is to measure how much these changed on his watch.

Narasimha Rao and Manmohan Singh spent their first year improving India's public finances by conserving rupees. In return for fresh loans, the IMF demanded that Rao reduce existing subsidies. Most of these (for example, cheap fertilizers) went to politically connected groups. It was therefore courageous of Rao and Manmohan to reduce them. Subsidies accounted for 11 per cent of all Central government expenditure in 1990-91. By the time Rao left office in 1996, it had reduced to around 7.5 per cent.[10]

Not only did Rao limit subsidies in the early months of his premiership, his speeches made little mention of the welfare schemes—for education, health, farmers and students—that were the rhetorical staple of every new prime minister. Soon after the 1992 budget, the journalist Sanjaya Baru wrote a news piece on how 'education and health saw the largest squeeze'.

'Manmohan Singh read it,' Baru remembers. 'He was very upset.'[11]

Even as Rao and Manmohan were avoiding spending on schemes, they were quietly altering taxation policy—alterations that would eventually benefit the poor. One of the consequences of liberalization was that it expanded middle class and corporate incomes, as well as rationalized tax policy. This has led to higher revenue from direct taxation. It is a subtle but progressive change, ensuring that the rich and middle class now contribute more to tax revenue, compared to the poor.[12]

The less subtle improvement that economic reforms brought about in the lives of the marginalized was that total government revenue—necessary to fund welfare schemes—went up. When Rao became prime minister in 1991, Central government income[13] (in real terms) was just 302 billion rupees. By the time he left office, there had been a 22 per cent increase.[14] More spectacular has been the revenue rise since the Rao years. In 2010, total revenue was 946 billion rupees in real terms[15]—a tripling in the size of government income since the onset of liberalization. This increase in revenue—primarily due to liberalization-led growth—is a necessary condition for welfare schemes the world over.

It is, however, not a sufficient condition. Between 1986 and 1991, Central government revenue actually grew at a higher percentage than during the Rao years—thanks to Rajiv Gandhi's deficit-led growth. But that additional money had not spurred the governments of Rajiv Gandhi, V.P. Singh or Chandrashekhar to craft better schemes for the poor.

Unlike these predecessors of his, Narasimha Rao was well placed to use increased revenues to fund schemes on education, health, food and social security. No Indian prime minister could match his experience on these issues. He had overseen education and health in both Delhi as well as Hyderabad. His private archives are full of handwritten notes and underlined articles on social policy.[16] Rao may have been a neophyte on the economy, but when it came to welfare schemes, he was a walking encyclopaedia.

By the middle of 1992, India's foreign exchange was back to safe levels, and the need for fiscal discipline had somewhat eased. Free to pursue his passion, Rao began laying out his vision for a social democracy. 'No multinational will build a primary school in India, no foreign investor will set up a health centre. These are jobs for the government. Let the multinationals handle the top sector, we will manage the grassroots. This is the way forward as I see it.'[17] When Rao visited South Korea, he noticed how economic growth had taken place alongside improvements in well-being. He told the diplomat Prabhakar Menon, 'This is what we have to do. We have to emphasize education and health at home. Look at the way young people are coming up.'[18]

Like everything else about the man, this welfare vision was shaped as much by idealism as it was by self-interest. Rao knew that economic growth would take long to 'trickle down' to the voter. He decided, instead, to channel the increased revenue from economic growth to straightaway help the poor. He told a bureaucrat working on the public distribution system, 'You are the man who will sell my [liberalization] policies.' Rao also had an eye on the cycle of state elections held every year, each of which would be seen as a referendum on his national government. As one of his closest aides put it, 'He was sincere about the [welfare schemes]. But the electoral impact . . . that was important also.'

As we saw in the chapter on rescuing the economy, the fact that prime minister Rao kept the industry ministry for himself shows how seriously he took industrial reform. Similarly, Rao decided to also serve as rural development minister (the first prime minister to do so) signalling his commitment to welfare.[19] He gathered an unusual team of bureaucrats who would implement these reforms. His initial rural development secretary was S.R. Sankaran, a man 'completely wedded to social causes'.[20] After his retirement, Sankaran shared his meagre pension with SC/ST students.[21] He was succeeded by another socialist B.N. Yugandhar. The sharp-featured Yugandhar was described by an Andhra politician as 'pro poor [with] strong left leanings'.[22] K.R. Venugopal was the other leftist official whom Rao tasked with working on food and employment security. Reed thin, energetic and uncompromising, Venugopal had decades of experience with the public distribution system in Andhra Pradesh.

These men were as different as could be from the pro-marketers who manned Rao's economic turrets. They were, however, rather like the younger Rao. When Rao was minister in Andhra Pradesh in the 1960s, he too believed in the obligation of the state to transform India's ills. That Rao had morphed into a pragmatist when it came to the economy. But when it came to welfare schemes, his choice of stubborn socialists as point men indicated which model he had in mind.

The primary way in which countries provide subsidy to the poor is through affordable food. In India, the availability of foodgrain had been solved through the Green Revolution, and by 1991, government godowns were bursting with rice and wheat. The problems of the public distribution system (PDS) were subtler, and in his first months as prime minister, Rao spoke about them candidly: 'The stuff doesn't reach the fair price [ration] shop. That has been the most important bottleneck so far. I have a long experience . . . both at that state level and here; I think that if you are able to reach the stuff to the last village where there is a fair price shop, you can expect some results, some relief to the people. But if you are sold out at the wholesale point, then it only means that you are spending your money and driving the stuff into the big black market.'[23]

Rao knew that PDS money was being siphoned off by corrupt middlemen and bureaucrats. Also benefitting were the rich farmers from whom the government procured rice, wheat and other grain. Since these farmers were politically connected, Rao ensured a steep increase in the procurement price which his government had to pay. To balance this increase, he simply raised the sale price at 'ration' shops. This ensured that while the farmers made more money, many consumers were driven by increased costs to abandon these fair-price shops.

Political scientist Rob Jenkins sees in this a general strategy of the Rao government: maintaining the appearance of continuity (in terms of the unchanging level of overall subsidy) while radically altering the PDS system.[24]

Having subtly starved this system, Rao sought to replace it with a more sophisticated form of food subsidy: the Renewed Public Distribution System, or RPDS.[25] The RPDS would focus on the poorest parts of India—around one-fifth of all districts—where rice and wheat would be sold at a rate even lower than in the normal 'ration' shop.[26]

The scheme was monitored directly from the prime minister's office, aided by the zealous K.R. Venugopal. Rao's private papers are full of his notes on the subject. On the back of one such note, he wrote, in red ink, 'In the RPDS blocks, rice and wheat are at present being sold at Rs. 0.50 per kilo less than the prevailing price. It is proposed to increase the concession in price to Re 1/-.'[27] Rao was especially concerned with the implementation of RPDS in election-going states. A bureaucrat working in civil supplies remembers: 'He told me I should go in advance and monitor. There should be no complaints.'

RPDS did not win Narasimha Rao any elections. It also did little for the poor. A survey found that 'Not a single consumer [in the twenty-one RPDS villages surveyed] had ever got subsidised food grain from the ration shop.'[28] As the Congress politician Jairam Ramesh put it, 'RPDS was not successful. Total offtake from the PDS declined between 1992-93 and 1995-96 . . .'[29]

Rao's failure to ensure that inexpensive food reached the hungry is instructive. Money was not the principal constraint; in absolute terms, food subsidy doubled during Rao's term.[30] The problem was in part the design of the RPDS. 'Why should only the poor in the RPDS areas alone benefit, and not the poor everywhere? And why should the wealthy in the RPDS areas benefit?' Venugopal asked Rao. He wanted the government to universalize the PDS to all districts, while targeting only the genuinely deserving. The main reason why RPDS failed, however, was that it did not reform the corrupt lower-level bureaucracy—such as storage officials—who prevented affordable food from crossing the 'last mile'. This had been the problem of the original PDS; it remained the problem of its 'renewed' avatar. As we saw in the last chapter, Narasimha Rao had similarly balked from reforming public sector firms. He judged he was too weak to take on government employees.

Another welfare measure on which Rao expended much rhetoric was on employment guarantee. 'The prime minister and I had sessions of conversations on this,' K.R. Venugopal remembers.[31] Rao's private secretary, Ramu Damodaran, adds, 'This was something Rao spoke a lot about.'[32] There had been previous schemes where the government guaranteed a job to a poor person,[33] but these had been confined to isolated states (such as Maharashtra). For the first time, Narasimha Rao made it a national-level scheme. He announced 100 days of assured employment in the 1700 RPDS blocks in the country, and devoted a lengthy paragraph to it in his 1993 Independence Day speech.[34]

'It was all talk,' says Venugopal. 'There was not enough money in it, and it wasn't justiciable.' Rao's was still the first national employment scheme, a precursor to the more famous NREGA, passed in 2005. Unlike NREGA, however, those who were denied employment under Rao's scheme had no form of redress. This inattention to detail ensured that Rao's employment assurance, like his RPDS, had little impact on the lives of the poor.

A WELFARE STATE?

'Rao understood the problems,' Venugopal says. 'He knew the kinds of schemes needed. But when it came to action . . .' Venugopal was also angry that, in the tussle between the fiscally cautious officials in the finance ministry and socialist bureaucrats who wanted larger entitlements, Rao sided with the former. Venugopal submitted his resignation in 1993. Rao sat on it, only accepting it two years later. The PM was perhaps reluctant to lose a man who was a portrait of his younger self.

To show that he supported his socialist bureaucrats personally (if not policy-wise), Narasimha Rao decided to 'gatecrash' the engagement ceremony of Venugopal's daughter, Anupama Priyadarshini, in 1992. Anupama was marrying the son of B.N. Yugandhar, Rao's other left-leaning official. The groom's name was Satya Nadella. Despite a father and father-in-law who were committed socialists, Nadella would go on to become the global head of that quintessentially capitalist empire, Microsoft.

The engagement ceremony was set in Venugopal's official bungalow in Lutyens Delhi. It was a simple affair, and the prime minister had not been invited.[35] Rao, however, decided to make an appearance. Choosing not to travel in his entourage of several dozen cars, he and Ramu Damodaran got into an Ambassador with blackened windows and drove with just one escort car for protection. Since the streets had not been cordoned off, Rao was stuck in traffic, an unusual experience for the prime minister. He ever so gently complained to Ramu.[36]

'I had forgotten what traffic is like.'

⁓

While Narasimha Rao's interventions in employment guarantee and food security were less than effective, his forays into education were more successful. As we saw in an earlier chapter, Rao had pushed through radical policies as Union education minister in the 1980s. He also had a reverence for education that was Brahminical as well as socialist. The journalist Sanjaya Baru remembers travelling with Rao on his official plane once. A teacher from his Nagpur days had just died, and Rao flew all the way for a condolence visit. 'We landed at Aurangabad, went to a small house in the village. Rao addressed a small meeting where he paid tribute to the man in Marathi. That's it. We flew back without any fuss.'[37]

The most dramatic change that prime minister Narasimha Rao brought to education was in funding. Central spending on education[38] was just 951 crore rupees in 1990. By 1995, it had risen to 2042 crores.[39] Rao also went out of the way to cultivate bureaucrats like Anil Bordia, and brought expertise on schooling from the states to the Centre. In the words of education expert Akshay Mangla, 'Rao handpicked babus, and made education into a prestige posting.'[40]

As we saw earlier, education minister Narasimha Rao had first operationalized Rajiv Gandhi's idea of Navodaya boarding schools for poor children. Now, as prime minister, Rao expanded the number of such schools. The bureaucrat Keshav Desiraju, who was education secretary in Uttarakhand in 2008, says: 'The Navodaya idea was one of the few that worked. By making it a residential school in rural areas, it ensured that teachers lived on campus, and helped solve teacher absenteeism.'[41] Rao's liberalization policies also allowed states to directly get World Bank and foreign funding for primary education. 'More than the money, a lot of new ideas poured in,' an education expert says. 'Many of those ideas would later become national policy.'

Education policy since Rao has sharpened these strengths. A series of Central government schemes—such as the Sarva Shiksha Abhiyan—have poured money into schools. This has improved the quality of facilities as well as enrolment rates.[42] Yet, many of Rao's blind spots, such as the inability to reform the education bureaucracy, persist in later administrations. By the late 2000s, while teacher and student enrolment figures were officially high, only one-third of students *actually* attended school, and teacher absenteeism was rife.[43]

This incapacity is reflected in learning outcomes. A 2006 survey found that only 37 per cent of children in classes four and five could 'read fluently'; a 2011 study found that only 58 per cent of students in classes three to five were able to read a class one text.[44] This lack of quality is why, studies show, poor parents prefer to send their children to private schools (at exorbitant costs even) rather than free government ones.[45]

Yet, education policy refuses to acknowledge this 'private exit' by the poor, a denial that can be traced back to Rao's era. When it came to economic sectors like banks, mobile phones and airlines, Rao empowered consumers to choose efficient private options over government ones. But when it came to education, Rao made little attempt to open up schooling to the private sector (he could have still ensured state funding—through vouchers, for example). The result is a licence raj that endures in education, with all its attendant ills.

Where Narasimha Rao deserves credit is for improving India's public finances, ensuring higher revenue, which has, in turn, improved the scale of welfare schemes. Compared to the heyday of Indian 'socialism', absolute—and percentage[46]—amounts spent on education, health, food and rural development increased during his tenure. The trend persists. The health budget in 1996 was double what it was in 1990.[47] Food subsidy has risen from less than 50 billion rupees in 1991 to more than 800 billion rupees in 2013.[48] Budgetary allocation for six major social protection programmes increased from 5 per cent of revenue in 1991–92 to 13 per cent in 2008–09.[49]

This expenditure—as well as the direct impact of growth—has reduced the ill-health, illiteracy and poverty levels[50] of the average Indian. Poverty among scheduled castes and tribes has also lessened,[51] and reforms have increased income levels across almost all percentiles.[52] The change in attitudes and opportunities for entrepreneurship (hitherto confined to the Bania, or mercantile castes) is typified in the rise of Dalit entrepreneurs.[53] Tax reforms have ensured that the poor pay less towards government revenue, compared to the middle class and the rich. The evidence also suggests that general inequality has worsened only marginally during the reform period[54]—though some kinds of inequality (for example, malnutrition levels) are more worrying than others. The claim that 'neo-liberal' growth has made Indians worse off is not borne out by data.

Critics such as the economists Amartya Sen and Jean Drèze are, however, right to point out that India has a long way to go.[55] What is particularly egregious is that while social protection schemes (like employment guarantee) have improved, preventive schemes (such as on health and education) have been less impressive.[56] For example, even after two decades of economic growth, malnutrition rates among India's children are twice those from sub-Saharan Africa.[57] This is unconscionable, and shows that liberalization-generated funding alone—while essential—does not guarantee social outcomes. No less vital are committed officials, smartly designed policies, and 'last mile' delivery.

This 'last mile' is controlled by state and district officials, not the Central government. As a result, the implementation of central schemes has varied vastly between regions. States with competent local bureaucracies and political will—such as Tamil Nadu and Kerala—have converted increased funding into individual well-being, while Uttar Pradesh and other sloppily managed states continue to implement the same schemes poorly. This variation within India shows that the problem is not only at the level of prime minister. But Rao and his successors must accept their share of blame.

Narasimha Rao did understand the importance of 'decentralisation and micro-level planning' to prevent corruption.[58]

A WELFARE STATE?

His passage of the 73rd and 74th amendments to the Constitution, devolving power to village-level panchayats,[59] was an attempt to create what he called 'a bypass model' where money directly reached the poor. But this decentralization has given power to both virtuous as well as venal local politicians, exacerbating inequalities between regions.

Even worse, the Rao years saw a decline in public recruitment, from doctors to teachers.[60] While it is not clear why this happened, one explanation could be that Rao and other politicians found it easier to shrink the inefficient public sector by curtailing future employees rather than firing well-entrenched current ones. These frontline bureaucrats are indispensable to improving the well-being of India's poor. Their dwindling has rendered the state machinery understaffed as well as corrupt.

Where history will judge Rao more kindly is for being the first Indian premier to *attempt* a genuinely social democratic vision—one where the state encourages private entrepreneurship, and pours the resultant revenue into the social sector. This vision persists not just in the economic reforms that later governments have followed, but in the well-funded schemes they have crafted. The sheer size of schemes (possible only because of high growth) has enabled them to touch the ordinary Indian, even after leakage on the way. This has turned the quality of development programmes into election issues—especially at the regional level—in a way that did not happen before Narasimha Rao. Like Willy Brandt, Rao was his country's first social democratic leader, the first to realize that growth and redistribution were not in conflict. They were, and are, necessary for the other.

10

Surviving Party and Parliament

Narasimha Rao would wake up at 5 a.m. in bungalow number three on Race Course Road, his official residence as prime minister. Still in checked lungi and white banyan, his sparse, white hair ruffled upwards, he would walk to the adjoining room and fiddle with his computer until the newspapers arrived at 6 a.m. An hour later, his personal physician, Dr Srinath Reddy, would arrive to take the prime minister's pulse, blood and urine samples.[1] Rao would then walk on the treadmill for half an hour, and breakfast by 8.30 a.m.

His cook, Rajaiah, a Yadav by caste, had lived in Rao's ancestral village, Vangara, and benefitted from chief minister Rao's land reforms in the 1970s. When Rao became prime minister, he craved the *upma* and *pitla* of his childhood, and brought Rajaiah to Delhi.[2] The prime minister could now relive his favoured Andhra and Maharashtrian tastes for breakfast.

Rao would then bathe, don a silk kurta and white starched dhoti, and leave for the day's work. He would return for a 5-p.m. snack—sugarless tea, noodles and pasta. Rao would reappear for dinner, then retire to his room. With Hindustani classical music playing in the background, the prime minister would type his thoughts into his laptop before turning in for the night. On occasion, Rao would invite his closest for a one-on-one dinner.

SURVIVING PARTY AND PARLIAMENT

Prabhakara, Rajeshwara, P.V.R.K. Prasad, A.N. Varma, Ramu Damodaran or select others were at various times treated to okra, dal fry, and rice. If they were lucky, they would sample Rao's favourite dish, karela—a vegetable with an acrid taste, which is good for you nonetheless.

Through his five long years as prime minister, Narasimha Rao was a ship that sailed out every day into a storm. In pushing economic reforms or welfare schemes, he would routinely encounter gales in Parliament or gusts from his own party. The fixed routine at home—familiar food, familiar faces—was his safe harbour, giving Rao a few hours of happiness before he floated off.

~

That the ship of state remained afloat for five full years was itself a wonder. In the Lok Sabha elections of 1991, Narasimha Rao's party had won only 232 of the 521 seats on offer. Even with allies, the Congress was around ten seats short of a majority. The parliamentary opposition was split between the right-wing BJP and the left-wing National Front (a coalition of parties headed by the Janata Dal). If they voted together against Rao even once, he would have to go. No minority government in India had ever completed a full term in office; the previous two governments, both minority, had collapsed within a year. This wobbly mandate presented Rao with challenges no other democratic reformer had ever faced. Ronald Reagan, Franklin D. Roosevelt, Margaret Thatcher and Jawaharlal Nehru were all voted in with substantial majorities. History foretold that Rao's collapse was only a matter of time.

To add to his political impotence, Rao had been chosen as prime minister *because* he was politically weak. The public scarcely knew who he was, and no faction rooted for him within the Congress. He threatened no one: not Sonia Gandhi, not his rivals Sharad

Pawar, Arjun Singh and N.D. Tiwari, and not Rajiv's sycophants. Narasimha Rao had been made chief minister of Andhra Pradesh in 1971 for this very quality. That Rao had lasted little more than a year.

Another political constraint for the new prime minister was that his party organization was a shadow of its former self. The Congress of the 1950s and '60s had penetrated every village. It was now a shell at the village level, with the party's ground associations—the Seva Dal, for example—having long ceased to attract idealists. While the grass roots had dried up, the leadership had become 'a railway platform', in Narasimha Rao's words. 'Anyone can come and go as he likes, and can push others aside to place himself in a better position.'[3] Any semblance of inner-party democracy had also long been displaced by a 'high command' hand-picked by the Nehru-Gandhis. The conversion of the 106-year old party into a family enterprise had resulted in its 'de-institutionalisation'.[4] It had also diminished its regional leadership. Mindful of a glass ceiling above, state bosses either chose to leave or plotted in the shadows. A final feature of the Congress of 1991 was that the party 'system'[5]—where ideological debate would take place through opposing groups within the Congress—had since been replaced by personality-centric factions squaring off at the state and Central level. These struggles involved very little principle; they were simply squabbles over patronage.

This was the organization that Narasimha Rao inherited: absent in the periphery, bloated in the middle, hollow to the core.

Prime minister Rao's first move was to choose his Cabinet. In a rare act of courage, he appointed the reformers Manmohan Singh and P. Chidambaram as finance and commerce ministers, and appointed himself industry minister. After that, Rao took care to accommodate the party's various factions. Congress old-timers Balram Jakhar, B. Shankaranand, C.K. Jaffer Sharief and S.B. Chavan were included in the Cabinet; as were Rao's rivals for prime ministership, Arjun Singh and Sharad Pawar. For ministers of state, Rao chose younger faces like Madhavrao Scindia from Madhya Pradesh and Salman Khurshid from Uttar Pradesh. Khurshid remembers, 'Mr Narasimha Rao was more than generous with those from the younger generation. But he felt a degree of comfort with those he had worked with in his own time.'[6] Rao appointed fifty-three ministers in all,[7] prompting a comment from BJP leader L.K. Advani that it was odd for a minority government to have such an outsized ministry.[8]

While Rao pandered where he had to, he was also firm enough to assert his authority. Arjun Singh wanted to be home minister—the effective number two in the Cabinet. Rao made him human resource minister instead. He turned down Sharad Pawar's demand for deputy prime ministership. Instead, the Maharashtra chief minister was given defence. Rao also refused to include N.D. Tiwari (another claimant for the top spot) in his Cabinet, on the grounds that Tiwari had just lost his elections from Uttar Pradesh. This delicate balancing act calmed the Congress while upholding the prime minister's authority.

Rao's work was just beginning. Every new prime minister has to prove through parliamentary vote that he enjoys the confidence of the House of the People. The confidence motion was set for 15 July 1991. Five days earlier, astrologer N.K. Sharma received a message that the prime minister wanted to see him. Narasimha Rao was meeting with his Cabinet when Sharma was driven in. Rao interrupted his meeting to talk to Sharma in an antechamber. 'When the ministers saw that,' Sharma remembers with a chuckle, 'they asked, "Who is this pandit N.K. Sharma whom the prime minister listens to?"'[9]

Sharma then left for Calcutta to meet Jyoti Basu, the communist chief minister of West Bengal. He says he spoke to Basu about the upcoming confidence motion. He then returned to Delhi and briefed the prime minister.

On the morning of the confidence motion, MPs streamed into the circular Parliament building. Narasimha Rao rose to speak from the front row of the treasury benches. He had a clear message for the Opposition: 'So, let us start with consulting each other. In the process of consultation we will immediately find out, we will come to know what is to be discussed, what is to be kept aside. The area of agreement we will concentrate on, the area of disagreement we will keep aside, if possible.'[10]

Narasimha Rao's seemingly humble attitude to the Opposition, not-so-humble deal with Jyoti Basu, and the National Front's distaste for fresh elections, worked. While the BJP voted against the government, the National Front and Left parties abstained. The Rao government won the confidence motion by 241 votes to 111.[11]

Soon after the confidence motion, the Janata Party politician and former commerce minister Subramanian Swamy says he got a call from the prime minister. 'I don't like the tag "minority government,"' Swamy remembers Narasimha Rao saying. 'You have to help me get a majority. You did it for Rajiv Gandhi, you broke the V.P. Singh government.' Swamy replied, 'Janata Dal is rudderless. V.P. is a failed leader. You can break it. But it will cost you.' 'That is not a problem,' Rao replied.[12]

Soon after, a document was placed on the prime minister's desk. It was titled 'Record of discussion with A.S.' Ajit Singh was a senior leader of the Janata Dal, and was at odds with his party leader, V.P. Singh. The paper is unsigned, and forms part of Rao's archives.[13] It reads:

'AS said that he was absolutely clear in his mind that the parting of ways of VPS has reached the final stage and even though conciliatory efforts were going on at different levels. . . he had decided to bid good-bye to VPS and have an understanding with Cong(I). AS then mentioned the following points on which an understanding had to be reached before the announcement: 1. mode of joining—coalition or merger; 2. share of power; 3. common programme; 4. finance help; 5. long term arrangements, such as allotment of tickets etc at the time of next elections.'

Two months later, in November 1991, Rao contested from the Nandyal Lok Sabha seat in Andhra Pradesh. Following Rajiv's orders, Rao had not fought the May elections. In order to continue as prime minister now, the law required him to become a member of Parliament. Rao could have avoided the rigmarole of campaigning by being nominated to the upper house of Parliament, the Rajya Sabha. Manmohan Singh would choose this unelected route through his decade as prime minister. But Rao had won seven consecutive elections, and considered himself a people's politician. Given his lack of control over party and Parliament, this would be his one claim to legitimacy.

Telugu pride trumped electoral maths, and Andhra opposition leader N.T. Rama Rao chose not to oppose the prime minister's candidacy from Nandyal. Rao won by 5.8 lakh votes, at the time the largest-ever margin for a Lok Sabha victory.[14] By-elections had also been held in several other constituencies. The Congress won a majority. A few months later, Congress also did well in the Punjab elections, which had been postponed due to the threat of violence.

By March 1992, Rao had not only lasted nine months in office, he had ended the foreign exchange crisis, overseen elections in Punjab, and—as we shall see in a later chapter—steered India through the collapse of the Soviet Union. His party had also increased its numbers in Parliament. Rao had also sought to build consensus within Parliament, briefing them on key economic changes, and offering the Padma Vibhushan (India's second-highest civilian honour) to the BJP's Atal Bihari Vajpayee and the communist leader E.M.S. Namboodiripad.[15] His was still in a minority government, however, and Rao's situation remained rickety.

He faced his second parliamentary hurdle that very month. After the yearly President's address to Parliament, convention required a 'vote of thanks'. This was usually a routine event, but so precarious were the government's numbers that even this nicety turned into a referendum. If Rao lost, or if anti-government amendments were successfully introduced by the Opposition, he would have to resign.

The debate over the 'vote of thanks' began on 9 March 1992. Narasimha Rao stressed the seriousness of the economic crisis, squarely defending his government from charges of selling out to the IMF. Less eloquently, he ensured that seven Janata Dal MPs close to 'AS', Ajit Singh, as well as nine Telugu Desam MPs, skipped the vote.[16] It is not known what allurements were offered. Suffice to say that their absence helped Rao sail through. The front page of the *Times of India* the next day announced: 'Rao govt. wins first test of strength'.[17]

The secret to Narasimha Rao's steady climb up the Congress ladder was simple and bears repeating. He lacked a power base, a coterie that threatened others. As he told a confidant, 'You have known me for so long. The party and party leader are supreme to me. Never have I attempted to build a base of my own . . . I have never drawn anybody closer or kept anybody at a distance.'[18]

Now that he was finally at the top of the ladder, Narasimha Rao realized that he needed a team of his own.

His economic line-up had been assembled in the first months of his premiership, as we saw in the chapter on how Rao rescued the economy. By March 1992, his political team was taking shape. Principal Secretary Amar Nath Varma and Cabinet Secretary

Naresh Chandra were as central to Rao's politics as they were to his economics. He also brought back two advisors from the past. P.V.R.K. Prasad had served chief minister Rao in the 1970s. Twenty years later, he was appointed the prime minister's voice to mediamen, businessmen and godmen. Prasad would go on to administer the Tirupati temple, become the monk that Rao never could, and remain on good terms with Rao's children in Hyderabad.

If Prasad represented the older, Hindu world that was central to Rao's disposition, Ramu Damodaran embodied Rao's more modern side. Damodaran had previously served under foreign minister Rao in the 1980s. He was scrupulous, urbane, and had spent years working in New York. He came back to work as the prime minister's private secretary. 'Ramu was like family,' Prabhakara Rao remembers. While Rao treated Damodaran as his son, he was careful to insulate his earnest protégé from his more Machiavellian schemes.

In the durbar culture of Delhi, blessed are the gatekeepers. Jawaharlal Nehru's secretary, M.O. Mathai, controlled access to India's first prime minister. Indira Gandhi's stenographer, R.K. Dhawan, rose to power because he was in charge of her appointments. So it was with Vincent George, secretary first to Rajiv, then Sonia Gandhi. Narasimha Rao's gatekeeper was R.K. Khandekar. Given to wearing safari suits and thick, black-rimmed glasses, Khandekar was entirely loyal and utterly discreet. He was an officer from the Maharashtra civil service, and knew leaders from across the political spectrum, including the RSS.

Bhuvanesh Chaturvedi, from Rajasthan, was another of Rao's conduits to the right wing, especially to BJP leader Atal Bihari Vajpayee. When it came to managing Parliament, Rao deployed V.C. Shukla and Subramanian Swamy. And he cultivated M.S. Bitta, Matang Sinh, Kumaramangalam, Rajesh Pilot and Jitendra Prasada as his eyes and ears within the Congress.[19]

These relationships were as unsentimental as they were instrumental. Jairam Ramesh, whom Rao used only to later discard, says that Rao 'had contempt for Congressmen. He never had a kind word for anyone.' As K. Natwar Singh—a friend whom Rao eventually sidelined—put it, '[Rao was] capable of radioactive sarcasm. He smiled without a smile.'[20]

Rao tolerated, perhaps even encouraged, rivalry within his inner circle. A.N. Varma and Naresh Chandra were larger than life, filling any room they occupied. Though Rao knew they did not see eye to eye on many issues, he insisted on retaining both in his 'room'. Rao encouraged P.V.R.K. Prasad and Ramu Damodaran to compete for his attention, even if it caused tension between the two. The prime minister's economic team was full of pro-western reformers like Manmohan Singh and Montek Ahluwalia. His welfare schemes, on the other hand, were run by the socialists S.R. Sankaran, K.R. Venugopal and B.N. Yugandhar. Even his home ministry was a nest of conflict. The minister of state, Rajesh Pilot, was forever squabbling with the senior minister, S.B. Chavan. Pilot confided to a friend, 'Every time I am with Chavan, he [Rao] looks at me and addresses me as "home minister". [This ensures that] for the next month, Chavan is angry with me.'

Rao even set his godmen against one another. N.K. Sharma and Chandraswami cordially disliked each other. Now sitting in a large house in west Delhi, N.K. Sharma says, 'When Chandraswami was sent to jail, some Congressmen thought I was behind it.'[21] When asked about Sharma, Chandraswami says, 'I would meet Rao two-three times a day, N.K. Sharma [would meet him] one-two times a month. Who do you think was closer?'

The compulsions of politics left Rao's political team bubbling in poison. This may have made for clever politics, but it meant that the ageing widower had no one he could completely rely on. He had always kept his family at a distance from his politics; Lakshmi Kantamma had long left him and was now a sadhvi. The solitary Rao needed one person who was completely dependable.

That person was Kalyani Shankar.

SURVIVING PARTY AND PARLIAMENT

Kalyani was a senior political journalist in the country's capital. It was a position that gave her access to the whispering gallery of Lutyens Delhi. Kalyani and Rao would talk politics. He would also share confidences with her that he told no one else.

Ramu Damodaran recalls their relationship. 'Narasimha Rao found it hard to trust anyone in politics. Kalyani was one person whom he could trust. When they were not discussing politics . . . once I saw them listening to Hindustani music together.'[22]

'She brought him happiness.'

~

By March 1992, the 'big bang' economic reforms of devaluation, trade liberalization and delicensing had become policy; the foreign exchange crisis had passed. The prime minister had survived a 'confidence' and 'vote of thanks' motion, and his economic, welfare and political teams were in place.

Rao was also fitter than he had ever been. He had left active politics in early 1991, driven away in part by diabetes and heart disease. In the year since, Rao had reclaimed his vigour.[23] How had his health improved so noticeably in his one year as prime minister? His doctor, Srinath Reddy—now one of the world's foremost public health experts—considers the question, then replies, 'Vitamin P.' Power.

An energetic Narasimha Rao addressed the Tirupati session of the All India Congress Committee (AICC) in April 1992. Ramu Damodaran remembers why the prime minister chose the temple town as venue. 'By choosing Tirupati, he made it clear that he was proud to be Andhra as well as Hindu.'[24] As chronicled in a previous chapter, Rao successfully deployed Nehru's name and Manmohan Singh's image to sell liberalization to his doubting party. His attempts at inner-party democracy, however, had mixed results.

The CWC is the party's apex decision-making body. Its members are conventionally selected by the party president, without ordinary workers ever having a say. Narasimha Rao was pained at how anarchic the Congress organization had become. He ordered that CWC members be elected by party workers. The move was altruistic: the party president was knowingly ceding his grip over the party in order to make it more transparent.

The CWC elections were held during the Tirupati session. Rao expected his hand-picked nominees to win anyway. To his surprise, his competitor Arjun Singh won by the largest margin. Sharad Pawar was also elected to the CWC.

Arjun Singh was the heavyset former chief minister of Madhya Pradesh, every kilogram a looming Thakur from the plains of North India. He spoke, however, in a soft voice that emerged from a mouth always set to half-smirk. Sharad Pawar, on the other hand, was direct and aggressive. They were dangerous in their own ways.

Rao responded to the triumph of his rivals with a masterstroke. Some of his supporters had also been elected to the CWC. He made them resign, on the grounds that the elections were flawed since not a single woman or Dalit had won. These staged resignations forced both Arjun Singh and Sharad Pawar to also step down; after all, they could hardly risk appearing to condone social exclusion. Rao explained his actions in a newspaper interview: 'Nobody wanted the Scheduled Caste candidates to be kept out but the method of election itself, and the pressure of election resulted in that. As Congress president, I was under an obligation to tell the AICC that this is not good.'[25] Rao then reconstituted the CWC the old way, by selecting the members himself. He picked women and Dalits; he also shrewdly chose both Arjun Singh and Sharad Pawar. This time, however, they were not elected leaders in their own right; they were mere nominees of the party president. Arjun Singh accepted the appointment, announcing, with heavy irony, that he was 'doubly blessed'.[26]

Before the Tirupati session, Narasimha Rao's upayas had been performed backstage. This was the first upfront evidence that the diminutive prime minister was thoroughly Machiavellian. 'Until [the] Tirupati session,' P.V.R.K. Prasad says, '[Rao's enemies] were sure that they would get rid of him.' They now realized that the happenstance prime minister was here to stay.

After April 1992, Arjun Singh began attacking Rao openly, even as Sharad Pawar continued to bide his time. Singh, who met Rao several times a week as his Cabinet minister, began writing him public letters on matters as damaging as threats to the Babri mosque and problems with economic liberalization. He was also rumoured to have paid priests in Ujjain, Madhya Pradesh, to cast a spell on Rao. When the prime minister heard about this from his network of informants, he laughed out aloud. 'Who worshipped which forces and made me prime minister. Would I lose my position if somebody propitiates evil forces today? And if I am destined to lose it, can I prevent it by resorting to rituals?'[27]

A year into Rao's premiership, the opposition parties were coming to the same conclusion as Arjun Singh: the prime minister was not going to fall on his own; he needed to be pushed. On 30 June 1992, the National Front and Left parties decided to bring a 'no-confidence motion' against the government for 'all round' failure and 'anti-people' economic policies.[28] Rao had already survived two opposition votes in Parliament. This was to be the first of three official 'no-confidence motions'. The BJP joined in. The numbers, it seemed, were stacked against Narasimha Rao. After days of debate, the motion was put to vote on 17 July.

Against the odds, Narasimha Rao won by fifty-two votes.[29] Jayalalithaa's AIADMK had voted for Rao, along with sections of the TDP, and four of Ajit Singh's MPs. The parliamentary affairs minister, V.C. Shukla, was active in splitting the Opposition. 'I had made [an] informal arrangement with [Ajit]

Singh that he would never issue whip. He kept his word and I used to draw from his 20 MPs,' Shukla later said.[30]

Around the same time, the five-year terms for the President and vice president of India ended. Though the posts were largely ceremonial, a prime minister as weak as Rao could have done with a friendly Raisina Hill. The vice president, Shankar Dayal Sharma, was the obvious choice for the presidency.

The problem was that, by 1992, vice president and prime minister, thick friends in the past, had grown weary of each other. Sharma—a senior of Rao's in the Congress hierarchy—expected the prime minister to brief him regularly when it came to affairs of state. A former professor, Sharma had a long-winded and didactic style of conversation; Rao had grown tired of wasting entire afternoons over tea with the vice president. Sharma had noticed. An aide to Rao says, 'Sharma knew he was being ignored. He resented it.' On the occasion that the prime minister would phone on some official work, Sharma would sometimes refuse to answer, demanding that the prime minister call in person. Rao's archives contain snappy exchange of letters between the two of them.[31] Rao was tempted to offer the presidency to someone else. But he considered the alternatives, and eventually realized that he could not refuse the man who had turned down the chance to be prime minister before him.

That selection left open the post of vice president. Rao was keen to offer it to P.C. Alexander, who had played a key role in turning the monk into monarch a year earlier. But since the Congress was in a minority in Parliament, they needed the support of opposition MPs in filling these posts. The communists agreed to support Sharma for President, but wanted K.R. Narayanan, a left-leaning diplomat and a Dalit, as vice president.[32] To add to the clamour, V.P. Singh swore he would resign from Parliament unless a scheduled caste was elected vice president.

Narasimha Rao reluctantly appointed Shankar Dayal Sharma as President and K.R. Narayanan as vice president. He was to have a tense relationship with them both.

Parallel to these failed negotiations over constitutional appointments, Rao was negotiating in secret with Ajit Singh and his faction of Janata Dal MPs, hoping to muster a permanent majority in Parliament. These parleys were more successful. By 7 August 1992, a series of defections had reduced the Janata Dal from fifty-nine seats to thirty-nine.[33] This meant there were now around twenty floating MPs who could prop up the Rao government if enticed. Subramanian Swamy worked hard to engineer these defections.[34] Helping him was a familiar tantrik from Rao's past. 'I worked with Subramanian Swamy to get to Ajit Singh [and] his group,' Chandraswami remembers. 'I was in touch with the Janata Dal MPs.'[35]

Narasimha Rao had behaved less than honourably in Tirupati, as well as in dealings with the Janata Dal. He had also chosen to retreat from the battle over the presidency and vice presidency. It is a measure of the complexity of the man, however, that once in a position of strength, he could be high-minded—even when his party preferred otherwise.

In October 1992, the Andhra Pradesh chief minister, N. Janardhana Reddy, was censored by the high court for corruption in the granting of permissions for private engineering colleges.[36] Though the prime minister insisted that Janardhana Reddy resign, he had no wish to name his successor. Two decades earlier, chief minister Rao had been a victim of the Congress 'high command' culture; he had no desire to now victimize others. The party, however, was still in feudal mode. The Congress general secretary Janardhana Poojary called up Ramu Damodaran to check who the prime minister had chosen as the new chief minister of Andhra Pradesh. Ramu communicated the response back to Poojary: 'You decide, even if it is any man on the street.' The next day, Poojary sent Ramu a follow-up. 'Does he have any particular man on the street in mind?'[37]

At the end of that month, October 1992, a crisis was in the making that even Narasimha Rao seemed unable to solve. On 30 October, a BJP-affiliate, the Vishwa Hindu Parishad (VHP), announced that it would perform prayers near Babri Masjid on 6 December. As we shall see in detail in a later chapter, the threat to the mosque was real.

Rao's rivals in party and Parliament sensed this was the perfect opportunity to topple the prime minister. Arjun Singh wrote several public letters to Narasimha Rao, warning him about dangers to the mosque. The letters were cleverly worded. While expressing concern, Arjun Singh stopped short of recommending Central rule in Uttar Pradesh.[38] Narasimha Rao tried hard to shift the responsibility for the decision to others, from the Supreme Court and National Front leaders to his rivals within the party. But they were playing the same game that he was, and refused to make the decision for him. When the mosque fell on 6 December 1992, it seemed Rao's reign was over.

The BJP immediately brought a no-confidence motion against the government. Over four days of acrimonious debate in Parliament, Narasimha Rao blamed his inability to impose Central rule on a 'lacuna' in the wording of the constitutional provision which allowed for Central rule in states—'It has to be made good.'[39] Worried that fresh elections might help the BJP, as many as forty-seven members of the National Front abstained from voting, while most of the remaining non-BJP opposition sided with Narasimha Rao. The no-trust vote was defeated on 21 December, 334 votes to 106.[40] Like he had done with his post-Babri economic reforms, Narasimha Rao was able to turn the tragedy into a secular rallying cry.

Having survived his own demolition in Parliament, Rao turned his attention to his party. The Congress was terrified that it had lost the Muslim vote in north India. M.L. Fotedar—a Nehru-Gandhi loyalist—had shouted at Rao during the Cabinet meeting on 6 December 1992. This was a *Lakshman rekha*, an uncrossable line, even for the unflappable Narasimha Rao. He decided to shuffle his Cabinet.

Among Rao's private papers is a large chart, the combined size of four A4 sheets. Written in green felt-tip pen is a cost-benefit analysis of each of the ministers in Rao's Cabinet. There are fourteen names. Some of them have a 'reputation for corruption', others are inefficient. Under the heading, 'Ministers to be Dropped' the chart lists 'M.L Fotedar', and under "reasons" it says 'Political'. It also names 'Rameshwar Thakur and Uttam Bhai Patil', and provides as reason, 'political no utility'.

Rao met Captain Satish Sharma just before he announced his new Cabinet. Sharma was Rajiv Gandhi's best friend, the sitting MP from Amethi, and had played a role in prime minister Rao's anointment. 'I want you to be in my government,' Rao said. 'It should have happened long time ago.' Sharma, a former pilot, wanted the aviation ministry. Rao cut him short. 'No aviation. [This is the] first time you are holding a ministry. Half the time, the airhostesses you knew will waste your time. Other half your pilot friends. So what work will you do?'[41]

In the final Cabinet reshuffle, announced a month after the demolition of Babri Masjid, Satish Sharma was made petroleum minister.[42] Pranab Mukherjee, once Rao's equal in Indira's Cabinet, was brought back as commerce minister. Apart from sacking Fotedar, Rao dropped several other Cabinet members. Partymen wondered who was next.

The destruction of Babri Masjid led to riots across India, turning the financial capital Bombay into a war zone. Narasimha Rao turned even this crisis into an opportunity. He told his defence minister, Sharad Pawar, to go back to Bombay as chief minister. Amidst Rao's private papers lies a set of stapled pages. It contains a note from Rao declaring that 'by virtue of the resolution passed by the Maharashtra congress legislative party, I nominate Shri Sharad Pawar to be the leader of the legislative party'. He continues, 'For almost a week, I have had detailed consultations and discussions with several important leaders of Maharashtra as well as AICC observers.'[43] Rao then scratched out this sentence in blue ink, replacing it with, 'I appeal to everyone in the Congress to unite behind Shri Pawar.' Though Pawar realized that Rao was getting rid of a rival, he could not refuse to help his city in its hour of need. Ramu Damodaran says of Rao, 'He knew how to make an offer you could not refuse.'[44]

That same month, March 1993, Narasimha Rao headed to another Congress session in Surajkund, Haryana. Unlike at Tirupati the previous year, the prime minister was now firmly in control. He ignored protests at the venue from dissenting Congressmen, angry that the prime minister had not kept his promise to step down as president of the party.

Years later, Sonia Gandhi as Congress president would emerge as a dual power centre to prime minister Manmohan Singh. Prime minister Rao foresaw the problems with that arrangement. When loyalist Bhuvanesh Chaturvedi asked him in 1993, 'Why don't you give up the Congress presidentship? It will give a greater comfort to everyone,' Rao replied, 'You want the prime minister to take a file and go to the Congress president. Are you serious?'

The Surajkund session marked the moment when Narasimha Rao became his own man in the Congress. He had cajoled or cut down rivals, while deploying Nehru and secularism to win the support of his party. His economic reforms were chugging along, and new social schemes on RPDS and employment were being announced.

Ramu Damodaran remembers the moment of change.[45] 'The first time I got a sense of how self-assured he was becoming was when he started referring to himself in third person. He would say, "This is a situation where the prime minister has to act." That's when I knew.'

On 12 June 1993, Narasimha Rao was basking in his new-found power when he received a call from N.K. Sharma, his astrologer and firefighter. 'I have information that Harshad Mehta is going to hold a press conference,' Sharma predicted. 'He is going to say that he gave you a bribe.'[46]

The banking scam of 1992 had not only hit the headlines, it had hit Rao's liberalization policies as well. The man himself, however, had so far escaped taint. That changed on 16 June 1993 when Harshad Mehta told a packed press conference that he had paid the PM one crore rupees in return for 'political patronage'. Mehta claimed that Sat Paul Mittal (then a Congress MP from Haryana) and his son Sunil (now the chairman of the telecom company Bharti Airtel) had accompanied him to the prime minister's house. Mehta alleged that Rao was given a suitcase full of cash.[47]

The Opposition had finally found a link between corruption, liberalization and Narasimha Rao. The BJP and the Left parties demanded that the prime minister resign.

The latter announced that they were moving yet another no-confidence motion in Parliament. The National Front and the BJP supported the motion. Voting was scheduled for 28 July 1993, and as before, the numbers were not with Rao. The *Times of India* wrote, 'In a house with an effective strength of 530, the Congress and its allies account for 255 members, while those belonging to opposition parties . . . number 261.'[48] A newspaper commentator told the *New York Times*, 'I think the old man is in serious trouble.'[49]

The government needed to 'persuade' some opposition MPs to switch teams. This posed a quandary for Narasimha Rao. His closest aides swear that 'personally he was not corrupt'. In his dying years, he even considered selling his house to pay his legal fees.[50] But Rao understood that any political party needed money to survive. As Andhra chief minister, he had given his secretary, P.V.R.K. Prasad, a bundle of cash to be given to partymen in Hyderabad. When Prasad realized what the bundle contained and balked, Rao had told him, 'Such work is equally unpalatable to me. I too suffer from a feeling of guilt. But these days, you can't be in politics without doing such things.'[51]

That was in 1972. By the time Rao became prime minister in 1991, bribe money was measured in crores, not lakhs. From being incidental to politics, money was now central to it. Prime minister Rao's qualms were no longer ethical, they were practical. The last time he had been part of the Congress organization was in 1976, and he did not now know where the party treasure was buried. To assist the prime minister in managing party funds were treasurer Sitaram Kesri and another Congressman who does not want to be named. This Congressman remembers a businessman once offering Rao a one-crore-rupee 'donation' for the party. Rao directed the businessman to the temporary party treasurer, at that time the squeaky clean A.K. Anthony. Anthony refused the money. When Rao heard of this, he said, 'It's not for him. It's for [the] party. This is how it happens.'

Two days before the no-confidence motion, on 26 July 1992, Rao's appointment diary shows that he met Subramanian Swamy. 'I helped break [the] Janata Dal. I had a problem. All these people wanted money. If I gave the money and they complained, I would go to jail,' Swamy remembers.[52] The next day, Swamy met members of the Ajit Singh faction. This meeting, it seemed, had little effect. The twenty-member Janata Dal (Ajit) announced that it would side with the Opposition and support the no-confidence motion.[53]

That very day, 27 July, Narasimha Rao met N.K. Sharma at 10.30 a.m. His diary shows that at 4 p.m., he met the director of the intelligence bureau. It is not known what was discussed, but the meeting—just before the no-trust motion—begs the question. Sometime during that day, Narasimha Rao also spoke to the Congressman tasked with 'winning' over opposition MPs. Twenty-six years later, this Congressman remembers the conversation with glee: 'We spoke about vitamin M.'

Urdu Scholar: The fourteen-year-old Narasimha Rao (standing third from left) in an Urdu-medium school in 1936. He was one of Hyderabad state's finest Urdu and Persian students.

With family in 1944: Rao is holding his eldest son, Ranga, while wife Satyamma stands by his side. Rao's parents are to his left, along with his two younger brothers.

Mentor: Newly appointed Andhra Pradesh state minister Narasimha Rao along with his guru Ramananda Tirtha (centre) in 1962. On the right is Maharashtra Chief Minister Y.B. Chavan.

Companion: Rao's relationship with Lakshmi Kantamma would define his personal and political life.

With Family as CM: Rao, along with his mother (seated), children and grandchildren. He has just become chief minister.

Raging Bull: Chief Minister Narasimha Rao announcing his radical land reform plan on radio, 1972.

Exile: Rao visits New York in 1974, his first time abroad. The trip was to impact the staunch socialist's view of the West.

The Emergency Crew: Prime Minister Indira Gandhi in 1975 with senior Congressmen. General Secretary Rao is sitting at the centre.

Marathi Campaigner: Rao canvassing from Ramtek in 1984. The garlanded photo of the recently killed Indira Gandhi is in the background.

Still Number Two: Narasimha Rao with Prime Minister Rajiv Gandhi in 1987.

Best Friend: Rao first used a computer in 1986, and swiftly learnt three computer languages. As he contemplated retirement in 1990, he turned once again to his most trusted ally—his personal computer.

The Fox: The PM welcomes PLO Chairman Yasser Arafat in January 1992. Rao orders this photo to be publicized. Soon after, he opens up full diplomatic relations with Israel.

The Mouse: Rao with Sonia and Rahul mourning Rajiv Gandhi.

With Confidantes: The prime minister on Air India One, returning from a visit abroad. His trusted principal secretary, Amar Nath Varma, is standing (in white shirt) on the left. To Varma's right is Foreign Secretary J.N. Dixit. Rao's close confidante, Kalyani Shankar, is first from right.

Team PMO: Rao with Naresh Chandra (second from left), R.K. Khandekar (third from left), Bhuvanesh Chaturvedi (fourth from left), Manmohan Singh, Amar Nath Varma (to Manmohan Singh's left) and P.V.R.K. Prasad (second from right).

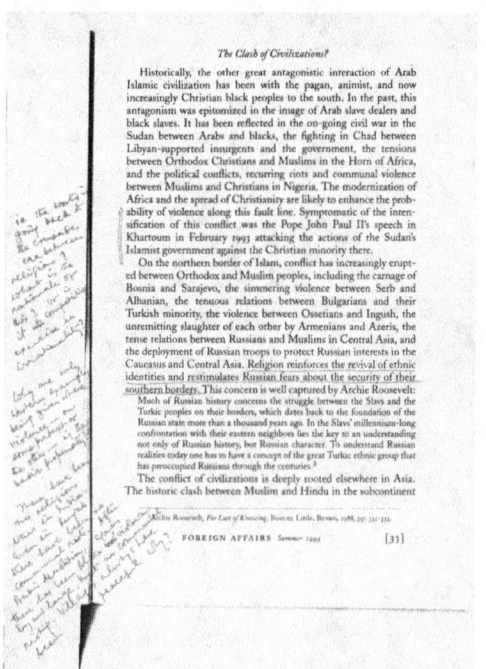

Philosopher King: Rao's personal notes on the article 'Clash of Civilizations' by Samuel Huntington in 1993. Rao was a constant consumer of academic articles on foreign policy.

Across Party Lines: Narasimha Rao hugging his close friend Atal Bihari Vajpayee soon after Vajpayee battled Pakistan in Geneva, 1994.

Going Nuclear: The chairman of the top-secret nuclear weapons committee, Naresh Chandra, with Member Secretary APJ Abdul Kalam and Prime Minister Narasimha Rao. They are at the DRDO lab in Hyderabad.

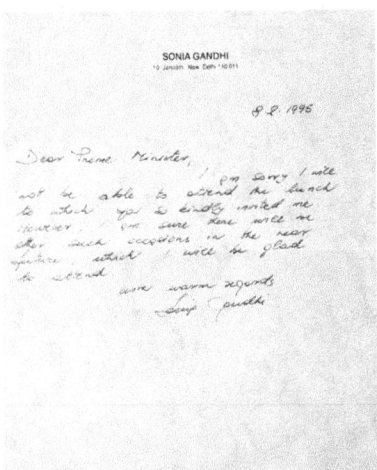

Managing Sonia: Sonia Gandhi sends Rao a polite letter of refusal in February 1995. A few months later, she would publicly accuse him of going slow on the investigation into her husband's assassination.

Lone Loyalist: Prime Minister Manmohan Singh is one of the few Congressmen to attend Rao's birth anniversary celebrations in 2011.

SURVIVING PARTY AND PARLIAMENT

On the morning of the motion, Rao made Arjun Singh defend him in Parliament from Harshad Mehta's allegations. Rao then got up—wearing his silk kurta and dhoti, with a white *angavastram* twirled round his neck—and gave a lengthy defence of his government. Narasimha Rao was well aware that it was the Left that had moved the motion, and his speech was tailored to their concerns. His economic policies had not resulted in a single job loss; 'liberalisation here has a human face'. He cited the social schemes his government had introduced, including 'a sudden jump of four times, 400 percent in rural development . . .' He then spoke about his legislation meant to prevent the mixing of religion with politics.[54] This could have well been his swansong, and Rao sang it well. He finished to loud applause from the treasury benches and left Parliament soon after. Months ago, he had set aside this day to feature in a documentary being made on him.[55] And so, on the most precarious day of his government, Rao seemed unconcerned about the outcome of the vote, instead choosing to star in a film about himself.

The motion was put to vote later that day. Apart from 248 Congressmen and their allies, seven of Ajit Singh's MPs—itself a breakaway group from the Janata Dal—broke further to vote for Narasimha Rao. Four MPs from the Jharkhand Mukti Morcha (JMM)—a regional party from what was then the tribal part of Bihar—also voted for Rao. The government won the motion by 265 votes to 251. It was at the time the narrowest margin of victory in the country's parliamentary history.[56]

The Communist Party of India-Marxist called it a 'political and moral defeat', alleging the 'shameless use of money power and horse trading'.[57] Seven years later, Narasimha Rao would be convicted by a special court for his part in a conspiracy to bribe the four JMM MPs. Though Rao's conviction would be set aside by the Delhi high court,[58] the blot continues to stain his legacy.

This ignominy would come later. For now, Narasimha Rao had survived his third formal test (the fifth, if one counts all challenges) in Parliament. He would continue to be beset by party, but his government would never again be threatened from outside. Soon after the vote, 'surrounded by jubilant party men in his Lok Sabha office, the prime minister gestured with both hands but offered no comments'.[59]

In November 1993, state elections were held in Madhya Pradesh, Uttar Pradesh, Himachal Pradesh, Rajasthan and Delhi. Voters were more likely to be influenced by local factors during state elections. But they were inevitably seen—by the media, by the Congress and by Parliament—as a referendum on the prime minister in Delhi. A poor result for the Congress—or a strong showing by the BJP—might have even forced Rao, exactly midway into his term, to resign.

When the state elections results were announced, the Congress had won in Rajasthan, Madhya Pradesh, and Himachal Pradesh. Even though the Congress had lost Uttar Pradesh, N.D. Tiwari had been humbled, and so had the BJP. The results were seen as a victory for Narasimha Rao. *India Today* put a smiling Rao on its cover, with the heading, 'Rao's Revival'. They wrote, 'After sort of having fizzled in two years ago with a majority thinner than his own hair, the man has begun to pop and crackle. He seems to have broken the cyclical curse and is enjoying a political rebirth in his mid-term.'[60]

Narasimha Rao's political renaissance coincided with the revival of India's economy, as we saw in an earlier chapter. The stock market was booming by 1994, exports and industrial production were up, and the foreign exchange crisis seemed a faint memory. N.D. Tiwari had been chastened in Uttar Pradesh—and other party rivals had been unable to displace him. Narasimha Rao, it seemed, was going to lead the first minority government to complete five years in office.

Sometime during this second wind, the special RAX phone rang at Dr Srinath Reddy's residence. It was 10.30 p.m. Reddy picked up the phone and realized that his VIP patient was on the line. 'Doctor gaaru, can you come over? I am not feeling well.'[61]

Reddy rushed to Race Course Road. Rao was sitting in a chair in his room. 'I am feeling numb in arm and side of the face,' he said. Reddy examined him. His motor movements—speech, hands, and vision—were all clear. But when Reddy pricked the right side of Rao's face and right arm, there was no sensation. The prime minister of India had just suffered a stroke.

Rao had been a diabetic for many years, and also had high blood pressure and heart disease. Months before his stroke, he had felt fleeting sensations, warm and prickly, on the right side of his face. When Reddy realized that Rao had undergone only a sensory stroke and his other vital parameters were normal, Reddy consulted a senior neurologist on the phone. It was decided that Rao's condition would be reviewed in the morning. For the remainder of the night, Reddy slept in the sofa in Rao's bedroom, while the prime minister continued to sleep on his bed. The next morning, a range of doctors trooped in, followed by Rao's son Prabhakara[62] and Kalyani Shankar. The consensus was that Rao had been lucky. He had only suffered a sensory stroke, not a motor one.

Narasimha Rao ordered that his illness be kept hush-hush (it remains secret to this day). If news spread that the seventy-two-year-old prime minister had experienced a stroke, the din to replace him would reach a high pitch. So Rao spent the next few months in meeting after meeting, speech after speech, with a face without sensation. A friend joked, '[Rao's] face anyways looked unmoving. Who would know when it really was?'

If 1994 was Rao's most successful year as prime minister, it was also the beginning of the end. State elections were held in Andhra

Pradesh in December of that year. Narasimha Rao campaigned extensively in his home state. It made no difference. The Congress lost to the TDP. The results emboldened Rao's critics, from Arjun Singh to N.D. Tiwari. If the prime minister could not carry his own backyard, of what use was he? Rao had had enough. In December 1994, Arjun Singh was asked to quit the Cabinet. He was soon suspended from the Congress party.

A few months later, the Congress split with the formation of the All India Congress (Tiwari). N.D. Tiwari was made the president of the breakaway party, Arjun Singh became its working president.[63] Singh organized a rally at Talkatora stadium in Delhi, where speaker after speaker attacked the leadership of Narasimha Rao, his role in the demolition of Babri Masjid, mortgaging of the 'nation's economic sovereignty' and compromise 'on Nehruvian principles'.[64]

Amidst Rao's private papers are a series of secret letters that report on Arjun Singh's every move at the time. One such letter was from an informant who wrote to Rao that Arjun Singh had arrived in Indore to meet the state's chief minister, Digvijay Singh. 'In the meeting, Arjun Singh categorically asked Digvijay Singh to announce once and for all whether he was standing by him or his opponent PV Narasimha Rao. [Digvijay replied that] he had no other option but to stand by the central leadership . . . Sir, this entire episode was narrated to me by the chief minister Digvijay Singh.'[65] Another 'white paper on Arjun Singh' was sent to the prime minister by a lawyer in the Supreme Court. In sixty-five lurid pages, it levelled a series of allegations against Singh.

It is not known how Rao acted on this information. But the evidence is clear that after mid-1995, Narasimha Rao began to slow down reforms. His focus shifted to unifying his party—as a litany of letters sent to him during this period reveal.

On 22 July 1995, the chief minister of Kerala, A.K. Anthony, wrote a short complaint to the prime minister. 'Respected Congress President, AICC General Secretary Sri Madhav Singh

Solanki visited Kerala yesterday. He addressed two party meetings and left for Delhi the same day. I was not informed of his visit. I am bringing this to your attention.' The Bengal Congresswoman Mamata Banerjee wrote him a fiercer letter on the 19th of that month 'to lodge a formal complaint with you and to inform you about the manner in which I was deliberately sidelined . . . In the selection of Congress Candidates.' Veteran Congressman H.K.L. Bhagat wrote a whining letter to his party president in October. 'I am sorry to bother you about [the] Delhi Congress. Unfortunately, it is a ramshackle Congress with dozens of office bearers, and the PCC under the present president is defunct.'[66]

Of all these letters, the one that best shows Rao's new focus after mid-1995 was written by 'Mahesh & Sons, manufacturers and suppliers of Flags & Election Publicity Materials'. They wrote to tell the prime minister of India that the Congress owed them Rs 1,95,000 for election publicity. 'I met Shri Rajiv Gandhi too and he promised to get these bills paid just after the 1991 General elections. But unfortunately he died during those elections, and could not honour his promise.'

This was neither lion, nor fox, nor even mouse. Prime minister Narasimha Rao had officially become a lame duck. All reforms on the economy—and even foreign policy—had stopped, and Rao's attention was now on the national elections scheduled for May 1996. Opinion polls suggested a resurgent BJP, with the Congress certain to fall from its current position. Would Narasimha Rao quietly waddle out of power, as seemed likely, or did he have any more tricks up his kurta sleeve?

On 16 January 1996, four months before the national elections, the solicitor general of India rose to address the Supreme Court.[67] He announced that the Central Bureau of Investigation (CBI)—run directly from the prime minister's office—was filing charges against several politicians in the hawala case. Those named included many Union ministers, the BJP's L.K. Advani and Arjun Singh. There was commotion in court and tumult across the country. Corruption was everywhere, it seemed, and here was a prime minister finally acting on it.

These CBI charges were a long time in the framing. In 1991, two arrested Kashmiri militants had revealed, on interrogation, that they had received foreign funds through an alternative system of bank remittances known as hawala.[68] Investigations into this hawala network led to the businessman S.K. Jain. The CBI raided Jain's farmhouse on the outskirts of Delhi soon after. Ninety lakh rupees in cash was recovered, as well as a diary recording bribes worth 60 crore rupees paid to various politicians and bureaucrats.[69] Here the matter rested, with the CBI unwilling to act.

Two years later, India was enthralled by another corruption scam that implicated the political class. Harshad Mehta had accused the prime minister of accepting a bribe, and newspapers breathlessly speculated on corruption in high places. In this atmosphere, the journalist Vineet Narain filed a public interest litigation in the Supreme Court, asking it to directly monitor the hawala investigation.

In few other countries would a case like this have directly reached the Supreme Court. But judicial activism the world over is closely tied to the fragmentation of legislative power.[70] Correctly assessing that Parliament was too divided to unite against the judiciary in 1993, the Indian Supreme Court took control over judicial appointments, held that the Centre's decision to impose President's rule must be subject to judicial review, and began directly monitoring the hawala investigation.

At the heart of this judicial coup was Justice J.S. Verma. Unlike Rao, Verma did not inhabit grey areas and had a clear, even zealous, sense of right and wrong. He accused the government of shielding politicians. He even ordered the heads of the CBI and enforcement directorate to attend court.[71] Verma told them, 'Who are you to decide whether there is clinching evidence or not. Your job is to have filed the chargesheet against all the suspects going by the entries in the diaries. Why are you not doing it?'[72] The CBI filed its charges soon after, in January 1996.

Four BJP leaders were named in the case, L.K. Advani and Yashwant Sinha included. As we shall see in a later chapter on Babri Masjid, Advani had given Rao his word that the mosque would remain standing on 6 December 1992. When the mosque fell, Rao assumed that Advani had lied to him. Corruption charges against its top leader put the BJP on the defensive. The party with a difference was now 'tarred with the same brush'.[73]

Advani resigned from the Lok Sabha. An associate—now estranged—remembers sitting in Advani's living room the day he was named. '[Advani] paced up and down . . . we were all there . . . some of us said not to resign . . . the old man was adamant.' This may have been one reason why Advani did not push his own case for prime minister in 1996, instead propping up Rao's friend Atal Bihari Vajpayee.

The principal shock from the CBI chargesheet, though, was felt by the Congress. The CBI had named Arjun Singh, who swore to 'fight it legally'.[74] Government ministers were also implicated. On 16 January 1996, an opposition leader said, 'Now, nobody will be able to say that Rao shields his corrupt colleagues. What he has done today is bound to stand him in good stead in the elections.'[75]

Narasimha Rao met with the CBI director, Vijaya Rama Rao, regularly during this period. His appointment diary shows that at 9 p.m. on 1 February, the CBI director, along with P.V.R.K. Prasad, met the prime minister. The two Raos met again on 9 February at 7.30 p.m. and again on 18 February at 9 p.m.[76] Newspaper reports quoted sources saying that Narasimha Rao was not just monitoring the investigation, he was clearing raids and the interrogation of suspects.[77]

The hawala case sullied many political careers. The case turned out to be a fabrication, as the courts themselves would say later.

Whatever the CBI's motive, their decision to file charges must have surely been approved by the prime minister—who controlled the CBI, and who was monitoring the case closely. Why did Narasimha Rao agree to the filing of charges, on such flimsy evidence, against his colleagues and rivals? Two competing answers have emerged over time.

The first is that the CBI was bullied by the Supreme Court, and '[Rao] did not want to be seen as soft on corruption . . . so close to elections.'[78] This answer is favoured by every one of Rao's aides. Rajeshwara Rao, Prabhakara Rao, Chandraswami and P.V.R.K. Prasad are adamant that Rao was compelled by circumstance rather than opportunity. Even Arun Jaitley of the BJP says, 'I think [Rao] had lost control over the case. Because, by that time, the case was being managed by Justice Verma.'[79] In an interview to a journalist—a copy of which lies in Rao's archives—Narasimha Rao called the hawala cases 'a millstone round my neck'. 'I could neither suppress them [the cases] nor allow them without harming the interests of so many colleagues who perhaps felt that I did not save them. Even now, I cannot see what I could have done," Rao said, 'except leave the matter to Providence.'[80]

A second theory is less providential and more Machiavellian. In the run-up to the national elections, Rao wanted to portray himself as a crusader against corruption. That he was still furious with Advani for misleading him on the Babri Masjid demolition provided added motive. The claim is not that Rao falsified the Jain diaries. Rather, he made cynical use of this minor evidence to foist cases against his opponents. The fact that the CBI director was a fellow Andhra man, selected by Rao, adds credence to this claim.

There is no conclusive way to privilege one theory over the other. But hindsight does tell us that the move boomeranged on Narasimha Rao. As P.V.R.K. Prasad writes, 'It is PV who suffered the most because of this decision, by losing a number of loyal supporters within the party, and that too, just before the elections.'[81] Those named in the chargesheet kept their vendetta against Narasimha Rao alive even after his death, ensuring that the memory of Rao is anathema to the Congress party today. His own son Rajeshwara says that 'Hawala was a total miscalculation. You can fight with one party. But you can't fight inside and outside [the] party.'[82]

It was the worst political decision of Narasimha Rao's career.

~

The 1996 national elections were scheduled for May. The polling agency MARG predicted that the BJP would emerge as the number one party.[83] The only hope the Congress had was to strike favourable pre-poll alliances.

Rao swiftly grasped that one state was the key to his re-election. This was Tamil Nadu, India's southern-most state with thirty-nine Lok Sabha seats. Since 1969, Tamil Nadu had been alternatively ruled by the two Dravidian parties: the AIADMK, run by the movie star Jayalalithaa; and the DMK, run by the scriptwriter Karunanidhi. Tamil voters had a reputation for siding completely with one party or the other. Narasimha Rao knew that whichever party he allied with would win him all thirty-nine seats—making him prime minister—or none at all.

Both options presented risks. The AIADMK was running the state and was unpopular. The head of the party was the mercurial Jayalalithaa, loathed by Congress leaders from Tamil Nadu. Jayalalithaa was also accused by her rivals of being involved in corruption scandals. That Rao was aware of these accusations is seen from a document found amidst his private papers, titled 'Yearwise Credits in Bank Accounts of J.Jayalalithaa'. The document lists bank account holdings, as also the properties of Jayalalithaa's supporters 'Smt Sasikala' and other senior AIADMK politicians.

Aligning with the DMK presented its own complications. The historical legatee of the Dravidian movement had links with the

LTTE. Going with the DMK would mean that Narasimha Rao was condoning the killers of Rajiv Gandhi.

It is a measure of how conscious Rao was of not being seen to abandon Rajiv's legacy that he decided to back Jayalalithaa. Even the faraway *New York Times* noticed that this was a bad idea, carrying the headline, 'Political Pact With Ex-Film Star May Bring Down India's Premier'.[84] Rao, however, felt he had no choice, telling his partymen, 'We are a hundred-year-old party. For short-term gains, we should not sacrifice our principles.'[85] The local Congress protested. As Rao wrote in his diary, 'At the marathon meeting of the CWC, the TN Congress leaders pleaded their case thoroughly and left nothing unargued. The leaders had always said the final decision of the High Command would be implemented—after everyone had his or her say, of course. I did not figure anywhere in that meeting but left them to thrash it out. And the CWC decision was categorical as final.'[86]

For the May 1996 elections, Narasimha Rao contested from Behrampur, Orissa, and canvassed in Oriya. In the first two weeks of the campaign, he addressed fifty meetings and covered twelve states.[87] While the BJP made hard-line Hindutva its main plank, Rao did not counter them by citing economic reforms. Instead, as we saw earlier, he campaigned on the stability his government had provided and the welfare schemes it had unleashed. Rao's Congress was also bruised by rebellion in various states. To shore up support from those who remained in his Congress, Rao gave tickets to the wives and relatives of leaders.

None of this worked. When the election results were announced on 10 May, the BJP had emerged as the single largest party with 161 seats. The Congress had collapsed to its worst-ever tally of 140 seats. The Congress and AIADMK had together won zero seats in Tamil Nadu. Narasimha Rao's term as prime minister was over.

Though the BJP was the single largest party, it was well short of a majority. N.K. Sharma says that BJP leaders contacted him, asking him to convince Narasimha Rao to support the BJP government. Sharma says that Rao considered the plan.[88] But after five decades in the Congress, he could not stomach abandoning his cherished party. On 12 May 1996—while the President of India was still determining whom to invite to form the government—Congress president Rao sent him a copy of the CWC resolution 'regarding the Committee's unequivocal decision not to have anything to do with the BJP in the current process of formation of the central Government'.[89]

Four days later, Atal Bihari Vajpayee took office as the eleventh prime minister of India. Narasimha Rao sat in the front row, in the same hall where he had been sworn in five years ago. Rao and Vajpayee, old friends, were similarly clad in white silk kurta and dhoti.[90] The only difference was that the new prime minister's shoulder cloth was orange, and on his forehead was a saffron tilak.

The government of Atal Bihari Vajpayee lived for just thirteen days; the next three governments lasted barely a year each. Buffeted thus by two failed minority governments before and four after, Narasimha Rao's mere survival for a full term is significant.

More astonishing is the fact that Rao did more than just survive. He transformed India in those five years, from its economy and welfare schemes to, as we shall see, foreign policy and national security. All the while, he managed a restless party, annual state elections, a hostile Parliament and a largely apathetic public. There are few reformers in world history who achieved so much with so little.

As if these chains were not enough, prime minister Rao had to deal with one more. This constraint was neither elected politician nor party member. Yet, she could have dismissed Rao with a single word. The story of how Narasimha Rao managed Sonia Gandhi is central to his transformation of India.

11

Managing Sonia

Sonia Maino was born in Italy in 1946, the year Narasimha Rao was an earnest twenty-five-year-old fighting the Nizam. Her family was intensely Catholic; her father was a building contractor who had spent World War II fighting for Mussolini's army. In 1964, Sonia travelled to the city of Cambridge in the United Kingdom to learn English. It was here that she met Rajiv Gandhi, a student at Cambridge University. They married in 1968, and Sonia Gandhi moved to New Delhi.

Rajiv was an Indian Airlines pilot with no interest in the family profession. Sonia and Rajiv moved in anglicized circles in Delhi[1]—light years removed from the world of Narasimha Rao. Rajiv Gandhi joined politics only in 1981. Rao had by then spent close to four decades in active politics, had served as state legislator, chief minister, party general secretary, and was at the time foreign minister of India.

Sonia Gandhi was afraid of politics. She had taken her bullet-riddled mother-in-law to hospital in 1984, and was worried that her husband and two children would suffer the same fate. She had begged Rajiv not to become prime minister. When he was killed in 1991, the crown was summarily placed on her head. She declined to wear it. When her party surprisingly won the 2004 national elections thirteen years later, Mrs Gandhi listened to her 'inner voice'[2]—or son Rahul's voice, depending on whom you believe[3]—and again refused to lead the world's largest democracy. The evidence is clear. Sonia Gandhi never wanted to sit on the throne.

She preferred, instead, to be the power behind it. Sonia Gandhi selected Manmohan Singh as prime minister in 2004 precisely because he lacked a power base. Manmohan Singh's press secretary, Sanjaya Baru, writes that Manmohan confessed to him: 'There cannot be two centres of power . . . I have to accept that the party president [Sonia Gandhi] is the centre of power.'[4]

Sonia's choice of Narasimha Rao as prime minister in 1991, on the advice of P.N. Haksar and Satish Sharma, was for much the same reason. As with Manmohan, Rao's virtue was that he threatened no one—not her, not her coterie, not any of the party factions. This was also why Indira Gandhi had 'nominated' Narasimha Rao as Andhra Pradesh chief minister in 1971. That Rao had failed to grasp the paradox inherent in his selection: he was chosen because he was powerless, but implementing Indira's will required him to be powerful.

Prime minister Narasimha Rao now faced a similar conundrum with Sonia Gandhi. If he roared, she would remove him. If he whispered, he would lose his prime ministerial authority and achieve little. To manage Sonia, Rao needed to project weakness as well as strength.

―

The prime minister's first action to please Mrs Rajiv Gandhi was to link his reforms to her husband's legacy. Most economic policies that Rao and Manmohan Singh pushed in the first months of their government had Rajiv's name associated with it. They took care, however, not to let this rhetoric change the substance of their policies.

On 22 August 1991, Rao released the fifth volume of the collected speeches of Rajiv. The prime minister was all honey, implausibly crediting Rajiv with pushing for global disarmament and the 'idea of a non-violent world' for the first time since Mahatma Gandhi.[5] At the same time (and as we shall explore in detail in a later chapter), Rao met with V.S. Arunachalam and Naresh Chandra—architects of India's nuclear programme—and ordered them to continue with weaponization. A year later, the prime minister spoke on the release of the book *Rajiv* written by Sonia Gandhi. 'I had occasion to see Soniaji with our late prime minister Rajivji,' Rao said. 'I sensed how unique and perfect their union was.'[6]

Rao announced that Rajiv Gandhi would be awarded the Bharat Ratna, India's highest civilian award. This was a curious honour for someone even Narasimha Rao privately considered a 'praise addict'[7] who was too inexperienced to run India. As we saw earlier, the government even donated 100 crore rupees to the newly formed Rajiv Gandhi Foundation,[8] which was being run by Sonia Gandhi.[9]

Rao complemented this public demonstration of respect for Rajiv with private discussions with his widow. Rao usually spoke on the phone with Sonia Gandhi twice a week. Once in a while, Sonia's aide would make the prime minister of India wait on the line for a few minutes. Rao complained to his secretary P.V.R.K. Prasad, 'I do not mind. It is the prime minister who minds.'[10]

Every week or so, Rao would meet Sonia Gandhi in person. His secretary, R.K. Khandekar, would coordinate with Sonia's secretary, Vincent George, and the prime minister would make the short journey to 10 Janpath. Narasimha Rao's son Rajeshwara says, 'Whether he talked to his own family, we don't know. But every time, he used to talk to Rajiv Gandhi's family.'[11]

Mrs Gandhi does not appear to have spoken much during these conversations. She was withdrawn and aloof during her entire first year in mourning.[12] Delegations visiting her were warned to avoid talking politics.[13] In October 1991, Sonia Gandhi refused to contest the Amethi by-election, necessitated by the death of the sitting MP, Rajiv Gandhi. It was a signal to Rao's detractors in the party that Mrs Gandhi was not planning to challenge the prime minister any time soon.[14]

Sonia Gandhi's one concern in those early months was the lives of her two children, Priyanka and Rahul. When she voiced her anxieties to Rao, he amended the law and extended SPG-level security—meant to protect the sitting prime minister—to former prime ministers and their family.[15] Sonia and Priyanka, who lived in Delhi, now enjoyed the same protection as Rao did. The prime minister then turned his attention to the security of Rahul Gandhi, who was studying at Harvard in faraway United States.

In his archives lies a letter written by the prime minister on 19 September 1991—three months after Rajiv's funeral. The letter is addressed to George H.W. Bush, the President of the United States, and relates to the 'security of Rahul Gandhi, the son of our late Prime Minister, Mr. Rajiv Gandhi'.' 'I had ventured to do so,' Rao wrote, 'knowing the warmth of your friendship as also the affection that Mrs Bush and you had for Mr. Rajiv Gandhi and his family.' He noted that the US authorities had 'been most helpful in providing a certain level of security assistance to Rahul Gandhi . . . In normal circumstances these arrangements would have been deemed satisfactory.' But Rao went on to write that Indian security agencies believed that Sikh extremists were plotting to kill Rahul. He then requested the US President for more security. 'The minimum, I believe, would be the availability of one trained person with him, who has also the necessary intelligence backing of various agencies, and effective means of communication.'[16]

This request for tighter American security for Rahul, enhanced protection for Sonia and Priyanka, regular visits to 10 Janpath, and ritualistic invocations of Rajiv's legacy—all had the desired effect. A close of friend of Rao says that in early 1992, Mrs Gandhi trusted Rao enough to tell him, 'People are asking me to come to politics. If I was your daughter, what would you advise?'

'Since you are asking as my daughter, I would say don't come.'

⁂

In April 1992, Narasimha Rao presided over the Tirupati session of the Congress, the first non-Family prime minister to do so. With Sonia Gandhi still in mourning, Rao had a free hand. As recounted in the previous chapter, the Tirupati session marks the moment when Rao's rivals within the Congress realized that he was more fox than mouse. They began taking their complaints about Rao directly to Sonia. Salman Khurshid, then a junior minister, remembers that 'Rao was seen as an intruder into what was seen as an exclusive Nehru-Gandhi preserve. Sonia consciously opted out. The trouble was you can take a noble decision, but in the daily functioning there will be any number of people who will say that enough respect was not being paid to 10 Janpath.'[17]

Rao knew that his adversaries were telling tales. His regular conversations with Sonia Gandhi, in person and on phone, were aimed at fighting those fires. The prime minister also went out of the way to address the few requests of the taciturn Sonia, on Rajiv's legacy, on her family's security—and on Bofors.

When it came to the Bofors corruption scam, a senior Congressman says that even though Sonia believed in Rajiv's innocence, she wanted the new government to lighten the taint on her dead husband. Just how keen the Narasimha Rao government was to oblige was revealed in the early months of 1992, when foreign minister Madhav Singh Solanki was found to have given a misleading letter to his counterpart in Switzerland asking him to scuttle the Bofors probe.[18] It is improbable that Solanki was acting without the knowledge of his prime minister, who had every incentive to please Sonia Gandhi.

For a year and a half, Rao's relationship with Mrs Gandhi remained without incident. She refrained from interfering in politics; he obliged her few requests. All of this changed on

6 December 1992, when the Babri mosque was demolished. Sonia Gandhi issued a statement condemning the destruction.[19] It was her first political act.

Though Sonia's statement did not blame the Rao government, the prime minister took note. He asked the intelligence bureau to keep tabs on 10 Janpath. On 18 December 1992, twelve days after the demolition, the IB replied, 'The important visitors of Smt. Sonia Gandhi, since December 7, included Arjun Singh (Dec.7 & 14), Digvijay Singh, MP . . . (Dec. 7 & 8) . . . N.D. Tiwari . . . Madhavrao Scindia . . . and Ahmed Patel.' The report went on to say, 'During the course of the discussions with Smt. Sonia Gandhi, Arjun Singh, Digvijay Singh, A.K. Jogi, Salamutallah and Ahmed Patel . . . reportedly expressed their unhappiness with the handling of the situation, including by the prime minister . . .'

Narasimha Rao realized he was facing a revolt within his party. As we saw in the previous chapter, Rao responded by turning crisis into an opportunity to consolidate his position. He rallied the non-BJP opposition behind him, reshuffled his Cabinet, and eased out critics. By July 1993, Rao had survived his third and final no-confidence motion in Parliament. The economy was doing well, and the prime minister felt he was finally in control. Rao's greatest skill was that he could dispassionately analyse his faults and frailties, objectively assess the precariousness of his own position. But political success in 1993 clouded his judgement. It led him to the principal misstep in his relationship with Sonia Gandhi.

Until 1993, Narasimha Rao met Sonia Gandhi almost once every week. Their conversations were brief, but they ensured that Rao could clear any doubts expressed to Sonia by disgruntled Congressmen. These meetings were, however, criticized by opposition parties. Why should a duly elected prime minister brief a private citizen, they asked.[20] Rao had ignored the jibes during his first two years in office. Now, he appeared to listen. In mid-1993, he stopped visiting Mrs Gandhi in her house.

For Rao to end his visits to 10 Janpath merely because he had gained temporal power seems uncharacteristic. He had spent his career bowing before Jawaharlal, then Indira, Sanjay and Rajiv. Unlike most other senior Congressmen, he had never once rebelled against the party's first family. He had even accepted his own forced retirement with equanimity. But perhaps it is not in human nature to always play second fiddle, especially when absolute power seems within grasp. Narasimha Rao always had little respect for Sonia's political abilities, as his diary entries soon after Rajiv's death in May 1991 reveal. Rao was opposed to Sonia Gandhi running the party and country. Finally in control by the middle of 1993, the prime minister was perhaps beginning to imagine the unimaginable. That he could sever the engine from the train and finally rid himself—and the party—of the Nehru-Gandhis.

If this was the intention behind Rao's decision to stop briefing Mrs Gandhi in her house, it had the opposite effect. Rao's absence created a situation where his many detractors—Arjun Singh, Natwar Singh, M.L. Fotedar, Sheila Dixit and Vincent George, among others—would incessantly complain to Sonia, while the prime minister lacked a forum to present his side of the story. Far from excluding Sonia Gandhi, it made her an alternative power centre. Kalyani Shankar says, '[Sonia's] chamchas, the middlemen and touts, also wanted to be important. Unless someone depended on them, they couldn't be reliable. As long as they [Sonia and Rao] were meeting regularly, the chamchas could not do much. Once they stopped [meeting], these middlemen created distance.'[21]

Rao increased that distance by sidelining bureaucrats and politicians close to Rajiv. An aide remembers, 'The prime minister was careful to follow rules, but he ensured [that] no bureaucrat close to Rajiv was given an extension.' Mani Shankar Aiyar was Rajiv's schoolmate and close friend in the Congress. Rao was polite to Aiyar but never gave him a job in government. As a senior bureaucrat remembers, 'Anybody associated with Rajiv Gandhi, he saw to it that none of them got anything.'

As dissent within the party increased through 1994, Rao's rivals flocked to Sonia Gandhi. Arjun Singh wrote her letter after letter.[22] Sonia was led to believe that Rao was deliberately going slow on the investigation into her husband's death. She suspected he was subtly removing her family from its central position in the Congress. By 1995, she was ready to speak out.

In May 1995, Narasimha Rao sent for K. Natwar Singh. The PM was a worried man. Sonia Gandhi had been sending him heated letters on Rajiv Gandhi's assassination. Apart from the criminal probe headed by a special investigation team, the Verma and Jain judicial commissions had been set up to investigate the lapses that led to the killing. Sonia felt these efforts were inadequate. Rao had tried to meet Sonia Gandhi to convince her otherwise. He even suggested installing a special RAX phone at 10 Janpath so he could speak to her on a secure line. After initially agreeing, Mrs Gandhi turned down the idea. "It was like a slap on my face," Rao told K. Natwar Singh.[23]

'I can take on Sonia Gandhi. But I do not want to do so. Some of her advisers have been filling her ears against me. I don't take them seriously. Sonia's case is different. Her attitude towards me is affecting my health.'[24]

When Natwar told Rao that Sonia thought the investigation into Rajiv's assassination was being delayed, Rao snapped. Natwar remembers Rao saying that 'he had sent P. Chidambaram to her with the necessary papers. He had also sent Home Minister S.B. Chavan to brief her . . . he said he himself had gone with the necessary files and explained to Mrs Gandhi the legal difficulties in hastening the trial. According to him, she had listened and said nothing.'[25]

That Rao took Sonia Gandhi's charge seriously is proved by a note that the director of the Central Bureau of Investigation sent Narasimha Rao on 22 May 1995. The note is titled, 'Comparative study of the assassination of Smt. Indira Gandhi and Shri Rajiv Gandhi'. It points out that despite Rajiv's assassination being much harder to solve, progress on the case, in terms of chargesheets filed and suspects arrested, was far better.

Sonia Gandhi remained unconvinced. On 20 August 1995, she gave a speech in Amethi, her dead husband's constituency. 'You can understand my anguish,' she told the assembled crowd of 10,000. 'My husband has been dead for four years and three months, but the inquiry into his assassination is moving at such a slow pace.'[26] She tellingly added that a 'vacuum' in leadership had developed since her husband's death.[27] It was her first political rally, and the crowd responded with cries of 'Remove Rao, bring in Sonia.'[28]

Was there any truth to the accusations against Rao? Satish Sharma dismisses the charges. 'The Jain commission and Verma commission were well implemented,' he says. '[Her advisors] were poisoning Sonia's mind against Rao.'[29] One of the senior-most policemen at the time—who is also close to Sonia—says that the charges are 'ridiculous'. 'It was all done by Arjun Singh. I think the entire discord between him and Sonia was because of Arjun Singh. He is the chief villain.'

Meanwhile, the Congress formally split, with N.D. Tiwari, Arjun Singh, K. Natwar Singh and Sheila Dixit forming a new party. 'The Congress Tiwari faction was Sonia's creation,' a Rao supporter alleges. 'She wanted the rest of Congress to migrate there, and then kick out Rao.' In her book on female Indian politicians, Kalyani Shankar says that Sheila Dixit put it slightly differently. 'Those days Sonia used to keep very quiet. She was a wonderful listener. She understood everything but spoke very little. I can't say she was the one who had given the signal to break away. She never said anything to me, but these people claimed they had her blessings. I had no reason to believe that I should check the facts.'[30] K. Natwar Singh agrees with Sheila Dixit. 'Sonia never gave any express support.'[31]

Rumours swirled that Sonia Gandhi had asked Narasimha Rao for his resignation. Around this time, there was an iftar party in Delhi's Hyderabad House. Rao's astrologer N.K. Sharma was invited. Sonia walked in and stood quietly in a corner, unwilling to engage with anyone. Sharma says he walked up to her and asked, 'Do you want Rao's resignation.' 'No, no, who asked you?' Mrs Gandhi replied, 'Please continue supporting Mr Narasimha Rao.'[32]

When Sharma reported back to the prime minister, he was not believed. Rao was paranoid that Sonia Gandhi was plotting a coup. Subramanian Swamy claims that Rao began collecting material on Sonia, especially her citizenship documents.[33] There is no way to confirm this, and Rao's private papers contain no evidence to support this assertion. What they do contain is a booklet published on 21 May 1995 by one Brahm Dutt Tiwari. The booklet is titled Vatican-Teresa-Sonia' and argues that Sonia is part of a Catholic conspiracy to destroy India.

At around the same time, Rao was provided a curious note by the intelligence bureau. It provided a list of twenty-one aspirants who wanted to become ministers, as well as the names of nine party leaders. Next to the names are details of the person's 'state', 'caste', 'age', 'loyalty', and 'comments'. Under the heading 'loyalty', there are two categories, 'pro-High Command' [i.e. pro-Rao] and 'pro-10 Janpath' [i.e. pro-Sonia].

For example, next to 'M.S. Aiyar', it is written: 'tamil nadu, brahmin, 52, pro-10 janpath, was critical of handling of the Ayodhya Issue by the PM. Took care of party interests in JPC on Bank scam.' Next to 'Pawan Bansal', it is written, 'chandigarh, bania, 47, pro-high command, enjoys good reputation for character and integrity.' Next to 'Smt. Margaret Alva', it is written, 'Karnataka, christian, 53, pro-high command, political lightweight. Could be dropped if adjusted suitably in the organisation other-wise christians of Karnataka may react adversely.'

The note ends with a list of leaders to be considered for 'appointment to organisational posts'. Topping the list is 'Sharad Pawar', who is 'Maharashtra, maratha, 54, doubtful, a good organiser and influential leader. Does not enjoy good reputation for integrity. Could prove useful.'

Rao had used the IB before to further economic reforms. He was now using it to keep tabs on support for Sonia Gandhi within the party. By late 1995, Rao had become wary of Sonia, very wary.

Around this time, Gopalkrishna Gandhi was heading the Nehru Centre in London. One evening, he was told that Narasimha Rao wanted him to serve as high commissioner to South Africa—an unusual honour for an IAS officer. Gopalkrishna Gandhi—the man whom Rao had called just hours after Rajiv died in 1991— was the grandson of Mohandas Gandhi and C. Rajagopalachari. He represented a lineage that was even more central to the freedom struggle than that of the Nehru-Gandhis.

'I do not think that the political significance of that was lost on Narasimha Rao,' Gopalkrishna Gandhi recalls. 'This was the first time a member of the family with a political heritage which is very different from the Nehru-Gandhi family was being honoured.'[34] Years later, in 2004, when Gandhi was appointed governor of West Bengal, an ailing Rao sent a message of delight through the loyal Khandekar: 'I think he had some political ambitions for me. It is possible that he was trying to wean off the Congress from the Nehru-Gandhi family.'[35]

MANAGING SONIA

Despite his private misgivings about Sonia, Narasimha Rao was careful to maintain a public façade of respect. They met at least four times at public functions in the last months of 1995. Each time, Rao greeted Mrs Gandhi with the appearance of regard. On 23 November, he even drove to 10 Janpath—breaking a tradition he had ended two years ago—for a twenty-minute meeting.[36] Though the visit was ostensibly to invite Sonia to his granddaughter's wedding, it was actually to neutralize disgruntled Congressmen such as 'Sharad Pawar, K. Karunakaran, Rajesh Pilot, Ahmed Patel, Balram Jakhar' who 'want[ed] to rope in Sonia Gandhi to force Rao to step down from party presidentship'.[37] On 9 December 1995, Rao sent a letter to Mrs Gandhi on her birthday, wishing her 'success in all your endeavours to fulfil Rajivji's dreams'. She replied two days later, on a simple thick white paper. A perfunctory sentence of thanks.

The national elections were scheduled for May 1996. As we saw in the last chapter, Narasimha Rao realized the importance of winning Tamil Nadu. Electoral logic dictated that the Congress tie up with the popular DMK, which was expected to sweep the state. But, in Prabhakara Rao's words, 'A case was being built up [by his enemies in the Congress] that Rao was trying to support the people who killed Rajiv Gandhi.'[38] It is a sign of how sensitive Rao was to this charge that he sided with the unpopular AIADMK instead of the DMK. 'He would have come back to power in 1996,' P.V.R.K. Prasad says, 'but he chose to follow his principles. It cost him.'[39]

In his five years as prime minister, Rao had kowtowed to Sonia Gandhi, yet never altered government policy to please her. Even when their relationship deteriorated after 1993, prime minister Rao discarded Rajiv's associates and contemplated sidelining Sonia, but he did not publicly challenge her. He had imagined a

Congress without the Nehru-Gandhi family, but had never fully acted on his imagination. Unlike chief minister Rao's misreading of Indira in the 1970s, prime minister Rao had *simultaneously* played both lion and mouse with Sonia.

Rao was less successful in managing his post-prime ministerial relationship with her. When Rao presided over his party's worst-ever (at the time) result in the 1996 national election, his partymen began to look back towards the Nehru-Gandhis to rescue them. When Sonia Gandhi became Congress president in 1998, Rao's enemies also returned. Narasimha Rao was not given a ticket to contest the 1999 elections. As he lay ill in his house on 9 Motilal Nehru Marg, few Congressmen came visiting, terrified of what 'Madam' would say.

Worried that Rao's legacy would compete with her family's within the party pantheon, Rao was not cremated in Delhi, his body not allowed to enter the Congress headquarters. Egged on by Sonia's advisors, Rao was even erased from official Congress history. The party version of the history of economic reforms does not mention the name of the man who did it.[40]

Sonia Gandhi's relationship with Rao was therefore complex. She suspected that Rao had made attempts—however feeble—to fashion a Congress without the Nehru-Gandhis. This view was intensified by those around her, who deserve much blame for ruining Rao's relationship with Sonia Gandhi. For all her anger towards him, however, Sonia Gandhi was too apolitical in those early years after her husband's death to interfere with the policies of his government. It was only after Rao's premiership that she began dismantling his legacy.

While maintaining the veneer of civility, Mrs Gandhi made it known that Rao was persona non grata, Latin for 'unwelcome person'. The party to which Rao devoted six decades of his life heard the message loud and clear. He remained unwelcome since.

12

The Fall of Babri Masjid

6 December 1992. Narasimha Rao woke up at 7 a.m., later than usual since it was a Sunday. He read the day's newspapers. The *Times of India* reported that more than '2.25 lakh VHP [Vishwa Hindu Parishad] volunteers are poised to' perform prayers right next to the Babri Masjid. The article quoted the VHP spokesman promise that 'volunteers would not violate the court orders'.[1]

The prime minister then spent thirty minutes walking on a specially installed treadmill. His personal physician, K. Srinath Reddy, arrived soon after. They chatted in Telugu and English, while Reddy took samples of Rao's blood and urine.[2]

Since it was a Sunday, Reddy, a cardiologist at AIIMS hospital, spent the rest of the day at home with his family. At around noon, he switched on the television. Channels showed calm in Ayodhya—the three domes of Babri Masjid visible. At 12.20 p.m., Reddy saw live on television, the assault on the first dome by thousands of Hindu activists. By 1.55 p.m., the first dome had collapsed. Reddy watched, numb. His father, K.V. Raghunatha Reddy, was an inveterate socialist, and this had rubbed off on the son. Reddy remembers, 'It was the worst day for Indian secularism.'

Almost immediately after, Reddy thought to himself, 'The prime minister is a heart patient. How will he be feeling?' A bypass surgery in 1990 had nearly caused Rao to retire from politics.

Reddy rushed to the prime minister's office. Rao was standing when he entered, a gaggle of officials and politicians around him. They were all staring at the television. The third dome of the mosque had just fallen. 'Why have you come now?' Rao angrily asked Reddy. But the doctor insisted that his patient be examined. Rao moved to a small anteroom. 'His mind was elsewhere,' Reddy remembers, 'but he was an obedient patient.'

Srinath Reddy checked the prime minister's pulse and blood pressure. 'As I expected, his heart was racing away . . . pulse was very fast . . . BP had risen. His face was glowering red, he was agitated.' Dr Reddy gave Rao an extra dose of beta blocker, and left only when the PM had visibly calmed.

Twenty-three years later, Reddy recalls Rao's physical state: 'I am fairly convinced as a doctor that his personal reaction to the demolition was one of honest agitation. It is not that of a person who would have planned it or been complicit in it.'

'The body does not lie.'

~

The Babri mosque was built in 1528 by a courtier of the Mughal emperor Babur, who named it after his overlord. It was located in the north Indian town of Ayodhya, revered in Hindu tradition as the city where the god Ram was born.[3] The three-domed mosque was housed in an inner compound, while the outer compound contained smaller buildings, including two Hindu structures of worship.[4] Since at least the nineteenth century, there are records of religious violence around the mosque—which local Hindu groups claimed was built atop the remains of a temple commemorating the birthplace of Ram.[5]

In 1885, the dispute entered the courts, with a local Hindu priest demanding that a temple be built in the outer courtyard, adjacent to the Babri mosque. The colonial administration dismissed the suit, worried that a temple built so close to the mosque would threaten

THE FALL OF BABRI MASJID

the peace.[6] In 1949, soon after Indian Independence, idols were surreptitiously installed inside the mosque by Hindus.[7] Afraid of sparking a riot, the Congress-run administration did not remove the idols,[8] and a local judge permitted Hindu pilgrims to enter the compound and pray. The judge, however, banned pilgrims from approaching the idols, which could be worshipped only through locked gates.[9] Here the matter rested for forty years.

Ayodhya is located in Uttar Pradesh (UP), India's most populous state. With the highest number of Lok Sabha seats, the path to power in Delhi traditionally passed through this state. The Congress party had dominated UP (and north India more generally) through a rainbow coalition of upper-caste Hindus, Muslims and Dalits. By the 1980s, however, these groups were looking elsewhere. Mulayam Singh Yadav's Janata Dal was attracting the state's 18 per cent Muslims, while the recently formed Bharatiya Janata Party was wooing upper- and backward-caste Hindus. The BJP campaigned on Hindu victimhood from centuries of Muslim domination. For them, no symbol captured this better than Babri Masjid. In 1984, the VHP, working with the BJP, began a movement to demolish the mosque and build a temple in its place.[10] The mosque was now a symbol of India's commitment to constitutional pluralism.

The Congress under prime minister Rajiv Gandhi could have responded by harking back to secular principle. It did not. As we saw in an earlier chapter, Rajiv catered to both Muslim and Hindu extremism in a bid to protect his electoral majority. He overturned the Shah Bano judgment of the Supreme Court; he also banned Salman Rushdie's *Satanic Verses*. Rajiv simultaneously sought to out-Hindu the VHP by ensuring that Babri Masjid was 'unlocked' for Hindu prayer in 1986. Three years later, he allowed a symbolic foundation ceremony for a temple right next to the Babri mosque.[11]

Rajiv's competitive communalism did not bring his party electoral dividends. The Congress lost power in UP in 1989, with the state's Muslims voting for Mulayam Singh Yadav. In the national elections held at the same time, Rajiv was dethroned, and the BJP's tally jumped from two seats to eighty-five. Sensing the wind behind his back, the BJP's L.K. Advani launched a new political campaign. He rode through north India on a van decked like a chariot, whipping up support for a Ram temple at Ayodhya. It polarized Hindus and Muslims as never before.

In October 1990, Hindu activists attempted to take over the mosque. Mulayam Singh Yadav, who had come to power with Muslim votes, ordered the police to open fire. As per the Constitution, the police and Central forces reported directly to the chief minister. They followed his orders. Sixteen activists died, and the mosque remained standing. Determined to protect the Babri Masjid at any cost, Mulayam swore, *'Yahan parinda bhi par nahin maar sakta.'* ('Even a bird cannot flutter its wings here.')[12]

As Mulayam would later admit, the firing may have protected the mosque, but it cost him Hindu votes.[13] State elections were held in Uttar Pradesh a year later. The BJP campaigned on two issues: the demolition of the Babri mosque (and the 'martyrdom' of the Hindu activists) and the wooing of backward-caste Hindus. It swept the elections, easily winning more than half the seats.[14] Kalyan Singh became the new chief minister. Singh was a backward-caste leader who was involved in the Ayodhya agitation. The BJP also did well in the national elections held at the same time. The new prime minister, says Ramu Damodaran, 'knew and respected the fact that the BJP had risen so quickly. He could not ignore them.'[15]

Narasimha Rao's own solution to the Babri dispute was straightforward: both religious groups should negotiate and build a temple near the mosque, while leaving the mosque intact. If no agreement could be reached, the decision of the courts would be final.[16] While Muslim groups seemed agreeable to this eventuality, the BJP and its allies did not think this was a matter for the courts, and wanted the temple built atop the destroyed mosque, not near it.

THE FALL OF BABRI MASJID

The BJP's victory in the UP state elections was especially vexing for Narasimha Rao. The Indian Constitution lists some powers that are exclusively the province of the state, one of them being 'law and order'. This meant that the police protecting the Babri mosque were constitutionally required to report to the UP chief minister only, not the prime minister. Even Central troops sent to the state would have to report to the state government. The Constitution provided only one exception to this. Article 356 dealt with 'provisions in case of failure of constitutional machinery in State'. It permitted the prime minister to dismiss a state government and impose 'President's rule' if 'a situation has arisen in which the government of the State cannot be carried on in accordance with . . . this Constitution.'[17] This had been used many times before,[18] but by 1992, Article 356 was being criticised by non-Congress parties as a tool through which the Congress perpetuated its dominance over the states.

The use of Article 356 had not been necessary to protect the Babri mosque as long as Uttar Pradesh was run by the Congress or Mulayam Singh. After June 1991, however, the very party that wanted the mosque destroyed was now in charge of securing it.

Prime minister Rao thus came to power facing three dilemmas over Babri Masjid. Since he needed both Hindus and Muslims to return to the Congress, he did not want to alienate either group. Second, while Narasimha Rao opposed the BJP's position on the mosque, his party was a minority in Parliament. If the BJP moved and won a no-confidence motion, Rao would have to resign. A third, critical, predicament was whether to dismiss the UP government by invoking Article 356. Could chief minister Kalyan Singh be trusted to place constitutional duty above ideological inclination?

Kalyan Singh's initial actions seemed to indicate that the answer was 'no'. Almost immediately after Singh's swearing-in ceremony as chief minister in June 1991, the UP government acquired 2.77 acres of land around Babri Masjid.[19] That October, it began demolishing ancient structures on the acquired land (the main mosque was left untouched).[20] It was only when the Supreme Court stepped in that the demolition stopped. In November, Kalyan Singh assured the National Integration Council (a group of senior politicians from across parties) that 'the entire responsibility for the protection of the disputed structure is ours, we will be vigilant . . .'[21]

Meanwhile, between September and November 1991, Rao ensured that Hindu and Muslim groups met around ninety times. There had been three prior attempts at negotiations, but they had failed[22] since Muslim groups were suspicious of the BJP. They were right to be. On 6 January 1992, the intelligence bureau sent Rao a note titled 'Ram Janma Bhoomi-Babri Masjid—Retrospect & Prospects'. It warned that 'notwithstanding the present impasse on account of legal obstacles, the BJP government in U.P. is considering how best to circumvent those hurdles that are standing in the way of the construction of the temple'.

Meanwhile, after the Congress session in Tirupati in April 1992, Rao's rivals within the Congress realized that Rao might last his full term. As we saw in an earlier chapter, Arjun Singh, in particular, decided to make Babri Masjid a wedge issue and unseat Rao. Through the year 1992, he sent Rao a series of public and private letters warning of the dangers to the mosque. He also advocated a strong line against the BJP.[23]

The BJP began a fresh set of provocations in July. Newspaper reports indicated that though the main Babri mosque was unharmed, the BJP had resumed construction in the outer compound. This was a direct violation of Supreme Court orders.

Many Congressmen were alarmed. On 9 July 9 1992, twenty Congress MPs—including Mani Shankar Aiyar and Prithviraj Chavan—signed a handwritten letter to Rao pleading that he take 'all necessary steps to protect the masjid by preventing construction, by taking physical possession of the masjid and the premises, and by deploying the Army to that area if necessary'. A few days later, the Allahabad high court directed the UP government to stop construction.[24] But the construction continued. It was only when the Supreme Court ordered suspension on 23 July 1992 that construction ceased[25] and the immediate threat to the mosque dissipated. Kalyan Singh had demonstrated once again that he was not a man of his word.

Though Rao decided not to impose Central rule in UP that July, he was confronted with the possibility that he would have to do so at short notice. He asked Madhav Godbole, his home secretary, to draw up a contingency plan to take over the mosque. Godbole, a Maharashtrian IAS officer, had a reputation for hard work, rectitude as well as acrimony. 'When he speaks, it is as if God-*bole* [God speaks],' a batchmate of his remembers. Godbole would later resign in a huff, and write a tell-all memoir criticizing Rao and other decision-makers for failing to prevent the demolition of Babri Masjid. But in July 1992, he was a bureaucrat who did as he was told. He sent Rao a secret contingency plan.

The plan contained the modalities for Central forces to take over Babri Masjid. It specified that Article 356 had to be invoked, and talked about 'Danger to security of RJB-BM' structure for 'a period of a few hours when the structure would be quite vulnerable. Ground realities preclude any fool-proof operational plan to avoid this.'[26] Rao did not go through with the plan in July. As Godbole puts it, '. . .there was no clear view within the government on whether the Centre should get so fully involved'.[27]

Meanwhile, July 1992 saw the retirement of Cabinet secretary Naresh Chandra, since he had crossed fifty-eight years of age. Chandra had been handling the business of government as well as economic reforms and, as we shall see later, the growing nuclear programme. A bachelor, he was a permanent presence in South Block, eating lunch, dinner and even breakfast there. 'I don't want to lose him,' Rao told an official. That very month, Rao announced in Parliament that a special 'Ayodhya cell' would be created in the prime minister's office. Its proposals would be submitted to the prime minister through Naresh Chandra, who was designated as a 'senior advisor'.[28] The creation of the Ayodhya cell signalled that the prime minister's office was directly dealing with the matter. But the home secretary, Madhav Godbole, felt that it was 'a wrong move . . . it weakened the MHA (ministry of home affairs), depriving it of initiative, without in any way . . . finding a solution . . .'[29]

The matter was now reaching boiling point and Rao personally monitored negotiations between Hindu and Muslim groups. In his Independence Day speech that August, he declared, 'It is our desire that a grand temple be built there, but the mosque must remain intact.'[30] This formula—of a protected mosque with a temple adjacent—was part of the 1991 Congress election manifesto[31] (drafted by Rao) and seemed just the kind of balancing act that had worked for him elsewhere. The VHP and Muslim leaders began talking again. Rao's patience appeared to be paying off.

Then on 30 October 1992, the VHP lobbed a bombshell. It declared that *kar seva,* or religious service, would be performed right next to the disputed structure on 6 December—on land that the UP government had taken over. The VHP promised that the mosque itself would be untouched, and the symbolic puja would be confined to the outer compound. But that meant around 100,000 Hindu kar sevaks in proximity to Babri Masjid on 6 December 1992.[32]

A few days later, Narasimha Rao asked Madhav Godbole to prepare yet another secret contingency plan to take over the mosque. On 4 November, Godbole replied, estimating that a large contingent of central forces would be required: 'CRPF: 90 Coys [companies]; RPF 25 Coys; CISF 54 Coys. Total 169 coys.' This strike force would gather in Delhi airport, fly to Lucknow, and make their way by road to Ayodhya.

THE FALL OF BABRI MASJID

The report made two points forcefully. First, the 'imposition of president's rule under article 356 of the constitution may be necessary just before the actual intervention'. Second, there would be a danger to the mosque while it was being taken over by Central forces. 'One major concern, in the backdrop of developments since July, 1992 would be the safety and security of the Ram Janma Bhoomi—Babri Masjid structure in such a situation.' Come 6 December, the activists around the mosque would constitute 'a target of 10 lakh *kar sevak*s, though the actual number is not expected to be so large'. For Central forces to take control of the mosque while it was surrounded by so many activists would mean 'likely bloodshed in Ayodhya' as well as a threat to the mosque. For this reason, the home ministry advocated that if a decision be taken to impose President's rule (the note was careful not to recommend it), it should be made well before 6 December. '[A] date prior to 24 November, 1992 may be considered.'

The note—which had never been made public before[33]—made clear that Rao effectively had only until 24 November 1992 to impose Central rule in UP. Any takeover after that date would imperil the mosque. The prime minister had just twenty days to decide.

Unlike Indira Gandhi, Narasimha Rao preferred to avoid violent confrontation. He had seen, up close, the disasters that sending troops to the Golden Temple and to Sri Lanka had proved. When he realized that he had a twenty-day window for taking control of the mosque, his first instinct was to consult and negotiate.

The Cabinet Committee on Political Affairs (CCPA) is the inner Cabinet, consisting of the prime minister, ministers from the top four ministries (home, external affairs, defence and finance) as well as senior officials. Rao immediately scheduled a meeting of the CCPA. He craftily invited the HRD minister Arjun Singh to join—so that he could not absolve himself of responsibility later.

At least five CCPA meetings were held that November. During these meetings, Rao repeatedly asked whether Article 356 could be legitimately invoked. In his memoirs, Madhav Godbole denies that there was any definite opinion voiced on Article 356 during discussions in the CCPA.[34] However, his version is contested by *two officials as well as one minister* who attended the meetings— but who do not want to be named. They remember distinctly the consensus articulated in the meetings: that Article 356 applied only when 'a situation has arisen', not when it is anticipated. Naresh Chandra, one of the few officials willing to speak on record, adds: 'The general feeling in government was that it would not be possible to justify recourse to Article 356 since it did not permit action in anticipation of a breakdown. All concerned, including P.C. Rao [the law secretary] shared this view.'

Arjun Singh later claimed that Rao dithered during those meetings, while he himself pushed for stronger action.[35] This is not supported by the minutes of the CCPA, where not a single minister— not Manmohan Singh, not Sharad Pawar, and certainly not Arjun Singh—demanded the only 'action' constitutionally permissible: the dismissal of the Kalyan Singh government. Since minutes of the meetings do not always capture all that was discussed, this key fact has also been confirmed in interviews with bureaucrats and a politician present. Naresh Chandra says, 'Members of the CCPA, while urging all steps to be taken to prevent damage to the building, did not propose or press on Rao for the imposition of the President's rule.'

The clearest evidence that Rao's Cabinet was unwilling to invoke Article 356 lies in the CCPA meetings around 20 November 1992. Narasimha Rao was not present, since he was travelling on an official visit to Senegal. One of the meetings was even held in the office of Arjun Singh. Godbole remembers the prime minister telling S.B. Chavan, Arjun Singh and Sharad Pawar that they could take a decision to impose Central rule in UP in his absence.[36] They chose not to do so. After the demolition of the mosque, Pranab

Mukherjee told complaining Congressmen, 'All of you were members of the Cabinet and some of you were members of the CCPA. All decisions were taken in the meetings of the Cabinet and CCPA. Responsibility is collective; the onus cannot only be on the prime minister or home minister.'[37]

The natural supporters of any bid to impose President's rule in UP should have been the left-leaning opposition: Janata Dal and the communist parties. The communists were resolutely anti-BJP. The Janata Dal, riven by factional feuds, was more complicated. They had accepted the support of the BJP at one time, but were now at daggers drawn. On 23 November 1992, Rao met the leaders of these secular parties during a meeting of the National Integration Council (the BJP boycotted it). The Janata Dal and communists could have declared President's rule justified in UP, given Kalyan Singh's untrustworthiness. They did not do so. Instead, pushing the decision on to Rao, the NIC unanimously backed the prime minister in his bid to protect the mosque.[38] The Left's Jyoti Basu later claimed that 'On our party's behalf we proposed that even Article 356 of the Constitution may be used if there is no other way to protect it [the mosque], though we have been opposing its use.'[39] Crucially, Basu did not provide a categorical declaration that, as there was no other way to protect the mosque, Article 356 was justified in the present circumstance.

With his Cabinet and the Opposition unwilling to make the decision for him, Rao turned to the Supreme Court. Kalyani Shankar says, 'Rao badly wanted the Court to hand over receivership'[40] of the mosque to the Central government. This legally elliptical manoeuvre would have given Rao control over the mosque without having to dismiss the Kalyan Singh government. The Supreme Court started hearings in late November. In the course of these hearings, Kalyan Singh—through his lawyers—swore to protect the mosque. The Supreme Court chose to believe him, and dismissed Rao's request for receivership.[41]

The intelligence bureau was Rao's own detective force—to keep tabs on his Cabinet colleagues, on his enemies, and even on Sonia Gandhi. It is no surprise then that he asked the IB to send him reports from Ayodhya. The IB sent two reports that November. The first claimed that the mosque was under threat, but stopped short of recommending President's rule. The second report, around early December, contained rumours that a VHP suicide squad was being trained to blow up the mosque on 6 December. This was an explosive claim, and the IB took great pains to stress that it was unverified. The lack of a clear message was typical of IB reports, a confidante of Rao says. 'All IB reports present both arguments. If the mosque fell, they would say we predicted. If it didn't, they would say we predicted.'

Yet another factor that played in Rao's mind was his relationship with the President of India, Shankar Dayal Sharma. As we saw in an earlier chapter, it was a relationship so poor that Rao's archives chronicle strained, even rude, letters between the two. Sharma resented the fact that Rao would avoid spending hours in consultation with him; Rao found the President to be long-winded and professorial—an irony given that Rao himself could devolve into abstruse verbiage. On a previous occasion, when Rao had wanted to dismiss a state governor, Sharma had simply refused to answer the phone.[42]

As per the Constitution, the Union Cabinet decision to dismiss the UP government would have to be approved by the President. Presidents are mostly paper tigers and have to eventually acquiesce to a Cabinet decision. But a President who sent back the recommendation for reconsideration—as Rao was afraid Sharma might—would have fuelled accusations that the Central government was acting against the Constitution.

A final justification Rao could have employed to dismiss Kalyan Singh was a report by the Uttar Pradesh governor advocating President's rule—something which Article 356 suggests. State governors are appointed by the Central government, and are usually not of independent mind. Unfortunately for Rao, the UP governor at the time, B. Satyanarayana Reddy, had been appointed by his predecessor V.P. Singh. He was not amenable to influence from the Centre. On 1 December 1992—five days before the kar seva—governor Reddy sent a letter recommending *against* Central rule. '[The] general law and order situation, especially on the communal front,' he wrote, 'is satisfactory.'[43]

Narasimha Rao realized he was being checkmated. Kalyan Singh had not made one false move through the whole of November. The Union Cabinet—including rivals Sharad Pawar and Arjun Singh—were worried about Kalyan Singh's intentions, but had stopped short of recommending his dismissal. The Supreme Court, the state governor and law ministry officials, all seemed against Central rule.

Were Rao to invoke Article 356, the Supreme Court may well have held the decision to be unconstitutional since law and order had not yet broken down. As Rao told P.V.R.K. Prasad, 'How could a democratically elected Government be dismissed as a precautionary measure without any valid reason? Would it be constitutional? Won't we attract the odium of having resorted to a blatantly unconstitutional act?'[44] The BJP would have cried Central tyranny and moved a no-confidence motion in Parliament—as they eventually did after 6 December. There was no certainty that the non-BJP opposition would back Rao, or that his own party would support him.

On the other hand, not imposing Central rule carried risks. There was a significant chance that Babri Masjid would fall on 6 December. Though Kalyan Singh had publicly and legally sworn to protect the mosque, he had previously shown he could not be trusted. If the mosque fell, Rao's government might fall too.

Faced with these two options—both of which carried political risks—Rao decided not to impose Central rule, even though Godbole repeatedly asked him to operationalize the contingency plan.[45] He decided, instead, to find a method to protect the mosque without imposing President's rule. That way, his government and the mosque would both remain standing. What he proceeded to do has never been revealed before. Before detailing this alternative strategy, however, it is important to grasp where Rao was coming from, and look through the lens that coloured his view of India.

Narasimha Rao was born into an observant Brahmin family. He came of political age fighting against the Muslim ruler of Hyderabad state, where he worked alongside the Hindu Mahasabha, Arya Samaj and the communists. His guru, Ramananda Tirtha, exemplified these contradictions: he was a Hindu swami, communist and Congressman—all rolled into one. Rao's entire life had been wrapped around morning pujas and yearly pilgrimages. In April 1991, two months before becoming prime minister, he had accepted the post of the religious head of a Hindu order in Courtallam. For some, this religious past opens Rao up to charges of being anti-Muslim.

There is no evidence for this accusation. It wasn't just Rao who worked with Hindu groups during the liberation of Hyderabad in 1948; so had the entire state Congress. More than any Indian prime minister, Rao had grown up around Islam and Muslims. He was well read in Koranic text, and could speak Urdu and Persian better than he could Sanskrit. 'There was no communalism in the man,' his Muslim foreign secretary Salman Haidar says. 'He was clean in heart.'[46]

The difference lay in his idea of secularism. As Haidar puts it, 'He was well aware of India's communality.'[47] Unlike the westernized Jawaharlal Nehru, Rao did not see India as a nation of individuals but as a federation of caste and religious groups.

Rao's Hindu self-identity also led him to a naïve portrait of the BJP. Rao had to fend off communists through his electoral career, never Hindu nationalists. On the other hand, Rao's rival within the Congress, Arjun Singh, had battled with (and lost to) the BJP in his home state of Madhya Pradesh. In his memoirs, Arjun Singh recalls lying in a hospital bed in Bhopal when he heard Advani's rath yatra pass by, its menacing slogans adding to his sense of siege.[48] Rao had never had this experience; he thought of the BJP as misguided Hindus rather than dangerous adversaries.

Rao was also blinded by personal chemistry. He was close to several BJP leaders, from Atal Bihari Vajpayee and Murli Manohar Joshi, to Bhairon Singh Shekhawat. The one leader Rao did not care for was L.K. Advani, at the time the BJP's most prominent voice. Advani had fled Sindh in Pakistan during the partition of India. Unlike Rao, Advani was not a practising Hindu. As humourless as Vajpayee was jovial, he was also more disciplined. Advani's organizational skills were almost solely responsible for the rapid rise of the BJP.

For Narasimha Rao, this rise represented less a visceral threat to secularism than a threat to the Hindu vote bank that had historically voted for the Congress. While he was worried that Muslims were leaving the Congress, he was equally concerned that the majority—upper- and backward-caste Hindus—were moving towards the BJP. 'If only minorities vote for the Congress, how can we win?' Rao said to a friend. In his book on Ayodhya, Rao blames Congressmen for a 'subconscious inhibition that any expression of [Hindu] religious sentiment on our part, even if we felt it strongly, would be seen as "non-secular". As a result, the BJP became the sole repository and protector of the Hindu religion in the public mind.'[49]

'You have to understand,' he once told an unconvinced Mani Shankar Aiyar, 'this is a Hindu country.'[50]

This belief in India's Hindu-ness as well as his own led Rao to his master stroke (or so, he thought) in protecting the mosque without imposing Central rule.

As Indira and Rajiv's chief negotiator with various dissident and separatist groups in the 1980s, Rao had specialized in backchannel talks, where pragmatic deals could be made away from the public glare. Starting in the middle of November 1992, prime minister Rao began similar backchannel talks with various Hindu groups, convincing them to protect the Babri mosque.

While these groups had a somewhat common agenda, they were distinct organizations with their own leaders. The BJP was the political face, while the RSS was a nominally apolitical organization, as were the Vishwa Hindu Parishad and Bajrang Dal. The Shiv Sena was an entirely separate political party. Besides, a profusion of religious sects and monasteries each had their own leaders. Narasimha Rao—scholar of Hinduism—was confident he could convince them all.

Rao had personal relations with a number of swamis, from the Sringeri Shankaracharya to the Pejawar Swami. In addition, he deployed the Tamil Nadu Congressman R. Kumaramangalam to reach out to gurus from south India,[51] while his astrologers N.K. Sharma and Chandraswami dealt with north Indian godmen. Rao's appointment diary shows that he frequently met with N.K. Sharma, for example at 9.30 a.m. on 2 November and 8.45 p.m. on 16 November.[52] Chandraswami remembers meeting Rao many times that November. 'I took the Shankaracharya to meet the PM . . . also Acharya Ram Vilas Vedanti.'[53]

In each of these meetings, Rao would press for an assurance that the Babri mosque would be unharmed. He would even break into Sanskrit and quote Hindu scriptures to make his point. A senior intelligence bureau official assisting Rao remembers being present. 'They were frauds, some of them,' he says. 'I told the PM that these are men of straw.'

'I am a Brahmin,' Rao replied to this official. 'I know how to deal with these people.'

Since Rao had studied in Nagpur, knew Marathi, and had represented nearby Ramtek in Parliament, he knew many RSS leaders. N.K. Sharma says, 'Most of the RSS leaders were Brahmins. They respected Rao who was also a Brahmin.'[54] Rao's old friend Madhukar Dattatraya 'Balasaheb' Deoras, was the head of the RSS. Rao spoke to him on the phone many times that November. He also met with the RSS leader (and Deoras's eventual successor) Rajendra Singh. Singh, known as 'Rajju bhaiya', was less in the thrall of the prime minister. N.K. Sharma says, 'Rajju bhaiya was a Thakur, so he was against Narasimha Rao.'[55]

Rao also negotiated in secret with the VHP, whose messianic leader Ashok Singhal was an architect of the Ayodhya movement. Singhal came from a wealthy family of Allahabad, and lived close to Jawaharlal Nehru's ancestral home. Their ideas of India, however, could not have been more different. Naresh Chandra recalls a meeting in 7 Race Course Road where Rao pressed Ashok Singhal to have more patience and not insist upon a showdown on 6 December. When Rao asked the BJP leader Bhairon Singh Shekhawat to speak to the VHP, Shekhawat confessed to Naresh Chandra that his efforts were not having much effect.[56]

Finally, Rao spent much of November 1992 in secret meetings with the leadership of the BJP. Since Rao's friend Vajpayee was less involved in the Ayodhya movement, Rao focused his attention on L.K. Advani—the party's organisation man. If anyone in the BJP could protect the mosque, Rao felt, it was Advani. He asked B. Raman, from the spy agency RAW, for a 'safe house' where he could meet Advani in secret.[57] Raman located a guest house that had been used by Rajiv Gandhi to meet the leadership of the Akali Dal right before Operation Blue Star in 1984.

On 18 November 1992, Rao met Advani for a secret conversation. In preparation for the meeting, the home ministry sent him a memo, asking Rao to clarify with Advani the 'plans for the resumption of Kar Seva at Ayodhya from 6.12.1992'. The memo asked that the BJP postpone either the kar seva until the Supreme Court resolved the feud, or issue a public statement saying that the proposed temple would not be built on the disputed land. Rao also met with Kalyan Singh that day, and once again the day after, on 19 November.[58] A week later, he met the entire BJP leadership at one go. P.V.R.K. Prasad remembers, 'Around November 25th, Advani, Vajpayee and Kalyan Singh visited house number five on Race Course Road. The meeting was top secret. I was in the room then. They assured him the mosque would be intact.'[59]

In parallel, the prime minister sought reassurance from Bhairon Singh Shekhawat, the chief minister of Rajasthan who had been representing the BJP during the negotiations with Muslim groups.[60] A courtly and courteous Rajput, Shekhawat prided himself as a man of his word. Rao and Shekhawat shared a medical doctor. On 2 December, this doctor walked into Rao's home and—within earshot of several others—said, '*Shekhawat sahib se baat ho gayi hai.* All is good.' Chandraswami too spoke with Shekhawat. 'He said nothing will happen to the mosque. Narasimha Rao believed him. Even I believed that the mosque will not be broken.'[61]

The contents of Rao's meetings—with a constellation of religious and political Hindu leaders —have remained undisclosed until now. They are not recorded in Rao's appointment diary. He did not even mention them in his book on Ayodhya, published after his death. However, the fact that at least some meetings between the prime minister and Hindu groups occurred in November 1992 has made it to the press. They have been interpreted as proof that Rao had, what the legal scholar A.G. Noorani calls, a tacit 'understanding' with the BJP.[62] The truth, unearthed here, reveals the opposite. Far from secretly conniving to demolish the mosque, Rao was, in fact, secretly conniving to protect it.

They also demonstrate his miscalculation. 'All these people who were consulted had a heightened sense of their importance. Rao misjudged that,' Naresh Chandra says.[63] 'The people who were really creating the problem were the Bajrang Dal and Shiv Sena,' a home ministry official adds. But these were the two groups that Rao did not reach out to, in the belief that they could be controlled by his friends in the BJP, RSS and to a lesser extent, the VHP. As Jairam Ramesh puts it, 'My own reading is that he overestimated his ability in dealing with these Hindu groups.'[64]

―

The 24 November deadline before which Central rule in UP could be imposed without damaging the mosque came and went. In the meantime, the crowd around the mosque had increased, from 500 on 25 November 1992 to 175,000 on 30 November and over two lakh by 5 December.[65] An army takeover at this point, in the midst of a hostile state government and crowd, would threaten human life as well as the mosque. The prime minister's options had severely reduced.

The sea of saffron-coloured humanity pouring into Ayodhya raised temperatures across the country. Though there was no violence as yet, mistrust between Hindus and Muslims in Uttar Pradesh began deepening. The UP Brahmin leader N.D. Tiwari told the young Muslim MP Salman Khurshid, 'You can't imagine somebody you could trust even months ago, ordinary Congressmen, now you can't trust them.'[66] When Salman Khurshid landed in Lucknow airport in early December, he remembers sensing helplessness. 'We were worried about communal violence.'[67]

In early December, a few days before 6 December, Arjun Singh travelled to Uttar Pradesh. He met with Kalyan Singh in Lucknow, and spoke on the phone to Rao describing the meeting. Arjun Singh says that Rao ordered him not to proceed to Ayodhya, which is why he returned to Delhi.[68] A senior Congressman from UP presents a different version. 'Arjun Singh didn't even want to go to Ayodhya. All he did when he met Kalyan Singh was to ask for security for a favourite [Muslim] politician of his from UP. He did not talk about Babri at all.'

On 3 December 1992, three days to go, Rao phoned Mani Shankar Aiyar, who had taken a sturdy stance on secularism.

Rao sounded upset, telling Aiyar, 'I've tried everything.' Aiyar replied, 'At this stage, let us please fly in all of Parliament into Faizabad airfield, hold a day-long public rally. Have this shown on television.' Rao suggested that Aiyar draft a speech. 'I gave it to him that day itself,' Aiyar says. 'He did not use it.'[69]

Around 4 December, two days to go, Rao wrote a little note to himself on the pros and cons of imposing President's rule. This was a clarification of his thoughts to his own self, and has remained untouched in his private archives since. The note, written in red ink and his small, neat script, is titled, 'reasons for and against trusting the government of uttar pradesh'.

In reasons for trusting, Rao wrote on the left column, 'CM gives assurance to NIC and SC' and 'Statements of local VHP leaders that kar seva will only be symbolic'.

In reasons against trusting Kalyan Singh, on the right column in the page, Rao put down, 'Kalyan Singh has consistently shown its disinclination to use force against religious leaders and kar sevaks', 'In his letter on november 17th, 1992, Kalyan Singh rejected central supervision over security forces', 'Intelligence report [that] mentioned, in passing, and using unconfirmed reports, that "balidani jathhas" were present in Ayodhya who were trained for the demolition of the structure', and 'Contra to state government assurance, MM Joshi and Advani increasing mobilisation for december 6th'.[70]

Narasimha Rao must have spent the day considering his note, then reconsidering it. On 5 December 1992, his schedule shows he had a normal day. He met with N.K. Sharma at 10 a.m. 'I had some information that the mosque might fall,' Sharma claims. 'I told the prime minister about threats to the mosque, and also the games that Arjun Singh was playing. I was keeping tabs on him.'[71] That evening, Rao met a close friend of his. The friend says, 'He talked about [Operation] Blue Star [when Indira Gandhi sent troops into the Golden Temple], saying that sending army into [a] religious place only made more problems.' The prime minister seemed withdrawn, the friend adds. At 7.30 p.m., Rao's diary shows that he met with 'Naresh Chandra etc'. Chandra confirms this. 'I met Rao along with [Cabinet secretary] Rajgopal and [IB chief V.G.] Vaidya. We spoke about the law and order situation. Godbole was a hard-working man. He had the [information] on his fingertips.'

'We had an assurance from Kalyan Singh,' Chandra adds. 'That was our misjudgement.'[72]

Rao returned home, where his cook Rajaiah made him a frugal meal in bungalow number three.[73] He then retired to his room, sat on his bed, laptop perched on his stomach, and punched away while strains of Hindustani music played in the background.

He went to sleep, having been convinced by the arguments on the left column of his note. He decided to trust Kalyan Singh.

On the morning of 6 December 1992, Rao met Dr Srinath Reddy. He also met with his astrologer. 'I cannot share what I said there,' N.K. Sharma says. Since it was a Sunday, Rao remained in his house in bungalow number three.

Meanwhile, at 9.30 a.m., Madhav Godbole spoke to the head of the Central paramilitary forces in Ayodhya, telling him that if the state government required his help he did not have to wait for formal orders from the Central government. This sequence of events is chronicled in a clandestine note that Godbole sent Rao after 6 December.[74] By 11.30 a.m., a large but peaceful crowd was being addressed by leaders of the BJP and VHP. Between 11.45 a.m. and 12 noon, the chief of police and administration for Ayodhya walked around the perimeter of the Babri Masjid. Everything was in order.

At about noon, a teenaged kar sevak jumped across the boundary and vaulted on top of the mosque dome.[75] He was not stopped by any one of the policemen present. That first kar sevak was joined by thousands of others, who began chipping away at the domes. There was a galaxy of BJP leaders present who had spent the past year whipping up passion on the issue. L.K. Advani made requests on the public address system for the kar sevaks to come down.[76] He was ignored.

Rao's home telephone began to ring. 'I called up Kumaramangalam immediately,' Jairam Ramesh remembers. 'Kumaramangalam said that Rao was not to be reached.' Another Congressman called up the PM's house. 'Khandekar picked up. He told me that the prime minister was in his room. He did not want to be disturbed.' Arjun Singh later claimed that he had tried to reach Rao at his house, but was told '. . . he has locked himself in his room and our directions are not to disturb him under any circumstances.'[77] Many other politicians called, none of whom could get through. This inability to reach Rao led to the rumour that the prime minister was sleeping while Babri was under attack. A senior journalist even claimed—on the basis of a conversation he claimed he had with a socialist politician who, in turn, claimed he had heard it from someone else, who, in turn, claimed he was witness to the fact—that Rao was doing puja when the mosque fell.[78] Is there truth to these allegations?

That Rao was sleeping is verifiably false. From 12.15 p.m., when the first dome was under attack, Rao was on the phone with several of his officials. Naresh Chandra and Madhav Godbole were both in the home secretary's office, monitoring developments. 'The prime minister was being informed on a regular basis,' Chandra says. The Cabinet secretary S. Rajgopal was also present.[79] In his memoirs, Godbole adds that during this time period, V.G. Vaidya had 'already spoken to the PM'.[80]

Around 2 p.m., Rao was joined by a host of officials. Two of them, P.V.R.K. Prasad and the law secretary, P.C. Rao, later gave a press conference confirming this. P.C. Rao even listed other officials who could vouch for the fact that Rao was awake and monitoring the situation.[81]

One might still wonder why Narasimha Rao refused to take calls from some politicians between 12 and 2 p.m.. Even though he was awake and on the phone with officials, why did he remain within his locked room?

A friend provides the answer. 'I was with him in the room throughout,' this person says. He was 'normal until 12 [noon]. As he saw [what was happening] on TV . . . for a few minutes he couldn't talk. He was not speaking. He trusted all those people very much.'

'After a few minutes,' this person says, 'he began calling. He called the DIB [director of the intelligence bureau, Vaidya], then [home minister] S.B. Chavan. He was not asleep at all.'

This testimony—along with the evidence of those whom Rao spoke to in those critical hours —is critical to disproving the myth of Nero playing the fiddle while Rome burnt. Why then has this friend of Rao not spoken in his defence?

'He promised me to keep it a secret. He made me swear.'

Rao was not the only one stunned by the attack on the Babri Masjid. 'It was like watching an India-Pakistan match' one senior official recalls. 'Of course, there is a chance that Pakistan will win. Obviously some people thought it [the demolition of the mosque] would happen. But that was guessing only. No one was sure.' Salman Khurshid adds, 'The destruction of the mosque came as a shock and a surprise. None of us were braced and ready for it.'[82]

As soon as the mosque was under attack, the Central government put pressure on Kalyan Singh to use the troops stationed nearby. These troops consisted of '35 companies of the PAC, 4 companies of CRPF . . . 15 tear gas squads, 15 police inspectors, 30 sub-inspectors, 2300 police constables . . .' apart from around 25,000 paramilitary forces nearby. These were all under the control of the district police chief and magistrate, who was 'acting on a direct, minute-to-minute control of the chief minister'.[83]

At around 2.30 p.m., three battalions of the Central paramilitary forces stationed outside Ayodhya marched towards the mosque. They were met by the magistrate, who asked them in writing to return. They turned back, since the Constitution was clear that Central forces could only act on orders of the state government. Meanwhile, in the words of the home ministry note: 'The commissioner had been contacted who had informed that the CM, U.P. had ordered that there will be no firing under any circumstances.' Kalyan Singh had even given an order in writing 'not to resort to firing under any circumstances'.[84]

Around this time, Rao left for the prime minister's office, where more politicians and officials joined him. It was here that Dr Srinath Reddy came to check up on Rao.

The Cabinet meeting was scheduled for 6 p.m., since Arjun Singh was travelling outside Delhi, and Rao wanted him to be part of any decision made. When the Cabinet met, 'No one could say anything. We were so shocked,' one minister remembers. 'Then [C.K] Jaffer Sharief [the senior-most Muslim leader] began to talk. He said what happened was terrible.' Many Congressmen were inclined to blame Rao. Nehru-Gandhi loyalist M.L. Fotedar shouted at the prime minister for failing to protect the mosque. Rao said little, but later told an aide, 'I will never sit with that man again.' A decision was taken to dismiss the UP government at 6.30 p.m.[85]

Almost simultaneous to the Cabinet meeting, at 6.45 p.m., Kalyan Singh announced his resignation as chief minister of UP.[86] At 7 p.m., Rao's diary shows, he met with 'Sh. Shahabuddin and Others'. By this time, riots had broken out across India. Thousands of Muslims flocked to Delhi's historic Jama Masjid for the evening prayers, worried that the sun was setting on the India they knew. The Shahi Imam of the Jama Masjid called for Muslims to react peacefully, adding, 'It is a major tragedy. Our hearts are broken.'[87]

THE FALL OF BABRI MASJID

That night, Rao gave an emergency broadcast to the nation.[88] 'I am speaking to you this evening under the grave threat that has been posed to the institutions, principles and ideals on which the constitutional structure of our republic has been built.' He added, 'What has happened today in Ayodhya where the Babri Masjid has been demolished, is a matter of great shame and concern for all Indians . . . I would like to say very clearly that we shall no longer suffer the Machiavellian tactics of the communal forces in this country.' He blamed the Kalyan Singh government, 'which has totally failed in its primary duty, to which they had pledged themselves time and again, to protect the structure'.

'I appeal to you,' he ended, 'to maintain calm, peace and harmony at this grave moment of crisis.'[89]

At 9 p.m., the President of India signed the proclamation for Central rule in UP. At 10 p.m., Rao went to meet him at Rashtrapati Bhavan to apprise him of the situation.[90] The Central forces had yet to take over the Babri Masjid complex. It was only the next morning, 7 December 1992, that they entered the complex. They faced no resistance. The kar sevaks, delirious with success, were receding. They were leaving behind the pickaxed ruins of Indian secularism.

As if to make up for lost time, Rao swung into action on 7 December. He met a series of Muslims leaders—who were all furious at his inability to protect the mosque.[91] On 8 December, his appointment diary shows, he met the 'Naib Imam, Jamma Masjid + 8'.[92] Two days after, the Rao government banned the RSS, VHP and Bajrang Dal, declaring them as 'unlawful' organizations.

There was pressure on Rao to rebuild the mosque on the same spot. In another error of judgement,[93] he decided not to. But he was not the only one who thought so. The minister of defence, Sharad Pawar, sent Rao a private memo on 12 December, cautioning against building the mosque on the same place. 'If the masjid is rebuilt at the same site . . . [the] issue is likely to be exploited again and again for spearheading mass movements. In such a situation the minority community will have to continuously face insecurity and tension.'[94]

On 15 December, Narasimha Rao dismissed the state governments of three BJP-ruled states in north India: Madhya Pradesh, Rajasthan and Himachal Pradesh. The ostensible reason was that the chief ministers of all three states were members of the just-banned RSS.[95] Newspapers criticized the move, with the *Times of India* calling it an 'overreaction', and the *Hindustan Times* terming it a 'political blunder'.[96] These dismissals were challenged in the Supreme Court. The court held that secularism was part of the basic structure of the Constitution, and states that violated secularism could be lawfully dismissed under Article 356. The court, however, laid out a new, higher, standard of scrutiny which the invocation of Article 356 would be subject to, in effect limiting the Centre's discretion to dismiss a state government.[97] Had this new, tougher, standard been applied to a hypothetical decision of Rao's to remove Kalyan Singh before 6 December, the Supreme Court may well have held it to be unconstitutional.

On 16 December 1992, Rao set up the Justice Liberhan Commission to inquire into the demolition. The Liberhan Commission would submit its report a staggering eighteen years later—exonerating Rao but detailing a planned conspiracy involving L.K. Advani, M.M. Joshi and other BJP and VHP leaders.[98]

As we examined in an earlier chapter, the BJP brought a no-confidence motion against the Rao government the next day. The prime minister ensured that his nemesis Arjun Singh was tasked with defending him in Parliament. When Rao's chance came to speak, his self-defence was that he had trusted the word of Kalyan Singh, and that Article 356 did not allow him to dismiss a state government 'in anticipation' of law and order breaking down.[99]

The BJP's no-confidence motion failed, with the secular opposition supporting Rao's government. Rao soon reshuffled his Cabinet, bringing in more loyalists and dropping Fotedar.

A man who nurtured grievances, Rao felt betrayed by the Hindu saints and politicians. He was convinced that Advani knew of the conspiracy and had lied to him. When Arjun Singh, N.D. Tiwari and others in the Congress began openly criticizing Rao, an aide told the prime minister he should take action. Rao replied, 'After what Advani has done to me, what can Arjun Singh do?'

On 24 October 1994, the Supreme Court passed judgment on the 6 December case. It found no fault with the prime minister, pinning the blame entirely on the Kalyan Singh government. By then the rest of the Congress was publicly rallying around Rao, even as Arjun Singh and others were being sidelined. A rare exception was Mani Shankar Aiyar, the public school-educated Congressman with a penchant for British wit. Critical of Rao's failure to protect the mosque, Aiyar quipped, 'Death is not a precondition for rigour mortis.'[100] This comment reached Rao. Aiyar was never taken into government.

While Arjun Singh had publicly supported the prime minister right after 6 December, he was privately manoeuvring. In February 1993, the government tabled a 'white paper' in Parliament on the events of 6 December. Naresh Chandra, who wrote the report, says, 'The finalization of the paper had posed difficulties because Arjun Singh kept suggesting changes that had the potential to unnecessarily embarrass the prime minister.' When Arjun Singh, Natwar Singh, N.D. Tiwari and others later began criticizing Rao's leadership, they brought up his failure to protect the mosque as evidence that Rao was communal.

This accusation got a fillip after 1998 when Sonia Gandhi joined the Congress. As we saw in the last chapter, many of those whom Rao had sidelined or foisted hawala cases on had by then returned to the party. Blaming Narasimha Rao for Babri Masjid killed two birds with one stone. Sonia's Congress could escape blame, which would allow it to reach out to the Muslims who had left the party. And Rao, who posed a threat to the Nehru-Gandhi legacy, would stand discredited. Gradually, the belief took hold within the party that Rao had wanted to destroy the mosque. 'Every Congressmen believes that Rao and Jiten Prasada, Brahmins both, plotted,' Jairam Ramesh says.[101] Salman Khurshid remembers: 'There was a time when saying pro-Rao [statements] was a problem. If I said it in my constituency I would be accused of being pro-demolition.'[102] Rahul Gandhi even publicly claimed that 'Had the Gandhi family been there in politics [in 1992], Babri Masjid demolition would not have taken place.'[103]

In 2002, anti-Muslim violence broke out in Gujarat. The violence killed around 1272 people, most of whom were Muslim. The police and state officials looked on, in some cases aiding the mobs. This was eerily similar to the UP government's actions a decade earlier. Fingers were pointed at the BJP chief minister of Gujarat, Narendra Modi, since the Constitution vested in him power over the police and administration. The prime minister at the time was Atal Bihari Vajpayee. He could have either imposed President's rule or dismissed Modi using intra-party mechanisms. He did neither. Yet, unlike Narasimha Rao, Vajpayee is rarely blamed. The central question of the Gujarat riots has never been the culpability of the prime minister.

In 2014, the website Cobrapost did a sting operation on several BJP and VHP leaders at the frontlines of the demolition. They reported that these leaders spoke of a well-planned conspiracy[104] and 'openly acknowledge' Rao's supportive role.[105] These leaders did not claim to have spoken to Rao, and the website provided no corroborative evidence. The allegations were not, however, rebutted. The demolition of Babri Masjid has become the principal taint on Narasimha Rao's legacy.

THE FALL OF BABRI MASJID

Meanwhile, Kalyan Singh was awarded a day's imprisonment for deceiving the Supreme Court. He was later re-elected as chief minister of Uttar Pradesh, and in 2014, became governor of Rajasthan—a constitutional gift for a man who had so blithely disregarded the Constitution. L.K. Advani rose to become deputy prime minister, but never became king. Arjun Singh returned to the Congress, and served as human resource development minister from 2004 to 2009—the same ministry he had held under Rao. Singh died in 2011, his dream of becoming prime minister unfulfilled.

The Allahabad high court passed judgment on the original title dispute in 2010. It declared that the Babri mosque was built above a Hindu temple, and that the God Ram was indeed born on that exact spot. The court ordered that the disputed land be divided three ways, with a portion each to two Hindu and one Muslim group.[106] The order was soon stayed by the Supreme Court. As of 2016, the matter drags on in the courts, mosque destroyed, temple unbuilt.

There is no question that Rao made the wrong decision on Babri Masjid. He should have imposed President's rule between 1 November and 24 November 1992. This decision would have been constitutionally suspect and politically fraught. The Supreme Court might have held the move illegal; the BJP would surely have brought a no-confidence motion in Parliament, Rao's rivals in the Congress would have blamed him, and the prime minister might have lost his job. But it was a risk that should have been taken. The fall of Babri Masjid was an event that shook the foundations of independent India like few others. Many Indians woke up to a different country on 7 December, and still blame the prime minister of the day. History has judged Narasimha Rao harshly.

But this is a judgement made with the benefit of hindsight, after knowing how events unfolded on 6 December. Knowing only what Rao did *before* 6 December, what can we fairly accuse him of?

To accuse him of plotting the demolition is a lie, and will remain one until contrary evidence emerges—which it has not in the twenty-four years since. Not only is there no hard proof that Rao aided the conspiracy, there is plenty to indicate that he tried to protect the mosque through secret talks with Hindu leaders.

To accuse Rao of indecision is also untrue. As we saw on the economy, Narasimha Rao could speedily make up his mind if he felt the right decision also made for good politics. In the lead-up to 6 December, all options carried political risks. Faced with such difficult choices, Rao *did* decide. By mid-November 1992, Rao had weighed the pros and cons and decided that he would not take over Uttar Pradesh. He did this because no one was willing to take a stand and push for Central rule—not his Cabinet colleagues in the Congress, not his law officers, not the state governor, not even the Supreme Court. For Rao to impose Central rule in these conditions would have risked the stability of his own government. Even Pranab Mukherjee—who is critical of Rao's handling of the Babri Masjid episode in some respects—says that Rao faced a 'Hobson's choice', since the decision to dismiss Kalyan Singh might not have been backed by Parliament, where the Congress was in a minority.[107] As Rao himself put it, 'The centre's plight was that of a person whose child has been abducted by the enemy.'[108] He therefore decided to protect the mosque by securing secret deals with an array of Hindutva groups. On the night of 5 December, he went to sleep believing he had protected the mosque without the political risk of invoking Article 356.

What then can Rao be legitimately criticized for?

His error was that, against the judgement of his officials (and, it must be admitted, Arjun Singh), Rao reposed his faith in members of the VHP, BJP, RSS and sundry Hindu gurus. To be

THE FALL OF BABRI MASJID

fair to Rao, he began these informal talks only when he realized he had few formal options. But he should have known that people like L.K. Advani were either in on the conspiracy (as the Liberhan Commission says they were) or were riding a tiger they could not control. For a statesman with a preternatural instinct for his own weaknesses, Rao's overconfidence in his ability to convince Hindu groups must go down as a serious failure of judgement.

Rao's desperation to protect his own minority government also clouded his instincts. Salman Khurshid says, 'The tragedy about Rao sahib is that his attempt to do consensus building is what destroyed him.'[109] This 'consensus building' was driven by Narasimha Rao's interest in appeasing both the Hindu as well as Muslim vote bank, instead of a single-minded focus on protecting the mosque. Rao wanted to protect the mosque *and* protect Hindu sentiments *and* protect himself. He ended up with the mosque destroyed, Hindus unattracted to the Congress, and his own reputation in tatters.

How grave has this error proved for India? It led to the killing of many innocents, mainly Muslims, in the riots that followed. It also symbolized for many the passing of Nehruvian secularism.

But that demise was not caused by the destruction of a disused mosque, symbolic and symptomatic though that may have been. It stemmed from the rise of the BJP. As long as the mosque stood, the BJP could play on the Hindu humiliation they claimed it symbolized, and rise from a party with two seats in 1984 to 120 seats in 1991. Ironically, the end of the mosque also ended its deployment as a campaign issue. In the national elections held in 1996, the BJP did not campaign on building a temple in Ayodhya, nor has it done so in any subsequent election. As Salman Khurshid argues, 'If you look at it in a tragic way, with the destruction of Babri Masjid, the mobilizing potential of the BJP reduced. I think the intensity or passion against the structure ended.'[110]

The demolition of the mosque was also not the reason for the Congress's decline in north India. The party had already lost the

Muslim vote in Uttar Pradesh by 1989 and the Hindu vote by 1991. Though the demolition angered Muslims, it did not change voting patterns in India.

In the final analysis, therefore, the enduring political victim of the Babri demolition was Narasimha Rao himself. Some of this was his doing, much of it deliberate defamation by his own party. As Narasimha Rao put it so presciently in his book on the events of 6 December, '. . . those responsible for the vandalism had got not only the Babri Masjid demolished, but along with the Babri Masjid it was me whom they were trying to demolish.'[111]

13

Look East, Look West

When it came to both the Babri Masjid and the economy, Narasimha Rao had inherited an inbox from hell. When he became the PM in June 1991, Kalyan Singh had just been elected UP chief minister, and India had foreign exchange reserves for just two weeks' worth of imports.[1] Rao faced intense political scrutiny on these two issues. Opposition parties and his own Congress had ideological stakes on the economy and Babri Masjid, and this limited Rao's ability to find solutions. It is under these weighty political constraints that Rao made the right call on the economy and the wrong one on 6 December.

Foreign policy was the other noxious bequest the prime minister inherited. But unlike with the economy and Babri Masjid, international affairs resonated less in domestic politics. To be sure, Israel would always be seen through the lens of the Muslim voter, and the Left would resent any chumminess with the United States. But there were plenty of hidden corners for Rao and his diplomats to play their games.

The world was the one stage where Narasimha Rao could write his own script.

For much of India's independence, the world was divided into two armed camps: the United States and the Soviet Union. India had taken sides in the Cold War, with the Soviet Union supplying it with armaments, ideology, as well as a veto in the United Nations. When Narasimha Rao became prime minister, however, revolutions in the Soviet Union were tearing at India's safety net in the world. An added problem was that the balance of payments crisis required loans and investments from the United States, a country previously on the other side of the Berlin Wall. Even India's neighbourhood looked uncertain. China—with whom India shared a long border and had fought a war—had spent the last decade refashioning itself into an economic powerhouse. India's mortal enemy, Pakistan, was both sponsoring terrorism in the Kashmir valley as well as alleging human rights abuse in global fora. The countries of East Asia, whom Jawaharlal Nehru had termed 'Coca Cola governments',[2] had since entered the First World, shattering Indian pretensions of Third World leadership. And the sands of the Middle East were shifting westward, leaving India in no man's land.

The idealism and liberal internationalism that had powered Nehruvian foreign policy was no more in tune with India's diminished role on the world stage. Bound by its own licence raj, India's foreign relations were in need of liberalization.

Unlike in the case of the economy, Narasimha Rao was himself an expert on international affairs. He had been foreign minister in the 1980s under both Indira Gandhi and Rajiv. Of the ten languages he knew well, three were foreign: Spanish, Persian and of course, English. Rao's personal library included books by the international relations theorist Henry Kissinger, as well as essays by Samuel Huntington and Zbigniew Brzezinski.[3] He would painstakingly mark important passages. On his overseas trips as foreign minister, he would spend the day in meetings and evenings roaming the streets unescorted. 'Before you go to a country,' he lectured his grandson Shravan, 'you should read about it fully.'[4]

LOOK EAST, LOOK WEST

Like with the economy, the realization that its foreign policy needed a new orientation had come to India a while back. Prime minister Rajiv Gandhi, especially, had reached out to the United States, China, and Israel.[5] But these were baby steps, more changes in attitude than reorientation of policy. Rao needed to convert these blueprints into concrete buildings.

Prime minister Rao's first months on foreign affairs were as decisive as his economic management. He appointed J.N. Dixit—a South Asia expert—as foreign secretary. The diplomat Salman Haidar, who would become foreign secretary in 1995, noticed more confidence in Rao. 'As foreign minister, he was not the sort of person who could make people walk with fear. As prime minister, he demonstrated a very different kind of authority.'[6] His choice of foreign minister, the politically busy Madhav Sinh Solanki, meant that it was the prime minister's office that called the shots.

The traditional approach to Indian diplomacy was posting career bureaucrats from the IFS as ambassadors to other countries. These IFS officers were polished and diligent, but were trained in a Nehruvian past that was ill-suited to a changing world. Rao wanted to signal a new approach. He thought of sending the movie star Dilip Kumar as Indian ambassador to the Bollywood-crazy Soviet Union, cricketer Tiger Pataudi to London, music conductor Zubin Mehta to the US, and the businessman Russi Mody to Germany. J.N. Dixit protested that only professional diplomats could do justice to these sensitive posts. Dixit won the argument, but not before Rao told him, 'Zubin Mehta would be able to get an appointment with [the CEO of General Electric] Jack Welch not only for me but for himself.'[7]

To convey that economic diplomacy was to be his priority, Rao's first overseas visit, in late 1991, was to Germany, the economic engine of Europe. Ramu Damodaran remembers: 'Before going, Rao read all the briefs given to him . . . he planned for it six weeks in advance.'[8] Once in Germany, Rao made sure to extoll the virtues of investing in India—something almost no prime minister had done before. A businessman in the audience remarked that Rao's style 'reminded us of a corporate chief executive'.[9]

He also met with Indologists, a pattern that would mark his other visits abroad. Two decades earlier, during his visit to the University of Wisconsin in the United States, Rao was struck by how out of tune western scholars of India were.[10] 'As these countries opened up to India,' Ramu Damodaran says, 'their governments would first reach out to the India experts in their universities. Rao wanted to make sure they had an updated impression.'[11]

In another pattern that the prime minister was to set, he took his cook with him. As we saw in an earlier chapter, the scrawny, bare-footed Rajaiah was from Rao's ancestral village of Vangara and had benefitted from chief minister Rao's land reforms in 1973. He would cook a simple meal of rice, dal, curry, chutney and sambar for Rao in his hotel room.[12] Home-cooked dinner over, Rao would then grace the official banquet, where he would feast on fruits, nuts and the occasional desert.[13]

Narasimha Rao's German visit took place amidst chaos in the Soviet Union. In August 1991, there had been a coup attempt against the reformist Mikhail Gorbachev. Rao had a phone conversation with him on 23 August 1991. The prime minister began by saying, 'Mr President, with God's grace and the will of the Soviet people, you have with your inimitable courage and confidence faced the ordeal of the past seventy-two hours.' Rao went on to assure Gorbachev that India stood by him against the 'elements in the USSR that could act so rashly and so diametrically opposed to the will of the Soviet people'.[14]

Rao had misjudged the 'will of the Soviet people'. In December 1991, the Soviet Union was formally dissolved. India's defence contracts were now spread between a variety of nations, from Russia to Belarus to Ukraine. As the Indian ambassador to the Soviet Union put it with classic understatement, 'Things have changed a great deal. We are learning to change too.'[15]

The end of the Soviet Union made it agonizingly clear that India needed to renew its relationship with the sole remaining superpower: the United States of America. It was a relationship mired in decades of mistrust and missed calls. India's new outlook needed to be broadcast to America. Rao decided to relay it through the Middle East.

~

India had historically supported the Palestinian quest for nationhood, and refused full diplomatic relations with Israel. There were three reasons for this: the need for Arab oil; fear of the Muslim vote bank within India; and an anti-colonial ideology that opposed white settlements on brown land. In 1986, Rajiv Gandhi had asked his favoured diplomat Ronen Sen to list a series of steps culminating in full diplomatic relations with Israel.[16] But so distracted was Rajiv by corruption allegations after 1987 that economic and foreign policy reforms lost momentum. 'Rajiv was worried about the Muslim vote,' says an official close to him. 'My assessment was that associating the Palestinian issue with concerns of only Indian Muslims was wrong,' Ronen Sen counters. 'The assumption that Indian Muslims are not as concerned with the national interest as other citizens are is untrue.'[17]

Now in 1991, prime minister Rao realized that the road to Washington, D.C., ran through Tel Aviv. Krishnan Srinivasan, eventually Rao's foreign secretary in 1994, says, 'I think he felt he could never get a good relationship with the US going while he did not have a diplomatic relationship with Israel.'[18]

Rao's chance came in December 1991, the same month that the Soviet Union was dissolved. The United States wanted an earlier resolution in the United Nations, equating Zionism with racism, to be rescinded. Rao grasped the significance of the vote. He sought advice from retired diplomats— 'old warhorses', he called them.[19] They all counselled that India should establish diplomatic relations with Israel. Narasimha Rao also asked a senior official from the intelligence bureau: 'What would be the impact on Muslims [if India opens up to Israel]?' 'It would have no impact,' the official replied.

Rao instructed his diplomats to vote in favour of the resolution. The United States noticed.

That very month, Narasimha Rao invited the chairman of the Palestine Liberation Organization (PLO), Yasser Arafat, for a state visit. Rao sensed that Arafat was on a weak wicket. His support for Saddam Hussein had left him isolated even within the Middle East.[20]

Narasimha Rao prepared in advance for Arafat's visit. Just how much is evident from his archives, where there are four drafts of his speech welcoming Arafat, each heavily pencilled by Rao. His final speech began with flattery: 'The man we honour today needs no introduction. He has become a legend in his lifetime and a household name not only in the Arab world but in my country, and, indeed, the world over.' The speech goes on to demand that 'Israel withdraw from all occupied territories.'

When Arafat came in January 1992, Rao welcomed him with a bear hug. That photograph—of a smiling Rao embracing an Arafat clad in olive-green military suit, and black-and-white keffiyeh—was plastered all over the Indian press. India was not abandoning an old friend.

In private, however, Rao told Arafat that India could only put pressure on the Israelis if it had an ambassador in Tel Aviv. Arafat, a man as wily as Rao was, grasped the subtext. At a press conference in Delhi, he said, '[The] exchange of ambassadors and recognition are acts of sovereignty on which I cannot interfere . . . I respect any choice of the Indian government.'[21]

LOOK EAST, LOOK WEST

On 29 January 1992, India announced full diplomatic relations with Israel. The exultant headline of the *Jerusalem Post* announced, 'India joins the World'.[22]

Rao moved to douse domestic fires. On 22 March 1992, he got up in Parliament and used Nehru to justify his decision, just as he had done for his liberalization policies. 'When we talk of recognising Israel, I do not know what the honourable members really mean. Because we have recognised Israel long time ago when Panditji was alive. What we have now done is to have diplomatic relations. We have a Consulate already in Bombay.'[23]

In order to balance his outreach to Israel, Rao decided to pay an official visit to Iran.[24] India also needed Iranian help in combating Pakistan on Kashmir, and clearing the debris in the Muslim world from the Babri Masjid demolition. Worried that opposition parties would attack him for this, Rao sent the diplomat M.K. Bhadrakumar to brief the BJP leader L.K. Advani. Given their bitterness over Babri Masjid, this showed dispassion and pragmatism on the prime minister's part. Advani rose to the occasion. He listened carefully before saying, 'I wish all success for the PM's visit to Iran.'[25]

Ties between Israel and India have strengthened much since Narasimha Rao's time. In 2012, defence contracts alone were worth nine billion dollars a year.[26] India no longer automatically votes against Israel in the United Nations. That this friendship has been able to flower without affecting India's relationship with the Iranians and Arabs owes much to Rao's efforts to disguise change in the garb of continuity.

~

With economic liberalization at home, foreign capital was now officially allowed into India. But convincing sceptical countries and corporates required more than a rule change. It required economic diplomacy. This had almost never been attempted before. Indian diplomats were used to either pontificating about Third World solidarity in the United Nations or petitioning the West for wheat and dollar loans. They had little experience selling the economy to private investors abroad.

A few months after he took over power, Rao sent a note to all Indian missions, asking them to promote India as an investment destination. On foreign visits—including to Germany and Iran—Rao took with him a planeload of businessmen. 'Tarun Das and CII especially, were well liked in government circles. He was often on the plane,' Krishnan Srinivasan remembers. 'These businessmen could access top politicians from that country in a way they could not do otherwise.'[27]

The most visible example of Rao's economic diplomacy was his two visits to the World Economic Forum in Davos. As we saw in the chapter on growing the economy, these visits were the first by an Indian prime minister. Though politicians abound, Davos is famous for hosting money men from around the globe. As Rao put it in a speech in February 1992, 'I have come here not so much to make a speech, but to know and learn something at this Economic Mecca. I am told that just about everyone who is anyone in the world of business and industry is here. This is a sort of pilgrimage for me. You don't go and lecture on a pilgrimage.'[28]

During these visits, Rao—who lacked the handshaking and backslapping routine of a Bill Clinton—was nonetheless able to convey that he meant business; as of 2015, international trade accounted for more than 40 per cent of Indian GDP.[29] 'He was not a person interested in a personal legacy,' Ronen Sen remembers.[30] He said that when it came to the integration of the [Indian] economy to global markets, he would be judged by results.'

In 1993, Narasimha Rao prepared to travel across the border—3500 kilometres of it.[31] The boundary with China had been demarcated by the British in 1914, and India took that line to be non-negotiable. The Chinese had never accepted the value of the British line, and this difference of opinion led to border hostilities in 1962. India had been pounded in the war, and relations had since chilled.

When prime minister Rajiv Gandhi decided to break the ice and visit China in 1988, his foreign minister Narasimha Rao had concerns, but soon fell in line. Rajiv established three working groups with the Chinese: on the boundary dispute; technology; and the economy.[32] But it was the sheer optics of the visit that improved ties. The then director of the intelligence bureau, M.K. Narayanan, says, 'There is no denying the fact that the Rajiv Gandhi visit created a major change.'[33]

Narasimha Rao had been part of the Indian delegation to Beijing in 1988. As foreign minister once before in the early 1980s, he had watched Deng mouthing Mao while moving towards the market. Rao had learnt from this doublespeak and was looking forward to finally meeting his idol. But—as we saw in an earlier chapter—Rajiv chose not to take either his foreign minister or foreign secretary with him to meet Deng. He only took along two relatively junior officials, one of them being Ronen Sen. 'Rao was very, very hurt,' a bureaucrat present remembers. 'He felt he had been slighted.'

In December 1991, soon after Rao became prime minister, Chinese premier Li Peng had visited India. In preparation for the visit, a former Indian ambassador to China had sent Rao a 'personal note on India China relations'. The note sketched out the personality of Li Peng, ending with 'Multi-party democracy, political pluralism, human-rights of a western kind, social permissiveness among youth etc. are all anathema to him'.[34] Rao underlined that sentence, as he did the conclusion of the note: 'He is still the man with whom we must do business at least for a little more time to come.'

So nuanced is global diplomacy that most prime ministers defer to their mandarins. Not Rao. In the note, the former ambassador had recommended that 'India and China could cooperate for South Asian prosperity. Why not think of Joint Sino-Indian projects in Nepal and Bangladesh.' On the margins, in precise, slanted handwriting, Rao wrote: 'On the other hand, this will only tend to enhance Chinese influence in these countries to our detriment. The ganging up of our neighbours against us will get a shot in the arm. This may not be tried just now.'

Two years after Li Peng's visit, Rao returned the favour. When he travelled to China in September 1993, he spoke to President Ziang Zemin of civilizational links.[35] As the diplomat Prabhakar Menon (at the time a joint secretary in the PMO) put it, 'Rao felt that India and China were bound by deeper, philosophical ties more than by a grocery list of things to sell and buy.'[36] The highlight of the visit was the signing of the 'Agreement on the Maintenance of Peace and Tranquillity along the . . . India-China Border Areas'. The pact created a separate mechanism to resolve the dispute, while laying out a series of measures—such as reducing troop movement on the border—designed to defuse tensions.[37]

The agreement was classic Rao. Faced with a border dispute that seemed irreconcilable, Rao isolated it from other aspects of the Indo-China relationship. This logic has worked well. Trade relations have boomed while, as Ronen Sen says, 'Factually, China is the most peaceful border we have with any country, thanks to Rao.'[38] 'I do think the peace and tranquillity agreement is a landmark,' M.K. Narayanan agrees. 'You can keep arguing [about the border] while delinking it from the rest.'[39]

While the trip was a diplomatic triumph for Rao, it was a personal failure. Rao wanted to meet Deng, something that Rajiv had denied him in 1988. Deng had by now retired from active politics. He declined to meet with the visiting Indian prime minister. The gossip was that Deng would have agreed to meet someone from the Nehru-Gandhi family.[40] Rao was not considered worthy enough.

Narasimha Rao's Air India One took off from Beijing airport on 9 September 1993. It headed east, to South Korea. Salman Haidar was in charge of the trip. He remembers: 'India was slow in reacting to the countries east of China. We were clouded by China.'[41]

I had heard the phrase, 'Go West, Young Man,' Haidar says. 'I coined the term "Look East".'

Rao became the first Indian prime minister to travel to Korea. In the 1950s and '60s, the newly decolonized countries of South Korea, Indonesia, Thailand, Singapore and Malaysia were poor and weak. Nehruvian India, large and democratic, was the leader of the post-colonial world. Indian foreign policy towards East Asia had been a mix of unfamiliarity as well as paternal pomposity. In 1967, when these countries grouped together to form ASEAN, they excitedly invited India to join. India had refused. By the 1980s however, these 'Coca Cola governments' had several times the per capita income of India, boasted soaring education and health standards, and were able to project global influence. Narasimha Rao's daughter Vani travelled with him to Korea as first lady. She remembers her father asking, 'This is such a small country. Why are they able to have such roads? Why can't we do that? The basic thing is education. We are behind by thirty years.'[42]

On 10 September 1993, at a banquet hosted by the Korean President in Seoul, Rao played travelling salesman. 'The Indian economy is the second largest in the developing world. Its 250-million strong middle class provides a market for manufactured goods which is potentially among the largest in the world . . . We would welcome more Korean businesses to come to India . . .'[43] He met with Korean business families. The head of the chaebol Daewoo was particularly keen to chat with Rao. They met in Seoul and within a few weeks again in Delhi. Daewoo cars were soon being driven on Indian roads.[44]

Rao visited Bangkok in that same year and met with a swathe of leaders, including Buddhist monks and corporate titans. He even had a two-hour session with the revered king,[45] the right tactic given the king's influence over Thai politics. As he got off his plane, a journalist watching through the window called Rao 'Ninja Turtle'. 'He purses his lips, walks with a slight stoop, has a back that brushes off everything, listens to a guru, walks fast and hits hard without seeming to.'[46]

The turtle visited another Asian tiger in 1994. Singapore was considered the gateway to East Asia, and in Tarun Das's words, 'an important listening post for multinationals'.[47] Rao began the visit routinely, giving a typical speech with Lee Kuan Yew in the audience. But he sparkled in the question-answer session.[48] When asked about the Indian economy, Rao—in mock humility—pointed to Montek Singh Ahluwalia and Lee Kuan Yew, and said that there were many Oxbridge intellectuals on stage who were better equipped to answer. The evening's most memorable moment was when the Pakistani high commissioner, present in the audience, asked Rao a brusque question on Kashmir.[49] Rao did not condescend to reply, telling the high commissioner that he was wrong, and the Indian high commissioner to Singapore (i.e. his counterpart) would give him a fitting reply. His answer was greeted with applause from the partisan audience.

Lee Kuan Yew, an astute judge of leadership, said that he had rarely been so delighted and impressed by a foreign leader.[50] But it is to his successor Goh Chok Tong that the credit for furthering Indo-Singapore relations goes.[51] As Congress leader Jairam Ramesh puts it, 'India can look East all it wants. But the East also has to look back. Goh played a critical role in that.'[52]

When India began to liberalize in 1991, the US and Europe were expected to provide the much-needed capital for industrialization. Rao's 'Look East' policy led countries like Singapore, Malaysia and Korea to provide money, cars, and expertise to the Indian economy. As of 2015, Singapore was the top destination for foreign direct investment entering India.[53]

It was not just this capital that Rao found in East Asia; it was also an alternative economic model. East Asian growth had been based not on free-market policies, but on what the Princeton political scientist Atul Kohli calls 'state-directed capitalism', i.e. the government assisting big business houses to achieve growth.[54] Rao—who had been a fervent believer in the redemptive power of the state for much of his career—was instinctively attracted to this aspect of the model.

He was less attracted to another facet. On a visit to Indonesia, Rao sent his secretary, P.V.R.K. Prasad, to have a vegetarian lunch with Mohan Lal Mittal, father of steel baron Lakshmi Mittal. Mittal told Prasad, 'In these countries, we have an understanding with the political boss, and everything falls in line. In India, just because the PM is saying something, does not mean the rest will agree.' When Prasad relayed this gripe back to the prime minister, Rao shrugged. 'This is the price of democracy.'[55]

Of all the foreign policy hurdles that Rao faced, the tallest was unquestionably Pakistan. This was not unique to his premiership. As he said to Parliament a few months after he became prime minister, 'Every time there is a change either in Pakistan or India, there is a sense of euphoria created, some new hopes are aroused. But subsequently these hopes are dashed to the ground. My own experience during the last three months has been more or less the same.'[56]

Rao's solution was to keep the conversation flowing while never taking Pakistan at its word. As Ramu Damodaran says, 'On Pakistan, Rao felt that one-on-one talks were critical. He always persisted. Despite his deep cynicism that anything can happen.'[57] Narasimha Rao met his Pakistani counterpart, Nawaz Sharif, six times in his first two years in office. He even met the Pakistani President and conversed in chaste Urdu.[58] Little was achieved, but the finest Urdu speaker in all of the Nizam's Hyderabad was probably the better of the two.

One such set of seemingly pointless conversations almost led to a breakthrough. Siachen is the world's highest, most inhospitable battlefield—a freezing glacier along the Line of Control. It has little military value. But so low is the trust between these two countries, that between 1984 and 2014, 2700 Indian and Pakistani troops died trying to secure the glacier. India pays the heavier cost, around a million dollars a day. One former military officer estimates that this amount could have been used instead to provide clean water and electricity to half the country.[59]

Between 2 and 6 November 1992, the sixth round of talks on the Siachen Glacier was held in New Delhi. The Indian side was led by N.N. Vohra, the defence secretary, who would eventually become governor of Jammu and Kashmir. In the draft agreement, Pakistan agreed to India's demand to mark the existing positions—in India's favour—before recording demilitarization. In N.N. Vohra's words, 'We had finalised the text of an agreement . . . by around 10 pm on the last day . . . . Signing was set for 10 am [the next day].'[60]

Through the negotiations, Narasimha Rao's office on Raisina Hill was crowded with olive-green military uniforms and dark lounge suits. When the room cleared for a break, Rao remained seated on his desk, pondering alone. When his joint secretary, the diplomat Prabhakar Menon, entered to get a file cleared, Rao looked up and said, 'This is serious. Tell them to be absolutely sure.'[61]

Rao decided to walk away. He was aware that concessions to Pakistan could be exploited by the opposition BJP. Rao's gut also told him that 'Pakistan were pulling a fast one.'[62] N.N. Vohra remembers, '. . . later that night, instructions were given to me not to go ahead the next day . . .'[63]

There have been many attempts since to reach a deal on Siachen, but with no success. India continues to bleed money and personnel. In 1999, Pakistan did to another part of Kashmir what Rao was afraid they would do to Siachen. Pakistani troops took control of the uninhabited Kargil mountains on the Indian side of the Line of Control. India had to go to war to wrest back the territory. Rao's instinct—that the Pakistanis could not be trusted to keep their side of any bargain—turned out to be true.

Matters with Pakistan flared up again two years later. Pakistan had exploited popular resentment against the rigged Kashmir state elections of 1987 to fuel unrest, mainly by training militants and sending them across the border. The increase in terrorist violence—and the ensuing human rights abuses by the Indian Army—gave Pakistan the excuse to corner India in various international fora. In the spring of 1994, Pakistan sponsored a resolution on Kashmir at the UN Commission on Human Rights in Geneva. Had the resolution gone in Pakistan's favour, political parties would have pilloried Rao for presiding over India's international disgrace.

Rao decided to send a heavyweight delegation to Geneva: his minister of state for external affairs, Salman Khurshid; and the BJP's Atal Bihari Vajpayee. 'It was Rao's decision to send Atal Bihari Vajpayee,' Salman Khurshid says. He speculates that Rao might have asked Bhuvanesh Chaturvedi—who was close to Vajpayee—to convey the message. 'And to his credit, Vajpayee agreed.'[64]

Just before the vote in March 1994, the Indian foreign secretary, Krishnan Srinivasan, estimated that seven countries would side with India and four with Pakistan, with the rest abstaining. Srinivasan remembers that 'Narasimha Rao became very shaky.' 'Was there some other way out?' he asked. Running a minority government, Rao was terrified that a loss in Geneva would result in his loss in Delhi. When Srinivasan assured him that the numbers were on the Indian side, 'he looked dubious, but mercifully allowed matters to take their own course'.[65]

Srinivasan's estimate turned out to be accurate. Afraid that they would lose, Pakistan took back its resolution. *India Today* magazine put on its cover a jubilant Atal Bihari Vajpayee hugging

Salman Khurshid.⁶⁶ When the Muslim Congressman and Hindu BJP-wallah returned to Delhi airport, they were greeted by a cheering crowd.

At the end of that very month, March 1994, a summit of the G-15 developing countries was held in Hyderabad House—the Nizam's Delhi palace which had since become the state guest house of the prime minister. More than a dozen heads of state and foreign ministers shared ideas about the ways of the world. It was boring, even by the standards of these summits. Two Indian journalists were invited for the post-summit banquet. They were Sanjaya Baru, now with the *Times of India*, and the *Hindustan Times*'s Kalyani Shankar. Rao had also invited Atal Bihari Vajpayee, his friend and political rival, to express gratitude for Geneva.

After the day-long session, just before the banquet, the guests were shepherded into a long anteroom for a glass of sherbet and *kokum* juice—since the prim Indians had decided not to serve alcohol. Sanjaya Baru, formally dressed, entered this anteroom and surveyed the scene.⁶⁷ At one end of the room, Rao and other world leaders sat drinking kokum juice.

At the other, journalists and officials formed a congregation. Baru moved towards this group, only to see Kalyani Shankar in animated conversation with Atal Bihari Vajpayee. He joined the two of them, but his eyes continued to scan the room. He noticed the prime minister of India staring at them.

The prime minister then got up, and made his way towards them. He walked towards Vajpayee, still in animated discussion with Kalyani Shankar, and put his arm on Vajpayee's shoulder. '*Kya ho raha hai?*' Rao asked in a mock-gruff manner. ('What is happening?')

Vajpayee replied, to ensuing laughter, 'Nothing for you to worry about.'

Two months after, in May 1994, Narasimha Rao journeyed to the United States. He had first travelled to the U.S. in 1974—also his first trip abroad—to visit his daughter Saraswathi. As we saw in an early chapter on his years in exile, that trip had exposed the Andhra socialist to the virtues of American capitalism.

At the time, India and the United States were on opposite sides of the Cold War divide. India was close to the Soviet Union, while Pakistan had gravitated to the United States. By the 1980s, however, Indian foreign policy was taking baby steps towards the US.[68] Now, as prime minister, Narasimha Rao was determined to leap forward. In anticipation of his visit, the *New York Times* gushingly described Rao as the 'Deng Xiaoping of India'.[69]

Krishnan Srinivasan remembers that Rao 'was unsure of himself, [and] perhaps felt inadequate to handle President Clinton'.[70] Srinivasan describes the core conundrum for Rao: '[He] had to steer a deft course between nationalist aspirations in the security field and the need to keep the USA in friendly and positive play.'[71]

Narasimha Rao flew to Washington, D.C., on board Air India One. He took along the AIIMS cardiologist Srinath Reddy. Reddy remembers watching Rao prepare on the plane. 'He was like a nervous student when he went to US. He would write and rewrite and correct his speeches in the plane. He was eager to impress. The cool aplomb that he had was missing. This was different from even other foreign visits.'[72]

Rao was scheduled for a fifteen-minute meeting with US President Bill Clinton. He read the official briefs, and deeming them inadequate, scribbled his own notes in red ink.[73] Rao was worried that Clinton, with a famously low attention span, was not a good listener.

There are varying versions of the actual meeting. Krishnan Srinivasan was 'reliably told' that Rao played the didactic intellectual, giving Clinton a windy and boring philosophical monologue.[74] There is some evidence for this. Clinton was strangely quiet after the talks. Photographs taken immediately after, show both looking pensive. Rao's son Rajeshwara, however, has an upbeat interpretation. 'When he went to meet Bill Clinton, [the] appointment was given only for fifteen minutes. But he came out in one and half hours. [Clinton] became fan of father.'[75]

Narasimha Rao was keen to meet CEOs of top American companies. He asked the Indian embassy in Washington to fix appointments. But the embassy, used to four decades of shunning capitalists, did not have the contacts. Rao turned to a man with even more connections in the US than his own diplomats. The tantrik Chandraswami had a network of American devotees, from CEOs to senators. Rao's secretary—and conduit to the corporate world—P.V.R.K. Prasad remembers Chandraswami putting up an impressive performance in arranging meetings.[76] Rao was able to sell India one-on-one to a host of corporates.

As a young man, Rao had dreamt of an academic career at Oxford. During his earlier visits to the US, he would vicariously live that dream, touring universities and debating with the academics Ralph Buultjens at New York University and Velcheru Narayana Rao at Wisconsin. Now visiting as prime minister, Rao spoke at Harvard University. He asked America to move beyond the Berlin Wall. 'The days of celebrating the demise of a system are over . . . But Cold War attitudes persist.'[77] He also laid out his economic vision. 'We have now assigned a large portion of infrastructure investment to private enterprise on a global scale, while the government takes on the bulk of the responsibility for investment in human resources, as also for rural development in general.'[78]

Rao returned home to a cool reception. The media complained that Rao had come back with nothing concrete. They had missed the point of the trip: to introduce predictable routine into a historically fraught relationship. His focus on trade made it clear that Rao expected a long-term relationship, as did the symbolism of inviting Bill Clinton to be the chief guest for the next Republic

Day parade in Delhi. While that President declined, another US President finally agreed, in 2015, to sit for hours in pouring rain as camels and cannons were paraded on Rajpath. It is a measure of how far the relationship has come.

Two months after his trip to the United States, Rao travelled West again, this time to Russia. The diplomats who organized the trip insist the timing was coincidental. It was surely propitious, then, that the great balancer was visiting Moscow so soon after Washington, D.C.

At the top of his agenda was defence. By late 1991, chaos in the former Soviet Union made spare parts and product support for the Indian Army hard to come by.[79] So seriously did Narasimha Rao take this that he appointed Ronen Sen, a relatively junior diplomat, as ambassador to Russia.[80]

Sen had served before in Moscow at a lower rank. He had a background in defence, had worked in the Atomic Energy Commission (AEC), and had been involved in the early stages of India's nuclear programme. Sen was also close to Rao. He had kept him company in April 1991 when Rajiv Gandhi had denied Rao a Lok Sabha ticket. Rao and Ronen Sen would engage in long discussions on Russian writers—the romantic poet Alexander Pushkin being a Rao favourite. Sen also placed an undiplomatic emphasis on action and delivery, making him the ideal man to 'fix' India's problems with the Russians. By the time Rao visited Moscow in 1994, India's supply chain was oiled, and Rao was able to sign new agreements. The former head of the Defence Research and Development Organization (DRDO), Dr V.S. Arunachalam, accompanied him to Moscow. Arunachalam remembers the prime minister asking him, 'How does the MIG 29 [plane] versus Mirage 2000 work?'[81]

Even as Rao emphasized defence ties, he was sending a deeper message. He told his officials, 'Never forget what the Indo-Soviet relationship was like, and how much we gained from it. We should never be ungrateful. You don't forget friends when they are less powerful or less influential or anything like that. You have to stand by them.'[82]

Rao's balancing act extended not just between the US and Russia, but also within the old Soviet Union. He was quick to accord diplomatic recognition to the new countries of Eastern Europe. As of 2015, India is one of the few countries with vibrant links to the United States, Russia, as well as Eastern Europe.

Rao's realistic assessment of shifting power was evident in his outreach to the US, Israel and East Asia. The border agreement with China showed a prime minister who had learnt—perhaps from his own domestic weakness—to set aside unresolvable conflicts and focus on common interests. This pragmatism was also visible in Rao's simultaneous suspicion of Pakistani intentions while keeping the conversation flowing.

Indian foreign policy since Rao has continued to move away from Nehruvian idealism to a more 'realist' and 'pragmatic' pursuit of national self-interest. India increasingly sees itself as a rising power that must shape its external environment rather than a non-aligned country seeking mere strategic autonomy within the international system.[83] These realist ideas were first visible in the 1980s. But—like with the economy—it was Rao who translated them into actual policy.

Rao did not advertise these policies as anything new. As a politically weak prime minister, he strategically—shall we say, pragmatically—defended them as mere extensions of Nehruvian idealism.[84] In retirement, Rao met the strategic affairs expert C. Raja Mohan on several occasions. Raja Mohan was at the time writing a book on the 'realpolitik' shift in Indian foreign relations since the 1990s. 'How are you saying all this?' Rao asked him.[85]

He did not want his foreign policy to be seen as a break from the past.

There is a sense in which he was right. Rao ensured that in making new friends, India did not abandon old ones. 'What was important to Rao was to demonstrate continuity,' Salman Haidar says. 'Of course it was conscious.'[86]

Rao also strived for bipartisanship. He reached out to the BJP's L.K. Advani before his visit to Iran, and sent Vajpayee to battle Pakistan in Geneva. The usually reticent prime minister also took care to brief Parliament on his foreign visits. This statesmanship has contributed to the political consensus on international relations since his tenure. As Raja Mohan says, 'After Rao, every possible ideological combination has held power in Delhi. Yet there has been broad continuity in foreign policy.'[87]

Narasimha Rao knew more about international relations than many diplomats, certainly more than most Indian politicians. In his archives is correspondence with various scholars abroad. Prime among them was Ralph Buultjens, from New York University. In an undated handwritten letter, Buultjens wrote, 'I enclose a review of Brzezinski's new book—The Grand Chessboard . . . I am sending the book itself to Kalyani [Shankar], who will give it to you.'[88]

This independent knowledge of international affairs taught Narasimha Rao to parlay on equal terms with his diplomats—his note exchange with the former ambassador to China about Li Peng being just one example. If Rao's success with the economy (something he knew nothing about before becoming prime minister) can be attributed to raw instinct, his success on foreign policy was due to cultivated expertise.

Rao's foreign travels were notable for the cultivation of both businessmen and Indologists. In that sense, he was a pioneer in economic as well as cultural diplomacy. At times, though, he misread his audience. 'Rao was a bit unpredictable,' Krishnan Srinivasan says. 'He could give long lectures to foreigners, with a historical or philosophical basis. Sometimes they were not appreciated.'[89]

The country that Rao inherited had a foreign policy nearing a crisis. India emerged from the Rao years with new global alliances as well as economic muscle. The one remaining hurdle to improved status in the world was India's pursuit of nuclear weapons. With the end of the Soviet Union, there was renewed pressure on India to cap its nuclear programme. In need of western support for his economic reforms, Rao could not disregard this pressure. Nor would national security compulsions allow him to abandon nuclear weapons. How Narasimha Rao navigated these contradictions is central to India's place in the world today.

14

Going Nuclear

Two days after Narasimha Rao's body was cremated in 2004, an emotional Atal Bihari Vajpayee paid his old friend a startling tribute. Rao was 'true father' of India's nuclear programme. Vajpayee said that, in May 1996, a few days after he had succeeded Rao as prime minister, 'Rao told me that the bomb was ready. I only exploded it.'[1]

'Saamagri tayyar hai,' Rao had said. ('The ingredients are ready.') 'You can go ahead.'

The conventional narrative at the time was that prime minister Rao had wanted to test nuclear weapons in December 1995. The Americans had caught on, and Rao had dithered—as was his wont. Three years later, prime minister Atal Bihari Vajpayee fulfilled his party's campaign promise by ordering five nuclear tests below the shimmering sands of Rajasthan.

Vajpayee's revelations unsettled this narrative with new questions.

How closely was Rao involved in India's nuclear programme? What prompted his decision to test in December 1995? Why did he change his mind? Was it US pressure or something altogether more mysterious? Why did he pass on the baton to Vajpayee six months later?

The journalist Shekhar Gupta asked Rao these questions months before he died. The former prime minister patted his belly. '*Arrey, bhai,* let some secrets go with me to my *chita* [funeral pyre].'²

These secrets are so delicate that this chapter avoids the footnoting and source attribution present in other parts of the book. It also takes a cautious view of what might impact national security, exercising restraint while letting the reader into the missile silos and underground bunkers of India's nuclear programme. Here, for the first time, are the secrets that Rao kept within his belly.

A credible nuclear deterrent requires two ingredients: nuclear technology to build atomic bombs and missiles (or aircraft) to deliver it to the enemy. In India, the Atomic Energy Commission (AEC) was tasked with developing nuclear technology, while the Defence Research Development Organization was charged with missile building.

Through most of the early years, India's research focus was on using nuclear energy from uranium and plutonium for civilian electricity, not for military weapons. This research was shrouded in secrecy, with the AEC and DRDO reporting only to the prime minister of the day. The lack of transparency, the Princeton physicist M.V. Ramana argues, created a civil nuclear energy programme that was wasteful and unable to fulfil India's electricity needs.³ It did, however, create indigenous capability to refine the plutonium into 'weapons-grade'—the essential ingredient for an atomic bomb.

This became evident on 18 May 1974 when prime minister Indira Gandhi authorized the testing of a nuclear fission device in the deserts of Pokhran in the western state of Rajasthan. Great care was taken to classify the test as a 'peaceful nuclear explosion' for civilian energy purposes only. What lent plausibility to this claim was that the detonated bomb was mammoth and unwieldy, and India did not have the missiles or aircraft to deliver the bomb to enemy targets.

This strategic ambivalence—of having nuclear technology without a deliverable weapon—continued through the 1970s and '80s. The 1974 test had triggered some western sanctions, and the Indian political establishment felt the heavier sanctions that overt nuclear weaponization would attract could damage the economy. Meanwhile, the team of scientists running India's nuclear programme discreetly worked on a smaller bomb, one that could be launched by missile or plane. In 1989, these scientists felt that the time had come to put bomb, missile and plane together to make India a nuclear weapons state.

They met prime minister Rajiv Gandhi, by then a lame duck hobbled by corruption charges. The meeting was attended by DRDO chief V.S. Arunachalam, a gaunt man who spoke in careful whispers. No log was kept of the meeting. When Arunachalam told Rajiv what the scientists wanted, the prime minister gave them permission to go ahead with weaponization. 'But I have to be informed. Every step you have to inform and seek approval.'

The land of the Mahatma had decided to pursue a nuclear deterrent.

As the scientists queued out of his office on Raisina Hill, Rajiv Gandhi mulled over the fact that the entire programme was being run by scientists. Since politicians would come and go, Rajiv wanted a civilian bureaucrat to permanently monitor the programme.

After conferring with Arunachalam, Rajiv called for the defence secretary, Naresh Chandra, who was sworn to secrecy. 'The thing about Naresh,' a colleague remembers, 'is that he knows how to keep his mouth shut.'

The nuclear weapons committee—so secret that no official record of it exists—would eventually consist of Naresh Chandra as chairman and A.P.J. Abdul Kalam as member secretary. The other members were V.S. Arunachalam, P.K. Iyengar and R. Chidambaram from the AEC, and the nuclear technologists Anil Kakodkar and K. Santhanam. K. Subrahmanyam—the doyen of Indian strategic experts—advised from the outside. The diplomat Ronen Sen had counselled Rajiv Gandhi on nuclear issues; he would continue to independently confer with the prime minister of the day.

Sen would go on to become one of the architects of the Indo-US nuclear deal as ambassador to the United States in 2005. So discreet was he that the then US national security advisor, Stephen Hadley, famously—and possibly apocryphally—described Ronen Sen to President George W. Bush as a 'bikini'. 'What he conceals is more important than what he reveals.'

What was remarkable about the nuclear weapons committee was that, except for Chandra, it was run almost completely by scientists. As a former nuclear official put it, 'One thing we learned is never to allow the military or the bureaucrats to have a role in the nuclear programme.'[4]

There were also no politicians involved. 'No one on the political level should know,' Rajiv had insisted.[5] The members of the nuclear weapons committee were bothered by this. They suggested two other politicians they wanted told. One was the President of India, R. Venkataraman. The other politician they wanted informed had spent nearly a decade as a Union minister. As defence minister in 1985, he had worked closely with Arunachalam. In the words of K. Subrahmanyam, he had previously been 'among the few in the decision-making loop on nuclear weapons'.[6] He was then foreign minister of India. His name was P.V. Narasimha Rao.

It was thus providential, what Machiavelli called *'fortuna'*, that when Rao became prime minister in 1991, he was one of the few politicians who knew of the existence of the nuclear weapons programme. Had any of his competitors—N.D. Tiwari, Arjun Singh or Sharad Pawar—become prime minister instead, the programme might well have taken a different turn.

Rao became prime minister at a time when India's policy of strategic ambivalence on its nuclear capability was under threat.

On the one hand, the Pakistanis were pursuing their own weapon, with help from the Chinese. Arunachalam estimated in 1991 that Pakistan had the capability to produce ten atomic bombs.[7] The BJP's hawkish president Murli Manohar Joshi declared that India 'must waste no time to go nuclear'.[8] Narasimha Rao, running a minority government, could ill afford to ignore the BJP's bluster.

On the other hand, changes in the global disarmament regime were narrowing India's options. In January 1992, the United Nations Security Council recognized the threat that the proliferation of nuclear weapons constituted to international peace and security.[9] The Non-Proliferation Treaty (NPT) of 1970 had allowed the US, China, Russia, UK, and France to keep their weapons; all other countries (including India) were banned from possessing them. India had resisted this treaty for decades, alleging that it legitimized 'nuclear apartheid'. But with the collapse of the Soviet Union and end of the Cold War, the United States renewed efforts to limit the spread of nuclear weapons—the one threat to its unipolar hegemony. Rao could not disregard this American pressure to cap India's nuclear programme. His economic reforms hinged on working with the US, and the collapse of the Soviet Union had weakened India's global alliances.

Narasimha Rao thus became leader at a time when India was being egged on to test nuclear weapons as well as being browbeaten into giving them up. The prime minister needed to be both ferocious as well as conciliatory. He needed to be half a lion.

A few days after he became prime minister, Rao's appointment diary shows that he met with Arunachalam.[10] 'The prime minister asked me some technical details,' Arunachalam remembers.

'I gave him a page of drawings, a sketch. He immediately read and understood, saying aloud, "So this is where the reaction takes place."'

Arunachalam told Rao that the bomb was ready for testing. But India was in the midst of a financial crisis, and Rao counselled patience, saying, 'We should wait for the economy to improve.'[11] Rao also understood that while India had the technology to detonate the bomb, its delivery systems were still in infancy. India was far from being a nuclear weapons state in 1991.[12] Time and funds were in short supply.

A few days later, Rao spoke to his Cabinet secretary who, fortuna again, happened to be the chairman of the nuclear weapons committee.

Naresh Chandra approached Manmohan Singh. The finance minister had just devalued the rupee, and was busy preparing for the 24 July 1991 budget—the most important of his life. Manmohan had earlier served as the finance member of the Atomic Energy Commission and had a low opinion of the commission's financial discipline.[13] Chandra asked Singh for additional funds under an innocuous budget category. 'What is it for?' Manmohan Singh asked.

'I don't think you want to know.'

As the nuclear programme progressed, Naresh Chandra would take 'black' flights out of Delhi to various 'black' nuclear sites so that he could give an independent report to Narasimha Rao on what the scientists were doing. Air traffic controllers were banned from recording these flight details. Chandra would be met on the tarmac by an unmarked car and driven directly to nuclear sites. He would scale down long shafts to inspect silos of weapons-grade plutonium. Technicians on site would joke that it was no easy task for a man of Chandra's girth to shimmy his way down a narrow hole.

Meanwhile, Narasimha Rao, along with Manmohan Singh, focused on economic growth. India would pursue nuclear deterrence, he decided, but would do so covertly without antagonizing the world. The Indian public shared its leader's contradictory strategy. An opinion poll of the period showed that 50 per cent of those surveyed 'would like India to sign the NPT', but 81 per cent 'would like India to develop nuclear weapons for defence purpose'.[14]

In 1992, Arunachalam decide to leave the DRDO for an academic position in the United States. 'Is he going there for his children to study?' Rao asked an official. 'If that is the case, I will help him out.' The official replied, 'That is not the reason. He has done the job for eleven years. He is tired.'[15]

Arunachalam was succeeded as head of the DRDO by A.P.J. Abdul Kalam. A Tamil Muslim from Rameswaram with a fondness for Carnatic music, Kalam had no PhD, nor was he a nuclear physicist. But he understood rockets and was easy to work with. His childlike enthusiasm, beaming from underneath white sheets of badly cut hair, made him a natural magnet for politician and technician alike.

There was soon a change of guard in the AEC, with the long-time head, P.K. Iyengar, being replaced by R. Chidambaram.[16] Chidambaram was a geeky, thick-glassed nuclear scientist, content to focus on the science while Kalam was absorbed with the delivery technology. While Chidambaram worked on producing a smaller nuclear weapon as well as the hydrogen bomb, the DRDO under Kalam made progress on building ballistic missiles that could carry nuclear warheads.

Rao was constantly consulted. One DRDO scientist says, 'The usual criticism [of Rao] was "analysis till paralysis". But I didn't find that. He would sit and analyse with me. Once we reached a decision . . . he would go through [with it].'

In February 1993, the Prithvi-1 missile was successfully test launched.[17] It was designed to carry a nuclear load to Islamabad and other Pakistani cities. Ronen Sen says, 'We had previously tested our nuclear [technology]. In 1993, we tested our ability to deliver. This is the day India became a nuclear power.'[18]

The Prithvi-1 tests were followed by the successful Agni missile tests of February 1994.[19] The Agni missile had a longer range than Prithvi-1. India was now confident that it could deliver nuclear weapons to both Pakistan as well as parts of China.

1994 was also the year India tested a delivery system of a different kind. In the mid-1980s, India had bought Mirage-2000 planes from France (as defence minister, Rao had overseen the final acquisition). In May 1994—twenty years after India's first nuclear test—a Mirage plane was fitted with a bomb—'slightly longer than two adult arms stretched out'.[20] This was a nuclear weapon, with the core and explosives charge inside, but without the plutonium. The plane flew to Balasore (India's missile test site) in Orissa and successfully dropped the bomb on a designated target.[21] India could now launch nuclear weapons by missile as well as from air.

The DRDO prepared to deploy the Prithvi missile within units of the Indian Army. The United States protested. In order to buy time, Rao delayed deployment until after his visit to the United States in May 1994. Rao was keen to talk economics for the entirety of that trip. But President Bill Clinton brought up the nuclear programme and demanded that India sign the NPT. Rao reiterated the official line: India would not sign any agreement that allowed some countries to keep their weapons. A month later, Rao ordered Prithvi missiles to be deployed into the Indian Army.

India's global isolation on nuclear matters continued. In May 1995, over India's loud objections, the NPT was extended in perpetuity. Discussions had also begun on a Comprehensive Test Ban Treaty (CTBT)—aimed at preventing *all* countries from carrying out nuclear tests. Unlike the NPT, the CTBT was superficially egalitarian: it did not contain any special privileges for the five nuclear states. But these five countries had already conducted close to 2000 nuclear tests,[22] and were confident of the reliability of their deterrent. The real effect of the treaty would be to prevent India and other countries from testing and becoming nuclear weapons states.

More than any other trigger, the extension of the NPT regime coupled with talks on the CTBT told India that time was running out. Added to this was wariness at China's nuclear tests and intelligence reports that it was providing Pakistan with nuclear-capable rockets.

Prime minister Rao had so far balanced the pursuit of nuclear weapons with the need to avoid antagonizing the West. This bluff was now being called. The man who had decided not to take a decision on nuclear weapons was being forced to make up his mind.

On 18 September 1995, four months after the NPT extension, Bill Clinton sent Narasimha Rao a letter. 'I understand that on some key elements of the Treaty your delegation . . . has taken positions different from ours . . . I ask that you give your negotiators the flexibility on those issues.'

Rao refused to respond to this harrying. A month later, he travelled to Cartagena in Columbia for a summit of the Non-Aligned Movement. There he complained of a nuclear oligarchy dictating terms to others.[23]

Immediately on his return to New Delhi, Rao sent a telling note to Naresh Chandra, R. Chidambaram, A.P.J. Abdul Kalam and other members of the nuclear weapons committee. He asked them to work on the assumption that their activities would be under surveillance from American satellites. The existence of this note has been confirmed by multiple sources. The 'activities' in question could only be one thing.

A few weeks later, in early November, the DAE and the DRDO sent a note to the prime minister. It was for the 'prime minister's eyes only'—the highest possible security level. The note discussed the pros and cons of the resumption of nuclear tests. It provided a clear recommendation: that India conduct two to three tests in Pokhran between December 1995 and February 1996. It ended by listing a process by which Rao's explicit approval would be sought at four different points: T-30 (thirty days prior to testing), T-7, T-3, and finally T-1 (one day before testing). At T-7, the bomb would be placed in an L-shaped shaft at Pokhran. Seven days later, India would be a nuclear weapons state.

Soon after the prime minister's eyes scanned this note, he began a series of actions indicating where his mind was headed. His appointment diary indicates that Rao spoke in person to Abdul Kalam. He also spoke to Ronen Sen—then ambassador to Moscow and previously Rajiv Gandhi's confidant on nuclear issues.

The diplomat Prabhakar Menon was at the time a joint secretary in the PMO. Rao—via his principal secretary Amar Nath Varma—asked Menon and another diplomat, Sujata Mehta, to provide a top-secret assessment on what the international response to a test would be.[24] Menon remembers, 'Within the PMO, the feeling was that if the decision was taken to test . . . we would be able to face the consequences, given our reserves.'[25]

Rao even asked the finance ministry—through his Cabinet secretary—what the economic consequences would be. 'We did say the international reaction would be very negative,' the then finance secretary Montek Singh Ahluwalia remembers. 'The [Indian] economy which had recovered from the crisis was still not very strong.'[26]

In end November, 'T-21', Naresh Chandra was ordered to fly to Delhi. Chandra had since retired from the bureaucracy and had been made governor of Gujarat. But such was his importance to the nuclear programme that he continued as its chairman. An encrypted red phone had been installed in his mansion in Gandhinagar so that Abdul Kalam or Narasimha Rao could reach him immediately.

A few days after that, in early December, Naresh Chandra made an official visit to a plasma physics institute in north India. K. Santhanam and Abdul Kalam 'happened' to be present. Making use of this coincidence, the three of them moved to a room that had luckily been soundproofed. Here they discussed, in hushed voices, the preparations under way in Pokhran. The tests were for a conventional atomic or nuclear fission bomb. While R. Chidambaram and his team at the AEC were also working on a hydrogen bomb—a more powerful fusion device that could flatten entire cities—it was still six months away from completion.

On 30 November 1995, Abdul Kalam wrote to the prime minister—again for his eyes only—criticizing the international non-proliferation regime, particularly the CTBT. He suggested to Rao that India test nuclear weapons while the CTBT was being negotiated and while China and France were still testing. India could then declare itself a nuclear weapons state and sign the CTBT in that capacity.

Around 12 December, Naresh Chandra rushed to Delhi. Rao had given his consent at T-7 and the bomb was being lowered into the L-shaped hole by a division of the army that did not exist on paper. The division had been trained to constantly dig around the area so that when this day arrived, satellites would not pick up anything different. Even so, one member of the secret committee wonders (and this person insists on calling it mere speculation): was the digging around the L-shaped hole a little more than necessary?

On the morning of 15 December 1995, the *New York Times* ran a sensational story. 'In recent weeks, spy satellites have recorded scientific and technical activity at the Pok[h]ran test site in the Rajasthan desert.'[27] The story quoted US government officials telling *The Times* that American intelligence experts suspected India was preparing for its first nuclear test since 1974.

A few days after the leaked story, the American ambassador to India, Frank Wisner, sought a meeting with Rao's principal secretary, Amar Nath Varma. Wisner walked into the PMO carrying photographs taken from American satellites.[28] Varma told Wisner he had no idea what he was talking about. He asked Wisner if he could keep the photographs and show them to the scientists. Wisner quickly hugged the photographs. 'These are part of my body,' he is reported to have angrily said. 'The only way you can take the photographs is if you take me along.'[29]

On 19 December 1995—the day the nuclear tests had been originally scheduled—the Indian foreign minister Pranab Mukherjee (who was not in the loop on the nuclear tests) was asked by Rao to make a statement of denial. The Americans were not satisfied. That same day, the President of the United States, Bill Clinton, sent a message to New Delhi. He wanted to speak to the prime minister. Narasimha Rao asked his closest nuclear confidant to prep him on possible questions from Clinton.

The call came in the morning to Rao's office in the PMO, sometime around 21 December. 'I want to tell you about progress in the CTBT negotiations,' Clinton began. After speaking in generalities for a couple of minutes, Clinton moved sideways. 'We are happy to note a clear statement by your foreign minister that the government of India is not testing.' Rao replied as planned, 'I saw the press clippings too. They are false.' 'But Mr Prime Minister,' Clinton interjected, 'what is this that our cameras have picked up?' Rao replied, again as planned. 'This is only a routine maintenance of facilities.' Rao then added, slowly, so that Clinton could understand him through his Indian accent.

'There is right now no plan to explode. But yes, we are ready. We have the capability.'

The nuclear tests should have been conducted on 19 December. It is not known when Rao stopped it—at T-3 or T-1. But here the matter rested until a few days after the Clinton phone call.

On 25 December 1995, a secret letter was delivered to Rao asking him to delay testing for four weeks, to keep the US at bay. It went on to suggest that by early February 1996, India should conduct two to three nuclear tests. The note ended by quoting K. Subrahmanyam: 'India's voice on nuclear disarmament is not heeded because it is like an elderly spinster espousing the virtues of chastity.'

Narasimha Rao ordered the bomb to be removed from the L-shaped shaft. Yet—contrary to the public narrative—he was far from done.

On 14 January 1996, Abdul Kalam wrote to Rao urging him to boycott the ongoing CTBT negotiations and test nuclear weapons as soon as possible. The note was prepared in consultation with other members of the secret nuclear committee. At 11 a.m. on 19 January 1996, Rao's appointment diary shows that he met with his principal secretary, as well as his foreign, atomic energy and defence secretaries to 'consider our stand on CTBT'.[30] A month later, Rao asked the finance ministry to prepare yet another analysis of the economic effects of a nuclear test.

In late March, Rao received a second call from Bill Clinton. The US President once again urged Rao to desist from testing. It is not known what exactly Clinton said. But the very fact of the call is more evidence that Rao was actively considering testing nuclear weapons in March 1996.

National elections were scheduled for May 1996, and Rao spent the next two months campaigning. On 8 May at 9 p.m., Abdul Kalam was asked to immediately meet with the prime minister. Rao told him, 'Kalam, be ready with the Department of Atomic Energy and your team for the N-test and I am going to Tirupati. You wait for my authorisation to go ahead with the test. DRDO-DAE teams must be ready for action.'[31]

Two days later, the election results were announced. Kalam recalls that Rao ordered him not to test, since 'the election result was quite different from what he anticipated'.[32]

The BJP's Atal Bihari Vajpayee took over as prime minister on 16 May 1996. Narasimha Rao, Abdul Kalam and R. Chidambaram went to meet the new prime minister 'so that', in Kalam's telling, 'the smooth takeover of such a very important programme can take place'.[33] Vajpayee's revelations of 2004 make clear what was discussed. Immediately afterwards, Vajpayee ordered nuclear tests, but rescinded that order when it was clear that his government would not last. In 1998, back as prime minister for the second time, Vajpayee was able to finally 'go ahead' and explode.

The evidence is overwhelming that Narasimha Rao gave the 'T-30' order to test nuclear weapons in late November 1995. Rao involved a large number of people in assessing the consequences, an unusual step for a man as secretive as he was. He knew that American satellites were hovering above Pokhran. They were nonetheless able to detect activity that indicated testing was imminent. US pressure followed, and Rao cancelled the tests.

It is also clear that India did not have a hydrogen or thermonuclear device in December 1995. A member of the nuclear committee confirms, '[This] became ready only by around March 1996.' Between April and May 96, Rao considered testing again. He backed off when he realized that he had lost the national elections.

Given that this is what we *know*, what can we deduce about Rao's intentions? Only three theories fit the known facts.

The first is that Rao had decided to test nuclear weapons in December 1995. But the American satellites caught on, and under pressure from the US, Rao chose to postpone testing. This is the explanation favoured by nuclear expert George Perkovich in his book on India's programme.[34] This theory, however, does not explain why Rao decided to test again only a few months later. American pressure—and sanctions—would not have varied significantly between December 1995 and April 1996.

The second theory is that Rao never intended to test in December 1995, and the Americans were mistaken. 'The truth is that Rao never cleared the tests,' the journalist Raj Chengappa says in his superbly sourced book on the nuclear programme.[35] This, however, leaves unexplained why Rao gave the order all the way till 'T-7' in December 1995, and why he wanted to test again four months later. What game was Rao playing?

A third, more sensational, theory attempts an answer. Rao knew he had only one chance to test before sanctions kicked in, i.e. he could not *both* test conventional atomic bombs in December 1995 as well as the hydrogen bomb separately in April 1996. As Shekhar Gupta—who has had unprecedented access to Rao as well as the nuclear team—speculates: 'By late 1995, Rao's scientists told him that they needed six more months. They could test some weapons but not others . . . thermonuclear etc. So Rao began a charade of taking preliminary steps to test, without intending to test then.'[36] He then *deliberately leaked* the information on the tests—by telling many people about it, and ordering observable digging in Pokhran. When the Americans found out—*as Rao wanted them to*—he ordered the tests to end.

In doing so, Rao made India's nuclear capacity clear while CTBT negotiations were ongoing, and gave his scientists breathing space to develop the hydrogen bomb. By April 1996, hydrogen bomb ready, Rao genuinely wanted to test, but decided against it since he had lost the mandate of the people.

For Rao to have gone ahead with this deception—only a whisker away from treason—there are three people he might have likely told: A.P.J. Abdul Kalam, R. Chidambaram and Naresh Chandra. Chidambaram and Chandra were both awarded the Padma Vibhushan, India's second-highest civilian honour, by later governments. Kalam was given the Bharat Ratna and made President of India. Did Narasimha Rao tell his successors something about these men that the public does not know?

Regardless of which of these theories is true, they all point to the fact that far from dithering, Rao was actively involved in the nuclear programme—a trait he also exhibited on the economy, welfare schemes and foreign policy. The portrait that emerges is of a hands-on manager. As Arunachalam puts it, 'I worked with five prime ministers. I would rate Rao very high. [He] was a rare politician who understood the importance of technology in building national policy.'[37]

Rao's magnanimity in letting Vajpayee revel in the glory of nuclear testing (including of the hydrogen bomb) is telling. As Abdul Kalam said, it 'reveals the maturity and professional excellence of a patriotic statesman who believed that the nation is bigger than the political system'.[38]

When India finally tested nuclear weapons in 1998, western sanctions followed. Yet—as Rao judged—it has not harmed India in the long term (its effects on India's security is more contested)[39]. Subsequent prime ministers have also followed Rao in refusing to sign the CTBT and NPT.

In 2005, US President George W. Bush decided to make an exception to the international non-proliferation regime. Under the Indo-US nuclear deal, India would separate its civilian and military nuclear facilities, placing only its civilian facilities under international scrutiny. The US would help with India's civilian nuclear energy. The deal made India the only country not part of the NPT framework that is still allowed to do nuclear commerce with the rest of the world.

This deal would have been impossible had not India been both an acknowledged nuclear weapons state *as well as* an emerging economic power.

GOING NUCLEAR

The 1998 nuclear tests—sanctioned by Vajpayee with the help of Narasimha Rao—forced the West to concede that India would never cap its nuclear programme. They could, of course, have treated India as a renegade—as they have Iran, North Korea, and to some extent, Pakistan. But the economic power of post-1991 India—for which Rao gets the lion's share of the credit—meant that the West could not afford to alienate India. This mix of economic might and an unbending nuclear programme is what has led to new status for India in the international system.

Seen thus, Narasimha Rao is not just the 'true father' of the 1998 nuclear tests. He is also the crafter of a fresh vision for India in the world. This new self-image, at odds with Nehruvian idealism,[40] emphasizes economic muscle alongside a conventional military and large nuclear programme. It is a vision not without its critics.[41] But for better or for worse, it is likely to be the dominant way in which India sees itself in the years to come.

15

Lion, Fox, Mouse

Narasimha Rao's end was swift, the fall steep. He was encircled by legal cases almost immediately after he resigned as prime minister in May 1996. On 21 September, a judge summoned Rao as an accused in a corruption case filed by a London-based pickle maker, Lakhubhai Pathak.[1] There was every chance that the former prime minister (who was still party president) would be arrested. There were predictable puns about pickles, and newspapers termed it "The beginning of the end for Rao".[2] He decided to resign as Congress president.

His astrologer, N.K. Sharma, told him that once he stepped down, 'all these people who are worshipping you, they will start kicking you'. Sharma says that Rao replied, 'If tomorrow I am arrested, I don't want the [newspaper] headline to read "Congress president goes to jail".'[3]

It took almost no time for the astrologer's prediction to come true. When Rao organized a tea party for his Congressmen on 25 September 1996, soon after his resignation as party chief, it had to be cancelled because not a single invitee was willing to attend.[4] Years later, unwell and ignored, Rao was visited by Congress leader Salman Khurshid and his wife. 'You know, Salman,' Rao said with a pause, 'I am accused of not taking a decision . . . the only decision I took in a hurry was resigning as Congress president. Look what has happened.'[5]

Apart from Lakhubhai Pathak's allegations, Rao was accused of forgery in the St. Kitts case, of corruption by stockbroker Harshad Mehta, and of conspiring to bribe MPs from the Jharkhand Mukti Morcha (JMM) to vote in his favour in Parliament. He was eventually convicted in one of those cases—the JMM affair—before being acquitted by a higher court. His son Prabhakara was arrested in connection with allegations of irregularity concerning the purchase of urea, before investigating agencies found no evidence against Prabhakara and the charges were dropped. The legal bills mounted, and in urgent need of 23 lakh rupees to pay his lawyers, the former prime minister considered selling his house in Hyderabad.[6]

Characteristically, Narasimha Rao turned even this court trauma into a learning experience, making detailed notes on the legal documents, originals of which are still mountain-stacked in his private archives. His lawyer, R.K. Anand, remembered, 'Rao himself used to study law books. His knowledge was immense.'[7] Meanwhile, Congressmen had moved on, turning once again to the Nehru-Gandhis to rescue them from political irrelevance. When Sonia Gandhi took over the party in 1998, she was determined to erase Rao from the party pantheon. 'That man is not a Congressman,' Rahul Gandhi told a senior Congress leader, 'because of him we have lost UP forever.' Rao's son Rajeshwara complains, 'I have been waiting for a full decade for a meeting [with Sonia Gandhi]. She refuses.'[8]

Sonia also brought back Congressmen who had left the party disgruntled—many of whom Rao had sidelined during his term as prime minister, some of whom he had even wronged. They now sought vengeance.

Almost no one accompanied the ex-prime minister on his many court appearances. The few who did, like Congress Rajya

Sabha MP Satchidananda Swamy, were punished by the party.⁹ 'He was a sad man. Only a few Congressmen visited him,' Swamy remembers. 'Manmohan Singh, Pranab Mukherjee and [M.S.] Bitta were some of the few.'¹⁰

Exile was not new for Narasimha Rao. As we saw in this book, he had been banished by Indira Gandhi in 1973 and 1976, and again by Rajiv in 1991. During these breaks from politics, Rao had worked on *The Other Half*, a fictionalized memoir of his time in Andhra politics. Each re-entry into politics had temporarily halted the writing of the book. Now, free once again, Narasimha Rao finished the book and published it as *The Insider*, released in 1998 by his friend Atal Bihari Vajpayee.

The book became famous for lurid descriptions of sex by an ageing former prime minister. But when first sketched in 1973, it was the silhouette of a thwarted career. Sentences were slow moving, the narrative meandered. And the disenchanted protagonist asked the same question that had confronted the Florentine courtier Niccolò Machiavelli four centuries earlier. How does one use power to do good, if gaining and wielding power requires one to do evil?

In his spare time, Rao brushed up on his Spanish, the last of ten languages he had learnt to speak with fluency. He also took to playing the piano. It kept his fingers nimble and warded off arthritis, he explained to his visiting son-in-law.¹¹ He began to read fiction once again. He would even write to authors he liked, commenting on their literary devices. Soon after the writer Arundhati Roy released *The God of Small Things,* Rao wrote her a letter. Her reply, in flowing black hand, is still preserved amidst Rao's private papers. 'I was touched by the fact that you wrote to me—but even more by the fact that you bothered to read the book before you wrote.'¹²

National elections were held in May 2004. The incumbent BJP government campaigned on the basis of its economic successes, essentially a deepening of Narasimha Rao's liberalization policies. The Congress, now headed by Sonia Gandhi, was expected to lose. Narasimha Rao's help was not sought.

Against expectations, the Congress emerged as the largest party. Sonia Gandhi declined the nation's most powerful job, and appointed Rao's finance minister Manmohan Singh as prime minister of India.

Rao was hospitalized soon after. Racked with ill-health, with disorders in his kidneys, heart and lungs, he was moved to a special ward of AIIMS hospital in New Delhi. His maid, Rosie—who had worked for him since 1977—assisted the hospital nurses. The only visitors were Manmohan Singh,[13] Sanjaya Baru and Rao loyalist M.S. Bitta. That was about it, his doctor Srinath Reddy remembers. 'Very few people came, except his family.'

Shubhranshu Singh, a corporate executive, was visiting his ailing mother in the adjacent ward. 'The lift door opened, and I saw Narasimha Rao. He looked like a scarecrow.'

'I paid him a goodwill visit since I was around,' Singh adds. 'He was on the bed, in a lungi. He was all alone.'[14]

In early November 2004, Rao left the hospital to pay his last respects to his beloved—and feared—principal secretary, Amar Nath Varma. They don't make them like him any more, Rao said, wiping tears.[15]

Some weeks later, on 24 November 2004, Rao was treated for a urinary infection. The strong medicines the doctors prescribed had side effects. Vani Devi, who was present, says of her father, 'He was usually a *sthithapragya*'—the description in the Bhagvad Gita of one 'undisturbed by distress, without desires'.[16] But that November, Rao lost his temper—something his children had never seen him do. He decided to stop eating.

'I don't want to take anything,' he announced. 'What's the point in living like this? Why do you people insist that this life should be prolonged?'

For twenty-four hours, the patient sat on a chair by his hospital bed, refusing to eat or drink. As the news spread, the family received a phone call from Shivraj Patil. 'Can we come and see him? Madam also wants to come.'[17]

At 10.30 p.m., Sonia Gandhi, along with Patil and Ahmed Patel, visited the hospital. Sonia sat quietly while Ahmed Patel offered Rao a glass of water. 'You people accuse me of breaking the mosque,' Rao told him angrily. 'Now you give me water.'

Rao argued with his guests late into the night, complaining about how the Congress had treated him. 'Who has not done a mistake? Why should I be blamed for something I have not done?'[18] Sonia and the others left only at 2.30 a.m., after which Rao was given a sedative. He woke up the next morning and resumed eating. He asked his children, 'Did I speak more than I should have last night?'[19]

Rao began to sink on 10 December. An aide to Sonia Gandhi came to the hospital. 'Where should we have the cremation?' he asked. The family was furious. 'He was still alive.'[20]

On 20 December 2004, Rao was visited in the hospital by prime minister Manmohan Singh and A.P.J. Abdul Kalam, who had since become President of India. The other visitor that day was Arjun Singh, a man who had done more than anyone to vilify Rao.

As Arjun Singh entered, Rao rose from his hospital bed. 'Please don't strain yourself. I have only come to wish you speedy recovery,' Singh said. He remembers tears welling in Narasimha Rao's eyes. 'Arjun Singhji, I will meet you at your house, since I owe you a visit.'[21]

The next day, Rao's condition worsened. He became unconscious. 'He was eyes closed, pipes everywhere,' Rajeshwara remembers. 'Then suddenly he opened [his] eyes and looked at me.'

'Where am I?" Rao asked, then answered himself. 'I am in Vangara. In mother's room.'[22]

He died a few days later, on 23 December 2004. Those were Narasimha Rao's last words.

―

P.V. Narasimha Rao's dying days were of a piece with his tattered legacy in the decade that followed. He has been removed from the pantheon of Congress leaders, criticized for the anti-Sikh riots, accused of letting the guilty escape after the Bhopal gas leak, and above all, blamed for complicity in the demolition of Babri Masjid. He has been portrayed as corrupt as well as communal, vacillating as well as vicious.

These political attacks on so consequential a figure have not been countered through academic research so far. While there are many explanations for this scholarly inaction, one major reason is that academics tend to discount the role that individual leadership plays in shaping the arc of history.

As the biographer Nigel Hamilton puts it, 'Biography is, simply, the orphan of academia.'[23] If a leader merely carried out what historical forces made inevitable, it is not the 'person' that mattered; it is the moment in 'time'. Seen this way, Narasimha Rao was simply in the right place at the right moment. It is not his actions that deserve study, it is his historical context.

This is an argument that deserves to be taken seriously. For, there is no question that India found itself at crossroads in the year 1991. The Soviet Union was in collapse, the balance of payments crisis was severe. India's social schemes were ineffective, a Nehru-Gandhi had just been assassinated, and separatist violence in Punjab, Kashmir and Assam threatened the integrity of the nation.

But India had been stuck at these crossroads for a decade before Rao's ascent. An IMF loan had been negotiated in 1981-82; but that had not jolted prime minister Indira Gandhi into liberalizing the economy. Foreign ministry mandarins knew that the Soviet Union was teetering since at least 1985,[24] and India's détente with the United States had first begun a decade prior to Rao becoming PM.[25] By the early 1980s, policymakers could objectively measure that welfare schemes were not reaching the poor, and India's nuclear programme had progressed steadily. Two Nehru-Gandhis had been killed in this decade, and violence in Punjab and Assam had already peaked. Even the specific ideas for foreign policy and economic reforms had been put down on paper some years prior to 1991.

Four prime ministers before Narasimha Rao had been presented with the right 'moment'—in terms of favourable external winds, well-sketched internal ideas, and opportunistic crises—to renovate India. They had been unable to make use of these opportunities.

For more proof that India's transformation was not ordained, consider the alternatives for premiership. What would have happened if Rajiv Gandhi had lived on? The idealistic reformer of 1985 had malformed, by 1987, into a cynical politician. It is unlikely he would have pursued meaningful change in his second term as prime minister. Had Rao's party rivals, Arjun Singh or N.D. Tiwari, replaced him, they may have temporarily liberalized the economy in 1991. But their instincts, and proclamations, were consistently against economic reforms or foreign policy changes. They would have likely halted reform after the foreign exchange crisis ended in February 1992. The transformations Rao brought about were far from inevitable.

They were also carried out in the most trying of circumstances.

P.V. Narasimha Rao worked in a fractious democracy and ran a minority government (the two before him and four after—all minority—lasted barely a year each). A usurper of the Nehru-Gandhi throne, Rao did not control his own party. He even lacked the charisma to appeal directly to the people.

No national leader who achieved his scale of transformation worked under such constraints. It makes Narasimha Rao the most skilled Indian prime minister since Jawaharlal Nehru, a twentieth-century reformer as consequential as Deng Xiaoping.

It also makes Rao's personality central to the transformation of India, a shift caused not by historical forces, but by the leadership of one man. 'You can use a biography to examine political power,' says Robert Caro, a prince among biographers. 'But only if you pick the right guy.'[26]

P.V. Narasimha Rao was born a fixer. When something didn't work, his first instinct was to open it up, figure out what was wrong, and make marginal improvements to solve the problem. As a young man in 1957, he noticed a malfunctioning water pump. He opened it, identified the problem, fixed it, and complained to the manufacturer. As chief minister in 1971, he had observed evasions of his cherished land reform policy. He had tweaked the law in ways that ensured their compliance. Two years later, he noticed that planting rice in his village was not remunerative. He bought more valuable cotton seeds from Gujarat. When he realized that the cotton plants self-pollinated and weakened the new crop, he ingeniously fixed a straw on the plant so that pollen would fly elsewhere. As Ramu Damodaran says, 'Rao was a *jugaad* reformer. He made the best of what he had.'[27]

What the early Rao had yet to grasp was that all reforms take place under political constraints, and are opposed by interest groups.

His failure to see this led to his dismissal as Andhra Pradesh chief minister. He had taken on too many enemies, used explosive language, and made his intent to reform clear. He had also misinterpreted his mandate: prime minister Indira Gandhi had wanted a minion both powerless as well as powerful, and that could never be.

Narasimha Rao learnt from his mistakes while in exile—it was this ability to introspect that made him so rare among his peers. He realized that reform is best carried out in silence, and opponents best countered singly. The arch-socialist also recognized that the state need not be the only vehicle for social reform.

His years in the Delhi durbar—more court than Cabinet—honed in him these lessons. He never cultivated a coterie, never favoured caste or kin. This was why he had become chief minister of Andhra Pradesh; this is why he rose to become Indira and Rajiv's factotum. His time in Delhi also gave him a ringside view of the colossal failure of Rajiv Gandhi in combating vested interests who resisted change. A liberalizer by instinct, Rajiv lacked the skills to manage the politics of reforms.

As prime minister, Rao inherited these same vested interests. The licence raj was upheld by businessmen who had prospered from monopolies, Left intellectuals and Congressmen who clung on to ideology, and unions and bureaucrats worried their sinecures would be threatened. It was not just anti-colonialism that prevented relations with Israel, it was also the unverified fear of losing Muslim votes that bound India to Palestine. Rich farmers, middlemen and corrupt officials siphoned off money from welfare schemes meant for the poor. They would agitate if their privileges were taken away.

Prime minister Narasimha Rao's genius in tackling these enemies of change was that he had learnt to assess political strength and weakness—his own, his opponents', and of India itself. The fact that Rao had informally accepted monkhood just two months before becoming prime minister shows the mental distance from power he had developed. It gave him an even clearer assessment of its constraints as well as opportunities. It gave him his unique ability to transform India.

This 360-degree view of politics means that, before initiating any reform, Rao had the measure of his opponents. When the prime minister invited Palestinian leader Yasser Arafat for an official visit in January 1992, he understood that India needed to normalize diplomatic relations with Israel without upsetting the Arab world. He also knew that Arafat, who had supported Saddam Hussein in the Gulf War, was politically weak. While advocating reforms to industrial policy, Rao knew that the principal critique would come from with his own party. In developing a nuclear deterrent, Rao grasped that he had to protect Indian national security without antagonizing the West (whom he needed for economic reforms). While facing Parliament, Rao saw that the right-wing BJP and left-wing National Front needed to stay disunited for his government to survive. While opening up the airline sector, Rao knew that if he attempted to disinvest Air India, well-entrenched unions might threaten his entire liberalization policy. In attempting to reform the public distribution system, Rao saw that rich farmers would agitate to protect their interests. The list could go on.

This cold-eyed assessment of his enemies gave Rao the ability to pick his disguises. He understood that the range and variety of his foes—indeed the contradictions of India itself—required him to occasionally retreat, sometimes fight, and often deceive. *This ability to assess the situation and play mouse, lion or fox—as need be—was Rao's paramount political skill.*

On industrial policy—Rao's supreme economic reform—he was able to assess the mood of his party, ensure the policy draft was peppered with enough references to Jawaharlal Nehru, play the cunning fox, and get his party behind his reforms. Before opening up to Israel, Rao first pampered Arafat, got his consent, then announced it to Parliament as a fait accompli. When opening up monopoly sectors like airlines, Rao simultaneously played lion in permitting private competition while playing mouse when it came to protecting state employees from retrenchment. On the PDS, he simply increased the price paid to both farmers and consumers, thereby subtly starving the system.

Rao's precise assessment of political context gave him not just a sense of *role*, but also a sense of *timing*.

He was horror-struck when he heard of Rajiv's death on 21 May 1991. But even in the disorienting hours following tragedy, Rao was able to see his stars realigning. After the fall of Babri Masjid on 6 December 1992, Rao realized he could use the tragedy to rally 'secular' forces around him and consolidate power. And perhaps most remarkable of all, it took the lifelong economic protectionist only a few hours on 19 June 1991 to see that the time had come for the economy to open up.

Contrary to the caricature of Narasimha Rao as chronically indecisive, he could make rapid decisions when he felt the timing was right, including choosing to alter long-held beliefs. Where he dithered, it was because he judged that the right decision was at the time not politically feasible.

It is this judgement that led Rao to conclude that certain reforms, while necessary, were not possible during his time as prime minister. These were on agriculture, labour, the bureaucracy, and welfare. Given his weak mandate, Rao estimated he would have lost office had he soldiered on. Critics accused him of underplaying his hand, but the fact that no prime minister after him has been able to implement these reforms proves Rao's calculation to be correct.

The few occasions where prime minister Rao misunderstood his role and misjudged the timing was when his analytical mind and unflinching eye failed him. His decision to not impose President's rule in Uttar Pradesh in November 1992 was an overestimation of his own strength in dealing with Hindutva activists. Where he had to play lion, he played fox. Rao's determination to play lion and ignore Sonia after 1993 overrated his own hold over the Congress party. And his decision to play fox and impose hawala charges on friend and foe earned him more enemies than it did votes.

These missteps blot Rao's record as prime minister. But they remain aberrations in a long line of correct calls. Most of the time, P.V. Narasimha Rao got the timing and role right.

Where did Rao obtain this sense of time and role? To answer that question, this book delved deep into Rao's political experience, information sources and personality quirks.

When Rao became prime minister, he had been in Congress politics for more than fifty years. Unlike Manmohan Singh, Rao had won eight consecutive elections before he became prime minister. For a man to campaign in three languages and win from three states, speaks of a grass-roots connect with the ordinary Indian. Unlike Rajiv Gandhi (who knew Delhi but not state-level administration) and Deve Gowda (who had worked at the state-level but never in Delhi), Rao had served as chief minister as well as Union minister. It gave him a sense of how Central as well as state politics worked. Rao had also held an unusual number of ministries—foreign, defence, home, education, health, law, to name a few. This range of experiences—and roles—afforded Rao multiple perspectives that informed his decisions as prime minister.

Rao also developed a world of informants that helped him determine when to play mouse, lion or fox. Curious as a child, his archives provide a glimpse of just how curious the older Rao continued to be. He kept notes on everyone—friends, enemies and rivals. As chief minister, he had relied on Lakshmi Kantamma and the tantrik Chandraswami. As prime minister, Rao deployed a more extensive range of informants. He had intelligence bureau reports on Sonia Gandhi, as well as every member of his party when it came to economic reforms. Rao also cultivated astrologers and godmen, brokers and journalists, friendly politicians as well as opponents. In his methodical mind, each nugget of data—a peccadillo about a Cabinet member, an enemy of an enemy—was tagged and filed. To be used at the right time.

Rao possessed a third trait that helped him weigh political context. In addition to learning from varied experiences and artfully cultivating sources, Rao was a man comfortable with extremes as well as ambiguity. His was a paradoxical personality.

In an essay written in 1860, the Russian writer Ivan Turgenev compared the two most famous fictional characters of the western world: Shakespeare's Hamlet and Cervantes's Don Quixote.[28] These contrasting personalities represented 'the fundamental forces of all that exists'.[29] Hamlet, educated and sensitive, is the epitome of the man who thinks so much that he cannot act. He is inward-looking, selfish even, and utterly sceptical of everything around him. Don Quixote, on the other hand, credulously believes the simplest of ideals and, motivated by selflessness, acts to achieve them. Hamlet was thoughtful and lethargic, Quixote an unthinking revolutionary.[30]

As a young man, Rao's personality contained both Hamlet as well as Don Quixote. Childhood loneliness—from his early adoption, arranged marriage, and separation from family—persisted into adulthood. An intellectual, he preferred books to actual friends, confidential diaries to confidantes. To his wife Satyamma, he tasked the care of their eight children and acres of village lands. Emotionally, he was a loner.

It is a measure of the contradiction of the man that such a personality was also an idealistic revolutionary. In Andhra of the 1960s, the young socialist was action personified, unsettling the ministries he took over. As chief minister, Narasimha Rao had unthinkingly charged at the windmill of land reform, uncaring of the stability of his saddle.

What was remarkable about the later Rao was that these contrasts merged into what became—at the best of times—a man who could be contemplative as well as action-oriented, cynical as well as idealistic. Rao could play for time, as he did with the nuclear programme in the initial years of his government. He could also act swiftly, as he did in a single day on economic reforms. He could project powerlessness, as he did when Sonia Gandhi chose him as prime minister. He could also project power, as he did after 1993.

When it came to God, Narasimha Rao reflected the contradictions of his guru, Ramananda Tirtha. He was a religious Hindu as well as a secular Congressman. He was devout enough to be offered the chance to head the Courtallam peetham; catholic enough to be versed in Urdu, Persian and Koranic scripture. His view of Hinduism may have given him a naïve view of the BJP, but he refused to split the Congress and support them in May 1996.

Narasimha Rao did not see these two parts of his personality as incompatible; he saw them as rooted in Hindu tradition. He loved the sixteenth-century Telugu poem *Raghava Pandaveeyam* that could be read as both Ramayana and Mahabharata, as the situation demanded. He even translated a book featuring Ardhanareeeshwara—the Hindu god who is half-man, half-woman.

Rao's dual disposition enabled him to be at once principled, at once immoral. Personally honest, he was no stranger to political corruption. Though the courts acquitted him in the JMM bribery case, the evidence available to this author suggests he was in on the conspiracy. While Rao could be sensitive to those he loved, he could also be petty to subordinates, distant to family, instrumental with friends, and vicious to his enemies.

Even Rao's association with women reflected a certain opacity. He lived away from his wife for much of their marriage. He had a relationship with Lakshmi Kantamma for more than a decade. From around 1976 till his death, he had a close friendship with Kalyani Shankar. 'He liked that people around him couldn't quite figure out the exact nature of these connections,' a friend of Rao says. 'He liked the ambiguity.'

Rao's varied persona also gave him hobbies when exiled from politics—as he was in 1973 and '76 by Indira, 1991 by Rajiv, and post-'98 by Sonia Gandhi. While the curse of politicians the world over is that they don't know how to 'exit' with grace,[31] Rao could distance himself from power. It contributed to his unique insight into it.

Rao's most adroit deployment of these skills is also perhaps the least acknowledged. Unlike in the case of economic reforms, welfare schemes, foreign policy or the nuclear programme—all dealt with in separate chapters in this book—Rao played only an indirect role in reducing separatist violence. But his interventions in Punjab, Kashmir and the North-east showcase perfectly, his ability to play lion, fox and mouse.

When Narasimha Rao became prime minister, Kashmir and Punjab were under Central rule, while Assam was ruled by a chief minister being undermined by state Congressmen. Rao's first act was to appoint his own team. When it came to Kashmir, he changed the governor. He would eventually give his home secretary, K. Padmanabhaiah, direct charge of Kashmir affairs. 'That was a smart decision,' the former RAW chief and Kashmir expert, A.S. Dulat, believes. 'He was reporting straight to the PMO.' Rao also enlisted the bureaucrat—and Sonia Gandhi favourite—Wajahat Habibullah to be his prime negotiator in Kashmir. When it came to Punjab, Rao appointed a new governor, and ensured that K.P.S. Gill was not moved out as police chief (despite constant complaints against him). He also gave the Assam chief minister, Hiteswar Saikia, his unconditional backing. Not only was Saikia under pressure from ULFA militants, he was facing dissent from within his own party. In November 1991, for example, Saikia sent Rao a secret letter—now archived amongst his papers—that state Congressmen were plotting to get him replaced.[32] Rao chose to stand by Saikia through his years as prime minister.

In addition to appointing his chosen men, Rao allowed some of the most ruthless assaults on militants during this period. Operations by the army and police wiped out the top militant leadership of ULFA in Assam and the Khalistanis in Punjab. 'Rao knew exactly what was happening,' an IB official coordinating the attacks remembers. 'He even knew we were targeting [militants'] families.'

Rao's condonation of human rights abuses shows a pitiless politician, willing to do what it took to preserve the integrity of India. What made him such a bundle of contradictions, however, was his simultaneous belief in freedom and democracy.

In the case of Punjab, Rao ordered elections to be held in 1992, despite every single official telling him not to.[33] Though the elections were boycotted by the Akalis and the chief minister eventually killed in 1995, this judicious mix of carrot and stick had the desired effect. By the time Rao left in 1996, Punjab was on the way to normalcy.

In the case of Kashmir, Rao was desperate to have elections in 1995. 'Rao knew that the rigged elections [of 1987] was the catalyst for the insurgency,' a police official from Kashmir says. 'He wanted to undo that.' His private papers are full of secret meetings he held with terrorists and freedom fighters of varying shades, imploring them to stand for elections instead.[34]

Rao also ordered an unusually large development package for Kashmir. His most equipped socialist official, K.R. Venugopal, remembers: 'The guiding and supervision of this effort was entrusted to me in the prime minister's office.'[35] Returning from one of his many visits to rural Kashmir, Venugopal told Rao, 'The cultural alienation could be compared to the feelings in Telangana, excepting for there being no hostile power sitting on the borders.'

Though Rao could not conduct elections during his tenure, they took place soon after, in 1996. And though Rao's policies have not made the local population any less hostile towards India, they have created a semblance of normalcy and democracy in that troubled state.

A.S. Dulat says, 'His role in Kashmir followed the pattern of his economic reforms. He wanted to look ahead. When he became

PM, it was the worst time in Kashmir. So obviously the old man believed this danda rule and military rule is OK up to a point. But he also believed: "We have to deal with the people, and we have to move on."[36]

As prime minister, Rao also encouraged peace talks in the North-east. The Bodoland Autonomous Council was set up during his time. Rao proved willing to talk to every dissident, though he had no illusions about his powers to persuade. He once called Bodo separatists for a secret meeting in his house on Race Course Road. They seemed amenable, but Rao later told an aide: 'Things always go well in the PM's office. The question is what happens when they go back.' Narasimha Rao also met—in secret—Naga separatist leaders in 1995 in Paris. Officials say that it helped lay the groundwork for peace talks undertaken by prime minister Narendra Modi twenty years later.[37]

In every one of these manoeuvres, the former chief minister of Andhra Pradesh revealed a skill in dealing with state politicians that Indira Gandhi and Rajiv lacked. He knew the details and the players intimately. His dual personality was also comfortable with deploying a range of options—from brute force, to monetary allurements, to electoral enticements—and manage these mutinies.

It is too much to credit one clever prime minister with reducing violence in Kashmir, Punjab and the North-east. Changes in external conditions, the exhaustion of locals with violence, effective counter-insurgency, and improved state governance mattered as much, if not more. But it remains to Rao's credit that his calibrated responses aided the process rather than setting it back. 'Rao was prepared to use sama, dana, bheda, danda . . . every technique,' the journalist Shekhar Gupta says.[38] It was a messy story, but it enabled perhaps Rao's most underrated achievement: preserving the territorial integrity of his country.

Rao's transformation of India was assisted by his ability to select the right team. For Punjab, Kashmir and Assam, he had his favoured governors, negotiators and chief ministers. On foreign policy, he selected pragmatists who delivered. He retained the old team when it came to the nuclear programme. He chose pro-market reformers for the economy, while staffing his welfare schemes with socialists. Many of his team members did not see eye to eye, but Rao tolerated, perhaps even encouraged, a team of rivals. This was in contrast to Indira Gandhi, who liked sycophants, and Rajiv, who appointed childhood chums. Flattery or conviviality, Rao believed, was not the same as effectiveness.

One of the reasons why Rao patronized talented people was that he was secure in his own abilities. He told an intelligence bureau man whom he turned to for advice, 'I don't like you. But you have insights I need.' A proactive manager, Rao's knowledge of files and rules was as good as his best bureaucrats. As Kalyani Shankar—his closest confidante—says, 'He would listen to everybody, take everyone's inputs. But he would always make up his own mind.'[39]

Of all his team members, historically the most important was Manmohan Singh, who would later go on to become prime minister. Manmohan was not the only pro-market reformer Rao selected; his principal secretary, Amar Nath Varma, was arguably as important to the liberalization process. Neither was Manmohan Singh the first choice for finance minister; that was the pro-market economist I.G. Patel. But Manmohan played the role Rao had anticipated for him: he was a scrupulously honest technocrat who could both deflect blame from Rao as well as prod the prime minister when Rao's instincts faltered. Unlike almost every other Congressman, Manmohan Singh never disowned his former boss, respecting him in retirement, attending his funeral, and gracing birthday celebrations held since. Manmohan also never belittled Rao's role in liberalization.

That was done by other members of the Congress, and by Narasimha Rao himself. Since economic reforms were politically dangerous in the 1990s, Rao found it convenient to 'blame' Rajiv Gandhi and Manmohan Singh for them. Rao's success in obscuring his own role has worked against him. Few credit him, as this book does, with being the principal architect of India's economic reforms.

This cannot be emphasized enough. For, though Manmohan was critical to Rao's team, he was not indispensable. Had I.G. Patel become finance minister in 1991, liberalization would have likely persisted. But had Narasimha Rao not become prime minister, India would have been a different country.

When the ex-chief minister Narasimha Rao returned to his village house in Vangara in 1974, he realized that the mud building was unsuited to the times. He decided to demolish it and build a brick and mortar structure in its place. Tellingly, and as we saw in an early chapter, Rao kept the original measurements—calculated according to *vaastu* architectural rules. Even while modernizing, Rao paid his respects to tradition.

This small incident captures Rao's larger philosophy. As foreign minister in the 1980s, he had noticed how Deng was able to reorient China towards the market by claiming he was only carrying out Mao's wishes. For a system as complex as China's, a sharp break from the past would have led to disarray. When Rao became prime minister, he too claimed that his economic and foreign policies were mere extensions of the past. And even as he moved towards the United States, Israel and East Asia, he balanced this with reassurances to old allies such as Russia.

When faced with the advent of new technology—like computers, satellite television or mobile phones—Rao's was not a Luddite's instinct to regulate; he, instead, sought to adapt and adopt. The prime minister's New Year greeting card for the year 1992 had a sketch of a spinning wheel smoothly turning into a mechanical gear. Typed below was the slogan 'Change is the only constant'.[40]

'How do you make a U-turn without making a U-turn? That's a special Narasimha Rao art,' Shekhar Gupta asked him in retirement. 'It's not like that,' Rao replied. 'If you understand that where you were standing is itself in motion, the turning becomes easier.'[41]

Such a philosophy was both strategic as well as ingrained. The psychologist Ashis Nandy argues that 'the tradition of India is to alter the dominant culture from within by showing dissent to be part of orthodoxy . . .'[42]

Rao spoke ten languages (seven of which were Indic) and was a skilled translator. It was a skill that reflected his world view. As he put it, 'We have this great tradition of interpretation, the *Bhashyakara* . . . [Nehru] took the text from Gandhiji. He moulded it, he interpreted it so as to be in continuity with Gandhiji and still different from what he started with. What we need today is persons who can imbibe Nehru not just as spongers.'[43]

This mix of tradition and modernity, continuity and change, places Rao in the mould of the eighteenth-century Irish liberal Edmund Burke. Burke was a political reformer: he had fought to limit the powers of the British monarch, supported the American revolution, and opposed the British mistreatment of colonial India. Where Burke was not a progressive liberal was in his respect for local customs and a hurtling suspicion of radical change. For Burke, modern enlightenment was a product of traditions evolving over time, not their abandonment. Reform had to be gradual, taking the best of the past while improving upon it.[44] If Chanakya, the fourth-century BCE Indian Machiavelli, best captures Rao's *skill* in politics, the eighteenth-century Burke captures his *vision*.

This political vision and skill enabled Narasimha Rao to reorient India's economic, foreign, welfare, nuclear and federal policies. Rao's idea of India was one that was open for business, sought to pragmatically shape the world order, pursued soft as well as hard power, stayed centralized while being sensitive to federal concerns, and used large social schemes to improve the lives of its marginalized. Later governments—inhabiting the entire range of ideological persuasions—have broadly followed his direction. But while they have built on, even improved, these ideas, it is Narasimha Rao who deserves credit for setting India off on a new direction.

Narasimha Rao's legacy also manifests in the everyday lives of most Indians. Real incomes of Indians across percentiles have increased. Most families—no matter how poor, how marginalized—are better off than they were before Narasimha Rao. Every time an Indian gives a missed call using her mobile phone, she has Rao to thank. The boom in private India—from corporate jobs to private airlines and toll roads—was possible largely because of Rao. The increase in social-sector schemes—from employment guarantee to better-targeted food subsidies—exemplifies Rao's vision (and warts), while incorporating the new technology developed since then. Even the way Indians think of politics has changed, with voters now demanding service and performance rather than just being content with patronage.[45]

Narasimha Rao lives on not just in this newer idea of India and the transformation of a billion lives, he persists in strategies that future prime ministers must use if they wish to succeed. This is because the contradictions that constrained Narasimha Rao continue to bind later Indian leaders. For, they are the paradoxes of Indians themselves.

It is the Indian voter who is half a lion.

We expect leaders who are all-powerful, without providing them a clear mandate. Five prime ministers since Rao were denied majority control of Parliament. It was only in 2014—almost twenty years after Rao's time in office—that a prime minister actually commanded a full majority, and he too only got one-third of the popular vote. The Indian voter is unsure whether to centralize power or devolve it. When states misbehave, the expectation is that the Centre will intervene. When they do, it is portrayed as a threat to federalism.

Indians have grown to expect the benefits of liberalisation—the large government schemes, the consumer options, the improvements in income. But voters are unwilling to reward political parties for espousing economic growth.

Indians complain that the bureaucracy is unresponsive. Their private mobile phone provider responds quicker than the police. Yet few Indians would support the radical restructuring of the state, the firing of administrators who don't perform. Most Indians know—and say so—that government schemes meant for them are siphoned off. But few are willing to agree that the pipeline needs refitting.

We expect the highest moral standards of politicians, yet make it impossible for them to win without spending black money. Every time a scandal erupts, we take to the streets. But we are unwilling to turn those blips into sustained activism.

Narasimha Rao's genius was that his own ambiguities matched those of his countrymen. 'India is destined to walk on [a] razor's edge,' he used to say. That India, that voter, has not changed, and the job of leading the world's largest democracy remains mired in contradiction. Every prime minister—no matter what his disposition—will have to learn from P.V. Narasimha Rao. For, as long as Indians remain half-lions, so must their representatives. Rao may have been denied a Delhi funeral, refused entry into his party headquarters, and abandoned at his own cremation. But his legacy lives on.

His half-burnt body continues to glow.

Acknowledgements

If there is a central theme that runs through Narasimha Rao's life, it is *fortuna*. So it is with this book. I was fortunate that my subject kept daily diaries, notes and letters. Few Indian leaders, if any, have left behind such a paper trail. When I began writing on Rao in early 2015, I had no idea that cartons of his papers even existed. I was also lucky that those who knew him—admirers as well as detractors—were alive (if barely) and willing to speak. Fortune smiled on me.

Luck alone, however, is insufficient to succeed. As Niccolò Machiavelli wrote, one needed virtu to make use of luck. Rao had his virtues. Mine were an eclectic team of mentors, colleagues and friends who converted my good fortune into the book you have just read.

Aditi Sriram read every chapter before I had the courage to show it to anyone else. She put up with Narasimha Rao the entire year I wrote this book, always a source of encouragement. Her aesthetic and insights permeate these pages. My brother Sudhir Sitapati, marketing genius, refashioned every word. He knows to never let detail and description obscure the larger point. If this book is easy to read and shorn of academic gobbledygook, you have him to thank. Ramu Damodaran helped me think through every idea, indulging me even when he disagreed. His perceptions, and fingerprints, are on every page. Neel Maitra was present at the creation: when, on a New Jersey train in 2014, we both felt Rao deserved a book. He improved every idea with a scholarly mind, read every word with a lawyer's eye. Maitra would often criticize a sentence with 'The only thing worse is the sentence before.'

Srinath Raghavan read with a historian's eye, providing detail and demanding more context. Srinath makes the mistake of presuming that others can be as meticulous as he is, work as hard as he does. Devesh Kapur, so nurturing of the young, has a love for cold facts I take seriously. His line-by-line remarks restructured this book. For anyone brave enough to write on India without pandering to university politics, Ramachandra Guha must be the inspiration. His comments have added reassurance as well as depth. Satyam Viswanathan, who dons the day garb of a market researcher with the nightdress of a deep thinker, provided this book's ideal reader: interested in politics but uninterested in differences between a joint and additional secretary. Aditya Iyer has the quirks of a writer; he also has the talent. He ensured that each para ending was premonition of the next.

Prabhakara and Rajeshwara, Narasimha Rao's sons, decided to trust me and reveal a treasure trove of private papers and archives. These have never been made public before. Prabhakara was also unstinting with rare photos. That they helped without expecting a hagiography would have made their father proud. Pramath Raj Sinha kindly made available Amar Nath Varma's papers. I must also thank the many anonymous sources who risked their careers in opening up. Your names are safe with me.

Kaushik Vaidya, polymath, prodded words until they fit. Lawyer K. Vivek Reddy set aside many billable hours hoping a Telugu *bidda* would get his due. Priya Krishnan gave line-by-line edits—an explanation here, a comma there—that has made the book measurably tighter. Aman Ahluwalia uses the few words he deploys to devastating effect. When I mentioned that a godman close to Rao indulged in human sacrifice, Aman interjected in a low voice, 'You mean murder. You mean murder.'

ACKNOWLEDGEMENTS

My understanding of politics has been shaped by a variety of people. Three stand out: Pratap Bhanu Mehta, Shekhar Gupta and Atul Kohli. The perfect mentor, Pratap helped think through this project from infancy to adulthood. He knows how to provoke without being provocative, critique without being critical. He is the primary influence on this book. Shekhar Gupta has an interviewer's ear for the telling quote, a reporter's eye for the revealing detail. He has taught me to respect the worm's view of politics. Atul Kohli, fabled professor at Princeton, has a bird's vision of the structures that produce and perpetuate power. His scholarship on the Indian political economy helped provide context to Rao's actions. This book would not have happened but for his support.

The same is true of Kim Scheppele and Ezra Suleiman, my other advisors at Princeton. Kim's dazzling range of disciplinary inquiry is an inspiration to those seeking to break out from departmental straightjackets. Ezra brings charm and cherishing to young researchers, a rarity in that most hierarchical of worlds. Jennifer Widner's course on the politics of development helped me structure this book. Christophe Jaffrelot taught me to take empirical detail and context seriously. Mark R. Beissinger, avuncular as well as exacting, was generous with funding.

Geoffrey Sigalet, Canadian philosopher, exacted context that a non-Indianist could grasp. My conversations with him on Machiavelli, Edmund Burke and Thomas Hobbes have helped frame the theoretical arguments in this book. B. Chandrasen Rao, from that vanishing tribe of selfless political workers, extended his altruism to this book. He has a preternatural feel for the mendacity of everyday politics, without ever being infected by it. Vivek 'Bongo' Trilokinath combines the analytical skills of a fund manager with the creativity of an aesthete. Bhanu Joshi provided insights on infrastructure, Nalin Mehta on the television industry, K.N. Vaidyanathan on capital markets. An IIT grad as a research assistant is a luxury. Thank you, Vikram Srinivas.

ACKNOWLEDGEMENTS

Rao had his eyes and ears. Mine are Vishnu Shankar, Madhav Khosla and Bipin Aspatwar. Vishnu's feel for foreign and nuclear policy speaks of a lost career; Madhav's grasp of academic writing speaks of a promising one. Bipin, that lover of mystery novels, has an eye for a good story. For an entire year, they were assaulted by constant references to Rao. This is atonement.

P.V.R.K. Prasad gave me much valuable time and encouragement. Sanjaya Baru munificently handed over his contacts and stories. As did Jairam Ramesh, whose admiration for Rao translated into assistance for this book. Unlike most politicians, Jairam is non-hierarchical. His big-heartedness proves that in the Hobbesian jungle that is Lutyens Delhi, not everyone is nasty or brutish.

A distinguished team of economists helped me. Rohit Lamba made sure I paid attention to theory and concepts. The always rigorous Shoumitro Chatterjee never let me overstate my conclusions. Partha Mukhopadhyay, budget man extraordinaire, was gracious with his expertise. As was Arvind Subramanian, who has the ability to be both friendly as well as inspiring.

The other technical field I received expert help on was foreign policy. Prabhakar Menon has written two excellent essays on Rao's international relations. I was led to Menon by another, Shiv Shankar Menon. K. Raja Mohan, doyen of strategic studies, helped structure the chapter. As did the only two living foreign secretaries of prime minister Rao, Salman Haidar and Krishnan Srinivasan.

Gautam and Gaurav Sabharwal helped with interviews, generously vouching for me to their vast network. 'To really understand India,' Gautam told me while pinching his wrist, 'you need a DNA.' Koppula Raju, from the Congress, kindly introduced me to Rao's family. A host of others, from Nandan Nilekani and K. Natwar Singh to Montek Ahluwalia and Yamini Aiyar, provided me with contacts. Needless to say, it doesn't implicate them in the opinions expressed in this book.

ACKNOWLEDGEMENTS

Throughout the 100-odd interviews I did, it was hard not be dazzled. Those interviewed had all been players in the 1990s. Twenty-five years later, facing death or dentures, they layered their reflections with hindsight. What emerged was wisdom.

My friends from the Left have blunted some of my sharper edges. Kanta Murali, as rigorous as I am prone to polemic, has reshaped my understanding of business-politics relations. Dinsha Mistree, as good-natured in the political as he is in the personal, is a fountain of joy. Sanjay Rupaleria, that careful scholar of contemporary India, is an ideal sparring partner. As are my two close Marxist friends, Sandipto Dasgupta and Arjun Sengupta. They are willing to argue, with voices raised even, without ever questioning the friendship that lies beneath.

I learnt writing from the works of George Orwell and V.S. Naipaul. Alia Allana, who writes some of the most moving sentences I know, mixes craft with general insanity (as, I predict, will Naira). Chinki Sinha's love for the lede, that burdensome first sentence, accosted me at the start of each chapter. Ananya Vajpeyi and Basharat Peer helped the transition to intellectual Delhi. Patrick French, whose life of Naipaul is the best biography I have read, was generous with trade tips. As was Dinyar Patel, that patient chronicler of Dadabhai Naoroji.

The *Indian Express* has taught me everything I know about journalism. I have learnt about north Indian politics from Seema Chishti and Vandita Mishra. Vandita has also made me take reporting seriously. Unni Rajen Shanker teaches me to never get hassled or hyperbolic. Saubhik Chakrabarti critiqued my early forays into opinion writing, Mini Kapoor was an effective first boss. The endearing Neeraj Priyadarshi helped with photographs; the delightfully opinionated Parth Mehrotra is a model of integrity. The *Express* has taught me to be hard-hitting as well as restrained. The man who exemplifies this is Raj Kamal Jha, whose sure touch reshapes every *Express* story. He made me promise never to use

ACKNOWLEDGEMENTS

'I' in my stories. The absence of the first person in this book is entirely his doing.

Shishira Rudrappa and Esther were kind hosts in Bangalore. Delhi has become home thanks to the Khoslas (Harish, Rajiv, Amita) and Sunitha Rangaswami (the best cook I know). M.R. Madhavan, Shyam Balganesh, Rushabh Sanghavi, Abu Mathen George, Shadan Farasat, Darshana Narayanan, Ashutosh Salil, Kartick Maheshwari, Averi Banerjee, Raeesa Vakil, Mohit Abraham, Rachael Israel, Jayadev Calamur, all provided emotional shelter. In Hyderabad, K. Pavan Kumar was especially supportive, as was Vijay Kumar of EMESCO books. The staff at IIC, Delhi, particularly Saandiip Biiswaas, provided helpful assistance.

This book began as the child of Nandini Mehta and Chiki Sarkar, who provided early nutrition. It passed on to Meru Gokhale and her team at Penguin Random House, including the resourceful and receptive Tarini Uppal and the hawk-eyed V.C. Shanuj. Meru showered attention, reading the draft with care. She has improved the book's flavour—from better-cooked side characters to more spice sprinkled over the early chapters.

Chandralekha and Sadanand Menon developed my early curiosity. B.N. Srikrishna has shown me that, more than any other body part, spine is required for public service. Lawrence Liang has taught me to pursue passion rather than profession. As has Satyajit Banerjee, guru in tennis as well as in life.

The other inhabitants of my Rishi Valley world—Radhika Herzberger, Alok Mathur, A. Kumaraswamy, Shailesh Shirali, M. Nandakumar—have also taught me to follow my heart, a lesson my fellow travellers have taken to their own. I mean you, Govind Naidu, Pranav Ullal, Saurabh Seth, Rachel Immanuel, Deepika Mahidhara and Malay Duggar.

My uncles and aunts motivate me: Tennis and Lalitha Krishnan, T.S.R. and Lalitha Subramanian, Janakiram, Vijaya and Venkatesh Mannar, Srinivasan and Uma, Krishnan and Shobha. As do A.V. Krishnan, Lalitha and their inspirational son Rajesh.

ACKNOWLEDGEMENTS

T.S.R. Subramanian and R. Srinivasan were watchfully involved with the book, providing insight as well as reassurance.

Kamala and Ganesh are the people most to blame for the author of this book. I have inherited my parents' love for ideas and argument, as well as their stubbornness. They have disciplined me as well as each word in this manuscript. Along with Ketki, Sudhir, Aditi and Sahaana, they are the rocks above which my castle hovers. Kanwal and Sushma Sachdev are pillars of support. In this last year, I have been lucky to gain a new family: Sriram, Rukmani, Aparaajit and Anusha. Mathuram Krishna provided much joy through the writing of this book. She blessed it before moving on.

I dedicate this book to the three grandparents who shaped me. Ramanathan, by his passion for knowledge; Chellam through her passion for people; and Padmavathi, who taught me to look beyond the Self.

Notes

EPIGRAPH

1. There is some dispute on the date of the *Bhagvata Purana* (though the myths themselves predate the books). Some scholars date it to 900 AD (see, for example, Ithamar Theodor, 'The Pariṇāma Aesthetics as Underlying the Bhāgavatapurāna', *Asian Philosophy* 17, no. 2, 109–25, 2007, 109). The *Encyclopaedia Britannica* dates it to around 1000 AD (see http://www.britannica.com/topic/Bhagavata-purana). Some Hindu scholars say it dates even earlier, to 6th century AD or before (see https://www.jiva.org/dating-of-the-bhagavat-purana/).

1. HALF-BURNT BODY

1. Interview with P.V. Prabhakara Rao in Hyderabad, 2015.
2. Interview with Chandraswami in Delhi, 2015.
3. Interviews with P.V. Rajeshwara Rao and P.V. Prabhakara Rao in Hyderabad, 2015.
4. Interview with Sanjaya Baru in New Delhi, 2015.
5. Interview with S. Vani Devi in Hyderabad, 2015.
6. Interview with P.V. Prabhakara Rao in Hyderabad, 2015.
7. 'Leaders pay last respects to Rao', *The Hindu*, 25 December 2004, http://www.thehindu.com/2004/12/25/stories/2004122504721200.htm.
8. Ibid.
9. 'Rao fails to get resting place in Delhi', the *Times of India*, 25 December 2004, 1.

NOTES

10. Interview with Manmohan Singh in New Delhi, 2015.
11. 'Rao fails to get resting place in Delhi', the *Times of India*, 25 December 2004, 1.
12. 'Cortege carrying PV's body arrives', *The Hindu*, 25 December 2004, http://www.thehindu.com/2004/12/25/stories/2004122509320400.htm.
13. Ibid.
14. 'Homage paid to Rao', *The Hindu*, 25 December 2004, 1, http://www.thehindu.com/2004/12/25/stories/2004122512810102.htm.
15. 'Manmohan to lead mourners at Narasimha Rao's funeral', *The Hindu*, 25 December 2004, http://www.thehindu.com/2004/12/25/stories/2004122503310600.htm.
16. Interview with K. Natwar Singh in New Delhi, 2016.
17. 'Nation bids adieu to Narasimha Rao', *The Hindu*, 26 December 2004, 1, http://www.thehindu.com/2004/12/26/stories/2004122605320100.htm.
18. Ibid.
19. 'Family revives Rao's funeral pyre', the *Tribune*, 26 December 2004, http://www.tribuneindia.com/2004/20041227/nation.htm#4.
20. Interview with P.V.R.K. Prasad in Hyderabad, 2015.
21. Interview with P.V. Prabhakara Rao in Hyderabad, 2015.
22. Interview with Sanjaya Baru in New Delhi, 2015.
23. Interview with Manmohan Singh in New Delhi, 2015.
24. Interview with Captain V. Lakshmikantha Rao in Warangal (now in Telangana state), 2015.
25. Interview with K. Natwar Singh in New Delhi, 2016.
26. Ramachandra Guha, 'The Great Unmentionable', the *Telegraph*, Kolkata, 27 March 2010, http://www.telegraphindia.com/1100327/jsp/opinion/story_12252417.jsp.
27. Interview with Jairam Ramesh in New Delhi, 2015.
28. 'Babri wouldn't have fallen if a Gandhi was PM: Rahul', the *Times of India*, 20 March 2007, http://timesofindia.indiatimes.com/india/Babri-wouldnt-have-fallen-if-a-Gandhi-was-PM-Rahul/articleshow/1781018.cms .
29. Arjun Singh (with Ashok Chopra), *A Grain of Sand in the Hourglass of Time: An Autobiography* (New Delhi: Hay House India, 2012), 179.

NOTES

30. Zoya Hasan, *Congress after Indira: Policy, Power, Political Change (1984–2009)*, (New Delhi: OUP India, 2012), 2.
31. Interview with Salman Khurshid in New Delhi, 2015.
32. Somnath Chatterjee, *Keeping the Faith: Memoirs of a Parliamentarian* (New Delhi: HarperCollins, 2010), 111.
33. 'Former Prime Minister PV Narasimha Rao's Life History to Be Taught in Telangana Schools', NDTV, 28 June 2015, http://www.ndtv.com/telangana-news/former-prime-minister-narasimha-rao-s-life-history-to-be-taught-in-telangana-schools-776083.
34. 'KCR bats for Bharat Ratna to P V Narasimha Rao on his 93rd birth anniversary; Naidu calls ex-PM a "legend"', the *Indian Express*, 28 June 2014, http://indianexpress.com/article/india/india-others/kcr-bats-for-bharat-ratna-to-p-v-narasimha-rao-on-his-93rd-birth-anniversary-naidu-calls-ex-pm-a-legend/.
35. Interview with Arun Jaitley in New Delhi, 2015.
36. 'Award Bharat Ratna to Rao: Swamy', *The Hindu*, 24 December 2004, http://www.thehindu.com/news/national/karnataka/bharat-ratna-for-pv-narasimha-rao-swamy/article7489611.ece.
37. Radhika Saraf, 'The myth of the great Indian Middle class: Roughly 30 per cent of India's population still lives below the poverty line', *Daily Mail*, 19 May 2013, http://www.dailymail.co.uk/indiahome/indianews/article-2327182/The-myth-great-Indian-Middle-class-Roughly-30-Indias-population-lives-poverty-line.html.
38. This is only one estimate, by the Asian Development Bank. But many other estimates place it at least over 120 million. See Sambuddha Mitra Mustafi, 'India's Middle Class: Growth Engine or Loose Wheel?', the *New York Times*, 13 May 2013, http://india.blogs.nytimes.com/2013/05/13/indias-middle-class-growth-engine-or-loose-wheel/?_r=0.
39. 'From 1947 to 2014: How the Indian economy has changed since independence', Firstpost, 15 August 2004, http://www.firstpost.com/business/data-business/from-1947-to-2014-how-the-indian-economy-has-changed-since-independence-1983853.html.
40. World Bank data, available at http://data.worldbank.org/indicator/IS.AIR.PSGR.
41. Ibid.

NOTES

42. Data from Department of Telecommunications and Telecommunications Regulatory Authority of India. Sunil Mani, 'India's Telecommunications Industry', available at http://www.nistads.res.in/indiasnt2008/t4industry/t4ind14.htm.
43. 'India Has 100.69 Crore Total Telephone Subscribers', NDTV, 1 September 2015, http://www.ndtv.com/india-news/india-has-100-69-crore-total-telephone-subscribers-1213248.
44. See http://telecomtalk.info/total-number-tv-channels-india/139844/.
45. Email exchange with Ramachandra Guha, 2016.
46. Interview with P.V. Rajeshwara Rao in Hyderabad, 2015.

2. ANDHRA SOCIALIST, 1921–71

1. V.R. Adiraju, *The Right Prime Minister: A Political Biography of P.V. Narasimha Rao* (Hyderabad: Satya Publications, 1992), 23.
2. A 'peer' is a Sufi master. Story from an interview with Venkat Kishen Rao in Hyderabad, 2015.
3. Adiraju, *The Right Prime Minister: A Political Biography of P.V. Narasimha Rao*, 24.
4. Convocation address at Telugu University, Hyderabad, on 7 July 1991. Available in *P.V. Narasimha Rao Selected Speeches 1991–1992*, Ministry of Information and Broadcasting, 1993, p. 239.
5. While Narasimha Rao had some knowledge of more than thirteen languages, the ones he could speak well were English, Telugu, Marathi, Tamil, Urdu, Sanskrit, Persian, Spanish, Hindi and Oriya.
6. Ramachandra Guha, *India After Gandhi: The History of the World's Largest Democracy* (New Delhi: HarperCollins, 2007), 53.
7. Milton W. Meyer, *Asia: A Concise History* (Maryland: Rowman & Littlefield, 1997), 218.
8. Ramachandra Guha, *India After Gandhi: The History of the World's Largest Democracy*, 66.
9. Quoting Smith in Lucien D. Benichou, *From Autocracy To Integration* (New Delhi: Orient Blackswan, Kindle edition, 2014), 374.

NOTES

10. N. Purendra Prasad, 'Agrarian Class and Caste Relations in "United" Andhra 1956–2014', *Economic&Political Weekly*, L(16), 18 April 2015, 78.
11. Interview with P.V. Prabhakara Rao (on phone) in 2016.
12. Adiraju, *The Right Prime Minister: A Political Biography of P.V. Narasimha Rao*, 24.
13. Benichou, *From Autocracy To Integration*, 752.
14. Author's visit to Vangara village, 2015.
15. P.V. Narasimha Rao, *The Insider* (New Delhi: Viking, 1998), 15.
16. Benichou, *From Autocracy To Integration*, 462–66.
17. Rao, *The Insider*, 13.
18. Interview with Venkat Kishen Rao in Hyderabad, 2015.
19. Ibid.
20. Interview with P.V. Prabhakara Rao in Hyderabad, 2015.
21. Rao, *The Insider*, 8–9.
22. Interview with P.V. Prabhakara Rao in Hyderabad, 2015.
23. Adiraju, *The Right Prime Minister: A Political Biography of P.V. Narasimha Rao*, 24–25.
24. Rao, *The Insider*, 51.
25. Ibid., 15.
26. Adiraju, *The Right Prime Minister: A Political Biography of P.V. Narasimha Rao*, 29.
27. Ibid., 28.
28. Narendra Reddy et al., *P.V. Narasimha Rao: Years of Power* (New Delhi: Har Anand Publications, 1993), 37.
29. Adiraju, *The Right Prime Minister: A Political Biography of P.V. Narasimha Rao*, 36.
30. Ibid., 37–39.
31. Benichou, *From Autocracy To Integration*, 1070.
32. Ibid.
33. Rao, *The Insider*, 426.
34. Interview with P.V. Prabhakara Rao (on phone), 2016.
35. Interview with P.V. Prabhakara Rao in Hyderabad, 2015.
36. Ibid.

NOTES

37. Sunil Purushotham, 'Internal Violence: The "Police Action" in Hyderabad', *Comparative Studies in Society and History* 57, no. 2 (2015): 437.
38. Official Congress party history, available at http://aicc.org.in/web.php/history/detail/16#.VvlaTxFN10c.
39. P.V. Narasimha Rao, 'Swami Ramananda Tirtha A Sacred Memory', *New Swatantra Times* (special annual number), 2014, 12.
40. Interview with Satchidananda Swamy in Bangalore, 2015.
41. Adiraju, *The Right Prime Minister: A Political Biography of P.V. Narasimha Rao*, 80.
42. Purushotham, 'Internal Violence: The "Police Action" in Hyderabad', *Comparative Studies in Society and History*, 442.
43. Ibid., 452.
44. Rao, *The Insider*, 105.
45. Rajni Kothari, 'The Congress "System" in India', *Asian Survey*, 4, no. 12 (December 1964): 1161–73.
46. Interview with S. Vani Devi in Hyderabad, 2015.
47. Ramachandra Guha, *India After Gandhi: The History of the World's Largest Democracy*, 143.
48. Ibid., 144.
49. Official Election Commission results of the 1951–52 General Election, available at http://eci.nic.in/eci_main/StatisticalReports/LS_1951/VOL_1_51_LS.PDF.
50. Rao, 'Swami Ramananda Tirtha A Sacred Memory', 14.
51. Interview with Venkat Kishen Rao in Hyderabad, 2015.
52. Ibid.
53. Ibid.
54. Interview with P.V. Prabhakara Rao (on phone), 2016.
55. Interview with villagers in Vangara (in 2015) and with Venkat Kishen Rao in Hyderabad, 2015.
56. These regions had formed Andhra state in 1953, which became Andhra Pradesh in 1956 after the merger of Telangana.
57. Rao, *The Insider*, 115.
58. Ibid., 243.
59. Adiraju, *The Right Prime Minister: A Political Biography of P.V. Narasimha Rao*, 92.

NOTES

60. Interview with P.V. Prabhakara Rao (on phone), 2016.
61. Interview with M. Narayan Reddy in Hyderabad, 2015.
62. Narendra Reddy et al., *P.V. Narasimha Rao: Years of Power*, 46.
63. Ibid., 47.
64. J. Vengala Rao, *Naa Jeevitha Katha (My Life's Story)*. English translation provided to the author by Jairam Ramesh in 2016.
65. Interview with Narsa Reddy in Hyderabad, 2015.
66. Interview with Venkat Kishen Rao in Hyderabad, 2015.
67. The phrase was used by Ram Manohar Lohia. See Shekhar Gupta, 'Turning Lohiaji on his head', the *Indian Express,* 1 March 2012, http://archive.indianexpress.com/news/turning-lohiaji-on-his-head/917582/.
68. Interview with Rakesh Mohan in Washington, D.C., 2015.
69. Ibid.
70. Atul Kohli, *State-Directed Development: Political Power and Industrialization in the Global Periphery* (New Delhi: Cambridge University Press, 2004).
71. Samanth Subramanian, 'Nostalgia sets in as time runs out for India's beloved watch', the *National,* 28 March 2016, http://www.thenational.ae/world/india/nostalgia-sets-in-as-time-runs-out-for-indias-beloved-watch.
72. Shankkar Aiyar, *Accidental India: A History of the Nation's Passage through Crisis and Change* (New Delhi: Aleph Books, Kindle edition, 2013), 478.
73. Ibid., 657.
74. Daman Singh, *Strictly Personal: Manmohan & Gursharan* (New Delhi: HarperCollins, 2014), 353.
75. The phrase was first coined by the economist Raj Krishna. See Meera Siva, 'What's a "Hindu" rate of growth', *The Hindu BusinessLine,* 8 June 2013, http://www.thehindubusinessline.com/portfolio/technically/whats-a-hindu-rate-of-growth/article4795173.ece.
76. Aiyar, *Accidental India: A History of the Nation's Passage through Crisis and Change,* 651.
77. This is dealt with in detail in chapter 9 ('A Welfare State?') of this book.
78. 'Poll manifesto: A.P. chief minister firm', the *Times of India,* 7 May 1972, 11.

NOTES

3. PUPPET CHIEF MINISTER, 1971–73

1. 'Implementation of land reforms: A Review by the Land Reforms Implementation Committee of the National Development Council 1966', 275, http://planningcommission.nic.in/reports/publications/pub1966land.pdf.
2. Ibid.
3. Interview with Atul Kohli in Princeton, 2015.
4. K. Srinivasulu, 'Caste, Class and Social Articulation in Andhra Pradesh' (2002), cited in N. Purendra Prasad, 'Agrarian Class and Caste Relations in "United" Andhra 1956–2014', *Economic&Political Weekly*, L(16), 18 April 2015, 78.
5. Interview with Captain V. Lakshmikantha Rao in Warangal, 2015.
6. Narendra Reddy et al., *P.V. Narasimha Rao: Years of Power*, 58.
7. P.V. Narasimha Rao, 'Change with stability: The Chief Minister's Burden', ed., B.N. Pandey, *Leadership in South Asia* (Noida: Vikas Publishing, 1977), 9–12.
8. 'Brahmananda has the last word', the *Times of India*, 26 September 1971, 1.
9. Interview with Narsa Reddy in Hyderabad, 2015.
10. Ibid.
11. Interview with K. Vivek Reddy in Hyderabad, 2015.
12. 'Biggest Ever Andhra Cabinet Sworn in', the *Times of India*, 21 March 1972, 12.
13. P.V.R.K. Prasad, *Wheels behind the Veil: PMs, CMs and beyond* (Hyderabad: Emesco Books, 2012), 19.
14. Ibid.
15. Interview with Narsa Reddy in Hyderabad, 2015.
16. Prasad, *Wheels behind the Veil: PMs, CMs and beyond*, 36.
17. 'Ramanand Tirth is Dead', the *Times of India*, 23 January 1972, 1.
18. Interview with P.V. Prabhakara Rao (on phone), 2016.
19. Interview with B.P.R. Vithal in Hyderabad, 2015.
20. Interview with P.V.R.K. Prasad in Hyderabad, 2015.
21. Interview with M. Narayan Reddy in Hyderabad, 2015.
22. Interview with Chandraswami in Delhi, 2015.
23. Ibid.
24. Ibid.

NOTES

25. Transcript of interview of P.V. Narasimha Rao with the journalist Neerja Chowdhary; copy found among Narasimha Rao's private papers in 2015.
26. Interview with M. Narayan Reddy in Hyderabad, 2015.
27. Ibid.
28. 'Land Bill Introduced in Assembly: STATE LEGISLATURES', the *Times of India*, 1 August 1972, 6.
29. Interview with M. Narayan Reddy in Hyderabad, 2015.
30. Interview with P.V. Prabhakara Rao in Hyderabad, 2015.
31. Interview with Narsa Reddy in Hyderabad, 2015.
32. 'Choice of C.M.s', the *Times of India*, 15 March 1972, 1.
33. Narendra Reddy et al., *P.V. Narasimha Rao: Years of Power*, 61.
34. Interview with P.V. Prabhakara Rao in Hyderabad, 2015.
35. Interview with Captain V. Lakshmikantha Rao in Warangal, 2015.
36. Narendra Reddy et al., *P.V. Narasimha Rao: Years of Power*, 64.
37. Interview with Narsa Reddy in Hyderabad, 2015.
38. Narendra Reddy et al., *P.V. Narasimha Rao: Years of Power*, 66.
39. 'Narasimha Rao welcomes court ruling', the *Times of India*, 4 October 1972, 6.
40. Narendra Reddy et al., *P.V. Narasimha Rao: Years of Power*, 66.
41. Prasad, *Wheels behind the Veil: PMs, CMs and beyond*, 37–38.
42. Ibid., 39.
43. 'President's Rule to be Imposed on A.P.', the *Times of India*, 17 January 1973, 1.
44. Prasad, *Wheels behind the Veil: PMs, CMs and beyond*, 41.

4. EXILE, 1973–74

1. Ezra F. Vogel, *Deng Xiaoping and the Transformation of China* (Massachusetts: Harvard University Press, 2011), 50.
2. Ibid., p. 53.
3. Interview with Narsa Reddy in Hyderabad, 2015.
4. 'Plea for government in AP under Narasimha', the *Times of India*, 29 October 1973, 7.
5. Interview with P.V. Sharath Babu, nephew of P.V. Narasimha Rao, in Vangara, 2015.
6. Vengala Rao, *Naa Jeevitha Katha (My Life's Story)*.

NOTES

7. Amarnath K. Menon, 'Revealing Rao', *India Today*, 30 September 1996, http://indiatoday.intoday.in/story/former-andhra-pradesh-cm-vengala-raos-autobiography-rips-apart-narasimha-rao/1/282385.html.
8. Interview with Narsa Reddy in Hyderabad, 2015.
9. Interview with P.V. Rajeshwara Rao in Hyderabad, 2015.
10. Ibid.
11. Interview with S. Vani Devi in Hyderabad, 2015.
12. Interview with M. Narayan Reddy in Hyderabad, 2015.
13. Ibid.
14. Interview with S. Vani Devi in Hyderabad, 2015.
15. Interview with Gopalkrishna Gandhi in Chennai, 2015.
16. Transcript of interview of P.V. Narasimha Rao with the journalist Neerja Chowdhary; copy found among Narasimha Rao's private papers in 2015.
17. Interview with M. Narayan Reddy in Hyderabad, 2015.
18. Interview with M. Narayan Reddy in Hyderabad, 2015.
19. P.V. Narasimha Rao, 'Change with Stability: The Chief Minister's Burden', 24–26.
20. Ibid.
21. Sanjay Chakravorty, Devesh Kapur and Nirvikar Singh, *The Other One Percent: Indians in America* (forthcoming).
22. Interview with P.V. Rajeshwara Rao in Hyderabad, 2015.
23. Ibid.
24. Interview with Saraswathi Kalvakota (on phone) in the United States, 2015.
25. Interview with Velcheru Narayana Rao (on phone) in Atlanta, 2015.
26. Ibid.
27. Interview with P.V. Prabhakara Rao in Hyderabad, 2015.
28. Interview with Narasimha Rao's eldest daughter in Hyderabad, 2015.
29. K. Natwar Singh, 'How PV became PM', *The Hindu*, 6 July 2012, http://www.thehindu.com/opinion/op-ed/how-pv-became-pm/article3592050.ece.
30. Sanjay Chakravorty, Devesh Kapur and Nirvikar Singh, *The Other One Percent: Indians in America* (forthcoming).

NOTES

31. Devesh Kapur, *Diaspora, Development, and Democracy: The Domestic Impact of International Migration from India* (New Jersey: Princeton University Press, 2010).
32. Interview with Montek Singh Ahluwalia in Delhi, 2015.
33. Adiraju, *The Right Prime Minister: A Political Biography of P.V. Narasimha Rao*, 141.
34. Interview with the manager of Rao's ancestral house in Vangara village, 2015.
35. Interview with P.V. Sharath Babu, nephew of P.V. Narasimha Rao, in Vangara, 2015.
36. Interview with villagers in Vangara (now in Telangana state), 2015.
37. Interview with Captain V. Lakshmikantha Rao in Warangal, 2015.
38. Interview with Mallaiah in Vangara village (now in Telangana state), 2015.
39. Interview with Kalyani Shankar in New Delhi, 2015.
40. Interview with Jairam Ramesh in New Delhi, 2016; confirmed by Kalyani Shankar via email, 2016.
41. Interview with K. Natwar Singh in New Delhi, 2016.

5. DELHI DURBAR, 1975–91

1. Draft chapter on the Emergency, found amongst Rao's private papers in 2015.
2. Ramachandra Guha, *India After Gandhi: The History of the World's Largest Democracy*, 467.
3. Adiraju, *The Right Prime Minister: A Political Biography of P.V. Narasimha Rao*, 143.
4. Interview with M. Narayan Reddy in Hyderabad, 2015.
5. Adiraju, *The Right Prime Minister: A Political Biography of P.V. Narasimha Rao*, 144.
6. Transcript of interview of P.V. Narasimha Rao with the journalist Neerja Chowdhary; copy found among Narasimha Rao's private papers in 2015.
7. Interview with Satchidananda Swamy in Bangalore, 2015.
8. Interview with Narsa Reddy in Hyderabad, 2015.

NOTES

9. Adiraju, *The Right Prime Minister: A Political Biography of P.V. Narasimha Rao*, 151.
10. Ibid., 151–52.
11. Ramachandra Guha, *India After Gandhi: The History of the World's Largest Democracy*, 492.
12. Official Election Commission results of the 1977 General Election, available at http://eci.nic.in/eci_main/StatisticalReports/LS_1977/Vol_I_LS_77.pdf.
13. Francine Frankel, *India's Political Economy 1947–2004* (New Delhi: Oxford University Press, second edition, 2006), 571.
14. Adiraju, *The Right Prime Minister: A Political Biography of P.V. Narasimha Rao*, 153.
15. Interview with K.L.N. Rao in Hyderabad, 2015.
16. 1980 General Election results data available at http://www.elections.in/parliamentary-constituencies/1980-election-results.html.
17. Interview with P.V. Prabhakara Rao in Hyderabad, 2015.
18. Ibid.
19. Ibid.
20. Interview with Ronen Sen in New Delhi, 2015.
21. Ministry of Home Affairs data, available at http://www.mha.nic.in/hindi/sites/upload_files/mhahindi/files/pdf/BM_Intro_E_.pdf.
22. Transcript of interview of P.V. Narasimha Rao with the journalist Neerja Chowdhary; copy found among Narasimha Rao's private papers in 2015.
23. Interview with Captain V. Lakshmikantha Rao in Warangal, 2015.
24. Voice recording of interview with Pranab Mukherjee (likely in the early 1990s) found in Rao's archives in 2015.
25. Interview with Ramu Damodaran in New York, 2015.
26. P.C. Alexander, *Through the Corridors of Power: An Insider's Story* (New Delhi: HarperCollins, 2004), 167–70.
27. Maya Chadda, *Ethnicity, Security, and Separatism in India* (New York: Columbia University Press, 1996), 135.
28. Pranab Mukherjee, *The Turbulent Years: 1980–1996* (New Delhi: Rupa Publications, 2016), 34.
29. Natwar Singh, *One Life Is Not Enough* (New Delhi: Rupa Publications, 2014), 232.

NOTES

30. Rao's deposition to the Ranganath Mishra commission of inquiry; copy found amidst Rao's private papers in 2015.
31. Ibid. In Pranab Mukherjee's biography, he states that Rao was already in Delhi by the afternoon of 31 October.
32. Manoj Mitta and H.S. Phoolka, *When a Tree Shook Delhi* (New Delhi: Roli Books, Kindle edition, 2008), 492.
33. Ibid.
34. Tacitus, *Annales*, 1.7, available at http://perseus.uchicago.edu/perseus-cgi/citequery3.pl?dbname=PerseusLatinTexts&query=Tac.%20Ann.%201.7&getid=1. Quote suggested by Neel Maitra, 2016.
35. Rashid Kidwai, *24 Akbar Road* (Gurgaon: Hachette India, 2011), 160.
36. Mitta and Phoolka, *When a Tree Shook Delhi*.
37. Ibid., 198.
38. 'Bhopal's deadly legacy', the *New York Times*, 4 December 2014, http://www.nytimes.com/2014/12/05/opinion/bhopals-deadly-legacy.html.
39. Alan Taylor, 'Bhopal: The World's Worst Industrial Disaster, 30 Years Later', the *Atlantic*, 2 December 2014, http://www.theatlantic.com/photo/2014/12/bhopal-the-worlds-worst-industrial-disaster-30-years-later/100864/.
40. Singh (with Chopra), *A Grain of Sand in the Hourglass of Time: An Autobiography*, 176.
41. Ibid., 179.
42. Hasan, *Congress after Indira: Policy, Power, Political Change (1984–2009)*, 13.
43. Interview with Captain V. Lakshmikantha Rao in Warangal, 2015.
44. Photograph given to the author by P.V. Prabhakara Rao in Hyderabad, 2015.
45. Interview with P.V. Prabhakara Rao in Hyderabad, 2015.
46. Voice recording of interview with Pranab Mukherjee (likely in the early 1990s) found in Rao's archives in 2015.
47. Singh, *One Life Is Not Enough*, 240.
48. Interview with Dr V.S. Arunachalam in Bangalore, 2015.
49. Interview with Ramu Damodaran in New York, 2016.

50. Ibid.
51. Jairam Ramesh, *To the Brink and Back: India's 1991 Story* (New Delhi: Rupa Publications, 2015), 137.
52. Akshay Mangla, 'Bureaucratic Politics and Universal Primary Education in India', unpublished draft, September 2015, 8.
53. Ibid., 9.
54. Ibid.
55. Interview with Sadanand Menon in Chennai, 2014.
56. Ibid.
57. P.V. Narasimha Rao, *Ayodhya: 6 December 1992* (New Delhi: Penguin Books, 2006), 49.
58. Singh, *One Life Is Not Enough*, 261–62.
59. Ibid., 262.
60. Sanjoy Hazarika, 'Indian army agrees to leave Sri Lanka', the *New York Times*, 19 September 1989, http://www.nytimes.com/1989/09/19/world/indian-army-agrees-to-leave-sri-lanka.html.
61. Arvind Panagariya, 'India in the 1980s and 1990s: A Triumph of Reform', IMF seminar paper, 6 November 2003, https://www.imf.org/external/np/apd/seminars/2003/newdelhi/pana.pdf.
62. 'These included the P. C. Alexander Committee Report on Import and Export Policies of 1978, the Vadilal Dagli Report of the Committee on Controls and Subsidies of 1978, the Abid Hussain Committee Report on Trade Policy of 1984 and the M. Narasimham Report on Industrial Licensing of 1985.' Shankkar Aiyar, *Accidental India: A History of The Nation's Passage through Crisis and Change*, 696.
63. Atul Kohli, 'Politics of Liberalization in India', *World Development* 17, no. 3 (1989): 308–11.
64. Hasan, *Congress after Indira: Policy, Power, Political Change (1984–2009)*, 48.
65. Kohli, 'Politics of Liberalization in India', *World Development*, 312.
66. Sumantra Ghoshal et al., *World Class in India: A Casebook of Companies in Transformation* (New Delhi: Penguin Books, 2001), 167.
67. Dani Rodrik and Arvind Subramanian, 'From "Hindu Growth" to Productivity Surge: The Mystery of the Indian Growth Transition', IMF working paper (May 2004), 5.

NOTES

68. Arvind Panagariya, 'India in the 1980s and 1990s: A Triumph of Reform', IMF seminar paper, 6 November 2003, https://www.imf.org/external/np/apd/seminars/2003/newdelhi/pana.pdf.
69. There is considerable debate between those who argue that this deficit-led growth of the 1980s was its primary problem (e.g. Montek Ahluwalia, T.N. Srinivasan) and those who disagree (e.g. Dani Rodrik and Arvind Subramanian). See Dani Rodrik and Arvind Subramanian, 'From "Hindu Growth" to Productivity Surge: The Mystery of the Indian Growth Transition', 17.
70. Kohli, 'Politics of Liberalization in India', *World Development*, 318–22.
71. Hasan, *Congress after Indira: Policy, Power, Political Change (1984–2009)*, 50.
72. Frankel, *India's Political Economy 1947–2004*, 587–88.
73. Interview with P.V. Prabhakara Rao in Hyderabad, 2015.
74. Ramesh, *To the Brink and Back: India's 1991 Story*, 5.
75. Letter dated 13 December 1990 to commerce minister Subramanian Swamy, found amidst Rao's private papers in 2015.
76. Interview with Prabhakar Menon in Delhi, 2015.
77. Printed diary entry dated 22 June 1991, found amidst Rao's private papers in 2015.
78. Television interview of Kiran Kumar Reddy, available at http://youtu.be/4FDcVeyvgIA.
79. K. Natwar Singh, 'Thatcher, Chandraswami and I', *The Hindu*, 9 April 2013, http://www.thehindu.com/opinion/op-ed/thatcher-chandraswami-and-i/article4595546.ece.
80. Interview with Chandraswami in Delhi, 2015.
81. Interview with Srinath Raghavan in Delhi, 2015.
82. Interview with Shravan, grandson of Narasimha Rao, in Hyderabad, 2015.
83. Interview with R. Srinivasan in Chennai, 2015. Full disclosure: He is the author's uncle.
84. Interview with Velcheru Narayana Rao (on phone) in Atlanta, 2015.
85. 1989 manifesto of the Congress party, 40–41.
86. Letter found amidst Rao's private papers in 2015.
87. Ibid.

NOTES

88. Ibid.
89. Note found amidst Rao's private papers in 2015.
90. Interview with Shekhar Gupta in Delhi, 2015.
91. Ramesh, *To the Brink and Back: India's 1991 Story*, 142.
92. Congressman, 'The Great Suicide', *Mainstream,* 27 January 1990, http://www.mainstreamweekly.net/article5438.html.
93. Interview with Dr Srinath Reddy in Delhi, 2015.
94. Interview with P.V. Rajeshwara Rao in Hyderabad, 2015.
95. Official website of Siddheshwari Peetham, http://www.siddheswaripeetham.org/peethadhipathi-parampara/.
96. Interview with P.V. Prabhakara Rao in Hyderabad, 2015, and Satchidananda Swamy in Bangalore, 2015.

6. MONK TO MONARCH

1. Interview with P.V.R.K. Prasad in Hyderabad, 2015.
2. Letter found amidst Rao's private papers in 2015.
3. Interview with P.V. Prabhakara Rao in Hyderabad, 2015.
4. Printed diary entry dated 22 June 1991, found amidst Rao's private papers in 2015.
5. Interview with Subramanian Swamy in New Delhi, 2015.
6. Interview with Kalyani Shankar in New Delhi, 2015.
7. Interview with Ronen Sen in New Delhi, 2015.
8. P.V. Prabhakara Rao says that his father got membership of IIC, Delhi in 1990–91; confirmed by Salman Haidar in New Delhi, 2015.
9. Appointment Diary 1991, written by Rao's secretary, Khandekar, and found amidst his private papers in 2015.
10. Printed diary entry found amidst Rao's private papers in 2015.
11. Interview with Ronen Sen in New Delhi, 2015.
12. Interview with P.V. Rajeshwara Rao in Hyderabad, 2015.
13. Interview with Gopalkrishna Gandhi in Chennai, 2015.
14. Interview with Rajeshwara Rao in Hyderabad, 2015.
15. Confirmed in interviews with Prabhakara Rao, Rajeshwara Rao, P.V.R.K. Prasad (all in Hyderabad) and Satchidananda Swamy (in Bengaluru) in 2015.

NOTES

16. 11 May 1991 entry in his 1991 Appointment Diary, maintained by Rao's secretary, R.K. Khandekar, and found amidst his private papers in 2015.
17. Official Election Commission results data of the 1991 General Election, available at http://eci.nic.in/eci_main/StatisticalReports/LS_1991/VOL_I_91.pdf.
18. 22 May 1991 entry in Rao's 1991 Appointment Diary, found amidst his private papers in 2015.
19. K.M.H.C.B. Kulatunga, 'When Tigers Killed Rajiv Gandhi 22 Years Ago', *Sunday Observer,* Colombo, 19 May 2013,http://www.sundayobserver.lk/2013/05/19/fea05.asp
20. Printed diary entry found amidst Rao's private papers in 2015.
21. Interview with Gopalkrishna Gandhi in Chennai, 2015.
22. 22 May 1991 entry in Rao's 1991 Appointment Diary, found amidst his private papers in 2015.
23. Ibid.
24. Ibid.
25. Singh (with Chopra), *A Grain of Sand in the Hourglass of Time: An Autobiography*, 240.
26. 22 May 1991 entry in Rao's 1991 Appointment Diary, found amidst his private papers in 2015.
27. Kidwai, *24 Akbar Road*, 151.
28. Alexander, *Through the Corridors of Power: An Insider's Story*, 402.
29. Ibid., pp. 402–03.
30. Robert Benjamin, 'Thousands mourn as Gandhi's body is cremated', *Baltimore Sun,* 25 May 1991, http://articles.baltimoresun.com/1991-05-25/news/1991145017_1_gandhi-rajiv-india.
31. Mukherjee, *The Turbulent Years: 1980–1996*, 131.
32. Robert Benjamin, 'Thousands mourn as Gandhi's body is cremated'.
33. Kidwai, *24 Akbar Road*, 156.
34. K. Natwar Singh, 'How PV became PM', *The Hindu,* 6 July 2012, http://www.thehindu.com/opinion/op-ed/how-pv-became-pm/article3592050.ece.
35. Ibid.
36. Interview with Satish Sharma in New Delhi, 2015.

NOTES

37. Ibid.
38. Ibid.
39. Kalyani Shankar, *Pandora's Daughters* (New Delhi: Bloomsbury India, 2013), 45. Confirmed in an interview, 2015.
40. Interview with Subramanian Swamy in New Delhi, 2015.
41. Letter found amidst Rao's private papers in 2015.
42. Adiraju, *The Right Prime Minister: A Political Biography of P.V. Narasimha Rao*, 189.
43. Interview with Jairam Ramesh in New Delhi, 2015.
44. Interview with Salman Khurshid in New Delhi, 2015.
45. Kidwai, *24 Akbar Road*, 161.
46. Alexander, *Through the Corridors of Power: An Insider's Story*, 406.
47. Ibid., 405.
48. Interview with Subramanian Swamy in New Delhi, 2015.
49. Interview with N.K. Sharma in New Delhi, 2015.
50. 17 June 1991 entry in Rao's 1991 Appointment Diary, found amidst his private papers in 2015.
51. George Perkovich, *India's Nuclear Bomb: The Impact of Global Proliferation* (New Delhi: Oxford University Press, 1999), 320.
52. R.D. Pradhan, *My Years with Rajiv and Sonia* (New Delhi: Hay House India, 2014), 170–71.
53. Alexander, *Through the Corridors of Power: An Insider's Story*, 407.
54. 'Pawar declares his candidature', the *Times of India*, 20 June 1991, 1.
55. Singh (with Chopra), *A Grain of Sand in the Hourglass of Time: An Autobiography*, 329.
56. Interview with Kalyani Shankar in New Delhi, 2015.
57. Interview with M.K. Narayanan in Chennai, 2015.
58. R. Venkataraman, *My Presidential Years* (New Delhi: Harper Collins, 1994): Jairam Ramesh, *To the Brink and Back: India's 1991 Story*, 23.
59. Ramesh, *To the Brink and Back: India's 1991 Story*, 6.
60. Interview with Jairam Ramesh in New Delhi, 2015.
61. Interview with Naresh Chandra in New Delhi, 2015.
62. Interview with Manmohan Singh in New Delhi, 2015.
63. Ibid.

NOTES

64. Interview with Montek Singh Ahluwalia in New Delhi, 2015.
65. Ibid.
66. 'Narasimha sworn in ninth PM', the *Times of India*, 22 June 1991, 1.
67. Cover, *India Today*, 15 July 1991.
68. Zafar Agha, 'New government: Back to the old guard', *India Today,* 15 July 1991, http://indiatoday.intoday.in/story/narasimha-rao-election-as-prime-minister-heralds-return-of-the-old-congress-guard/1/318487.html.
69. *P.V. Narasimha Rao Selected Speeches 1991–1992*, 3–4.
70. Interview with Naresh Chandra in New Delhi, 2015.

7. RESCUING THE ECONOMY, 1991–92

1. Aiyar, *Accidental India: A History of the Nation's Passage through Crisis and Change*, 1081–87.
2. The flight was caught by enterprising journalists of the *Indian Express*, led by Shankkar Aiyar.
3. Ramesh, *To the Brink and Back: India's 1991 Story*, 16.
4. Ibid., 11.
5. Quoted directly from Daman Singh, *Strictly Personal: Manmohan & Gursharan* (New Delhi: HarperCollins, 2014), 373.
6. Aiyar, *Accidental India: A History of the Nation's Passage through Crisis and Change*, 1048.
7. *P.V. Narasimha Rao Selected Speeches 1991–1992*, 106
8. Ramesh, *To the Brink and Back: India's 1991 Story*, 31.
9. Singh, *Strictly Personal: Manmohan & Gursharan*, 353.
10. Ibid., pp. 359–60.
11. Interview with Montek Singh Ahluwalia in Delhi, 2015.
12. Singh, *Strictly Personal: Manmohan & Gursharan*, 355.
13. Rob Jenkins, *Democratic Politics and Economic Reform in India* (Cambridge: Cambridge University Press, 1999), 41.
14. 1991 General Election manifesto of the Indian National Congress(I), 22.
15. Ibid., 24.
16. Mancur Olson, *The Logic of Collective Action: Public Goods and the Theory of Groups* (Harvard Economic Studies, revised edition, 1971).

NOTES

17. Interview with Naresh Chandra in Delhi, 2015.
18. Interview with Subramanian Swamy in New Delhi, 2015.
19. Interview with Jairam Ramesh in New Delhi, 2015.
20. Interview with Sanjaya Baru in New Delhi, 2015.
21. Interview with Manmohan Singh in New Delhi, 2015.
22. Ramesh, *To the Brink and Back: India's 1991 Story*, 18–19.
23. *Report of the South Commission: The Challenge to the South* (Oxford: Oxford University Press, 1990), http://www.southcentre.int/wp-content/uploads/2013/02/The-Challenge-to-the-South_EN.pdf.
24. Singh, *Strictly Personal: Manmohan & Gursharan*, 349–50.
25. Story narrated to the author by an official who had worked with Rao at the time, and who wishes to remain anonymous.
26. Interview with G.V. Ramakrishna in Chennai, 2015.
27. Full disclosure: Ahluwalia's second son is a friend of the author.
28. Yashwant Sinha, *Confessions of a Swadeshi Reformer: My Years as Finance Minister* (New Delhi: Viking, 2007), 40.
29. Interview with Rakesh Mohan in Washington, D.C., 2015.
30. Interview with Jairam Ramesh in New Delhi, 2015.
31. Sinha, *Confessions of a Swadeshi Reformer: My Years as Finance Minister*, 26.
32. Interview with Naresh Chandra in Delhi, 2015.
33. Interview with Rakesh Mohan in Washington, D.C., 2015.
34. *P.V. Narasimha Rao Selected Speeches 1991–1992*, 7.
35. Singh, *Strictly Personal: Manmohan & Gursharan*, 354.
36. Interview with Manmohan Singh in New Delhi, 2015.
37. *P.V. Narasimha Rao Selected Speeches 1991–1992*, 8.
38. T.N. Ninan, 'Story of Two Devaluations', *Business Standard*, 16 August 2013, http://www.business-standard.com/article/opinion/story-of-two-devaluations-113081601231_1.html.
39. Ramesh, *To the Brink and Back: India's 1991 Story*, 36.
40. Note found amidst his private papers in 2015.
41. 'Step in Haste: Opposition', *Times of India*, 2 July 1991, 1.
42. Ibid.
43. Note found amidst his private papers in 2015.
44. Interview with Manmohan Singh in New Delhi, 2015.
45. Ibid.

NOTES

46. Letter found amidst Rao's private papers in 2015.
47. His book, first published in 1993, gives some sense of his detailed rage at the licence raj. See Ashok V. Desai, *My Economic Affair* (New Delhi: Wiley Eastern Limited, second edition, 1994).
48. Shaji Vikraman, 'Commitment, quick decisions in making of new trade policy', the *Indian Express*, 13 August 2015, http://indianexpress.com/article/explained/express-economic-history-series-commitment-quick-decisions-in-making-of-new-trade-policy/.
49. Ibid.
50. *P.V. Narasimha Rao Selected Speeches 1991–1992*, 155.
51. Ibid., 156.
52. Interview with Rakesh Mohan in Washington, D.C., 2015.
53. Aiyar, *Accidental India: A History of the Nation's Passage through Crisis and Change*, 849.
54. Interview with Rakesh Mohan in Washington, D.C., 2015.
55. Ramesh, *To the Brink and Back: India's 1991 Story*, 77.
56. Interview with P.V.R.K. Prasad in Hyderabad, 2015.
57. Ramesh, *To the Brink and Back: India's 1991 Story*, 83.
58. Kalyani Shankar, 'Industrial Licensing to go', *Hindustan Times*, 12 July 1991.
59. Ramesh, *To the Brink and Back: India's 1991 Story*, 87.
60. *P.V. Narasimha Rao Selected Speeches 1991–1992*, 9.
61. Entry on 16 July 1991 in Appointment Diary 1991, written by Rao's secretary, Khandekar; found amidst his private papers in 2015.
62. Interview with Rakesh Mohan in Washington D.C., 2015.
63. Shaji Vikraman, 'Industrial policy and the importance of political context', the *Indian Express*, 24 June 2015, http://indianexpress.com/article/explained/express-economic-history-series-industrial-policy-and-the-importance-of-political-context/.
64. Tapan Dasgupta, 'Cabinet okays industrial policy', the *Times of India*, 24 July 1991, 1.
65. Interview with Manmohan Singh in New Delhi, 2015.
66. Interview with Rakesh Mohan in Washington, D.C., 2015.
67. Sinha, *Confessions of a Swadeshi Reformer: My Years as Finance Minister*, 42.

NOTES

68. Interview with T.S.R. Subramanian in Noida, 2015. Full disclosure: he is my uncle.
69. Sinha, *Confessions of a Swadeshi Reformer: My Years as Finance Minister*, 44.
70. *P.V. Narasimha Rao Selected Speeches 1991–1992*, 155–56.
71. Ramesh, *To the Brink and Back: India's 1991 Story*, 104.
72. Entry on 20 July 1991 in Appointment Diary 1991, written by Rao's secretary, Khandekar; found amidst Rao's private papers in 2015.
73. Letter found amidst Rao's private papers in 2015.
74. Interview with Manmohan Singh in New Delhi, 2015.
75. Swaminathan S. Anklesaria Aiyar, 'Unsung Hero of the India Story', 26 June, 2011, http://swaminomics.org/unsung-hero-of-the-india-story/.
76. Ramesh, *To the Brink and Back: India's 1991 Story*, 98.
77. Ibid.
78. 'A budget, a briefcase and expectations: Finance ministers on budget day', http://www.livemint.com/Multimedia/GyTLM3rVW8wPCsVA89j36H/A-budget-a-briefcase-and-expectationsFinance-ministers-on.html.
79. 1991–92 Union Budget, para 1. Available at http://indiabudget.nic.in/bspeech/bs199192.pdf.
80. Ibid., para 2.
81. Ibid., para 16.
82. Puja Mehra, 'Liberalisation (1991–92)', *The Hindu*, 7 July 2014, http://www.thehindu.com/business/budget/liberalisation-199192/article6186027.ece.
83. 1991–1992 Union Budget, para 153. Available at http://indiabudget.nic.in/bspeech/bs199192.pdf.
84. Entry on 24 July 1991 in Appointment Diary 1991; found amidst Rao's private papers in 2015.
85. Editorial, the *Times of India*, 25 July 1991.
86. 'Singh's new song', *The Economist*, 27 July 1991, 52.
87. Cover, *India Today*, 31 July 1991.
88. 'Anti-people, says opposition', *Times of India*, 25 July 1991, 1.
89. *P.V. Narasimha Rao Selected Speeches 1991–1992*, 16.
90. Ibid.
91. *P.V. Narasimha Rao Selected Speeches 1991–1992*, 164.

NOTES

92. Ibid., 158–59.
93. Interview with Rakesh Mohan in Washington, D.C., 2015.
94. Ramesh, *To the Brink and Back: India's 1991 Story*, 72.
95. Interview with Manmohan Singh in New Delhi, 2015.
96. Ramesh, *To the Brink and Back: India's 1991 Story*, 110.
97. Ibid., 60.
98. Ibid., annexure 6.
99. Hasan, *Congress after Indira: Policy, Power, Political Change (1984–2009)*, 53.
100. Ibid.
101. Interview with Sanjaya Baru in New Delhi, 2015.
102. Singh, *Strictly Personal: Manmohan & Gursharan*, 382.
103. Interview with P.V. Prabhakara Rao in Hyderabad, 2015.
104. Ramesh, *To the Brink and Back: India's 1991 Story*, 103.
105. Ibid.
106. Interview with P.V.R.K. Prasad in Hyderabad, 2015.
107. Kapil Komireddi, 'PV Narasimha Rao reinvented India—so why is he the forgotten man?', the *National*, 19 May 2012, http://www.thenational.ae/lifestyle/pv-narasimha-rao-reinvented-india-so-why-is-he-the-forgotten-man.
108. Ramesh, *To the Brink and Back: India's 1991 Story*, 108.
109. Interview with Mani Shankar Aiyar in New Delhi, 2015.
110. Singh, *Strictly Personal: Manmohan & Gursharan*, 366.
111. Jenkins, *Democratic Politics and Economic Reform in India*, 14.
112. Ramesh, *To the Brink and Back: India's 1991 Story*, 123.
113. Interview with Naresh Chandra in Delhi, 2015.
114. James Manor, 'The Congress party and the "Great Transformation"', in Sanjay Ruparelia et al., *Understanding India's New Political Economy: A Great Transformation?* (Abingdon: Routledge, 2011), 204–21.
115. Singh, *Strictly Personal: Manmohan & Gursharan* (New Delhi: HarperCollins, 2014), 384.
116. Devengshu Datta, 'The Budgets That Shaped India', *Huffington Post,* 28 February 2015, http://www.huffingtonpost.in/devangshu-datta/budgets-that-shaped-india_b_6773966.html.
117. From the Reserve Bank of India's database on the Indian Economy, available at dbie.rbi.org.in.

118. Interview with S. Rajgopal in Mumbai, 2015.
119. *P.V. Narasimha Rao Selected Speeches 1992–1993*, 161.
120. Jeremy Adelman, *Worldly Philosopher: The Odyssey of Albert O. Hirschman* (New Jersey: Princeton University Press, 2013), 262.
121. 'At a Glance—India and the IMF', available at https://www.imf.org/external/country/IND/rr/glance.htm.
122. Interview with Tarun Das in New Delhi, 2015.

8. GROWING THE ECONOMY, 1992–96

1. Roger Boesche, 'Moderate Machiavelli? Contrasting The Prince with the Arthashastra of Kautilya', *Critical Horizons* 3, no. 2 (2002): 257–58.
2. There is controversy on the date. Some scholars believe that it was more likely written in the 3rd century AD.
3. For a discussion on these techniques, see Rashed Uz Zaman, 'Kautilya: The Indian Strategic Thinker and Indian Strategic Culture', *Comparative Strategy* 25:3, 231–47 (2006), 238.
4. Akhilesh Pillalamarri, 'Chanakya: India's Truly Radical Machiavelli", *The National Interest*, 29 January 2015, http://nationalinterest.org/feature/chanakya-indias-truly-radical-machiavelli-12146.
5. Boesche, 'Moderate Machiavelli? Contrasting The Prince with the Arthashastra of Kautilya', 260.
6. Hasan, *Congress after Indira: Policy, Power, Political Change (1984–2009)*.
7. Interview with Kalyani Shankar in New Delhi, 201.
8. Note from P.C. Alexander dated 27 March 1992, found amongst Rao's private papers in 2015.
9. Note from V.N. Gadgil, found amongst Rao's private papers in 2015.
10. Interview with Montek Singh Ahluwalia in New Delhi, 2015.
11. Singh, *Strictly Personal: Manmohan & Gursharan*, 380.
12. Janak Singh, 'Rao Swears by Nehru', the *Times of India*, 17 April 1992, 1.
13. A. Devarajan, 'Tirupati Plenary—down memory lane', *The Hindu*, 21 January 2006, http://www.thehindu.com/todays-paper/tp-national/tp-andhrapradesh/tirupati-plenary-down-the-memory-lane/article3242772.ece.

NOTES

14. 'Congress Economics', the *Times of India*, 17 April 1992, 10.
15. Interview with G.V. Ramakrishna in Chennai, 2015.
16. Sucheta Dalal, 'Harshad Mehta scam broke 20 years ago. What has changed?' *Moneylife*, 3 May 2012.
17. Chapter 25 of Niccolò Machiavelli (translator: Harvey Mansfield), *The Prince* (Chicago: University of Chicago Press, second edition, 1998).
18. Dalal, 'Harshad Mehta scam broke 20 years ago. What has changed?', 3 May 2012.
19. Edward A. Gargan, 'Huge Financial Scandal Shakes Indian Politics', the *New York Times*, 9 June 1992, http://www.nytimes.com/1992/06/09/business/huge-financial-scandal-shakes-indian-politics.html.
20. Ibid.
21. Note found amongst Rao's private papers in 2015.
22. Gargan, 'Huge Financial Scandal Shakes Indian Politics'.
23. Dalal, 'Harshad Mehta scam broke 20 years ago. What has changed?'.
24. Interview with G.V. Ramakrishna in Chennai, 2015.
25. Ibid.
26. 'Foreign Institutional Investors in India', *Indian Securities Market, A Review*, November 2009, http://www.nseindia.com/content/us/ismr2009ch8.pdf.
27. Deepak Korgaonkar and Puneet Wadhwa, 'FIIs' net investment in equities set to cross Rs 1 lakh cr in 2014', *Business Standard*, 4 December 2014, http://www.business-standard.com/article/markets/fiis-net-investment-in-equities-set-to-cross-rs-1-trillion-in-2014-114120400151_1.html.
28. Interview with Pratap Mehta in New Delhi, 2015.
29. Letter found amongst Rao's private papers in 2015.
30. Interview with P.V. Prabhakara Rao in Hyderabad, 2015.
31. Interviews with Manmohan Singh and Montek Singh Ahluwalia in New Delhi, 2015.
32. Interview with P.V. Prabhakara Rao in Hyderabad, 2015.
33. Interview with Sanjaya Baru in New Delhi, 2015.
34. Interview with Manmohan Singh in New Delhi, 2015.
35. Interview with Prabhakar Menon in Delhi, 2015.

NOTES

36. 'India deploys 200,000 police as it braces for Hindu-Muslim race riots over 16th-century mosque ownership', *Daily Mail*, 30 September 2010, http://www.dailymail.co.uk/news/article-1316466/Ayodhya-verdict-India-braces-Hindu-Muslim-riots-Babri-mosque-ownership.html
37. *P.V. Narasimha Rao Selected Speeches 1992–1993*, 302.
38. Jenkins, *Democratic Politics and Economic Reform in India*, 201.
39. Hasan, *Congress after Indira: Policy, Power, Political Change (1984–2009)*, 58.
40. 'IDFC and Bandhan make the cut for banking licences', *Business Standard*, 3 April 2014, http://www.business-standard.com/article/specials/rbi-grants-bank-licence-to-idfc-bandhan-114040200963_1.html.
41. Prasad, *Wheels behind the Veil: PMs, CMs and beyond,* 120.
42. Infosys website, available at http://www.infosys.com/investors/investor-services/Pages/FAQs.aspx.
43. Data available at *https://ycharts.com/companies/INFY/market_cap*.
44. Interview with Devesh Kapur (on phone) in the United States, 2015.
45. Interview with Nandan Nilekani in Bangalore, 2015.
46. Ibid.
47. *P.V. Narasimha Rao Selected Speeches 1993–1994*, 237.
48. Ibid., 282.
49. Adiraju, *The Right Prime Minister: A Political Biography of P.V. Narasimha Rao*.
50. *P.V. Narasimha Rao Selected Speeches 1993–1994*, 422.
51. Interview with Montek Singh Ahluwalia in New Delhi, 2015.
52. *P.V. Narasimha Rao Selected Speeches 1993–1994*, 24.
53. Interview with Montek Singh Ahluwalia in New Delhi, 2015.
54. *P.V. Narasimha Rao Selected Speeches 1993–1994*, 131.
55. *P.V. Narasimha Rao Selected Speeches 1991–1992*, 185.
56. See generally, Kohli, 'Politics of Liberalization in India'.
57. CII website, available at http://www.cii.in/about_us_History.aspx?enc=ns9fJzmNKJnsoQCyKqUmaQ==.
58. Interview with Montek Singh Ahluwalia in New Delhi, 2015.
59. Montek S. Ahluwalia, 'Infrastructure Development in India's Reforms', 5, http://planningcommission.gov.in/aboutus/speech/spemsa/new/msa29.pdf.

NOTES

60. Ibid., 2.
61. Ibid., 4.
62. T.S. Ramakrishnan and T. Raghuram, 'Evolution of Model Concession Agreement for National Highways of India', Indian Institute of Management, Ahmedabad, July 2012, 4. Available at: http://www.iimahd.ernet.in/assets/snippets/workingpaperpdf/5564292122012-07-01.pdf.
63. Montek S. Ahluwalia, 'Infrastructure Development in India's Reforms', 5.
64. Data available at http://www.tradingeconomics.com/india/electricity-production-from-coal-sources-percent-of-total-wb-data.html.
65. Jenkins, *Democratic Politics and Economic Reform in India*, 189.
66. Ibid., 190.
67. *P.V. Narasimha Rao Selected Speeches 1992–1993*, 235.
68. Waquar Ahmed, 'From Militant Particularism to Anti-neoliberalism? The Anti-Enron Movement in India', *Antipode* 44, no. 4, (2012): 1059–80.
69. Singh (with Chopra), *A Grain of Sand in the Hourglass of Time: An Autobiography*, 306.
70. Ibid., 307.
71. Dilip Bobb, 'Fact or Fiction?', *India Today*, 15 July 1993, http://indiatoday.intoday.in/story/securities-scam-harshad-mehta-claims-to-have-paid-rs-1-crore-to-narasimha-rao/1/303698.html.
72. Singh, *Strictly Personal: Manmohan & Gursharan*, 389.
73. Interview with Montek Singh Ahluwalia in New Delhi, 2015.
74. Ibid.
75. Singh, *Strictly Personal: Manmohan & Gursharan*, 386.
76. Prasad, *Wheels behind the Veil: PMs, CMs and beyond*, 123.
77. Interview with P.V.R.K. Prasad in Hyderabad, 2015.
78. Interview with Sanjaya Baru in New Delhi, 2015.
79. Ibid.
80. Prasad, *Wheels behind the Veil: PMs, CMs and beyond*, 123.
81. Shanti Kumar, *Gandhi Meets Primetime: Globalization and Nationalism in Indian Television* (Champaign: University of Illinois Press, 2005), 4.
82. Ibid., 4–5.
83. Interview with P.V.R.K. Prasad in Hyderabad, 2015.

NOTES

84. Interview with Nalin Mehta in New Delhi, 2015.
85. *The Secretary, Ministry of Information and Broadcasting* vs *Cricket Association of Bengal*, 1995, SCC (2) 161.
86. Data available at http://telecomtalk.info/total-number-tv-channels-india/139844/.
87. World Bank data, available at http://data.worldbank.org/indicator/IS.AIR.PSGR.
88. 'Narasimha Rao govt asked Tata to start airline, then backed out', the *Times of India*, 31 January 2015, http://timesofindia.indiatimes.com/india/Narasimha-Rao-govt-asked-Tata-to-start-airline-then-backed-out/articleshow/46073074.cms.
89. Document found amongst Rao's private papers in 2015.
90. 'Sukh Ram, Vittal duel stalls Telecom reforms', *Economic Times*, 17 April 1994.
91. Letter from Sukh Ram dated April 20 1994, found amongst Rao's private papers in 2015.
92. Sinha, *Confessions of a Swadeshi Reformer: My Years as Finance Minister*, 161.
93. Data sourced from 'Highlights of Telecom Subscription Data as on 31st March, 2015', Telecom Regulatory Authority of India, available at http://www.trai.gov.in/WriteReadData/WhatsNew/Documents/PR-34-TSD-Mar-12052015.pdf.
94. Rohit Saran, '1995: Cell phones arrives', *India Today*, 26 December 2005, http://indiatoday.intoday.in/story/bengal-cm-jyoti-basu-made-indias-first-cell-phone-call-to-telecom-minister-sukh-ram-in-1995/1/192421.html.
95. Interview with Sanjaya Baru in New Delhi, 2015.
96. Interview with Tarun Das in New Delhi, 2015.
97. Interview with Manmohan Singh in New Delhi, 2015.
98. 'Defend GATT Aggressively', *India Today*, 15 May 1994, http://indiatoday.intoday.in/story/defend-gatt-aggressively/1/295403.html.
99. Resolution of 2 April 1994, found amongst Rao's private papers in 2015.
100. *P.V. Narasimha Rao Selected Speeches 1993–1994*, 234.
101. John F. Burns, 'Unlikely Reformer Coaxes India Towards a Market Economy', the *New York Times*, 8 May 1994, http://www.nytimes.

com/1994/05/08/business/unlikely-reformer-coaxes-india-toward-a-market-economy.html?pagewanted=all.
102. Sunil Jain, 'Slow Pace, Long Road', *India Today,* 15 October 1994, http://indiatoday.intoday.in/story/slow-pace-long-road/1/294199.html.
103. Daksesh Parekh, 'Basically Different', *India Today,* 30 September 1994, http://indiatoday.intoday.in/story/two-and-a-half-years-of-sulking-sensex-hits-new-high-with-cheery-nonchalance/1/294111.html.
104. *P.V. Narasimha Rao Selected Speeches 1994–1995*, 22.
105. Rachel Dwyer, '"Indian values" and the diaspora: Yash Chopra's films of the 1990s', *West Coast Line*, 32–34 (2, Autumn 2000), 6–27.
106. Singh (with Chopra), *A Grain of Sand in the Hourglass of Time: An Autobiography,* 310.
107. Inderjit Badhwar and Zafar Agha, 'Rao's actions are anti-secular', *India Today,* 15 June 1995, http://indiatoday.intoday.in/story/raos-actions-are-anti-secular/1/288952.html.
108. Zafar Agha, 'Fighting for survival', *India Today,* 15 June 1995, http://indiatoday.intoday.in/story/divided-denied-its-traditional-vote-banks-congress-turns-to-populism-and-regional-players/1/290438.html.
109. Jenkins, *Democratic Politics and Economic Reform in India,* 13.
110. Interview with Montek Singh Ahluwalia in New Delhi, 2015.
111. *P.V. Narasimha Rao Selected Speeches 1993–1994*, 468.
112. Kanta Murali, *Economic liberalization, electoral coalitions and private investment in India* (PhD dissertation, Department of Politics, Princeton University, 2013).
113. Interview with Devesh Kapur (on phone) in the United States, 2016.

9. A WELFARE STATE?

1. Chatterjee, *Keeping the Faith: Memoirs of a Parliamentarian*, 99.
2. Manor, 'The Congress party and the "Great Transformation"', 204–20.
3. Hindi phrase that means 'Remove Poverty'.
4. Satish Y. Deodhar, *Day to Day Economics* (IIM Ahmedabad Business Books, Random House India, 2012), 41.

NOTES

5. Ibid., 41.
6. Mihir Shah et al., 'Rural Credit in 20th century India: An Overview of History and Perspectives', 17, http://www1.ximb.ac.in/users/fac/shambu/sprasad.nsf/0/e78490ff090249d06525730c0030abf9/$FILE/Mihir%20Shah_rural_credit__April_2007__epw.pdf.
7. Jagdish Bhagwati and Arvind Panagariya, *Why Growth Matters: How Economic Growth in India Reduced Poverty and the Lessons for Other Developing Countries* (Public Affairs, Kindle edition, 2013), 33–35.
8. Census of India 1991 literacy rates, available at http://infochangeindia.org/education/statistics/literacy-rates-in-india-1951-2001.html.
9. 'Global Nutrition Report: India Country Profile', available at http://globalnutritionreport.org/files/2014/11/gnr14_cp_india.pdf.
10. Jenkins, *Democratic Politics and Economic Reform in India*, 23.
11. Interview with Sanjaya Baru in New Delhi, 2015.
12. Deodhar, *Day to Day Economics*, 41.
13. In terms of tax and non-tax receipts.
14. Figures computed by Vikram Srinivas. Data sourced from 'Handbook of Statistics on the Indian economy', Reserve Bank of India, available at http://dbie.rbi.org.in/DBIE/dbie.rbi?site=publications. Srinivas has used the year 1982 as base, and CPI for industrial workers as the deflator to calculate in real terms.
15. Ibid.
16. Notes and letters found amidst Rao's private papers in 2015.
17. Jenkins, *Democratic Politics and Economic Reform in India*, 178.
18. Interview with Prabhakar Menon in Delhi, 2015.
19. Interview with Jairam Ramesh in New Delhi, 2015.
20. Interview with Ramu Damodaran in New York, 2015.
21. '"People's IAS officer" S.R. Sankaran no more', *The Hindu*, 8 October 2010, http://www.thehindu.com/todays-paper/tp-national/tp-andhrapradesh/peoples-ias-officer-sr-sankaran-no-more/article818981.ece.
22. C.R. Sukumar, 'Satya Nadella's father a high achiever himself; has strong left leanings', *Economic Times*, 3 February 2014, http://articles.economictimes.indiatimes.com/2014-02-03/news/46963079_1_satya-nadella-yugandhar-rural-development.
23. *P.V. Narasimha Rao Selected Speeches 1991–1992*, 412.

NOTES

24. Jenkins, *Democratic Politics and Economic Reform in India*, 181.
25. Ibid., 182.
26. *P.V. Narasimha Rao Selected Speeches 1991–1992*, 412.
27. Note found amidst Rao's private papers in 2015.
28. Swaminathan S. Anklesaria Aiyar, 'The real path to social justice', 27 April 997, http://swaminomics.org/the-real-path-to-social-justice/.
29. Jairam Ramesh, 'New subsidy raj', *India Today*, 15 February 1999, http://indiatoday.intoday.in/story/the-pds-has-been-reformed-but-problems-remain/1/253199.html.
30. Jenkins, *Democratic Politics and Economic Reform in India*, 24.
31. Interview with K.R. Venugopal in Hyderabad, 2016.
32. Interview with Ramu Damodaran in New York, 2015.
33. Jenkins, *Democratic Politics and Economic Reform in India*, 185.
34. *P.V. Narasimha Rao Selected Speeches 1993–1994*, 54.
35. Sudipta Sengupta, 'When former PM PV Narasimha Rao "gatecrashed" Satya Nadella's wedding', the *Times of India*, 7 February 2014, http://timesofindia.indiatimes.com/india/When-former-PM-PV-Narasimha-Rao-gatecrashed-Satya-Nadellas-wedding/articleshow/29965083.cms.
36. Interview with Ramu Damodaran in New York, 2015.
37. Interview with Sanjaya Baru in New Delhi, 2015.
38. The budget also included spending on youth and culture.
39. *P.V. Narasimha Rao Selected Speeches 1994–1995*, 100.
40. Interview with Akshay Mangla (on the phone) in US, 2015.
41. Interview with Keshav Desiraju in New Delhi, 2015.
42. Jean Drèze and Amartya Sen, *An Uncertain Glory: India and its Contradictions* (Princeton: Princeton University Press, Kindle edition, 2013), 118.
43. Ibid., 118–19.
44. Ibid., 122.
45. Interview with Baladevan Rangaraju in Delhi, 2015.
46. This has been a smaller increase compared to the increase in absolute amounts.
47. This includes the budget for health and family welfare. See *P.V. Narasimha Rao Selected Speeches 1994–1995*, 100.

48. Devesh Kapur and Prakirti Nangia, 'Social Protection in India: A Welfare State Sans Public Goods?', *India Review* 14, no. 1, 73–90 (2015): 77.
49. Ibid., 83.
50. Bhagwati and Panagariya, *Why Growth Matters: How Economic Growth in India Reduced Poverty and the Lessons for Other Developing Countries*, 33–34.
51. Ibid., 33–35.
52. Pranjul Bhandari and Rohit Lamba, *On Twenty-five Years of Economic Liberalisation* (unpublished paper, 2016).
53. Devesh Kapur, D. Shyam Babu and Chandra Bhan Prasad, *Defying the Odds: The Rise of Dalit Entrepreneurs* (Gurgaon: Random House India, 2014).
54. See, for example, Pravin Krishna and Guru Sethupathy, 'Trade and Inequality in India', in Jagdish Bhagwati and Arvind Panagariya, eds, *India's Reform: How They Produced Inclusive Growth* (New Delhi: Oxford University Press, 2012), 247–78. There is, however, a debate on the quality of the data, and other metrics, such as malnutrition.
55. Drèze and Sen, *An Uncertain Glory: India and its Contradictions*.
56. Devesh Kapur and Prakirti Nangia, 'Social Protection in India: A Welfare State Sans Public Goods?'.
57. World Bank estimates, available at http://www.worldbank.org/en/news/feature/2013/05/13/helping-india-combat-persistently-high-rates-of-malnutrition.
58. *P.V. Narasimha Rao Selected Speeches 1991–1992*, 63.
59. Hasan, *Congress after Indira: Policy, Power, Political Change (1984–2009)*, 14.
60. Interview with Devesh Kapur in Philadelphia, 2015.

10. SURVIVING PARTY AND PARLIAMENT

1. Interview with Dr Srinath Reddy in Delhi, 2015.
2. Interview with Rajaiah in Vangara village (now in Telangana state), 2015.
3. Manor, 'The Congress party and the "Great Transformation"', 204–21.

NOTES

4. Atul Kohli, *Democracy and Discontent: India's Growing Crisis of Governability* (Cambridge: Cambridge University Press, 1991).
5. Rajni Kothari, 'The Congress "System" in India', 1161–73.
6. Interview with Salman Khurshid in New Delhi, 2015.
7. 'Narasimha Sworn in ninth PM', the *Times of India*, 22 June 1991, 1.
8. Ibid.
9. Interview with N.K. Sharma in New Delhi, 2015.
10. *P.V. Narasimha Rao Selected Speeches 1991–1992*, 11.
11. 'Rao wins trust vote', the *Times of India*, 16 July 1991, 1.
12. Interview with Subramanian Swamy in New Delhi, 2015.
13. Note found amidst Rao's private papers in 2015.
14. Gollapudi Srinivasa Rao, 'Seventh Highest Margin', *The Hindu*, 26 November 2015, http://www.thehindu.com/todays-paper/tp-national/tp-telangana/seventh-highest-margin/article7914610.ece.
15. While Vajpayee accepted the honour, Namboodiripad refused.
16. V. Krishna Ananth, *India Since Independence: Making Sense of Indian Politics* (New Delhi: Pearson Education India, 2010), 391.
17. The *Times of India*, 10 March 1992, 1.
18. Prasad, *Wheels behind the Veil: PMs, CMs and beyond*, 101–02.
19. Zafar Agha, 'The favourite five', *India Today*, 31 May 1993, http://indiatoday.intoday.in/story/five-trusted-aides-who-help-pm-narasimha-rao-run-the-party-and-the-government/1/302316.html.
20. Singh, *One Life Is Not Enough*, 290.
21. Interview with N.K. Sharma in New Delhi, 2015
22. Interview with Ramu Damodaran in New York, 2015.
23. Interview with Dr Srinath Reddy in Delhi, 2015.
24. Interview with Ramu Damodaran in New York, 2015.
25. *P.V. Narasimha Rao Selected Speeches 1991–1992*, 434.
26. Singh (with Chopra), *A Grain of Sand in the Hourglass of Time: An Autobiography*, 310.
27. Prasad, *Wheels behind the Veil: PMs, CMs and beyond*, 107.
28. 'NF-left plans no-trust move', the *Times of India*, 30 June 1992, 1.
29. 'Narasimha Rao wins trust vote', the *Times of India*, 18 July 1992, 1.

NOTES

30. Akshaya Mukul, 'How Shukla saved Rao govt in 1992', the *Times of India*, 23 September 2012, http://timesofindia.indiatimes.com/india/How-Shukla-saved-Rao-govt-in-1992/articleshow/16509278.cms.
31. Letters found amidst Rao's private papers in 2015; confirmed in interview with Sanjaya Baru in New Delhi, 2015.
32. Interview with Ramu Damodaran in New York, 2015.
33. Javed M. Ansari, 'Splitting endlessly', *India Today*, http://indiatoday.intoday.in/story/latest-defections-shock-v.p.-singh-but-could-bring-solace-to-narasimha-rao/1/307575.html.
34. Interview with Subramanian Swamy in New Delhi, 2015.
35. Interview with Chandraswami in Delhi, 2015.
36. Prasad, *Wheels behind the Veil: PMs, CMs and beyond*, 113–14.
37. Interview with Ramu Damodaran in New York, 2015.
38. Singh (with Chopra), *A Grain of Sand in the Hourglass of Time: An Autobiography*.
39. 'No-trust Motion Defeated', the *Times of India*, 22 December 1992, 1.
40. Ibid.
41. Interview with Satish Sharma in New Delhi, 2015.
42. Ibid.
43. Draft found amidst Rao's private papers, 2015.
44. Interview with Ramu Damodaran in New York, 2015.
45. Ibid.
46. Interview with N.K. Sharma in New Delhi, 2015.
47. 'I gave Rs 1 cr. to Rao, says Harshad', the *Times of India*, 17 June 1993, 1.
48. 'Ajit Singh faction to vote against government', the *Times of India*, 28 July, 1993, 1.
49. Edward A. Gargan, 'India's Prime Minister Faces a No-Confidence Vote', the *New York Times,* 28 July 1993.
50. Interview with P.V.R.K. Prasad in Hyderabad, 2015.
51. Prasad, *Wheels behind the Veil: PMs, CMs and beyond*, 41.
52. Interview with Subramanian Swamy in New Delhi, 2015.
53. 'Ajit Singh faction to vote against government', the *Times of India*, 28 July 1993, 1.
54. *P.V. Narasimha Rao Selected Speeches 1993–1994*, 17–30.

NOTES

55. Interview with P.V. Prabhakara Rao in Hyderabad, 2015.
56. 'Rao survives no-confidence move', the *Times of India*, 29 July 1993, 1.
57. 'Moral victory, says opposition', the *Times of India*, 29 July 1993, 1.
58. *Shri P.V. Narasimha Rao* vs *State Through CBI*, 2002, CriLJ 2401.
59. 'Moral victory, says opposition', the *Times of India*, 1.
60. Inderjit Badhwar, 'Rao's revival', *India Today*, 31 December 1993, http://indiatoday.intoday.in/story/raos-revival/1/303568.html.
61. Interview with Dr Srinath Reddy in Delhi, 2015.
62. Interview with P.V. Prabhakara Rao in Hyderabad, 2015.
63. Singh (with Chopra), *A Grain of Sand in the Hourglass of Time: An Autobiography*, 349.
64. Ibid.
65. Letter found amidst Rao's private papers in 2015.
66. Letters addressed to the Congress president, found amidst Rao's private papers in 2015.
67. 'CBI chargesheets Advani, Arjun, 5 others', the *Times of India*, 17 January 1996, 1.
68. US Department of Treasury document, available at https://www.treasury.gov/resource-center/terrorist-illicit-finance/Documents/FinCEN-Hawala-rpt.pdf.
69. 'Chronology of Hawala Case', the *Times of India*, 17 January 1991, 1.
70. Julio Ríos-Figueroa, 'Fragmentation of Power and the Emergence of an Effective Judiciary in Mexico, 1994–2002', *Latin American Politics and Society* 49, no. 1, 31–57 (2007); Tom Ginsburg, *Judicial Review in New Democracies: Constitutional Courts in Asian Cases* (New York: Cambridge University Press, 2003); Gretchen Helmke, *Courts under Constraints: Judges, Generals, and Presidents in Argentina* (New York: Cambridge University Press, 2005).
71. Prasad, *Wheels behind the Veil: PMs, CMs and beyond*, 190.
72. Ibid., 191.
73. N.K. Singh, 'Tarred with the same brush', *India Today*, 15 February 1996, http://indiatoday.intoday.in/story/tarred-with-the-same-brush/1/280827.html.
74. Mahendra Ved, 'Indicted ministers may resign', the *Times of India*, 17 January 1996, 1.

75. Janak Singh, 'Rao's hand seen in Hawala drama', the *Times of India*, 17 January 1996, 1.
76. Entries in Appointment Diary 1991, written by Rao's secretary, R.K. Khandekar; found amidst his private papers in 2015.
77. Janak Singh, 'Rao's hand seen in Hawala drama', 1.
78. Interview with P.V.R.K. Prasad in Hyderabad, 2015.
79. Interview with Arun Jaitley in New Delhi, 2015.
80. Note found amidst Rao's private papers in 2015.
81. Prasad, *Wheels behind the Veil: PMs, CMs and beyond*, 194.
82. Interview with Rajeshwara Rao in Hyderabad, 2015.
83. 'BJP gaining an edge', *India Today,* 15 May 1996, http://indiatoday.intoday.in/story/elections-1996-bjp-will-add-substantially-to-its-1991-lok-sabha-tally-opinion-poll-shows/1/281179.html.
84. John F. Burns, 'Political Pact With Ex-Film Star May Bring Down India's Premier', the *New York Times*, 3 May 1996, http://www.nytimes.com/1996/05/03/world/political-pact-with-ex-film-star-may-bring-down-india-s-premier.html.
85. Interview with P.V.R.K. Prasad in Hyderabad, 2015.
86. Diary entry found amidst Rao's private papers in 2015.
87. Raj Chengappa, 'Selling the Optimism Dream', *India Today*, 15 May 1996, http://indiatoday.intoday.in/story/selling-the-optimism-dream/1/281153.html.
88. Interview with N.K. Sharma in New Delhi, 2015.
89. Letter to the President of India, copy found amidst Rao's private papers in 2015.
90. Janak Singh, 'Vajpayee Sworn in as P.M.', the *Times of India*, 17 May 1996, 1.

11. MANAGING SONIA

1. See generally Tavleen Singh, *Durbar* (Gurgaon: Hachette India, 2012).
2. George Wright, 'Sonia Gandhi declines Indian prime ministership', *Guardian*, 18 May 2004, http://www.theguardian.com/world/2004/may/18/india.georgewright.
3. K. Natwar Singh says that he was present when Sonia decided not to become prime minister in 2004, at the insistence of Rahul

NOTES

Gandhi. See http://indiatoday.intoday.in/story/natwar-singh-sonia-gandhi-prime-minister-shankar-dayal-sharma-pv-narasimha-rao/1/374821.html.

4. Sanjaya Baru, *The Accidental Prime Minister: The Making and Unmaking of Manmohan Singh* (New Delhi: Penguin Books, 2014).
5. *P.V. Narasimha Rao Selected Speeches 1991–1992*, 24.
6. *P.V. Narasimha Rao Selected Speeches 1992–1993*, 33.
7. Congressman, 'The Great Suicide', *Mainstream*, 27 January 1990, http://www.mainstreamweekly.net/article5438.html.
8. Ramesh, *To the Brink and Back: India's 1991 Story*, 110.
9. Facing political opposition, she eventually rejected the donation.
10. Interview with P.V.R.K. Prasad in Hyderabad, 2015.
11. Interview with Rajeshwara Rao in Hyderabad, 2015.
12. Kalyani Shankar, *Pandora's Daughters*, 46.
13. Inderjit Badhwar and Zafar Agha, 'The Sonia factor', *India Today*, 31 August 1991, http://indiatoday.intoday.in/story/congressmen-push-sonia-gandhi-into-politics-for-their-own-political-survival/1/318730.html.
14. Prakash Joshi and Rajdeep Sardesai, 'Sonia's "no" disheartens dissidents', the *Times of India*, 15 October 1991, 1.
15. Sanjay Singh, 'Lessons from Rajiv: Congress must amend Modi's security', *Firstpost*, 7 November 2013, http://www.firstpost.com/politics/lessons-from-rajiv-congress-must-amend-modis-security-1215771.html.
16. Letter found amongst Rao's private papers in 2015.
17. Interview with Salman Khurshid in New Delhi, 2015.
18. 'Ex-minister to be tried for scuttling Bofors probe', Rediff, 7 July 2008, http://www.rediff.com/news/2008/jul/07bofors.htm.
19. Kidwai, *24 Akbar Road*, 180.
20. Interview with Rajeshwara Rao in Hyderabad, 2015.
21. Interview with Kalyani Shankar in New Delhi, 2015.
22. Singh (with Chopra), *A Grain of Sand in the Hourglass of Time: An Autobiography*, 247.
23. Singh, *One Life Is Not Enough*, 310.
24. Ibid., 309–10.
25. Ibid., 310.

NOTES

26. Shankar, *Pandora's Daughters*, 48.
27. John F. Burns, 'Speech Stirs Speculation of a Gandhi's Return', the *New York Times*, 25 August 1995, http://www.nytimes.com/1995/08/25/world/speech-stirs-speculation-of-a-gandhi-s-return.html.
28. Ibid.
29. Interview with Satish Sharma in New Delhi, 2015.
30. Shankar, *Pandora's Daughters*, 47.
31. Interview with K. Natwar Singh in New Delhi, 2016.
32. Interview with N.K. Sharma in New Delhi, 2015
33. Interview with Subramanian Swamy in New Delhi, 2015.
34. Interview with Gopalkrishna Gandhi in Chennai, 2015.
35. Ibid.
36. Zafar Agha, 'Damage control exercise', *India Today*, 15 December 1995, http://indiatoday.intoday.in/story/in-deft-move-rao-reaches-out-to-sonia-while-consolidating-position-in-congressi-in-disarray/1/289719.html.
37. Ibid.
38. Interview with Prabhakara Rao in Hyderabad, 2015.
39. Interview with P.V.R.K. Prasad in Hyderabad, 2015.
40. For details on economic reforms as recorded in the official Congress website, see http://www.inc.in/about-congress/history/literature/5-Journey-of-a-Nation/13-A-New-Political-Reality.

12. THE FALL OF BABRI MASJID

1. 'Sadhus call for kar seva', the *Times of India*, 6 December 1992, 1.
2. Interview with Dr Srinath Reddy in Delhi, 2015.
3. *Commission of Inquiry Report of the Liberhan Ayodhya Commission of Inquiry, 2009* (New Delhi: Akalank Publications, 2010), 9.
4. Ibid., 27.
5. Rao, *Ayodhya: 6 December 1992*, 4.
6. Ibid.
7. Krishna Jha and Dhiren K. Jha, *Ayodhya: The Dark Night, The Secret History of Rama's Appearance in Babri Masjid* (New Delhi: HarperCollins, 2012).
8. Rao, *Ayodhya: 6 December 1992*, 21–22.
9. Ibid., 9, 24.

NOTES

10. Hasan, *Congress after Indira: Policy, Power, Political Change (1984–2009)*, 19.
11. Ibid., 19–20.
12. Sharat Pradhan, 'Mulayam and the Muslim vote', *Tehelka*, 2 September 2013, http://www.tehelka.com/2013/09/mulayam-and-the-muslim-vote/.
13. Piyush Srivastava, 'Mulayam admits 1990 Ayodhya shooting lost him Hindu vote bank', *Daily Mail*, 23 March 2015, http://www.dailymail.co.uk/indiahome/indianews/article-3008147/Mulayam-admits-1990-Ayodhya-shooting-lost-Hindu-votebank.html.
14. Official Election Commission results of the 1991 Uttar Pradesh assembly election, available at http://eci.nic.in/eci_main/StatisticalReports/SE_1991/Stat_Rep_UP_91.pdf.
15. Interview with Ramu Damodaran in New York, 2015.
16. Rao, *Ayodhya: 6 December 1992*, 89.
17. Article 356 of the Constitution of India, 1950.
18. Harbir Singh Kathuria, *President's rule in India, 1967–89* (New Delhi: Uppal Publishing House, 1990).
19. *Commission of Inquiry Report of the Liberhan Ayodhya Commission of Inquiry, 2009*, para 30.11, 58.
20. Ibid., para 30.14, 59.
21. Rao, *Ayodhya: 6 December 1992*, 90.
22. Interview with P.V.R.K. Prasad in Hyderabad, 2015.
23. Singh (with Chopra), *A Grain of Sand in the Hourglass of Time: An Autobiography*, 251–69.
24. *P.V. Narasimha Rao Selected Speeches 1992–1993*, 8.
25. Ibid., 10.
26. Note found amidst Rao's private papers in 2015.
27. Madhav Godbole, *Unfinished Innings: Recollections and Reflections of a Civil Servant* (New Delhi: Orient Longman, 1996), 347.
28. Interview with Naresh Chandra in Delhi, 2015.
29. Godbole, *Unfinished Innings: Recollections and Reflections of a Civil Servant*, 351.
30. *P.V. Narasimha Rao Selected Speeches 1992–1993*, 30.
31. Godbole, *Unfinished Innings: Recollections and Reflections of a Civil Servant*, 334.

NOTES

32. Rao, *Ayodhya: 6 December 1992*, 99.
33. Godbole describes part of the contingency note in his memoir, though the entire note has not been made public elsewhere. Godbole, *Unfinished Innings: Recollections and Reflections of a Civil Servant*, 363–65.
34. Ibid., 396.
35. Singh (with Chopra), *A Grain of Sand in the Hourglass of Time: An Autobiography*, 249–50.
36. Godbole, *Unfinished Innings: Recollections and Reflections of a Civil Servant*, 368.
37. Mukherjee, *The Turbulent Years: 1980–1996*, 155.
38. *Commission of Inquiry Report of the Liberhan Ayodhya Commission of Inquiry, 2009*, 98.
39. 'Jyoti Basu's Deposition before Liberhan Commission', *People's Democracy* 36, no. 49 (9 December 2012).
40. Interview with Kalyani Shankar in New Delhi, 2015.
41. Rao, *Ayodhya: 6 December 1992*, 120.
42. Story told to the author by one of Rao's close aides, who demanded anonymity.
43. Girish Kuber, 'Narasimha Rao's book gives new twist to demolition', *Economic Times*, 28 April 2008, http://articles.economictimes.indiatimes.com/2006-04-27/news/27459247_1_kar-sevaks-central-rule-ayodhya.
44. Prasad, *Wheels behind the Veil: PMs, CMs and beyond*, 164.
45. Godbole, *Unfinished Innings: Recollections and Reflections of a Civil Servant*, 364–65.
46. Interview with Salman Haidar in New Delhi, 2015.
47. Ibid.
48. Singh (with Chopra), *A Grain of Sand in the Hourglass of Time: An Autobiography*, 228.
49. Rao, *Ayodhya: 6 December 1992*, 48.
50. Interview with Mani Shankar Aiyar in New Delhi, 2015.
51. Interview with P.V.R.K. Prasad in Hyderabad, 2015.
52. Entries in Appointment Diary 1992, written by Rao's secretary, Khandekar; found amidst Rao's private papers in 2015.
53. Interview with Chandraswami in Delhi, 2015.
54. Interview with N.K. Sharma in New Delhi, 2015.

NOTES

55. Ibid.
56. Interview with Naresh Chandra in Delhi, 2015.
57. Kidwai, *24 Akbar Road*, 175.
58. Rao, *Ayodhya: 6 December 1992*, 100.
59. Interview with P.V.R.K. Prasad in Hyderabad, 2015.
60. Godbole, *Unfinished Innings: Recollections and Reflections of a Civil Servant*, 352.
61. Interview with Chandraswami in New Delhi, 2015.
62. A.G. Noorani, 'Silent Spectator', *Frontline* 23, no. 10 (20 May–2 June 2006), http://www.frontline.in/static/html/fl2310/stories/20060602000707900.htm.
63. Interview with Naresh Chandra in Delhi, 2015.
64. Interview with Jairam Ramesh in New Delhi, 2015.
65. Hasan, *Congress after Indira: Policy, Power, Political Change (1984–2009)*, 26.
66. Interview with Salman Khurshid in New Delhi, 2015.
67. Ibid.
68. Singh (with Chopra), *A Grain of Sand in the Hourglass of Time: An Autobiography*, 272–75.
69. Interview with Mani Shankar Aiyar in New Delhi, 2015.
70. Note found amidst Rao's private papers in 2015.
71. Interview with N.K. Sharma in New Delhi, 2015.
72. Interview with Naresh Chandra in Delhi, 2015.
73. Interview with Rajaiah in Vangara village (now in Telangana), 2015.
74. Note found amidst Rao's private papers in 2015.
75. *Commission of Inquiry Report of the Liberhan Ayodhya Commission of Inquiry, 2009*, para 44.18, 119.
76. Ibid., para 44.24, 120.
77. Singh (with Chopra), *A Grain of Sand in the Hourglass of Time: An Autobiography*, 277.
78. The claim was made by the journalist Kuldip Nayar, who said that he was told by the socialist leader Madhu Limaye, who, in turn, claimed he heard it from someone present. See 'Narasimha Rao performed puja during demolition of Babri Masjid: Book', the *Times of India*, 5 July 2012, http://timesofindia.indiatimes.com/india/Narasimha-Rao-performed-puja-during-demolition-of-Babri-Masjid-Book/articleshow/14687884.cms.

NOTES

79. Interview with S. Rajgopal in Mumbai, 2015.
80. Godbole, *Unfinished Innings: Recollections and Reflections of a Civil Servant*, 383.
81. 'Absurd to say PV was incommunicado during Ayodhya demolition', Rediff, 9 July 2012, http://www.rediff.com/news/report/slide-show-1-arjun-singhs-story-on-ayodhya-demolition-cock-and-bull/20120709.htm.
82. Interview with Salman Khurshid in New Delhi, 2015.
83. *Commission of Inquiry Report of the Liberhan Ayodhya Commission of Inquiry, 2009*, paras 44.6–44.7, 117–18.
84. Ibid., para 44.42, 122.
85. Ibid., para 44.31, 121.
86. Ibid., para 44.30, 121.
87. M.G. Gupta and Vijay Jung Thapa, 'Kar Sevaks Destroyed Babri Masjid', the *Times of India*, 7 December, 1992, 1.
88. *P.V. Narasimha Rao Selected Speeches 1992–1993*, 63–65.
89. Ibid.
90. Entry in Appointment Diary 1992, found amidst Rao's private papers in 2015.
91. Interview with N.K. Sharma in New Delhi, 2015.
92. Appointment Diary 1992, written by Rao's secretary, R.K. Khandekar; found amidst his private papers in 2015.
93. Hasan, *Congress after Indira: Policy, Power, Political Change (1984–2009)*, 35.
94. Note found amidst Rao's private papers in 2015.
95. Edward A. Gargan, 'India, Acting on Militants, Ousts Local Rulers', the *New York Times*, 16 December 1992, http://www.nytimes.com/1992/12/16/world/india-acting-on-militants-ousts-local-rulers.html.
96. Quotes accessible at http://www.ucanews.com/story-archive/?post_name=/1992/12/23/experts-deplore-rao-governments-dismissal-of-prohindu-ministries&post_id=42523.
97. *S.R. Bommai vs Union of India*, AIR, 1994, SC 1918.
98. *Commission of Inquiry Report of the Liberhan Ayodhya Commission of Inquiry, 2009*, ch. 14.
99. 'No-trust Motion Defeated', the *Times of India*, 22 December 1993, 1.

NOTES

100. Interview with Mani Shankar Aiyar in New Delhi, 2015.
101. Interview with Jairam Ramesh in New Delhi, 2015.
102. Interview with Salman Khurshid in New Delhi, 2015.
103. 'Babri wouldn't have fallen if a Gandhi was PM: Rahul', the *Times of India*, 20 March 2007, http://timesofindia.indiatimes.com/india/Babri-wouldnt-have-fallen-if-a-Gandhi-was-PM-Rahul/articleshow/1781018.cms.
104. 'Babri demolition planned; Advani, P V Narasimha Rao knew of plot: Cobrapost sting, the *Times of India*, 4 April 2014, http://timesofindia.indiatimes.com/india/Babri-demolition-planned-Advani-P-V-Narasimha-Rao-knew-of-plot-Cobrapost-sting/articleshow/33202922.cms.
105. Ibid.
106. For the official judgments, see http://elegalix.allahabadhighcourt.in/elegalix/DisplayAyodhyaBenchLandingPage.do.
107. Mukherjee, *The Turbulent Years: 1980–1996*, 154.
108. Godbole, *Unfinished Innings: Recollections and Reflections of a Civil Servant*, 337.
109. Interview with Salman Khurshid in New Delhi, 2015.
110. Ibid.
111. Rao, *Ayodhya: 6 December 1992*, 181.

13. LOOK EAST, LOOK WEST

1. Ramesh, *To the Brink and Back: India's 1991 Story*, 11.
2. Sunanda K. Datta-Ray, *Looking East to Looking West: Lee Kuan Yew's Mission India* (New Delhi: Penguin Books, 2009), 78.
3. Letters found among Narasimha Rao's private papers in 2015.
4. Interview with Shravan, grandson of Narasimha Rao, in Hyderabad, 2015.
5. See Srinath Raghavan, 'At the Cusp of Transformation: The Rajiv Gandhi Years, 1984–89', in David M. Malone, C. Raja Mohan and Srinath Raghavan, eds, *The Oxford Handbook of Indian Foreign Policy* (New Delhi: Oxford University Press, 2015, first edition).
6. Interview with Salman Haidar in New Delhi, 2015.
7. Interview with Ramu Damodaran in New York, 2015.

8. Ibid.
9. Raj Chengappa, 'PM in Germany: Striking the right note', *India Today*, 30 September 1991, http://indiatoday.intoday.in/story/narasimha-rao-candid-approach-makes-an-impact-in-germany/1/318862.html.
10. Interview with Velcheru Narayana Rao (on phone) in Atlanta, 2015.
11. Interview with Ramu Damodaran in New York, 2015.
12. Interview with Rajaiah in Vangara village (now in Telangana), 2015.
13. Interview with P.V.R.K. Prasad in Hyderabad, 2015.
14. Transcript of conversation found among Narasimha Rao's private papers in 2015.
15. Shekhar Gupta, 'Indo-Soviet ties: cooling of an affair', *India Today*, 15 September 1991, http://indiatoday.intoday.in/story/balmy-days-over-indo-soviet-treaty-a-mere-ceremonial-document/1/318757.html.
16. Interview with Ronen Sen in New Delhi, 2015.
17. Ibid.
18. Interview with Krishnan Srinivasan (on phone) in Kolkata, 2015.
19. Prabhakar Menon, 'The Quiet Innovator: Foreign Policy under P.V. Narasimha Rao', in K.V. Rajan, ed., *The Ambassador's Club: The Indian Diplomat at Large* (New Delhi: HarperCollins, 2012), 302.
20. Nicolas Blarel, *The Evolution of India's Israel Policy: Continuity, Change, and Compromise since 1922* (New Delhi: Oxford University Press, 2014), 236.
21. Shubhajit Roy, '24 years on, why India looks set to finally come out of the closet on Israel', the *Indian Express*, 14 January 2016, http://indianexpress.com/article/explained/in-fcat-why-india-looks-set-to-finally-come-out-of-the-closet-on-israel/.
22. Shekhar Gupta, 'A pragmatic peace', *India Today*, 21 June 2013, http://indiatoday.intoday.in/story/india-israel-to-establish-full-diplomatic-relations/1/306258.html/.
23. *P.V. Narasimha Rao Selected Speeches 1991–1992*, 111.
24. J.N. Dixit, *My South Block Years: Memoirs of a Foreign Secretary* (New Delhi: UBS Publishers Distributors, 1997), 143.

NOTES

25. M.K. Bhadrakumar, 'As shadow of terror hangs over talks with Pakistan, Narasimha Rao has a lesson for Modi', Scroll.in, 4 January 2016, http://scroll.in/article/801319/as-shadow-of-terror-hangs-over-talks-with-pakistan-narasimha-rao-has-a-lesson-for-modi.
26. S. Samuel C. Rajiv, 'The Delicate Balance: Israel and India's Foreign Policy Practice', *Strategic Analysis* 36, no. 1, 128–44, 128.
27. Interview with Krishnan Srinivasan (on phone) in Kolkata, 2015.
28. *P.V. Narasimha Rao Selected Speeches 1991–1992*, 362.
29. Email interview with C. Raja Mohan, 2016.
30. Interview with Ronen Sen in New Delhi, 2015.
31. Ministry of Home Affairs data, available at http://www.mha.nic.in/hindi/sites/upload_files/mhahindi/files/pdf/BM_Intro_E_.pdf.
32. Srinath Raghavan, 'At the Cusp of Transformation: The Rajiv Gandhi Years, 1984–89', 125 (uncorrected proofs), in Malone, Mohan and Raghavan, eds, *The Oxford Handbook of Indian Foreign Policy*.
33. Interview with M.K. Narayanan in Chennai, 2015.
34. Note found among Narasimha Rao's private papers in 2015.
35. Prabhakar Menon, 'The Quiet Innovator: Foreign Policy under P.V. Narasimha Rao', in *K.V. Rajan*, ed., *The Ambassador's Club: The Indian Diplomat at Large*, 296–97.
36. Interview with Prabhakar Menon in Delhi, 2015.
37. Full text of agreement available at http://peacemaker.un.org/sites/peacemaker.un.org/files/CN%20IN_930907_Agreement%20on%20India-China%20Border%20Areas.pdf.
38. Interview with Ronen Sen in New Delhi, 2015.
39. Interview with M.K. Narayanan in Chennai, 2015.
40. Kidwai, *24 Akbar Road*, 179.
41. Interview with Salman Haidar in New Delhi, 2015.
42. Interview with S. Vani Devi in Hyderabad, 2015.
43. *P.V. Narasimha Rao Selected Speeches 1993–1994*, 402–403.
44. Interview with Salman Haidar in New Delhi, 2015.
45. Menon, 'The Quiet Innovator: Foreign Policy under P.V. Narasimha Rao', 301.
46. Sudeep Chakravarti, 'Rao's roadshow', *India Today*, 30 August 1993, http://indiatoday.intoday.in/story/pm-narasimha-rao-emerges-as-a-competent-diplomat-abroad/1/302131.html.

NOTES

47. Salil Tripathi, 'Rediscovering the East', *India Today*, 30 September 1993, http://indiatoday.intoday.in/story/rao-trip-opens-up-investment-opportunities-for-india-with-economic-tigers-of-east/1/294152.html.
48. Menon, 'The Quiet Innovator: Foreign Policy under P.V. Narasimha Rao', 302.
49. Interview with Prabhakar Menon in Delhi, 2015.
50. Menon, 'The Quiet Innovator: Foreign Policy under P.V. Narasimha Rao', 302.
51. Sanjaya Baru, 'Strongman who took Singapore to the first world', *The Hindu,* 24 March 2015, http://www.thehindu.com/opinion/op-ed/strongman-who-took-singapore-to-the-first-world/article7024865.ece.
52. Interview with Jairam Ramesh in New Delhi, 2015.
53. 'Singapore knocks off Mauritius as top FDI source into India in current fiscal, *Economic Times*, 6 December 2015, http://articles.economictimes.indiatimes.com/2015-12-06/news/68809344_1_india-singapore-mauritius-double-taxation-avoidance-agreement.
54. Kohli, *State-Directed Development: Political Power and Industrialization in the Global Periphery.*
55. Interview with P.V.R.K. Prasad in Hyderabad, 2015.
56. *P.V. Narasimha Rao Selected Speeches 1991–1992*, 323.
57. Interview with Ramu Damodaran in New York, 2015.
58. Menon, 'The Quiet Innovator: Foreign Policy under P.V. Narasimha Rao', 291.
59. Andrew North, 'Siachen dispute: India and Pakistan's glacial fight', BBC News, 12 April 2014, http://www.bbc.com/news/world-asia-india-26967340.
60. 'Siachen was almost a done deal in 1992', *The Hindu*, 10 June 2012, http://www.thehindu.com/news/national/siachen-was-almost-a-done-deal-in-1992/article3509787.ece.
61. Interview with Prabhakar Menon in Delhi, 2015.
62. Ibid.
63. 'Siachen was almost a done deal in 1992', The Hindu, http://www.thehindu.com/news/national/siachen-was-almost-a-done-deal-in-1992/article3509787.ece.
64. Interview with Salman Khurshid in New Delhi, 2015.

65. Krishnan Srinivasan, *Diplomatic Channels* (New Delhi: Manohar Publishers, 2012), 36–37.
66. Cover, *India Today*, 31 March 1994.
67. Interview with Sanjaya Baru in New Delhi, 2015. This story has also been confirmed via email by Kalyani Shankar.
68. See Raghavan, 'At the Cusp of Transformation: The Rajiv Gandhi Years, 1984–89'.
69. Burns, 'Unlikely Reformer Coaxes India Towards a Market Economy.
70. Srinivasan, *Diplomatic Channels*, 18.
71. Ibid.
72. Interview with Dr Srinath Reddy in Delhi, 2015.
73. Interview with Prabhakar Menon in Delhi, 2015.
74. Srinivasan, *Diplomatic Channels*, 20.
75. Interview with P.V. Rajeshwara Rao in Hyderabad, 2015.
76. Prasad, *Wheels behind the Veil: PMs, CMs and beyond*, 132–34.
77. *P.V. Narasimha Rao Selected Speeches 1993–1994*, 479.
78. Ibid., 472.
79. Interview with Ronen Sen in New Delhi, 2015.
80. Ibid.
81. Interview with Dr V.S. Arunachalam in Bangalore, 2015.
82. Prabhakar Menon, 'Reminiscences of a Fly on the Wall: Oral History', *Indian Foreign Affairs Journal* 8, no. 3, 317–36 (July-September 2013): 330.
83. Email interview with C. Raja Mohan, 2016.
84. *P.V. Narasimha Rao Selected Speeches 1991–1992*, 318.
85. Interview with C. Raja Mohan in New Delhi, 2015.
86. Interview with Salman Haidar in New Delhi, 2015.
87. Interview with C. Raja Mohan in New Delhi, 2015.
88. Letter found among Narasimha Rao's private papers in 2015.
89. Interview with Krishnan Srinivasan (on phone) in Kolkata, 2015.

14. GOING NUCLEAR

1. 'Rao was "true father" of Indian bomb, says Vajpayee', *Daily Times*, http://archives.dailytimes.com.pk/national/28-Dec-2004/rao-was-true-father-of-indian-bomb-says-vajpayee.

NOTES

2. Interview with Shekhar Gupta in New Delhi, 2015.
3. M.V. Ramana, *The Power of Promise: Examining Nuclear Energy in India* (New Delhi: Viking, 2013).
4. Perkovich, *India's Nuclear Bomb: The Impact of Global Proliferation*, 331.
5. Interview with Dr V.S. Arunachalam in Bangalore, 2015.
6. K. Subrahmanyam, 'Narasimha Rao and the Bomb', Institute for Defence Studies and Analysis, October 2004, http://www.idsa.in/strategicanalysis/NarasimhaRaoandtheBomb_ksubramanyam_1004.
7. Perkovich, *India's Nuclear Bomb: The Impact of Global Proliferation*, 324.
8. Ibid., 326.
9. Available at http://www.un.org/en/sc/repertoire/89-92/Chapter%208/GENERAL%20ISSUES/Item%2028_SC%20respons%20in%20maint%20IPS.pdf.
10. Entries in Appointment Diary 1991, written by Rao's secretary, Khandekar; found amidst his private papers in 2015.
11. Interview with Dr V.S. Arunachalam in Bangalore, 2015.
12. Raj Chengappa, *Weapons of Peace: The Secret Story of India's Quest to be a Nuclear Power* (New Delhi: HarperCollins, 2000), 370.
13. Perkovich, *India's Nuclear Bomb: The Impact of Global Proliferation*, 322.
14. Ibid.
15. Interview with Dr V.S. Arunachalam in Bangalore, 2015.
16. Chengappa, *Weapons of Peace: The Secret Story of India's Quest to be a Nuclear Power*, 381.
17. Data available at http://www.globalsecurity.org/wmd/world/india/prithvi.htm.
18. Interview with Ronen Sen in New Delhi, 2015.
19. Chengappa, *Weapons of Peace: The Secret Story of India's Quest to be a Nuclear Power*, 384.
20. Ibid, 382–84.
21. Ibid.
22. Ibid., 371.
23. Menon, 'The Quiet Innovator: Foreign Policy under P.V. Narasimha Rao', 303.

NOTES

24. Menon, Reminiscences of a 'Fly on the Wall': Oral History', 334–35.
25. Interview with Prabhakar Menon in Delhi, 2015.
26. Interview with Montek Singh Ahluwalia in Delhi, 2015.
27. Tim Weiner, 'U.S. Suspects India Prepares To Conduct Nuclear Test', the *New York Times*, 15 December 1995, http://www.nytimes.com/1995/12/15/world/us-suspects-india-prepares-to-conduct-nuclear-test.html.
28. Information corroborated from declassified US State Department documents. See http://nsarchive.gwu.edu/nukevault/ebb412/docs/doc%201.pdf.
29. Interview with Shekhar Gupta in New Delhi, 2015.
30. Entries in Appointment Diary 1996, written by Rao's secretary, Khandekar, found amidst his private papers in 2015.
31. Bharti Jain, 'Narasimha Rao had asked Kalam to be ready for nuclear test', the *Times of India*, 25 January 2013, http://timesofindia.indiatimes.com/india/Narasimha-Rao-had-asked-Kalam-to-be-ready-for-nuclear-test/articleshow/18173888.cms.
32. Ibid.
33. Ibid.
34. Perkovich, *India's Nuclear Bomb: The Impact of Global Proliferation*, 353–77.
35. Chengappa, *Weapons of Peace: The Secret Story of India's Quest to be a Nuclear Power*, 395.
36. Interview with Shekhar Gupta in New Delhi, 2015.
37. Interview with Dr V.S. Arunachalam in Bangalore, 2015.
38. Jain, 'Narasimha Rao had asked Kalam to be ready for nuclear test'.
39. See, for example, Praful Bidwai and Achin Vanaik, *South Asia on a Short Fuse: Nuclear Politics and the Future of Global Disarmament* (New Delhi: Oxford University Press, 1999).
40. See generally C. Raja Mohan, *Crossing the Rubicon: The Shaping of India's New Foreign Policy* (New Delhi: Palgrave Macmillan, 2004).
41. See, for example, Praful Bidwai and Achin Vanaik, *South Asia on a Short Fuse: Nuclear Politics and the Future of Global Disarmament*.

NOTES

15. LION, FOX, MOUSE

1. 'Chronology of Lakhubhai Pathak case', Rediff, http://www.rediff.com/news/2003/dec/22rao2.htm.
2. Rakesh Bhatnagar, 'The beginning of the end for Rao', the *Times of India*, 22 September 1996, 1.
3. Interview with N.K. Sharma in New Delhi, 2015.
4. Janak Singh, 'Rao isn't their cup of tea anymore', the *Times of India*, 25 September 1996, 1.
5. Interview with Salman Khurshid in New Delhi, 2015.
6. Prasad, *Wheels behind the Veil: PMs, CMs and beyond*, 205.
7. Man Mohan, 'Honourable acquittals satisfied Rao', the *Times of India*, 25 December 2004, 7.
8. Interview with P.V. Rajeshwara Rao in Hyderabad, 2015.
9. Interview with Satchidananda Swamy in Bengaluru, 2015.
10. Ibid.
11. Interview with Venkat Kishen Rao in Hyderabad, 2015.
12. Letter found amidst Rao's private papers in 2016.
13. Interview with Sanjaya Baru in New Delhi, 2015.
14. Interview with Shubhranshu Singh in Mumbai, 2014.
15. Email conversation with Pramath Raj Sinha, son-in-law of A.N. Varma, 2016.
16. Parkash Satti, *Futuristic Version of Geeta: The Ultimate Theory of Fate* (New Delhi: Partridge India, 2015).
17. Interviews with P.V. Prabhakara Rao and Rajeshwara Rao in Hyderabad, 2015.
18. Interview with P.V. Prabhakara Rao in Hyderabad, 2015.
19. Ibid.
20. Interview with P.V. Rajeshwara Rao in Hyderabad, 2015.
21. Arjun (with Chopra), *A Grain of Sand in the Hourglass of Time: An Autobiography*, 351–52.
22. Interview with P.V. Rajeshwara Rao in Hyderabad, 2015.
23. Nigel Hamilton, 'On biography', http://www.huffingtonpost.com/nigel-hamilton/on-biography_b_780976.html.
24. Interview with Ronen Sen in New Delhi, 2015.
25. See Raghavan, 'At the Cusp of Transformation: The Rajiv Gandhi Years, 1984–89'.

26. Brian Bulduc, 'Robert Caro: Political Power—How to Get It and Use It', *Wall Street Journal*, 4 May 2012, http://www.wsj.com/articles/SB10001424052702304743704577382450285971364.
27. Interview with Ramu Damodaran in New York, 2015.
28. Ivan Turgenev and Moshe Spiegel, 'Hamlet and Don Quixote', *Chicago Review* 17, no. 4 (1965): 92–109.
29. Gay Saul Morson, 'The intolerable dream', *New Criterion*, November 2015.
30. Ibid.
31. Devesh Kapur, 'Exit', *Seminar*, http://www.india-seminar.com/2016/677/677_devesh_kapur.htm.
32. Note found among Narasimha Rao's private papers in 2015.
33. Interview with Rajeshwara Rao in Hyderabad, 2015; also, interview with another bureaucrat in the PMO who wanted to remain anonymous.
34. Notes found among Narasimha Rao's private papers in 2015.
35. The amount was Rs 950 crore. Interview with K.R. Venugopal in Hyderabad, 2015.
36. Interview with A.S. Dulat in Delhi, 2015.
37. V. Balachandran, 'The Rao breakthrough', the *Indian Express*, 20 August 2015, http://indianexpress.com/article/opinion/columns/the-rao-breakthrough/.
38. Interview with Shekhar Gupta in New Delhi, 2015.
39. Interview with Kalyani Shankar in New Delhi, 2015.
40. Card given to the author by Ramu Damodaran in New York, 2016.
41. *Walk the Talk*, NDTV, http://www.ndtv.com/video/player/walk-the-talk/walk-the-talk-p-v-narasimha-rao/296375.
42. Jenkins, *Democratic Politics and Economic Reform in India*, 176.
43. *P.V. Narasimha Rao Selected Speeches 1991–1992*, 197.
44. Yuval Levin, *The Great Debate: Edmund Burke, Thomas Paine, and the Birth of Right and Left* (New York: Basic Books, 2013).
45. See Vinay Sitapati, 'What Anna Hazare and the Indian Middle-Classes Say About Each Other', *Economic&Political Weekly* 46, no. 30 (2011).

Index

AIADMK, 193, 209–10, 223
Advani, L.K., 5, 77, 185, 206–08, 228, 239, 241–42, 244, 246, 250, 253, 255, 277
Ahluwalia, Montek Singh, 50, 72, 103, 110, 116–17, 121, 143, 145, 147, 152–54, 157, 190, 268, 288
Aiyar, Mani Shankar, 66, 135, 218, 221, 230, 239, 243–44, 251
Akali Dal, 241
Alexander, P.C., 61, 67, 93, 99, 101–02, 113, 115, 142, 144, 194
Ali, Aruna Asaf, 95
All India Congress Party, 204
All India Congress Committee (AICC), 55, 191, 198, 204
Alva, Margaret, 222
Álvarez, Jorge Castañeda, 86
Ambani, Dhirubhai, 127, 134
Ambedkar, B.R., 19
Anand, R.K., 297
Anderson, Warren, 7, 65

Andhra Pradesh, 24–25, 41, 52, 57
  assembly elections, 43
  President's Rule, 41
Anthony, A.K., 200, 204
Arafat, Yasser, 262, 304–05
Aravindan, G., 69
Arora, Gopi, 109
Arunachalam, Dr V.S., 67–68, 214, 275, 281–85, 294
Arya Samaj, 17, 20, 238
Azad, Ghulam Nabi, 1, 99

Babri Masjid, 7–8, 149–50, 196, 207–08, 217, 225–33, 235, 240–43, 246–47, 249, 253, 255, 306
Bachchan, Amitabh, 93
Bajrang Dal, 240, 242, 249
Baker, James, 80
Banerjee, Mamata, 205
Bansal, Pawan, 222
Barooah, D.K., 56
Baru, Sanjaya, 2, 6, 100–01, 113, 148, 161, 171, 178, 272, 299

INDEX

Basu, Jyoti, 134, 161, 185–86, 235
Bhagat, H.K.L., 205
Bhagwati, Jagdish, 72, 114
Bharatiya Janata Party (BJP), 7, 21, 66, 71, 80, 100, 109–10, 116, 118, 120, 141, 149, 165–66, 183, 186–87, 189, 193, 196, 199, 202, 205–09, 228, 230, 235, 237–43, 245–46, 250, 254–55, 283, 299, 305
    electoral victory, 229
    Hindutva, 210, 227–28, 239
Bhindranwale, Jarnail Singh, 61
Bhushan, Shanti, 63
Bhutto, Benazir, 93
Birla, K.K., 127, 136
Bitta, M.S., 5, 189, 298–99
Boesche, Roger, 140
Bordia, Anil, 178
Brandt, Willy, 169, 171, 181
Brzezinski, Zbigniew, 258, 277
Burke, Edmund, 315
Bush, George H.W., 215
Bush, George W., 282, 294
Buultjens, Ralph, 274, 277

Camdessus, Michel, 161
Caro, Robert, 303
Central Bureau of Investigation (CBI), 205–08, 220
Chakravartty, Nikhil, 77, 111, 119
Chanakya, 140, 148, 154, 166–68, 315

Chandra, Naresh, 68, 102, 116, 137, 189–90, 214, 231–32, 234, 241–42, 245–46, 251, 281–82, 284, 287–89, 293
Chandralekha, 69
Chandraswami, 1, 21, 36–37, 77, 96, 190, 195, 208, 240, 242, 274, 307
Chatterjee, Somnath, 7, 169
Chaturvedi, Bhuvanesh, 189, 198, 271
Chavan, S.B., 21, 101, 185, 190, 219, 234, 247
Chavan, Prithviraj, 230
Chengappa, Raj, 293
Chidambaram, P., 117, 121, 147–48, 158, 184, 219
Chidambaram, R., 282, 285, 287, 292–93
China, 47, 59, 78, 258–59, 264–67, 286
Clinton, Bill, 264, 273–74, 286–87, 290–91
Communist Party of India (Marxist), 120, 133
Congress Party, 6–8, 13–14, 16, 28–29, 43, 57, 166, 205, 210
    and economic liberalization, 74, 135, 141, 143–44, 166
Congress Parliamentary Party (CPP), 112–13, 124
Congress Working Committee (CWC), 74, 91, 93, 97, 99, 125, 191–92, 210–11
Hyderabad State Congress, 17, 20

INDEX

Indian National Congress, 18, 20, 22
   land redistribution, 33, 38
   manifesto, 111
   pending bill, 205
   religious politics, 71
   Seva Dal, 184
   state elections, 165, 173, 187, 202
Chung–hee, Park, 110
Confederation of Indian Industry (CII), 134, 152, 154, 161, 163, 264
DMK, 209, 223
Dalal, Sucheta, 144
Damodaran, Ramu, 60, 68, 177, 183, 189–91, 195, 198, 228, 260, 269, 303
Das, Tarun, 134, 138, 152, 154, 161, 264
de Gaulle, Charles, 10
Deoras, Madhukar Dattatraya 'Balasaheb', 241
Desai, Ashok V., 120–21
Desai, Padma, 72, 114
Desai, Xerxes, 73
Desiraju, Keshav, 178
Devi, S. Vani, 2, 22, 44, 299
Dhawan, R.K., 58–59, 92, 189
Dikshit, Uma Shankar, 34, 41, 52
Dilip Kumar, 259
Dixit, J.N., 259
Dixit, Sheila, 218, 220–21
Drèze, Jean, 180
Dulat, A.S., 310–12
Dwyer, Rachel, 164

Enron, 156
Evans, Gareth, 80

Fotedar, M.L., 91–92, 125, 147, 196–97, 218, 248, 251

Gadgil, V.N., 142
Gandhi, M.K., 13, 18–20, 89, 214, 222, 315
Gandhi, Gopalkrishna, 45, 89–90, 222
Gandhi, Indira Nehru, 28–31, 33–34, 37, 39–40, 43, 45, 52–62, 64–66, 70, 90–93, 109, 111, 123, 125, 130, 141, 150, 170, 189, 213, 218, 220, 224, 233, 244, 258, 280, 298, 301, 303, 312–13
   currency devaluation, 111, 119
   Emergency, 54–55, 57
   Punjab crisis, 61–62
   rethinking strategy, 41
Gandhi, Rahul, 7, 93, 213, 215, 252, 297
Gandhi, Rajiv, 6, 9, 55–56, 62–71, 76–81, 84–86, 93, 97, 106, 109, 111, 114, 117, 122–23, 130, 132, 135, 143, 161, 172, 178, 186, 189, 197, 205, 210, 212–14, 218, 227–28, 258–59, 261, 265, 275, 281–82, 298, 302, 304, 306–07, 312–14
   assassination, 89–90, 215
   judicial probe, 219–20

INDEX

economic liberalization, 72–74, 142
vote bank politics, 71, 79
Gandhi, Sanjay, 54–55, 101, 218
Gandhi, Sonia, 1–6, 8, 34, 37, 55, 62, 90–96, 100, 132–33, 183, 189, 198, 211–24, 236, 251, 297, 299–300, 306–10
George, Vincent, 85, 189, 214, 218
Gill, K.P.S., 310
Godbole, Madhav, 231–32, 234, 237, 245–46
Gokhale, Gopal Krishna, 18
Gorbachev, Mikhail, 78, 97, 260
Gowda, H.D. Deve, 4, 10, 307
Guha, Ramachandra, 23, 56
Gulf War, 108–09, 305
Gupta, Shekhar, 280, 312, 315

Habibullah, Wajahat, 310
Hadley, Stephen, 282
Haidar, Salman, 238, 259, 267, 277
Haksar, P.N., 94–95, 213
Hamilton, Nigel, 301
Hasan, Zoya, 149
Herald, 135
Hindu Mahasabha, 17, 20, 238
Hindustan Machine tools (HMT), 29–30
Hindustan Times, 124
Hirschman, A.O., 138
Huntington, Samuel, 258
Hussain, Abid, 72
Hussein, Saddam, 262, 305

India,
and global terrorism, 258
annual budget, 126–31
Associated Chambers of Commerce and Industry of India (ASSOCHAM), 153
Atomic Energy Commission (AEC), 280, 282, 284–85, 289
bank nationalization, 141, 150, 170
bank privatization, 150
before and after Rao, 9
Bhopal gas tragedy, 65, 91
Bodoland Autonomous Council, 312
Bofors scandal, 70, 74, 96, 216
Bombay Stock Exchange, 163
Cabinet Committee on Political Affairs (CCPA), 233–35
Cash Compensatory Scheme (CCS), 121
caste politics, 32, 34, 39, 46
communal conflicts, 21, 62–63, 149, 225–30, 243, 255
Controller of Capital Issues (CCI), 144, 146
corruption, 174, 180–81, 206
Defence Research Development Organization (DRDO), 280–81, 285–87, 291
economic crisis, 101–04, 107–09, 112, 132, 258

INDEX

economic liberalization, 6, 8, 72–73, 141, 145, 167–68
   benefits from, 162–63
   criticism of, 156
economic socialism, 28–31, 41, 111, 142, 170–71
education, 178–79
Emergency, 54–58
Federation of Indian Chambers of Commerce and Industry (FICCI), 134, 153
Foreign Investment Promotion Board (FIPB), 148
foreign policy, 47–48, 78, 257–59, 264, 276–78
   promoting India, 264, 267–68
General Agreement on Tariffs and Trade (GATT), 162
Gujarat riots, 252
hawala scam, 206–09, 306
Hyderabad state, 24
income in real terms, 172
Indian Army, 22, 286
Independence, 20
Indo-US nuclear deal, 282
intelligence bureau (IB), 78, 85, 113, 135–36, 200, 217, 221, 230, 236, 240, 247, 262, 265, 307, 313
land reforms, 32–33, 38, 182
Land Reforms Act, 56
licence raj, 28, 30–31, 72, 75, 109, 114, 121, 123, 128, 141, 154, 159, 179, 258, 304

Maintenance of Internal Security Act (MISA), 57
National Education Policy, 69
national elections, 88, 291–92, 299
National Front, 79, 100, 109, 118, 132, 149, 183, 186, 193, 196, 199, 305
National Integration Council, 230, 235
malnutrition rates, 180
mulki rules, 40
Navodaya school system, 69, 178
nuclear proliferation, 68, 279–83, 288
   global isolation, 286–87
   missile testing, 285–86, 288–89, 292
personality/contradictions, 308, 311–12
Planning Commission, 120
poverty, 30, 54, 169–72, 180
privatization of media, 159–60
public distribution system (PDS), 174–75
   renewed (RPDS), 175–76, 198
Punjab separatism, 61, 310–11
'right wing' discourse, 8
rupee devaluation, 119–20
Sarva Shiksha Abhiyan, 178
Securities Exchange Bureau of India (SEBI), 144–45
Shah Bano case, 227

INDEX

Supreme Court, 40, 46, 55, 70, 159, 196, 204–06, 208, 227, 230–31, 235, 237, 241, 250–51, 253–54
taxation policy, 170–72
Telegraph Act, 158–59
welfare state, 169–70

India Today, 131
Infosys, 150
International Monetary Fund (IMF), 105, 108–09, 119, 133, 136, 138, 161, 164, 169, 171, 188, 301
Israel, 259, 261–62
Iyengar, P.K., 282, 285

Jain, S.K., 206
Jain Commission, 219–20
Jaitley, Arun, 8, 208
Jakhar, Balram, 136, 185, 223
Janata Dal, 100, 183, 186, 188, 195, 200–01, 227, 235
Janata Party, 52, 57, 186
  United Janata Opposition, 57–59
Jayalalithaa, 193, 209–10
Jenkins, Robert, 136, 175
Jethmalani, Ram, 63
Jha, L.K., 72
Jharkhand Mukti Morcha (JMM), 201, 297, 309
Jinnah, M.A., 19
Jogi, A.K., 217

Joshi, P.C., 18
Joshi, Murli Manohar, 239, 244, 250, 283
K., Saraswathi, 47, 49, 273
Kakodkar, Anil, 282
Kalam, A.P.J. Abdul, 282, 285, 287–89, 291–94, 300
Kamble, Prabhakar, 88
Kantamma, Lakshmi, 25–27, 34–37, 43–44, 52, 56, 83, 190, 307, 309
Kapur, Devesh, 50
Karunakaran, K., 223
Karunanidhi, M., 209
Kennedy, John F., 98
Kesri, Sitaram, 92, 98, 200
Khandekar, R.K., 124, 189, 214, 222, 246
Khashoggi, Adnan, 37
Khurshid, Salman, 7, 98, 185, 216, 243, 247, 252, 255, 271–72, 296
Kirpekar, Subhash, 101
Kissinger, Henry, 140, 258
Kohli, Atul, 73, 269
Kothari, Rajni, 22
Krishnan, N., 124
Kumaramangalam, R., 189, 240, 246
Kurien, P.J., 129

Lakshmikantha, Captain V., 6, 33, 51
Lal, Devi, 97
Liberation Tigers of Tamil Eelam (LTTE), 9, 71, 89, 210

INDEX

Machiavelli, 129, 140, 145, 166–68, 189, 193, 208, 249, 282, 298, 315
Mainstream, 77, 81, 111
Malkani, K.R., 120
Mangla, Akshay, 69, 178
Manor, James, 137, 169
Mathai, M.O., 189
Mathur, Suresh, 123
Mehta, Harshad, 137, 145, 157, 163, 199, 201, 206, 297
Mehta, Sujata, 288
Mehta, V.R., 146–47
Mehta, Zubin, 259
Menon, K.P.S. (Jr), 78
Menon, Prabhakar, 148, 173, 183, 266, 270, 288
Menon, Sadanand, 70
Mittal, Lakshmi, 153, 269
Mittal, Mohan Lal, 269
Mittal, Sat Paul, 199
Mittal, Sunil, 199
Modi, Narendra, 165, 252, 312
Mody, Russi, 259
Mohan, C. Raja, 276–77
Mohan, Rakesh, 117, 123–25, 132
Morita, Akio, 152
Mukherjee, Pranab, 2, 60, 67, 90–92, 99, 102, 113, 158, 197, 235, 254, 290, 298

NREGA, 176
Nadella, Satya, 177
Naidu, Chandrababu, 165
Namboodiripad, E.M.S., 77, 133, 188
Nandy, Ashis, 315
Narain, Vineet, 206
Narayan, Jayaprakash, 54
Narayanan, K.R., 194
Narayanan, M.K., 265–66
Nayyar, Deepak, 120
Nehru, Arun, 72
Nehru, Jawaharlal, 8, 10, 18–19, 21, 26, 28–29, 49, 111, 125, 130, 132, 135, 143–44, 152, 183, 189, 191, 218, 238, 258, 263, 303, 315
  Industrial Policy Resolution, 29
New Age, 18
Nilekani, Nandan, 150–51
Nixon, Richard, 47
Nizam Asaf Jah VII, 13–14, 17, 20–22, 31–32, 212
Noorani, A.J., 242

Obama, Barack, 164, 275
Olson, Mancur, 112

Padgaonkar, Dileep, 101
Padmanabhaiah, K., 310
Pakistan, 258, 269–71, 283, 286, 295
Palestine Liberation Organization (PLO), 262
Pataudi, Nawab Mansoor Ali Khan (Tiger), 259
Patel, I.G., 30, 102–03, 113, 313–14
Patel, Ahmed, 2, 217, 223, 300

INDEX

Patel, Sardar Vallabhbhai, 19, 21
Pathak, Lakhubhai, 296
Patil, Shivraj, 1, 3, 300
Patil, Uttam Bhai, 197
Patil, Virendra, 21
Pawar, Sharad, 80, 92, 94, 96, 98–101, 111, 183–85, 192–93, 197–98, 222–23, 234, 237, 249, 283
Peng, Li, 265–66, 277
Perkovich, George, 292
Pilot, Rajesh, 189–90, 223
Poojary, Janardhana, 195
Pradhan, R.D., 100
Prasad, P.V.R.K., 5, 35, 134, 154, 157, 159, 183, 189–90, 193, 199–200, 207–08, 214, 223, 237, 242, 246, 269, 274
Prasada, Jitendra, 189, 252
Priyadarshini, Anupama, 177
Pushkin, Alexander, 275

RAW, 241, 310
Raghavan, Srinath, 78
Rai, Aishwarya, 163
Rajagopalachari, C., 89, 222
Rajgopal, S., 137, 245–46
Rajaiah, 182, 245, 260
Rajiv, 214
Rajiv Gandhi Foundation, 133, 214
Ram, Sukh, 160–61
Ramakrishna, G.V., 115, 144–46, 166
Raman, B., 241
Ramana, M.V., 280

Ramesh, Jairam, 7, 75, 94, 98, 102, 109, 113, 117, 122–25, 134, 175, 189, 90, 243, 246, 252, 268
Rangarajan, C., 120
Rao, J. Vengala, 43
Rao, N.T. Rama, 36, 187
Rao, P.C., 234, 246
Rao, P.V. Narasimha, 1–2
   and Babri Masjid, 71, 149–50, 225–37, 240–42, 244–55, 306
   'Ayodhya cell', 231–32
   emergency broadcast, 249
   Justice Liberhan Commission, 250, 255
   protection of, 240–43, 255
   state governments dismantled, 250
   and Delhi riots, 62–65
   and gurus, 20–23, 37
   and socialism, 26–27, 55
   and Sonia Gandhi, 10, 217–24, 300, 306–09
   as prime minister, 9, 101–03, 162, 257
   and foreign investment, 151–53, 165, 263
   brokering change in attitude, 128, 163–64
   confidence motion, 185–86
   constraints, 104, 109–11
   diplomatic relations, 259–61, 266–69, 276
   Kashmir issue, 270–72, 310–11
   'Look East', 267–68

INDEX

Palestine question, 261–62, 304
with Iran, 263, 295
with Israel, 263, 305
with Russia, 275–76
economic liberalization, 118, 136–38, 141–46, 165–69
economic policy, 75–76, 102–06, 109, 143, 305
education policy, 178
global disarmament, 214
industrial policy reforms, 123–26, 129–31
legislative handicap, 110
no-confidence motion, 193, 196, 200, 217, 251
nuclear programme, 279–80, 283–84, 287–94, 305
political pressure, 120, 147
political strategy, 147–48, 192–93, 238–40
precarious national stability, 103–05
privatization, 155–56, 158
airlines, 159
media, 158–59
mobile telephony, 160–61
reduced subsidies, 171
reforms, 9, 72, 106, 117–18, 122–28, 143–44, 161, 172
jugaad, 303
shortcomings, 167–68
story behind, 95–100
team selection, 114–17, 184, 188, 313

partisanship, 218–19, 223
touring Japan, 152
winning Sonia's trust, 214–16
with businessmen, 134–35
with left parties, 133–34, 150, 166, 185
with Opposition, 118–19, 122, 124, 131, 167, 186, 193, 199, 235
birthday celebrations, 5–6
Cabinet minister, 26
Chief Minister, Andhra Pradesh, 34–35
intemperate speech, 40, 46
radical steps, 39, 46
Congress general secretary, 53
criticism for,
Babri Masjid, 7, 197, 204, 208–09, 217, 230, 251–56, 301
Bhopal gas leak, 7, 65, 301
corruption, 156–58, 164, 199, 201, 296–97, 301
Delhi riots, 7, 63–65, 301
criticism of Rajiv Gandhi, 81–82, 214
daily routine, 182–83
death, 301
defence minister, 66–67
diplomacy, 61–65, 259–61, 266–69, 276
early years, 10–14
given up for adoption, 14–15
education, 15–18
election campaigning, 88–89, 98

INDEX

foreign minister of India, 58–60, 78–79, 282
funeral, 1–5, 224, 279
higher studies, 19
honesty, 23–24
Human Resource Development Ministry, 68
ill health, 203, 299
in USA, 47–48, 75, 163, 273–74
in USSR, 275
inner transformation, 46–47
land reform, 31–33, 38–39, 45–46, 50–51, 56
language skills, 27, 58, 298, 315
computer languages, 67, 151
leaving Delhi, 87
legal cases against, 296–97
literary pursuits, 43–46, 48, 50, 77, 87
Lok Sabha elections, 23, 57, 65–66
loneliness, 31
loyalty to Indira Gandhi, 58, 218
Marathi, 17–18
marriage, 16
memorial, 4, 6
nationalist years, 17–18, 20–21
'nominated' chief minister, 33, 37, 45
party infighting, 10, 165
party solidarity, 99
personal notes, 76–77, 80, 85, 92, 99, 265–66

political career, 22–25, 65–69
political enemies, 40, 45–46, 158, 165, 216–19, 224
political exile, 42–44, 48–50, 56, 88, 298
political instinct, 113
political legacy, 316–17
political pacifism, 71–72, 95–96
political vision, 59–60, 173, 181, 316
Public Accounts Committee (PAC), 57
public image, 7–8
public service, 26
relationships outside marriage, 36, 309
role conflict, 37–38
secular nature, 238
scholarship, 48–49, 297, 309
Siddheswari peetham, 83, 88
technological skills, 67
The Insider, 77, 298
The Other Half, 298
welfare measures, 170–77
winning confidence, 66–68
Rao, Burgula Ramakrishna, 19–20, 22–23
Rao, Prabhakara, 1–3, 49, 58–59, 67, 75, 148, 189, 203, 208, 223, 297
Rao, Rajeshwara, 44, 47, 82, 87, 183, 208–09, 214, 274, 300
Rao, Ranga, 1, 5, 16, 18, 27, 43, 47
Rao, Sadashiva, 134

INDEX

Rao, Satyamma, 16, 18–19, 26, 35, 308
Rao, Shravan, 78, 258
Rao, Sitarama, 12, 14–15
Rao, Velcheru Narayana, 48, 79, 274
Rao, Venkat Kishen, 23–24
Rao, Vijaya Rama, 207
Rashtriya Swayamsevak Sangh (RSS), 54, 189, 240–41, 243, 249–50, 254
Razakars, 21
Reagan, Ronald, 10, 110, 183
Reddy, B. Satyanarayana, 237
Reddy, Dr Srinath, 82, 182, 191, 203, 225–26, 245, 248, 273, 299
Reddy, K. Brahmananda, 33–34, 39
Reddy, K.V. Raghunatha, 225
Reddy, M. Narayan, 36, 38, 45
Reddy, N. Janardhana, 196
Reddy, Y.S. Rajasekhara, 2
Reddy, Kiran Kumar, 77
Reddy, Narsa, 34–35, 39, 56
Reserve Bank of India (RBI), 75, 107, 114, 122, 150
Roosevelt, Franklin D., 10, 183
Roy, Arundhati, 298
Rushdie, Salman, 71, 227

Saifullah, Zafar, 160
Saikia, Hiteswar, 310
Salamatullah, 217
Salve, N.K.P., 85, 89
Sanjay Gandhi memorial trust, 101
Sanjivayya, D., 34
Sankaran, S.R., 173, 190
Santhanam, K., 282, 289
Savarkar, V.D., 18
Scindia, Madhavrao, 4, 94, 136, 147, 185
Sen, Amartya, 180
Sen, Ronen, 59, 85–86, 261, 264, 266, 275, 282, 286, 288
Sen, Sushmita, 163
Shahabuddin, 248
Shankar, Kalyani, 2, 52, 82, 85, 91, 97, 124, 142, 190–91, 203, 218, 220, 271, 277, 309, 313
Shankaracharya, 240
Shankaranand, B., 185
Sharief, C.K. Jaffer, 185, 248
Sharif, Nawaz, 269
Sharma, N.K., 21, 99, 185, 190, 199–200, 210–11, 221, 240–41, 244–45, 296
Sharma, Captain Satish, 66, 96–97, 197, 213, 220
Sharma, Shankar Dayal, 41, 95, 194, 236, 249
Shastri, Lal Bahadur, 10, 28
Shekhar, Chandra, 108, 116, 118, 132, 172
Shekhawat, Bhairon Singh, 239, 241–42
Shiv Sena, 165, 240, 242
Shukla, V.C., 189, 193–94
Singh, Ajit, 123, 186–88, 193–95, 200–01
Singh, Arjun, 65, 91, 94, 96, 99, 101, 111, 124–25, 136, 147,

INDEX

156, 158, 164, 184–85, 192–93, 196, 201, 204, 206–07, 217–20, 230, 233–34, 237, 239, 243, 246, 248, 250–51, 253–54, 283, 300, 302
Singh, Arun, 66, 72
Singh, Daman, 111
Singh, Digvijay, 136, 204, 217
Singh, Jaswant, 118, 131
Singh, K. Natwar, 4, 6, 49, 52, 61–62, 71, 94–95, 190, 218–21, 251
Singh, Kalyan, 228–31, 234–37, 242–45, 247–51, 253–54, 257
Singh, Manmohan, 2–4, 6, 30, 37, 57, 72, 75, 102–03, 108, 110–11, 113–21, 125–38, 141, 143–44, 146–49, 154, 157–58, 161, 164, 166–67, 171, 184, 187, 190–91, 198, 234, 284–85, 298–300, 307, 313–14
  as prime minister, 213
Singh, Matang, 189
Singh, Rajendra, 241
Singh, Shubhranshu, 299
Singh, Vishwanath Pratap, 79, 100, 109–10, 118, 131, 172, 186–87, 194, 237
Singh, Zail, 61, 77
Singhal, Ashok, 241
Sinha, Yashwant, 117, 207
Solanki, Madhav Singh, 204–05, 216, 259
Soviet Union, 9, 29, 47, 49, 78, 88, 104, 110, 128, 138, 170, 187, 258–61, 273, 275–76, 278, 283, 301–02
  Cold War, 258, 273, 283
  perestroika, 110
Srinivasan, Krishnan, 261, 264, 271, 273, 277
Subrahmanyam, K., 282, 291
Swamy, Mouna, 83
Swamy, Satchidananda, 56, 298
Swamy, Subramanian, 8, 75, 85, 97, 99, 112, 117, 186, 189, 195, 200, 221

Tata, J.R.D., 134
Tata, Ratan, 159
Telangana Rashtra Samithi (TRS), 6–7
Telangana state, 7, 20, 24–26, 32
  agitation, 33–34
  demand for separation, 40
Telugu Academy, 27
Telugu Desam Party (TDP), 165, 193, 204
Tendulkar, Sachin, 163
Thakur, Rameshwar, 197
Thatcher, Margaret, 10, 37, 77, 110, 169, 183
Tilak, Bal Gangadhar, 18
Tirtha, Swami Ramananda, 20–23, 26, 31, 33, 35, 101, 238, 309
Tiwari, N.D., 90, 94, 111, 164, 184–85, 202, 204, 220, 243, 251, 283, 302
Tiwari, Brahm Dutt, 221
Tong, Goh Chok, 268

INDEX

ULFA, 310–11
United Nations, 258, 262–64, 271
    Comprehensive Test Ban Treaty (CTBT), 286–87, 289–91, 293–94
    Non-Proliferation Treaty (NPT), 283, 285–87, 294
    Security Council, 283
United States, 47, 59, 257–59, 261–62, 282, 302
    Indian/Telugu immigrants, 50
    re-establishing ties, 273–75

Vadhra, Priyanka (née Gandhi), 215
Vaidya, V.G., 245–47
Vajpayee, Atal Bihari, 120, 132, 187, 189, 207, 211, 239, 241–42, 252, 271–72, 277, 279, 292, 294–95, 298
Varma, Amar Nath, 115–16, 123, 126, 134, 148, 154, 183, 188, 190, 288, 290, 299, 313
Vedanti, Acharya Ram Vilas, 240
Venkataraman, R., 60, 68, 77, 89–90, 102–04, 147, 282
Venugopal, K.R., 174–77, 190, 311
Verma, J.S., 206–08, 219–20

Vietnam War, 27, 47
Vishwa Hindu Parishad (VHP), 196, 225, 227, 232, 236, 240–41, 243, 245, 249–50, 254
Vithal, B.P.R., 36, 142
Vithal, N., 160
Vogel, Ezra, 42
Vohra, N.N., 270

Weber, Max, 140
Welch, Jack, 259
Wisner, Frank, 290
World Bank, 108, 116, 119, 136, 169, 178
World Trade Organization (WTO), 162

Xiaoping, Deng, 10, 42, 52, 59–60, 78, 110, 153, 163, 265–66, 303

Yadav, Mulayam Singh, 227–29
Yew, Lee Kuan, 110, 268
Yugandhar, B.N., 173, 177, 190

Zedong, Mao, 42, 59
Zee TV, 158
Zemin, Ziang, 266

www.ingramcontent.com/pod-product-compliance
Lightning Source LLC
LaVergne TN
LVHW022003060526
838200LV00003B/78